TRANSPARENCY AND CONSPIRACY

TRANSPARENCY

AND CONSPIRACY

Ethnographies of Suspicion in the New World Order

EDITED BY HARRY G. WEST AND TODD SANDERS

Duke University Press Durham and London 2003

© 2003 DUKE UNIVERSITY PRESS

All rights reserved. Printed in the United States of America on

acid-free paper ∞. Designed by Amy Ruth Buchanan. Typeset in Sabon

by Tseng Information Systems, Inc. Library of Congress Cataloging-in-

Publication Data appear on the last printed page of this book.

CONTENTS

Acknowledgments

This volume is the product of a workshop, entitled "Transparency and Conspiracy: Power Revealed and Concealed in (the) Global Village(s)," held on 28 and 29 May 1999 in the Department of Anthropology at the London School of Economics and Political Science (LSE). The workshop was organized by Harry G. West and Todd Sanders, with administrative assistance from Margaret Bothwell and Annick Saliman. Draft papers were presented at the workshop by Laurel Kendall, Misty Bastian, Harry West, Todd Sanders, Daniel Hellinger, and Karen McCarthy Brown (whose essays are included in this volume) as well as by Nancy Scheper-Hughes, Nancy Ries, Richard Tapper, and Tamara Teghillo. Jean and John Comaroff provided stimulating commentary in their role as discussants in the workshop and contributed an afterword to the volume. Additional papers were later solicited from Albert Schrauwers, Caroline Humphrey, and Susan Harding and Kathleen Stewart. Institutional support was provided by the Department of Anthropology at the LSE and, in particular, by the department convenor, Chris Fuller. For additional financial support, we thank the Economic and Social Research Council and the Suntory Toyota International Centres for Economics and Related Disciplines. We wish to thank Erin Koch for her help preparing the index. Finally, we are grateful to the two anonymous reviewers, arranged by Duke University Press, who provided engaged and insightful commentary on the manuscript.

trans par ent (trans pâr´ent, -par´-), *adj.* 1. having the property of transmitting rays of light through its substances so that bodies situated beyond or behind can be distinctly seen, as opposed to opaque, and usually distinguished from translucent. 2. easily seen through, recognized, or detected. 3. easily understood; manifest; obvious. 4. candid; frank; open.

There can be no doubt that distrust of words is less harmful than unwarranted trust in them. Besides, to distrust words, and indict them for the horrors that might slumber unobtrusively within them—isn't this, after all, the true vocation of the intellectual?
—*Václav Havel (December 1989)*

Take a whiff of the New World Odor
—*Sign displayed in a window in Madison, Wisconsin, on the first day of the U.S. military operation Desert Storm*

Power Revealed and Concealed
in the New World Order

TODD SANDERS AND HARRY G. WEST

Our world, and the exercise of power within it, is becoming more "transparent." Such, at least, is the conclusion that one might draw from listening to contemporary global-speak. In May 1993, for example, a group of government officials, representatives of international development agencies, and influential businesspeople gathered in Berlin to found Transparency International, an organization committed to reducing bribery and other forms of corruption in the realm of international commerce.[1] In 1998, the governing committee of the International Monetary Fund adopted new rules requiring its 182 member states to adhere to common standards of "financial transparency" in order to facilitate IMF surveillance and to create more stable environments for international investors around the world (Boxer 1998; Goozner 1998; Phillips 1998; Brown 1998; Larsson and Lundberg 1998; Marceau and Pedersen 1999). *Transparency* has become nearly synonymous with *good governance* for institutions such as the Carter Center, which has, since September 1998, operated a "Transparency Project" with the aim of assisting fledgling democratic institutions in Latin American countries (http://www.cartercenter.org/; see also Kopits and Craig 1998; Shukla 1998; Finkelstein 1999). In post–Cold War peacemaking and peacekeeping initiatives, the United Nations, Western bilateral donors, and international organizations have not only celebrated transparency as a strategic objective but also identified its pursuit by states emerging from civil conflict as a precondition for continuing assistance. The staging of multiparty national elections in countries such as Cambodia, Guatemala, and Mozambique has been described as a necessary measure in the campaign to establish political transparency (see also Dundas 1994; Scholte 1998), as has the establishment of war tribunals and "truth commissions" in countries such as Bosnia, Rwanda, El Salvador, and South Africa. In the arms trade, *transparency* has, in recent years, been employed as a euphemism for adherence to arms-reduction and nuclear-nonproliferation agreements (Wright 1993; Smith and Graham 1997; Safire 1998; United Nations 1993, 1994; Chalmers and Green 1994; Chalmers 1997; Gill and Mak 1997).

"Suddenly, everything is transparent," the *New York Times* columnist Sarah Boxer (1998) recently mused. Or is it? This, at least, is true: suddenly, much is being *called* transparent. So much that the term *transparency* featured in William Safire's "On Language" column in the *New York Times Magazine* in January 1998.

If we treat Safire's column as a contemporary language barometer, as many do, we cannot fail, however, to notice that, little more than two years previously, in November 1995, Safire wrote a column entitled "Conspiracy Theory." In that piece, not only did he define the conspiracy theorist as a "person who attributes an unexplained or unaccountable event to a sinister plot," but he also sardonically alluded to the ubiquity of such persons of late. How, we must ask, can transparency and conspiracy thrive simultaneously in William Safire's world? In our world? Perhaps the world, and the operation of power within it, is *not* becoming more transparent. Perhaps, amid all this talk of transparency, many people have the sense that something is not as it is said to be—that power remains, notwithstanding official pronouncements, at least somewhat opaque.

Consider this: Safire links the rise in global-speak currency of the term *transparency* to the "mutual veil dropping" coming with the end of the Cold War. Once the Berlin Wall came down and the Western world had the opportunity to establish eye contact with Russians formerly hiding themselves behind the Iron Curtain, U.S. president George Bush (the First) wasted little time in calling for a "New World Order"—a global power regime to be characterized by collective policing of open compliance with internationally agreed on norms and rules. Bush first mentioned the New World Order in a September 1990 address to a joint session of Congress with the Persian Gulf crisis brewing (Bush 1990; see also Ingwerson 1990); high on the president's immediate priority list was the exposure to light of covert Iraqi nuclear-weapons programs—the rendering "transparent" of Iraqi military capabilities. Within a very short time, however, Bush's New World Order was interpreted by substantial numbers of anxious Americans not in the language of transparency but, rather, in the language of conspiracy; the New World Order, many believed, was nothing short of a plot to undermine American sovereignty, to subordinate the will of the American people to that of an unelected transnational bureaucracy and an international elite that might dictate its governing objectives. Callers to talk radio shows across America argued that the United States should not pay its membership dues to the United Nations, and tales of the appearance of black UN helicopters in American skies circulated in many parts of the country, fueling right-wing militias and millenarian movements alike.[2] Randy Weaver (of Ruby Ridge), David Koresch (of Waco), and Timothy McVeigh (of the Oklahoma City bombing) shared a deep suspicion of power in the New World Order. "When President Bush spoke of 'a New World Order' in 1990, he scared the daylights out of . . . people," writes Ira Straus, U.S. coordinator of the Committee on Eastern Europe and Russia in NATO. "The rise of the militias was no accident. These people were utterly serious about organizing against the impending federal-NWO [New World Order] tyranny" (Straus 1996).

Just as serious about organizing against tyranny on a new global scale have been various groups opposing the World Trade Organization. As the "Battle in Seattle" demonstrated, this complex coalition highlights, not only the ways in which "free trade" benefits the rich and the powerful at the expense of the poor and the powerless, but also how trade agreements are brokered in closed-chamber dealings between unelected representatives and are shielded from public scrutiny by fast-track legislative review.

A propensity toward suspicion of political power is nothing new in America (Bailyn 1967; Davis 1969, 1971; Hutson 1984; Ostler 1995), be it what Richard Hofstadter (1965) has called "the paranoid style in American politics" or earlier Jeffersonian or Jacksonian popular mistrust of the state (Banning 1978; Robertson 1971). Today, however, conspiracy thinking is as vibrant as ever in the American popular imagination (Fenster 1999; Melley 2000; Knight 2001, 2002).

In his 1988 novel *Foucault's Pendulum* (which became an international best-seller), Umberto Eco tells the tale of a group of occult books publishing house editors who feed bits of rejected manuscripts into a micro computer that randomly reworks them into an all-encompassing conspiracy reaching across time and around the globe; the Internet today affords conspiracy theorists with a greatly more powerful tool than any Eco could have imagined little more than a decade ago. In the United States, right-wing militias have

used the Internet to recruit members and to garner sympathy for their movements, but they are not the only conspiracy theorists on-line (Belsie 1997;
James 2001; see also Bastian, Hellinger, and Harding and Stewart, chapters 2, 7, and 9 in this volume). Websites such as Conspire.com and Conspiracy Net provide wide audiences with a means to produce and consume
conspiracy theories about such diverse topics as the "Trilateral Commission"
and the "Illuminati" (both said to be covertly running world affairs), the
death of Princess Diana (said to have been killed by British Intelligence to
ensure that the future king of England not have an Arab stepfather; see also
Cullen 1997), the crash of TWA Flight 800 (said to have been shot down by
the U.S. Navy; see also Revkin 1996), and the events of 11 September 2001
(said to have been orchestrated by Israeli Intelligence and/or by the CIA).

Conspiracy theorists on the Internet are often dismissed as a "fringe"
group (James 2001), but evidence suggests that a broad cross section of
Americans today—traversing ethnic, gender, education, occupation, and
other divides—gives credence to at least some conspiracy theories (Crocker
et al. 1999; Glock 1988; Goertzel 1994; Melley 2000; Parsons et al. 1999;
Warner 1987; Waters 1997). This has been most persuasively demonstrated
in the literature on conspiracy theories among African Americans. Large
percentages of African Americans, from various social backgrounds, are reported to subscribe to a variety of conspiracy theories. Among those with
substantial support include theories positing that the Los Angeles Police Department framed O. J. Simpson for the murder of his ex-wife and her com-
panion; that the CIA introduced crack cocaine into American inner cities to
fund covert operations abroad (Webb 1999; see also Hellinger, chapter 7 in
this volume); that Church's Fried Chicken, the Brooklyn Bottling Company,
and other companies are fronts for the Ku Klux Klan, who use their products
to sterilize African American male consumers, among other things (Coombe
1997; Parsons et al. 1999; Sasson 1995; Turner 1993: 82–83; Waters 1997);
and that AIDS was produced as a biological weapon targeting Africans and
African Americans (Goertzel 1994: 734; Klonoff and Landrine 1999; Thomas
and Quinn 1991: 1499).

Yet conspiracy theories have broad appeal beyond the African American community. Consider Roswell (New Mexico), where the government is
said to have concealed evidence of a UFO crash in 1947 (see Saler, Ziegler,
and Moore 1997). This conspiracy theory has generated a veritable industry of tabloid articles, books, television programs, and films, all of which
are consumed with great relish by vast American audiences (Klass 1983;
Good 1987; Strieber 1987; Blum 1990; Randle 1998). *The Day After Roswell,*

written by the ex-military intelligence officer Colonel Phillip Corso, quickly made its way to the *New York Times* best-seller list when it was published in 1997 (Ziegler 1999: 18–19). The Fox Television series *The X-Files* has made the Roswell conspiracy a fundamental component to its ongoing macroplot, spinning it into other conspiracies, big and small. Not all viewers of the once-popular show necessarily believe in the Roswell conspiracy, but most have sufficient familiarity with, and tolerance for, such ideas to find entertaining and intriguing the show's many episodes exploring how state and supra-state powers collude with unknown, perhaps alien, forces to steer the path of American and global affairs (Bell and Bennion-Nixon 2001; Campbell 2001). Over the past decade, films such as *Total Recall*, *The Package*, *JFK*, *Bob Roberts*, *Wag the Dog*, *The Net*, *Conspiracy Theory*, *Enemy of the State*, and *Arlington Road* have all cashed in on the notion that conspiracies are a fundamental part of the operational logic of American, and global, politics. The point is this: even as President Bush proffered his vision for an American-led global glasnost, members of the American "Open Society" remained deeply suspicious of power.

To borrow a phrase from the opening sequence of *The X-Files*, "we are not alone." Conspiracy theories thrive around the globe, as Daniel Pipes (1996), Richard Tapper (1999), Jon Anderson (1996) and others have demonstrated in their work on the Middle East, for example. As the contributors to this volume show, however, conspiratorial thinking about power may take on vastly different forms in different global locales. Thus, for example, suspicion of IMF claims to produce a transparent economic environment in places like Korea or Tanzania may be expressed in the form of consultations with shamans (Kendall, chapter 1) or seers (Sanders, chapter 5). Beliefs that power continues to conspire even under a regime of electoral democracy may be expressed in Mozambique or in Indonesia in the form of references to the dark world of sorcery (West, chapter 3; Schrauwers, chapter 4). Among Buddhists in Russia, Mongolia, and China, lingering doubts about glasnost truths and "transitional justice" may come in the form of reincarnation stories (Humphrey, chapter 6). Suspicion, in Nigeria, of judicial and police complicity in dirty dealings may be articulated in the form of accusations of "ritual murder" directed at elite social classes (Bastian, chapter 2).

At the same time, conspiracy ideas in America may also be expressed in ways that transcend the bounds of a strict definition of *conspiracy theory*. Doubts in a Haitian American community about whether the American justice system or the media serve their mandates to expose social truths accurately may be expressed through the production of Vodou charms

(McCarthy Brown, chapter 8), for example. Lest we assume that it is only recent immigrants to America—"the Others among us"—who draw on occult cosmologies to express conspiracy ideas, we need only consider the members of the Calvary Chapel church, who decipher current events in accordance with their understandings of divine will and scriptural prophesy, or the members of the Heaven's Gate movement, whose suspicions of "the system" were expressed in a neology of their own conception (Harding and Stewart, chapter 9).

Readers may protest that we are comparing conceptual apples and oranges here—that conspiracy theories and urban myths, on the one hand, and beliefs in occult powers, on the other, are not at all the same. This has, indeed, been the general assumption in the existing literature on both conspiracy theories and occult cosmologies. It is, however, an assumption that we wish to challenge. While we recognize that the varied beliefs identified above are sustained in the midst of specific social and historical circumstances, we suggest that they share essential commonalties. In asserting such commonalties, we intend to subvert a number of problematic dichotomies whose maintenance, we suggest, is bound up with keeping conspiracy theories and occult cosmologies distinct. These include dichotomies between "the West" and "the rest," between the global and the local, between modernity and tradition, and between rationality and conviction. We suggest that the difference between conspiracy theories and occult cosmologies lies, not in the identity of the believer (e.g., Western vs. non-Western, modern vs. traditional, rational vs. religious), but, rather, in the ontological dimensions of belief: by definition, a cosmology concerns itself with how the world works, while a conspiracy theory may concern itself with only a small part of the world's workings.

In adopting the term *occult cosmologies,* we eschew any pejorative sense, defining these merely as systems of belief in a world animated by secret, mysterious, and/or unseen powers. Occult cosmologies suggest that there is more to what happens in the world than meets the eye—that reality is anything but "transparent." More specifically, they claim that power operates in two separate yet related realms, one visible, the other invisible; between these two realms, however, there exist causal links, meaning that invisible powers sometimes produce visible outcomes (Arens and Karp 1989; Comaroff and Comaroff 1999). Not only do occult cosmologies suggest that power sometimes hides itself from view, but they also often suggest that it conspires to fulfill its objectives (each an essential trait of conspiracy theories). In this way, occult cosmologies potentially contain within them theories of conspiracy. On the other side of the coin, although conspiracy theories are not necessarily fully fledged cosmologies, they constitute occult perspectives on the world, for they, too, concern themselves with the operation of secret, mysterious, and/or unseen powers. They, too, suggest that there is more to power than meets the eye.

In either case, occult cosmologies and conspiracy theories may express profound suspicions of power. Through them, ordinary people may articulate their concerns that others, in possession of extraordinary powers, see and act decisively in realms normally concealed from view.[3] They may suggest that, in a world where varied institutions claim to give structure to the "rational" and "transparent" operation of power, power continues in reality to work in unpredictable and capricious ways.

Transparency, we have suggested, is a term that has only recently gained global currency. It is, however, a term born of the self-reflexivity of a larger historical moment, namely, modernity. Transparency is invoked by those who think of themselves as modern as they talk about their vision of a modern society, and it is frequently juxtaposed, not only with conspiratorial ideas, but also, as we shall see, with the "ignorance" of "tradition." As such, transparency constitutes a fashionable buzzword that inflects ideas with a long historical legacy. Because *transparency* borrows from, and contributes to, modernity's broader assertions, we must situate our analysis of the term within a wide framework in order to understand its present-day salience in global discourse.

Enlightenment-era philosophers professed faith in man's ability to gain mastery over himself and his environment through reason and the scientific pursuit, and discovery, of truth. Fundamental to the Enlightenment view of modernity were the notions that human actions could be rationalized and that the workings of society could, thus, be rendered sensible to its members, one and all. Contemporary transparency claims constitute yet another way of celebrating the rationality of modern society. A social world whose workings are transparent to all is a social world that is amenable to the dictates of reason, arrived at openly through the public exercise of irrefutable logic validated by society's sovereign subjects themselves. In such a world, there is no place for suspicion and doubt; there are no dark recesses to harbor occult cosmologies, no closed chambers in which conspiracies might be hatched. Indeed, belief in indecipherable powers constitutes modernity's dark Other—an Other condemned, as "superstition," to fade under the light of historical progress.

Among the most influential scholars of modernity have been those, like Max Weber and Karl Marx, who suggest that man suffers consequences with the onset of modernity (Giddens 1990). Weber, for example, warned that the rationalization of society produces an "iron cage"—a bureaucratic nightmare leading to man's "disenchantment" with the world. Marx concerned himself with modern man's alienation from the products of his labor, from his fellow man, from himself, and from his species being. Not even such critics, however, challenged the inevitability of modernity's march or the assumption that modernity would eliminate local traditions and irrational convictions.[4] Their legacy has been influential. Compare, for example, the two guiding historical paradigms of the second half of the twentieth century—modernization theory in its neoliberal and Socialist variants. Neoliberal modernization theorists argued in the 1950s and 1960s that the peoples of the "Third World" could, and would, "develop" and become modern, breaking the shackles of tradition and ignorance through the intensification of urbanization and industrialization, commerce and education—albeit with the assistance and exemplary model of the West (Lerner 1958; Pye 1966; Rostow 1960). Socialist modernization efforts were animated by the conviction that the profound inequalities and injustices produced by global modernity could be resolved only through the intensification of its processes and the unification of those, worldwide, who suffered its consequences in common. In the post–World War II era, neither Cold War camp disputed the notion that modernity was a singular, teleological process that, eventually, would produce a homogeneous, modern "global village" (McLuhan 1964). What is more, neoliberal modernizationists were every bit the material determinists that their Socialist adversaries were. Both agreed, in fact, that, with the creation of specified social institutions and relations of production, modernity would materialize, washing over any and every cultural landscape.

In the post–Cold War era, we have ample evidence to question the bold assertions of both modernization paradigms (see Escobar 1995; Ferguson 1999; Donham 1999; Verdery 1996; West 2001). While it is undoubtedly true today that "modernity is everywhere" (Gaonkar 1999: 1), it is not everywhere the same. Our world has not been homogenized, nor does it appear to be headed in that direction. The shape that modernity has taken from one country and epoch to the next—even in "the West" (Wittrock 2000)—differs markedly. Indeed, with the intensification of the processes associated with modernization has come a proliferation of modern situations and conditions. Some

scholars have suggested that we can no longer speak meaningfully of modernity in the singular; instead, we must now speak of a multiplicity of modernities (Comaroff and Comaroff 1993; Fischer 1999: 459; Taylor 1999: 162–65).[5]

Not only does the notion of multiple modernities challenge globalization
mythology, which suggests that the world is fast becoming one. It also highlights the fallacy of modernizers' assumptions that modernity is first and
foremost a material project—one that *produces* cultural effects but that is
not, itself, culturally *produced*. The notion of multiple modernities suggests,
on the contrary, that the world is best seen "as a story of continual constitution and reconstitution of a multiplicity of cultural programs" (Eisenstadt 2000: 2). To this end, cultural historians, anthropologists, and others
have recently argued that, far from being an acultural or anticultural project,
modernity has always been deeply cultural (Comaroff and Comaroff 1993;
Taylor 1999)—that it has been animated in specific places and times by particular worldviews and ideological perspectives, particular truth claims and
culturally specific rationales.

"It is sometimes necessary," Marshall Sahlins writes, "to remind ourselves
that our pretended rationalist discourse is pronounced in a particular cultural dialect" (Sahlins 1993: 12). The idea of modernity, indeed, arose within
the context of Western European societies in the "age of discovery"—a moment of encounter with cultural Others provoking a search for self-identity
as well as a quest for means of asserting power vis-à-vis cultural Others. At
the same time, modernity has been taken up by Western Europe's Others in
distinctive ways and reconceived in relation to local cultural logics and practices. Hence, scholars now speak of "vernacular modernities": Indian modernity (Kaviraj 2000); Bengali modernity (Chakrabarty 1999); Sri Lankan
modernity (Lynch 1999); Confucian East Asian modernity (Weiming 2000);
Islamic modernity (Eickelman 2000; Gardner 1995; Göle 2000; Watts 1996);
Afro-modernity (Hanchard 1999), colonial-American modernity (Heideking
2000); Latin American modernity (Ortiz 2000); Soviet modernity (Arnason
2000); New Guinean modernity (Gewertz and Errington 1996); Nigerian
modernity (Bastian 2001); Chinese modernity (Lee 1999); and so on.

To imagine the world in this way is to problematize a host of previously
assumed dichotomies, including those between tradition and modernity, between the West and the rest, and between the local and the global. It is to suggest that global processes and local worlds are mutually constitutive (Robertson 1995: 40; Hannerz 1996). It is to suggest that modernity has escaped the
proprietorship of the West and that it has found new stewards among the

rest. It is to suggest that modernity is instantiated in moments of cultural reproduction and in the adaptation of varied local traditions to ever-changing historical circumstances.

Arjun Appadurai has provided a useful conceptual framework for exploring this complex world of multiple modernities. He suggests that we understand cultural interconnectivity in terms of what he defines as a variety of *-scapes*—for example, ethnoscapes, mediascapes, financescapes, technoscapes—formed of cultural flows that move over, and superimpose themselves on, geographical landscapes. Among these he includes *ideoscapes*— chains of ideas, terms, and images that can be condensed into key words (e.g., *freedom, welfare, rights, sovereignty, representation, democracy*) and exported to new contexts (Appadurai 1996: 36–37). In this volume, we treat *transparency* as a key-word component to ideoscapes that travel the globe conveying notions fundamental to the operative logic of globalizing economic and political institutions.

Appadurai's use of the suffix *-scape* has the decided analytical effect of decentering such global discourses as we seek to understand them. Ideoscapes are not only amorphous but also move at lightning speed; once unleashed, they may seem to be found everywhere yet to come from nowhere in particular. In Appadurai's language, ideoscapes, like modernity, are "at large" in the world (Appadurai 1996), flowing around us in every which way. As was suggested above, "suddenly, everything is transparent."

Tracing the idiosyncratic trajectories and unequal pathways of global ideoscapes requires that we do ethnography "on an awkward scale" (Comaroff and Comaroff 1999), seeing the global in the local and the local in the global. Yet tracing cultural flows around the globe is not without its difficulties. Chief among the dangers of such an endeavor is the possibility that accounts will suffer from a certain "ethnographic thinness" (see Ortner 1995). As Knauft has noted, "Concern with traveling cultural idioms easily comes at the expense of careful and systemic documentation, particularly in matters of social action, discourse, and belief" (1997: 286). Indeed, much of the literature on cultural aspects of "globalization" is based on fortuitous findings in taxicab conversations and popular media and literature, and it often takes the form of anecdotal storytelling devoid of rigorous ethnographic evidence. It is far too commonplace, in this literature, to speak in ill-supported generalities—to conjure evocative images of people, things, and ideas found in surprising new places, of CNN, mobile phones, and the Internet linking us in a single global village. Such analyses depoliticize cultural flows, leaving us with the shallow conclusion that "the world is becoming ever more intercon-nected" without telling us how and to what ends, or whom these processes marginalize and what sort of world *they* inhabit (Kearney 1995: 553).

Detailed ethnographic accounts are, we believe, required to enhance our appreciation of the myriad ways in which people around the world engage with globalizing processes, ranging from resistance to embrace, but includ-ing, most importantly, that vast and complex swath of strategies lying in be-tween (Broch-Due and Sanders 1999; Clough and Mitchell 2001; Comaroff 1989; Comaroff and Comaroff 1986; Grosz-Ngaté and Kokole 1997; Piot 1999; Robotham 1998). For most people around the globe today strive to "be modern," but they seek modernity on, and in, their own terms. As the authors whose work is collected in this volume compellingly show, an understanding of these terms comes only with rigorous ethnography.

Global ideoscapes, as Appadurai conceives of them, are appropriate foci for finely grained ethnography. Not only does the -*scape* suffix alert us to the potential for translocal movement of cultural elements with global preten-sions. It also suggests the possibility that these elements will be transformed in their varied new settings—that these -scapes will be manicured by their in-habitants. Ideoscapes travel pathways delineated by human institutions em-bodying complex and differential relations of power. In the varied locales through which they move, they are "decoded" by various people in accor-dance with diverse perspectives on, and experiences of, our modern world. Ideoscapes are read differently by people in different places (if people bother reading them at all).

Where Anthony Giddens has suggested that *trust*—that is, confidence in the operation of institutions that people cannot directly monitor and con-trol—is the lifeblood of modernity (1990), the contributors to this volume demonstrate with rich ethnographic detail how tenuous, even illusive, trust is, whether in the midst of the disorienting processes of Third World mod-ernization, the turbulent transformations defining post-Socialist societies, or moments of postindustrial drift and democratic ennui. While powerful forces in any of these settings may assert rationality and transparency as their operational logics, the volume's contributors find people reluctant to believe these claims. In the diverse settings examined, people express pro-found suspicions of the United Nations, the state, political parties, the police, courts, international financial institutions, banks, traders and shopkeepers, media, churches, intellectuals, and the wealthy. Their suspicions challenge and disrupt the flow of the global discourse of transparency and, with it, the confident claims of modernizing and globalizing institutions, even where

ek to make theirs the goods, institutional arrangements, and ideas of
nity.

:eover, the evidence presented in this volume suggests that people do
iply listen to, and assess, the ideas conveyed in global ideoscapes.
: quest for a meaningful modernity, people create and convey their
own terms and images, producing and sustaining ideoscapes that cohabit
the world along with those of global dimensions. These ideoscapes often
comprise ideas and images with long historical pedigrees—ones that mod-
erns and modernizers may look on with scorn. In any case, through the
production and maintenance of these ideoscapes, people assert their beliefs
that dominant forms of power—sometimes in combination with a "higher
power"—continue to work in obscurity, determining the course of social
events in ways not always "for the social good." These discourses of suspicion generally assert—contra transparency claims—that power is inher-
ently ambivalent and that it operates in ambiguous ways. Consequently, in
the globe's constituent localities, key words such as *transparency,* conveying notions of trust, openness, and fairness, must dance endlessly across the
same terrain as vernacular key words expressing suspicion, hiddenness, and
treachery. The depth of local wells of conspiracy ideas is as great, it would
seem, as the breadth of global transparency claims.

No one is more aware of conspiracy theories and/or occult cosmologies than
the purveyors of global transparency discourse. Ideas that power operates in
hidden ways make necessary their claims that it operates in the open. Quite
simply, conspiracy ideas and/or occult suspicions are the raison d'être for
transparency claims. Hence, policymakers preaching the merits of "fiscal accountability," "free trade," "the rule of law," "democracy," a "free press,"
"human rights," and other ideological positions bound up with the notion of
transparency expend a great deal of energy in attempts to paint Other ways
of seeing power with the brush of "ignorance," "irrationality," or "superstition." Conspiracy theorists are sometimes accused of "connecting too many
dots," of "mistaking metaphors for metonyms" (Harding and Stewart, chapter 9 in this volume), or of "backsliding" or "regression" (e.g., Zonis and
Joseph 1994). Conspiracy theories are typically cast as "fantastic" or as expressions of "paranoia"—sometimes subsumed under the term *conspiranoia.*
Descriptions of belief in witchcraft, sorcery, shamanism, and spirit possession, for their part, are often prefaced with descriptors like *persistent* or *re-
surgent* (see Kendall, chapter 1 in this volume) and are almost always tagged
traditional or, even, *antimodern* or *atavistic.*

Anthropologists, however, have long embraced a vaguely defined mandate to discover the "sense" in human belief systems, no matter how "strange" they seem. Evans-Pritchard's *Witchcraft, Oracles, and Magic among the Azande* set the standard here. In an implicit argument with Lévy-Bruhl ([1910] 1985), who saw evidence everywhere in non-Western society of a "pre-logical mentality," Evans-Pritchard argued that Zande beliefs were "eminently coherent, being inter-related by a network of logical ties" (Evans-Pritchard [1937] 1976: 150). Once the Azande "idiom" was adopted, he concluded, there was nothing "irrational" about Azande thought. Taking this notion one step further, Robin Horton argued that witchcraft beliefs did for the Azande what science did for Westerners; it explained happenings that direct observation and common sense could not, ordering an otherwise disorderly world of human experience (Horton 1970).

More recent anthropologists have searched for the sense, specifically, in diverse ways of understanding power, whether in Bolivian tin mines (Nash [1979] 1993), in Malaysian factories (Ong 1987), in Zimbabwean guerrilla camps (Lan 1985), or in other contexts (Comaroff 1985; Boddy 1989; Limón 1994; Kapferer 1997; Taussig 1980). Noteworthy is the fact that this anthropological sense making of "strange beliefs" has largely focused on non-Western peoples.[6]

Finding sense in the beliefs of more familiar folk has proved problematic. Philosophers, historians, and political scientists have been dismissive of the conspiracy ideas of Westerners. Richard Hofstadter (1965) set the tone for later scholars by suggesting that conspiracy theories were collective "paranoid delusions." Karl Popper (1966) equated conspiracies with secularized religious beliefs but concluded that, as such, they were *wrong*. "To modern scholarly ears," Ostler has written, "the language of conspiracy sounds bizarre and irrational" (1995: 25). "Most academics," Keeley has concluded, "simply find the conspiracy theories of popular culture to be silly and without merit" (1999: 109, n. 1).

Anthropologists might be expected to show more sympathy than social scientists working in other disciplines, but, even in a time when the discipline has embraced study in familiar places, anthropologists have manifested their indifference to occult beliefs and conspiracy ideas among familiar natives. In the introduction to his book on New Age religion in the United States, for example, Michael Brown tells us that his emerging interest in the topic was often greeted with raised eyebrows (Brown 1997).

We can only speculate on the reasons for this. Anthropologists are, after all, social and political beings in their own rights. "Close to home," where research subjects' beliefs actually have the potential to affect the anthropologist as a fellow member of society, it is, perhaps, harder to establish methodological empathy and easier simply to disagree with Other views of the world. Consider, for example, the dilemma faced by Harding and Stewart (chapter 9 in this volume), whose work brought them into encounter with fundamentalist Christians who espouse right-wing positions on issues ranging from abortion, to homosexuality, to gun control. Setting aside one's own opinions on these politically charged issues pushes the limits of "scientific objectivity." In recent years, anthropological discussions have identified the need to "study up," that is, to study the structures of power that affect anthropology's more conventional subjects. Studying up is generally understood as work "behind enemy lines," but this seems justified when one considers the balance of power. Studying behind enemy lines where one's subjects are not powerful actors and/or institutions appears much more complex. Where American anthropologists are told by the American Anthropological Association (1998) that they must "do everything in their power to ensure that their research does not harm the safety, *dignity*, or privacy of the people with whom they work," examining belief systems that one doubts or disagrees with poses intractable dilemmas. Perhaps, in part, for such reasons, no anthropologist (that we know of) has yet undertaken ethnographic study of right-wing militia movements in the United States.[7]

Even in the absence of politically informed disagreement, anthropologists working close to home have found it more difficult to attribute to next-door natives "traditional wisdom" or "indigenous knowledge" when these people theorize, across the grain of "scientifically established truths," about the workings of hidden powers in our midst. It is apparently easier to conclude that those who live in societies where the scientific paradigm constitutes a predominant interpretative schema "ought to know better." Consider the exasperated—albeit paternalistic—tone of scholarly discussions of "conspiracy theory" among African Americans, who are said to waste precious intellectual energy fighting fictive enemies, creating fantastic scapegoats, and, ultimately, victimizing themselves. To the extent that academics have taken such conspiracy ideas seriously, they have generally done so to disprove them (Pigden 1993; Pipes 1992, 1996; Keeley 1999).

Indeed, it has proved difficult for anthropologists studying anywhere ultimately to avoid assessments of the "truth" of the beliefs that they study. Evans-Pritchard found sense in Azande beliefs, but he tells us quite explicitly that he did not believe in witches and oracles even if, as a good participant observer, he did consult oracles while in the field. He wrote that "witches, as the Azande conceive them, clearly cannot exist." Azande beliefs "make sense," he tells us, only once one (erroneously) assumes the existence of witches and the efficacy of oracles, once one filters observation through the "idiom" of witchcraft (Evans-Pritchard [1937] 1976: 18, 150).

Subsequent anthropological treatments of the occult have sometimes been more nuanced about the issue of truth and have approached it in different ways. Many ask not simply if beliefs are "true" or "false," but, rather, if through believing people achieve "consciousness" of their situation or, instead, develop "false consciousness" (Comaroff 1985; Lan 1985; Limón 1994; Nash [1979] 1993; Ong 1987; Scott 1985; Taussig 1980).

Some of the contributors to this volume argue explicitly against accusations of falsehood or false consciousness leveled against the conspiracy ideas that they analyze. Some conclude, simply, that there is truth to be found in suspicions of power—that, in the cases they consider, power does, without a doubt, conspire (Bastian, chapter 2; Hellinger, chapter 7; McCarthy Brown, chapter 8) and that, consequently, the suspicious may be "paranoid within reason" (Marcus 1999). More broadly, however, these authors treat conspiracy ideas, near and far, as discourses that *construct* truths in contradistinction to the (also *constructed*) truths of discourses of transparency. Although recognizing that those making the transparency argument often hold considerably more power than those left to suspect these claims, the authors level the epistemological playing field between these truth-asserting endeavors. In what is perhaps the most poignant example of this, Karen McCarthy Brown playfully describes the narratives of the police officers, lawyers, and newspaper reporters involved in the trial of an officer for police brutality against a Haitian immigrant in New York as "word *wanga*"—*wanga* being the Vodou term for a magical charm.

In conceiving of transparency claims and conspiracy suspicions alike as ideological formations, the contributors to this volume raise questions larger than the veracity of these ideas. In doing so, they do not unproblematically celebrate any and every "oppositional" view as a successful form of "resistance"; they do not gloss over issues pertaining to the efficacy of the practical strategies of dealing with power nurtured by occult cosmologies and conspiracy theories. Rather, they place these concerns within a wider sociocultural framework. Collectively, they ask: What can we learn from occult cosmologies and conspiracy theories about the varied social experiences of power in our globalizing world? What do these diverse ideoscapes of suspicion tell us—that ideoscapes of transparency fail to express—about the operation of power in our world? And what social, political, and economic effects are produced by these alternative ways of understanding power?

The contributors to this volume provide persuasive evidence that modernity is experienced by many people as a fragmented, contradictory, and disquieting process that produces untenable situations and unfulfilled desires and that power is, in the modern world, perceived by many to be something that lies beyond their grasp. Modernity, paradoxically, generates the very opacities of power that it claims to obviate.[8] Rather than simply resist power, however, the peoples considered in this volume seek to reveal and to steer the hidden forces that they believe animate their world, to explore the nuances of power and to take advantage of its ambivalence. Through reading global ideoscapes of transparency and writing their own ideoscapes of suspicion, they assert themselves in a world whose rationalized systems would, if only they could, nullify their subjectivity and agency completely. Through articulation of their suspicions, people put modernity "on endless trial" (Kolakowski 1990), ensuring that it remain an unfinished project. At the same time, they " 'make' themselves modern, as opposed to being 'made' modern by alien and impersonal forces" (Gaonkar 1999: 16).

The analysis of power manifest in these varied discursive formations is often—in one sense or another—revealing. These revelations lead us to question the very meaning of transparency. What, after all, is claimed when the operation of power is described as transparent? What is *seen through,* and what, then, is *seen? Transparency,* as it is used in contemporary global-speak, presumes a *surface* to power that can be seen through and an *interior* that can, as a result, be seen. If the processes through which power functions constitute its interior, what, then, constitutes its surface? Its (ideological) representations? If so, can such surfaces ever be rendered transparent; can they ever be completely stripped away? Or can they only be transformed/replaced/covered over? And by whom?

As people around the globe consider transparency claims, they conceive of power's surfaces and depths in vastly different ways, as the contributors to this volume illustrate. In some cases, people understand themselves to shed light on the hidden recesses of power, exposing its concealed logic. In other cases, they claim not to be able to see how power works, but that is precisely the point; by expressing how the workings of power remain to them invisible or, at least, clouded, they decertify power's claims to transparency, calling attention to its hiddenness behind an impenetrable facade. Sometimes, the occultists and conspiracists considered in this volume enshroud themselves in secrecy, for fear that being seen by stronger forces might undermine their own power; they fight hidden power with hidden power (Scott 1990). At other times, they avowedly launch their campaigns against dark forces in the light of day, challenging regnant powers to meet them in the open, thus "flushing them out." In a variety of ways, the subalterns that interest us in this volume mime the powers that they suspect. This should come as no surprise, for, as they reveal the ideological nature of transparency claims, these people express their own ideologically informed views of power—views that *re-present* the world as they experience and understand it. These representations often invoke complex metaphors. In any case, they adorn the reality that they purport to describe with masks no more, and no less, constructed than those that they seek to tear off the inchoate face of reality.

The ideas about power ethnographically presented in this volume belie the notion, widely held, that conspiracy theories and occult cosmologies recklessly reduce the world's complexity at the expense of deeper analyses and accurate understandings (Groth 1987: 5). In fact, it would seem from the evidence here presented that they do precisely the opposite, rendering the world more complex by calling attention to its hidden and contradictory logics, by proposing alternative ways of understanding and engaging it (cf. Craig and Gregory 1999). Through expressing their suspicions that power works in complicated ways, these people "rake over the coals of events in search of the sense (and senselessness) of their sociability" (Taussig 1987: 394), or, put otherwise, they seek "to penetrate the impenetrable, to unscrew the inscrutable, to recapture the forces suspected of redirecting the flow of power in the world" (Comaroff and Comaroff 1993: xxx). Through their discursive imaginings, they sometimes seek to expose power, sometimes to reflect or refract it, and sometimes to further enshroud it. As often as not, however, they expound ways of better coping with the forces that animate their world.

Laurel Kendall's essay begins this volume by examining how people of diverse social classes in South Korea have read recent IMF-sponsored economic restructuring through a "shamanic lens." After the collapse of financial markets throughout Asia in the autumn of 1997, South Korea accepted terms from the IMF in return for financial assistance. While the South Korean government sought to persuade citizens that the resultant tightening of credit was necessary to "rationalize" the labor market and increase economic "accountability," many South Koreans suffered acute personal hardships with the slowing of the economy and widespread layoffs. Kendall tells us that, for most, "the future was illegible" in the midst of IMF-sponsored reforms and that the very term *IMF* took on ominous tones "as something more mythically potent than a body of global financial regulators." She continues, "[The word *IMF*] stood, not for transparency and fiscal accountability, but for a welter of concealed powers in distant places, both foreign and domestic, whose veiled operations had wreaked havoc, not only on the abstraction *nation*, but on many simple lives."

Shamanic rituals have long provided South Koreans with a means with which to make sense of individual fate in a capricious world. What is most interesting for our purposes, however, is that, in recent years, "mediumship has been reborn" (Morris 2000b: 460; see also Morris 2000a) across the region, within the context of profound economic and social crisis. And not only the downtrodden have turned to spirit mediums for assistance in these troubled times. The wealthy and well educated, too, have found mediums indispensable in coming to terms with an unsteady economy (cf. Geschiere 1997, 1998a; Hellinger, chapter 7 in this volume; Harding and Stewart, chapter 9 in this volume). If the fact that shamanic discourse cuts across class and status boundaries to include more "modern" Koreans were not alone sufficient to challenge the assumptions of the modernization paradigm that occult cosmologies thrive only on the receding margins of the modern world, Korean shamans accent the modernity of the shamanic tradition by calling on "*Official* Spirits" to aid their clients.

Koreans have always looked to the spirits with ambivalence, Kendall explains, because they sometimes bring good fortune and sometimes bring disaster. The unpredictability of Official Spirits in the IMF era powerfully reflects what most Koreans see in the IMF. Although neither are entirely trustworthy, one can, at least, engage with the spirits. Kendall tells us that "confrontations with gods and ancestors in playful and sometimes poignant rituals permit, if not a transparent aperture on the forces that drive Korean modernity, some critical lenses through which participants view the living out of modernity's consequences as they engage a capricious market." Tellingly, shamans do not often claim to be able to see, clearly, the hidden powers behind the generalized social condition referred to simply as *IMF*. What they *see,* instead, is the *obscurity* produced by the IMF. As a consequence, Kendall tells us, spirits are often rendered "mute and impotent—at least for a time." The silence and weakness of the spirits, however, is powerfully expressive of the experience of the moment for many Koreans, constituting a salient counterdiscourse to IMF claims to be producing a more "rational," more "transparent" economic climate.

In the next essay in the collection, Misty Bastian presents another case—this one drawn from Nigeria—of popular readings of the global IMF discourse of economic transparency. In the case that she describes, people seek to make sense, not simply of their own misfortunes, but also of the good fortunes of others in a generally difficult time. The story unfolds in Owerri, the capital town of Imo State, when a man named Innocent is found not so innocently transporting the severed head of a young boy in the trunk of his car. Before he can be tried, Innocent dies in the Owerri prison under mysterious circumstances, but only after being made to pose for television cameras holding the boy's head. The broadcast images spark riots in which the town's lower classes target the goods and persons of the town's elite.

To understand these events, Bastian suggests, we must take into account political and economic developments in Owerri over the past decade. Notwithstanding a post-oil-boom recession in the region and the 1987 adoption of an IMF Structural Adjustment Program, regional elites combined with outsiders in the early 1990s to secure government support for the building of an airport in Owerri, "opening up" the town to adventurous investors. Watching the comings and goings, and movements around town, of this new class, Owerri residents could not avoid wondering, as Bastian phrases it, "from where, in what was officially touted as an age of fiscal austerity, did the money for all this excess come?" (cf. Comaroff and Comaroff 1999, in press). As Owerri "opened up" to outsiders, it seemingly closed down to its own residents, who felt at a loss to comprehend the forces animating contemporary events and processes.

Simultaneous with these developments, however, Owerri reportedly experienced an epidemic of child theft and kidnapping. In popular discourse, Owerri residents suggested that the otherwise inexplicable successes of the nouveaux riches depended on the ritual murder of innocent children. The broadcast image of a man holding the severed head of a child served its audience as a corporeal trope that crystallized nagging suspicions of a supernatural "elite conspiracy to garner riches at the expense of the ordinary Nigerian people." Through her class-centered analysis, Bastian treats Owerri residents, not as homogeneous locals on the global landscape, but, rather, as a heterogeneous mix, paying close attention to politics *among* these global subalterns (see Ortner 1995: 179). Through her telling of the story of ritual murder in Owerri, she conveys the assertions of Owerri's poor that power hides itself *as well as*, sometimes, rendering invisible its victim-subjects. These stories echo with accounts of the poaching of bodies, body parts, and bodily fluids heard around the globe (Campion-Vincent 1990; Sanders

2001; Scheper-Hughes 1996, 1998a, 1998b, 2000; White 1997), not to mention stories of the "disappeared" in Latin America and elsewhere. By probing ritual murder, the Nigerian state risked exposing, not only criminal elements, but also state complicity in criminal phenomena, as is the case anywhere the state finds itself tightly bound up with the social forces—whether organized crime or paramilitary death squads—producing such "disappearances." The official investigation in Owerri might, as Bastian describes it, be better understood as an attempt to cloak a violent underworld in a *veil of transparency* than as an attempt to expose it. Predictably, soon after the Owerri riots, the probing eye of the Nigerian state turned away from the town's elite and onto Owerri's lower classes, whose bodies and persons were subjected to scrutiny by joint army-police patrols and security checkpoints.

In the moment of the riots, however, Owerri residents turned from their television screens to the marketplace—which served them, Bastian suggests, not merely as a venue for rumormongering, but as a place in which they could render *themselves* visible to *themselves*. The violent actions that they then took have been viewed with ambivalence by many Nigerians, who now invoke the term *doing Otokoto* (*Otokoto* is the name that the riots took from the hotel where Innocent worked and where his victim's body was found) to mean both "rioting and lawlessness" and "violently uncovering a hidden truth, making plain what everyone suspects but no one dares to see or to say."

In his essay, Harry West picks up the theme of citizens rendered visible to themselves in detailing the responses of residents of the Mueda Plateau, in northern Mozambique, to voter-registration efforts within the context of a United Nations–brokered peace process including preparations, in 1994, for multiparty elections. West suggests that the voting process was presented to Mozambicans as a vast material metaphor wherein voter-registration cards represented the political subjectivity of individual citizens and ballot cards represented individual political wills. Manipulation of these material artifacts would, Mozambican voters were told, allow observers and participants alike to see the collective will of the Mozambican people expressed and enacted.

To their surprise, election workers found Muedan elders reluctant to register. West suggests that this was not because these elders failed to understand the process but, rather, because they understood it all too well. This was clear in how they read voter-registration cards as metaphors; Muedans associated these cards with several other "identity tokens" with which they had had experience over the course of their lifetimes, including colonial-era labor passbooks and tax receipts, church-issued Virgin Mary medallions, and nationalist party membership cards. In their experience, West tells us, "voter cards echoed with messages embedded in identity tokens of the past . . . reminding [Muedans] that power works in both visible and invisible realms and that it reveals itself and/or its subjects when this serves its purposes but conceals itself and/or its subjects when this serves its purposes better." The root metaphor that saturated all these references was, West argues, that of sorcery. In the realm of sorcery, possession of a medicinal substance called *shikupi* allows sorcerers to cloak their predatory actions in invisibility; the same substance must be used by responsible authority figures who seek to police the invisible realm and to protect the commonweal. In associating voter cards with other identity tokens and with shikupi, West suggests, Muedans conjured up the specter of "dangerous games of hide and seek played with capricious forms of power" and reminded themselves that power in the here and now was no less complex, no less dangerous.

Most Muedans, West tells us, do not themselves claim to be able to see into the hidden realm of sorcery. Echoing Kendall (chapter 1), then, West argues that it would be misleading to conclude that Muedans' more complex metaphors allowed them to see more clearly into the realm of hidden political motives and activities—to "unmask" reality. Instead, in the language of sorcery, West argues, Muedans painted their own mask on reality, one that portrayed what lay beneath as obscure rather than clear.

Albert Schrauwers's account also deals with a new political order— namely, Suharto's Indonesian "New Order" state—and with popular readings of power that proliferate beyond official symbols. The New Order state derived legitimacy under the specter of its implied antithesis, which Schrauwers points out was not an Old Order but, rather, disorder. Even so, rampant corruption and abuse of state power created fertile terrain for alternative readings of the New Order—ones through which "discourses of 'open and transparent' bureaucratic process" were recast as "the multiplication of rules for the personal enrichment of those with 'connections'" (cf. Bastian, chapter 2). In addition to this, obscure state practices were also suspected by the Christian community of Central Sulawesi to be "signs of a larger project of enforced state Islamicization." Schrauwers tells us that such "conspiracy theories . . . sketch out an alternate, unseen terrain whose reality makes sense of, and transcends, the obscure workings of corruption."

Complicating matters, however, members of the Christian community often found the workings of the corrupt church bureaucracy as impenetrable as those of the state, and, in these circumstances, they turned to yet another interpretative framework to deal with powers hidden from view, namely, sorcery. The nested power bureaucracies of Indonesia were met with nested popular theories of conspiratorial power, evoking, for Schrauwers, the image of Russian-made dolls that bear within them ever-smaller replicas of themselves (cf. West, chapter 3). Schrauwers tells us, "Occult cosmologies, whether 'religious' or 'magical,' offer important conceptual tools to people confronted with the obscure workings of open government." Through them, political battles are understood as components to "an epic battle played out on a different plane." Schrauwers concludes that, where Weber predicted that the bureaucratization of power would disenchant the world, the Christians of Central Sulawesi reenchant it by doing exactly the opposite of that which Weber predicted, embracing "tradition" (*rebutan*). As they do so, they struggle to reassert themselves in the face of powerful forces by summoning up larger, more overly determinant powers to frame their individual and collective agencies. In their view, Schrauwers tells us, "The politics of [the] unseen realm always exceed the structural determinacies of . . . open and transparent bureaucracies."

In his essay, Todd Sanders presents a case that further challenges the idea—implicit or explicit in the works of countless social theorists—that "modernity" banishes "tradition." The Ihanzu of Tanzania, with which he deals, themselves distinguish between what they understand as "modern" and "traditional" economic spheres. Believing that modern goods are produced by modern people in modern places, the Ihanzu look on these goods with deep ambivalence owing to the subtle forms of social differentiation that have accompanied them into Ihanzu society, most intensively in the period following IMF structural adjustment in the late 1980s. The Ihanzu's ambivalence is expressed in their readings of the mysteries of the "open market"—an economic domain that strangely rewards traders and shopkeepers who, from an Ihanzu standpoint, do almost no "work." What is the source of this new wealth, the Ihanzu ask themselves (cf. Bastian, chapter 2)?

In search of an explanation, the Ihanzu turn to seers whose vision penetrates into the hidden realm of witchcraft. Ordinarily, seers are able to see how witches feed on victims, who lose the "traditional" forms of wealth—crops, livestock, children—that witches gain. This zero-sum game can be verified by ordinary Ihanzu, who may easily see the visible traces of witchcraft in the rise and fall of individual fortunes. However, the logic of translocal commodity flows—the movements of "modern" goods, as the Ihanzu classify them—resists the interpretative view of Ihanzu seers (cf. Kendall, chapter 1; West, chapter 3). Because traders and shop owners possess novel, "modern" forms of wealth, they cannot have taken these from their poorer fellow villagers, Ihanzu seers reason; the source and the manner of procurement of these "modern" goods consequently remain incomprehensible to most Ihanzu.

This is why, for many Ihanzu, "modern economic processes have, by spanning vast distances, become virtually unintelligible." Thus, contra earlier modernization theory and its more recent neoliberal reincarnations, the Ihanzu consider the modern sphere of the economy *less* visible and sensible than the traditional sphere. Sanders points out that Ihanzu views of the modernity/tradition dichotomy are as ideological as are those of modernization theorists. What is more, he shows that these concepts can be delinked from their purported sites of origin—the West and the rest—and reconfigured in imaginative ways. Even if the Ihanzu and their seers admit, then, that they are unable to decipher the logic of "modernity," their witchcraft beliefs provide them with insights into the globalizing world in which they live. Sanders concludes: "Rather than downplaying or ignoring [the] magicalities of modernity—the patently odd fact that hidden hands and other enigmatic economic processes drive, in some unspecified manner, our everyday world—the Ihanzu dwell on such absurdities. . . . They recognize and confront head-on [modernity's] deep-seated ambivalences. Not for a moment do they pretend, for convenience's sake, that our world can ever be rendered entirely transparent."

Caroline Humphrey's contribution takes us to Russia, where, much like Western champions of modernization, Soviet-era Communist Party leaders argued that the bright Communist future would supplant a dark, primitive past imbued with superstitious beliefs. In this way, they justified state persecution of Buddhism. Even so, today, Buryat Buddhists concern themselves with reading the historical events of their lifetime through the Buddhist lens of reincarnation beliefs rather than celebrating the political transparency of post-Soviet glasnost.

Humphrey suggests that, among Buryat Buddhists, dialectical materialism ironically nurtured a sense of historical overdetermination akin to reincarnation beliefs wherein individual action could be attributed to the near karmic forces of "historical conditions." In any case, where the Soviet-led project and, with it, Communist historical narratives failed, Buryats read between the lines, reworking Communist narratives in the language of reincarnation beliefs. Stalin, for example, is now widely said to have been the reincarnation of the mythic Blue Elephant who, after failing to receive due credit for aiding in the construction of a Buddhist temple, vowed to destroy Buddhism three times in subsequent lives. Buryats today consequently embrace neither Communist nor post-Communist official narratives, Humphrey suggests; they place their faith in neither scientific socialism nor the rationalized liberal state. Instead, they believe that the ethical weight of acts committed in previous lives constitutes a decisive force in ongoing historical processes.

Humphrey describes these reincarnation narratives as paranoid since, as Buryats talk about the past lives of others, they also talk about themselves, if only implicitly. In doing so, she moves well beyond Hofstadter (1965), depathologizing the collective paranoia that she describes. Humphrey reminds us that, in looking to the recent past, Buryats must come to terms with the roles they played in complex events such as the great purges. Hence, through investiture in reincarnation beliefs, Buryats metaphorically reproduce the historical overdetermination of Communist historical narratives—even as they supplant these (cf. West, chapter 3; Schrauwers, chapter 4)—to explain, not only their suffering in these years, but also their complicity with the state.

In his essay, Daniel Hellinger considers and dismisses a more conventional (pathological) definition of paranoia in relation to a number of conspiracy theories sustained by Americans in the post–World War II era. Among these are the varied theories suggesting that Lee Harvey Oswald did not act alone in assassinating John F. Kennedy as well as more recent conspiracy ideas suggesting U.S. government complicity in the introduction of crack cocaine into American inner cities in the 1980s and the use, by the CIA, of drug profits to finance covert operations in Central America. Hellinger tells us that most commentators see such conspiracy theories as a popular response to society's impersonal forces. The popular appeal of the major motion picture *JFK* and others in the conspiratorial genre has sometimes been attributed to "a sea change in Americans' trust in government and sense of civic efficacy." African Americans, in particular, are sometimes said to be "more susceptible to conspiracy theory because they harbor 'an endless supply of suspicion.'" However, in the end, most commentators conclude, conspiracy theorists only distract themselves from the task of gaining a true understanding of society's workings, displacing blame for their own ignorance of how "the system" works.

By contrast, Hellinger advocates moving beyond the "paranoid-style thesis," taking the belief in conspiracy seriously through identifying *who* believes *what* and *why* they believe it from *their* point of view. Hellinger does so for two reasons. First, as social facts, popular beliefs in conspiracy constitute a substantial political force on the American landscape—a form of resistance to hegemonic forces variously understood. "Conspiracies are not just for kooks," Hellinger tells us. Political survey work, for example, shows that, contrary to some opinions, the belief in conspiracy theories cuts across racial and class divides in American society; in fact, data show that higher education only deepens political mistrust. Hellinger writes that the wide-spread appeal of the television program *The X-Files* "put[s] in doubt the con-tention that conspiracy theory is attractive mostly to minorities and lower-income groups. Its plots fed off widespread doubts about the legitimacy of democratic processes and the possibility of citizen efficacy."

Beyond this, however, Hellinger suggests that conspiracy believers often have good reason to suspect hegemonic powers; for example, he argues that the history of U.S. foreign policy since World War II is replete with opera-tions undertaken behind a screen of secrecy and deception. Quite simply, conspiracy theorists may be on to something, even if they cannot clearly see the details; the fact that they cannot clearly see the details is precisely the point. Hellinger suggests that, where "parapolitical" analysis may allow for the belief that all is well in the world, a "deep political" analysis—one that recognizes the propensity of power to conspire—affords a truer understand-ing. Hellinger argues that African Americans in particular are apt to believe that the government is out to get them *because the facts seem to fit the theory* (cf. Pigden 1993).

In her contribution, Karen McCarthy Brown presents another case in which the facts seem to fit the theory that people of African descent in the United States are abused by dominant forces—this time forces hiding behind the mantra of "due process." Brown presents accounts of two different social responses to the brutalization of a Haitian immigrant named Abner Louima by New York City police officers. Louima was arrested outside a Brooklyn nightclub in August 1997 after being mistaken, Brown tells us, for someone who had taken a swing at a police officer in the midst of a melee. On the way to the police precinct, he was beaten, and, on arrival, during interro-gation in a precinct bathroom, a wooden stick (thought at the time to be a toilet plunger handle) was shoved into his rectum. Eventually, Louima's as-sailant was convicted and sentenced to prison. Justice for Louima came at a considerable price, however. Through official police accounts and media coverage of his assailant's trial, his "hypersexualized black body," Brown tells us, was subjected to racially informed scrutiny by the American public, who looked on him as both shamefully vulnerable and persistently dangerous (cf. Bastian, chapter 2). At the same time, the acts of Louima's assailant—and, perhaps, accomplices—remained enshrouded in the darkness of police cover-up.

Haitian Americans responded with vigor and creativity to these events, offering their own narratives to counter official accounts—to reveal what "actually happened" where "due process" had failed to do so. In particular, Mama Lola, the Vodou priestess with whom Brown has worked for many years, prepared *wanga* (charms) to "reconfigure Louima's reality"—to help ensure that jurors saw the case in Louima's favor. Beyond this, Haitian Americans assembled to demonstrate publicly against racial profiling and the brutality of the New York City police. In these endeavors, Brown notes, secrecy and transparency worked together, "evoking one another in a paradoxical dance of increasing complexity." As Mama Lola worked with Louima toward the goal of exposing the truth, she fought the hidden powers of the police with her own hidden powers. As she sought to ensure that jurors saw Louima for who he was, she was careful to keep her own activities secret for fear that they would be misunderstood, according to American stereotypes of Vodou, as ill intentioned. By contrast, Haitian American street protesters did not fight hidden powers with hidden powers; rather, they sought to render police power visible through their own highly visible actions, miming what had occurred in the interrogation room by brandishing toilet plunger handles painted blood red; in this way, they imaginatively pulled back the *veil of transparency* that enshrouded police activities, transferring the shame associated with this hidden moment from the victim to the perpetrator(s).

In the volume's final major essay, Susan Harding and Kathleen Stewart also take up the theme of paranoia, suggesting that "we have all glimpsed somewhere—in our families, schools, workplaces, and communities—that hypervigilant over-the-edge look in the paranoid eye, that bottomless rage against the system, that obsessive compilation of signs that 'they' are up to no good." They analyze this paranoia in relation to two distinct social groups. The first of these is the Calvary Chapel church of Orange County, California, whose members gather several days a week to decipher the signs in contemporary events of the battle between God's will and the forces of evil (e.g., federal gun control, "unisex" Bibles, environmentalism, sex education in public schools, media images of homosexuality) that stand in the way of the realization of His plan. Notwithstanding evidence of the workings of "the guy in the little red suit"—even, sometimes, in their own lives—and the resultant sense of siege, believers comfort themselves in the knowledge that "God [has] a plan that [will] turn it all around in the end." In fact, the worse things appear, the better they are deemed actually to be, given that, for those who know how to read it, bad news is a sign of the coming of the Lord.

The second group that Harding and Stewart consider is the Heaven's Gate movement, whose members committed suicide under the passing Hale-Bopp comet, behind which, they believed, was hidden a spaceship to carry them home to a higher plane. Harding and Stewart examine the lives and tenets of Heaven's Gate's leaders, showing not only how they led their members to spurn the "things of this world" but also how they cast themselves as heroes, able both to understand "the system" that constitutes our world and to get "outside" of it. Harding and Stewart conclude that conspiracy theories constitute "metadiscourses of modernity" and, as such, are "a new lingua franca" in the context of both the New World Order and "the long-standing sense of disjuncture between the American dream and an always already degraded reality."

Through theorizing about hidden powers, suggest Harding and Stewart, the members of Calvary Chapel and of Heaven's Gate seek/sought not only to understand a perplexing world but also to engage with it. They write that conspiracy theory constitutes a *structure of feeling* that both generates and registers the contradictions of contemporary social transformations—that actively works on, and works out, the world (cf. Schrauwers, chapter 4). In working out the world, however, members of both these movements are/were led to surveil not only the world around them but also themselves (cf. Bastian, chapter 2), producing within them, Harding and Stewart suggest, an obsessive urge to coax the world toward its overdetermined outcome, a paranoid drive to align themselves with the inevitability of coming events.

Notes

1   Among those in attendance were ex-World Bank president Robert S. McNamara, ex-Costa Rican president and Nobel laureate Oscar Arias Sanchez, and ex-U.S. delegate to the United Nations Andrew Young. See "A War on Global Corruption" (1993); http://www.transparency.de/index.html.

2   For a journalist's account of meetings attended by residents of Franklin County, Missouri, who feared that the United Nations planned to take over half of America and restore it to wilderness areas designated for "little or no human use," see Uhlenbrock (1997a, 1997b).

3   One could draw a distinction here between two types of unseen powers: *hidden* (or concealed) powers and *invisible* powers. The former implies some degree of agency—an active concealing of the powers that be—while the latter describes forces that remain unseen owing to impersonal structural forces. Conspiracy theories and occult cosmologies can subscribe to either view of unseen powers or

to both simultaneously in different temporal and social settings. The theoretical implications of this distinction depend greatly on the ethnographic contexts in which they are made.

4 We are well aware that Weber, more than Marx, was particularly concerned with ideal types when he spoke of "modernity" and "tradition." However, to the extent that Weber was concerned with the dynamics of social change, he did not always distinguish clearly between the "real" world and ideal models of that world. This is why he could discuss a "modern" capitalist world in which "religious and ethical reflections upon the world were increasingly rationalized . . . [and] primitive and magical notions were eliminated" (Gerth and Mills 1958: 275).

5 A number of scholars have viewed capitalism in this way: "Western capitalism in its totality is a truly exotic cultural scheme, as bizarre as any other, marked by the subsumption of material rationality in a vast order of symbolic relationships" (Sahlins 1993: 12; see also Sahlins 1976; Mintz 1985; Comaroff and Comaroff 2000). See also the interesting work by Mayfair Yang (2000) that deals with the question of "multiple capitalisms."

6 There have been some notable exceptions to this tendency, as when analysts have focused on popular notions of satanic child abuse in the United States (Comaroff 1997) and the United Kingdom (La Fontaine 1998) and on parallels between African "witch doctors" and American "spin doctors" (Geschiere 1998b).

7 For a historical overview of the American militia movement, see Pitcavage (2001).

8 This point has regularly been made clear in recent years to citizens around the globe protesting the policies of the World Bank, the International Monetary Fund, and the World Trade Organization, who have encountered an ever-widening no-protest zone that has made observation of, and engagement with, the activities of these organizations increasingly difficult.

References

American Anthropological Association. 1998. "Code of Ethics of the American Anthropological Association." http://www.aaanet.org/ethcode.htm. Accessed June 2000.

Anderson, Jon W. 1996. "Conspiracy Theories, Premature Entextualization, and Popular Political Analysis." *Arab Studies Journal* 4 (1): 96–102.

Appadurai, Arjun. 1996. *Modernity at Large: Cultural Dimensions of Globalization.* Minneapolis: University of Minnesota Press.

Arens, W., and Ivan Karp. 1989. Introduction to *Creativity of Power: Cosmology and Action in African Societies,* ed. W. Arens and I. Karp, xi–xxix. Washington, D.C.: Smithsonian Institution Press.

Arnason, Johann P. 2000. "Communism and Modernity." *Daedalus* (special issue: "Multiple Modernities") 129 (1): 61–90.

Bailyn, B. 1967. *The Ideological Origins of the American Revolution.* Cambridge, Mass.: Belknap.

Banning, Lance. 1978. *The Jeffersonian Persuasion: Evolution of a Party Ideology.* Ithaca: Cornell University Press.

Bastian, Misty L. 2001. "Vulture Men, Campus Cultists, and Teenaged Witches: Modern Magics in Nigerian Popular Press." In *Magical Interpretations, Material Realities: Modernity, Witchcraft, and the Occult in Postcolonial Africa,* ed. Henrietta L. Moore and Todd Sanders. London: Routledge.

Bell, David, and Lee-Jane Bennion-Nixon. 2001. "The Popular Culture of Conspiracy/the Conspiracy of Popular Culture." In *The Age of Anxiety: Conspiracy Theory and the Human Sciences,* ed. Jane Parish and Martin Parker. Oxford: Blackwell.

Belsie, Laurent. 1997. "UFOs? Secret Agents? On the Net, Conspiracy Theories Abound." *Christian Science Monitor,* 7 October, 12.

Blum, Howard. 1990. *Out There: The Government's Secret Quest for Extraterrestrials.* New York: Simon and Schuster.

Boddy, J. 1989. *Wombs and Alien Spirits: Women, Men, and the Zar Cult in Northern Sudan.* Madison: University of Wisconsin Press.

Boxer, Sarah. 1998. "Transparent Enough to Hide Behind." *New York Times,* 19 December, D7.

Broch-Due, Vigdis, and Todd Sanders. 1999. "Rich Man, Poor Man, Administrator, Beast: The Politics of Impoverishment in Turkana, Kenya, 1890–1990." *Nomadic Peoples* 3 (2): 35–55.

Brown, Gordon. 1998. "Reforming the International Monetary Fund." *Wall Street Journal,* 6 October, A22.

Brown, Michael F. 1997. *The Channeling Zone: American Spirituality in an Anxious Age.* Cambridge, Mass.: Harvard University Press.

Bush, George. 1990. "Bush: 'Out of These Troubled Times . . . a New World Order.'" *Washington Post,* 12 September, A34.

Campbell, John Edward. 2001. "Alien(ating) Ideology and the American Media: Apprehending the Alien Image in Television through the *X-Files.*" *International Journal of Cultural Studies* 4 (3): 327–47.

Campion-Vincent, Véronique. 1990. "The Baby-Parts Story: A New Latin American Legend." *Western Folklore* 49 (1): 9–26.

Chakrabarty, Dipesh. 1999. "Adda, Calcutta: Dwelling in Modernity." *Public Culture* (special issue: "Alter/native Modernities") 11 (1): 109–45.

Chalmers, Malcolm, ed. 1997. *Developing Arms Transparency.* Bradford, U.K.: University of Bradford, Department of Peace Studies.

Chalmers, Malcolm, and O. Green. 1994. "The UN Arms Register: An Emerging Global Transparency Regime?" *Contemporary Security Studies* 15 (3): 58–83.

Clough, Paul, and Jon P. Mitchell. 2001. *Powers of Good and Evil: Social Transformation and Popular Belief.* New York: Berghahn.

Comaroff, Jean. 1985. *Body of Power, Spirit of Resistance: The Culture and History of a South African People.* Chicago: University of Chicago Press.

———. 1997. "Consuming Passions: Child Abuse, Fetishism, and 'the New World Order.'" *Culture* 17 (1–2): 7–19.

Comaroff, Jean, and John L. Comaroff. 1986. "Christianity and Colonialism in South Africa." *American Ethnologist* 13 (1): 1–22.

———. 1993. Introduction to *Modernity and Its Malcontents: Ritual and Power in Postcolonial Africa,* ed. Jean Comaroff and John Comaroff, xi–xxxvii. Chicago: University of Chicago Press.

———. 1999. "Occult Economies and the Violence of Abstraction: Notes from the South African Postcolony." *American Ethnologist* 26 (2): 279–303.

———. 2000. "Millennial Capitalism: First Thoughts on a Second Coming." *Public Culture* (special issue: "Millennial Capitalism and the Culture of Neoliberalism") 12 (2): 291–343.

———. In press. "Alien-Nation: Zombies, Immigrants, and Millennial Capitalism." In *Forces of Globalization,* ed. Gabriele Schwab. New York: Columbia University Press.

Comaroff, John L. 1989. "Images of Empire, Contests of Conscience: Models of Colonial Domination in South Africa." *American Ethnologist* 16 (4): 661–85.

Coombe, Rosemary J. 1997. "The Demonic Place of the 'Not There': Trademark Rumors in the Postindustrial Imaginary." In *Culture, Power, and Place: Explorations in Critical Anthropology,* ed. Akhil Gupta and James Ferguson. Durham: Duke University Press.

Corso, Phillip J., with William J. Birnes. 1997. *The Day after Roswell.* New York: Simon and Schuster.

Craig, Traci, and W. Larry Gregory. 1999. "Beliefs in Conspiracies." *Political Psychology* 20 (3): 637–47.

Crocker, J., R. Luhtanen, S. Broadnax, and B. E. Blaine. 1999. "Belief in US Government Conspiracies against Blacks among Black and White College Students: Powerlessness or System Blame?" *Personality and Social Psychology Bulletin* 25 (8): 941–53.

Cullen, Kevin. 1997. "Conspiracy Theories Take Root and Flower." *Boston Globe,* 5 September, A28.

Davis, David Brion. 1969. *The Slave Power Conspiracy and the Paranoid Style.* Baton Rouge: Louisiana State University Press.

———. 1971. *The Fear of Conspiracy: Images of Un-American Subversion from the Revolution to the Present.* Ithaca: Cornell University Press.

Donham, Donald L. 1999. *Marxist Modern: An Ethnographic History of the Ethiopian Revolution.* Berkeley and Los Angeles: University of California Press.

Dundas, C. W. 1994. "Transparency in Organizing Elections." *Round Table* 329:61–76.

Eco, Umberto. 1988. *Foucault's Pendulum:* Ballantine.

Eickelman, Dale F. 2000. "Islam and the Languages of Modernity." *Daedalus* (special issue: "Multiple Modernities") 129 (1): 119–35.

Eisenstadt, S. N. 2000. "Multiple Modernities." *Daedalus* (special issue: "Multiple Modernities") 129 (1): 1–29.

Escobar, A. 1995. *Encountering Development: The Making and Unmaking of the Third World*. Princeton: Princeton University Press.

Evans-Pritchard, E. E. [1937] 1976. *Witchcraft, Oracles, and Magic among the Azande*. Oxford: Clarendon.

Fenster, Mark. 1999. *Conspiracy Theories: Secrecy and Power in American Culture*. Minneapolis: University of Minnesota Press.

Ferguson, James. 1999. *Expectations of Modernity: Myths and Meanings of Urban Life on the Zambian Copperbelt*. Berkeley and Los Angeles: University of California Press.

Finkelstein, Neal D., ed. 1999. *Transparency in Public Policy*. London: Macmillan.

Fischer, Michael M. J. 1999. "Emergent Forms of Life: Anthropologies of Late or Postmodernities." *Annual Review of Anthropology* 28:455–78.

Gaonkar, Dilip Parameshwar. 1999. "On Alternative Modernities." *Public Culture* 11 (1): 1–18.

Gardner, Katy. 1995. *Global Migrants, Local Lives: Travel and Transformation in Rural Bangladesh*. Oxford: Clarendon.

Gerth, H. H., and C. W. Mills, eds. 1958. *From Max Weber: Essays in Sociology*. New York: Oxford University Press.

Geschiere, Peter. 1997. *The Modernity of Witchcraft: Politics and the Occult in Postcolonial Africa*. Charlottesville: University Press of Virginia.

———. 1998a. "Globalization and the Power of Indeterminate Meaning: Witchcraft and Spirit Cults in Africa and East Asia." *Development and Change* 29 (4): 811–38.

———. 1998b. "On Witch-Doctors and Spin-Doctors: The Role of 'Experts' in African and American Politics." Working Paper no. 4. University of Leiden, Department of Cultural Anthropology.

Gewertz, Deborah, and Frederick Errington. 1996. "On Pepsico and Piety in a Papua New Guinea 'Modernity.'" *American Ethnologist* 23 (3): 476–93.

Giddens, Anthony. 1990. *The Consequences of Modernity*. Stanford: Stanford University Press.

Gill, Bates, and J. N. Mak, eds. 1997. *Arms, Transparency, and Security in South-East Asia*. Oxford: Oxford University Press.

Glock, C. Y. 1988. "The Way the World Works." *Sociological Analysis* 49 (2): 93–103.

Goertzel, Ted. 1994. "Belief in Conspiracy Theories." *Political Psychology* 15 (4): 731–42.

Göle, Nilüfer. 2000. "Snapshots of Islamic Modernities." *Daedalus* (special issue: "Multiple Modernities") 129 (1): 91–117.

Good, Timothy. 1987. *Above Top Secret: The Worldwide UFO Cover-Up.* New York: Morrow.

Goozner, Merrill. 1998. "IMF Seeks Money System Shapeup: Agency Moves toward a Financial Police Role." *Chicago Tribune,* 17 April, sec. 3, p. 1.

Grosz-Ngaté, Maria, and Omari H. Kokole, eds. 1997. *Gendered Encounters: Challenging Cultural Boundaries and Social Hierarchies in Africa.* New York: Routledge.

Groth, D. 1987. "The Temptations of Conspiracy Theory; or, Why Do Bad Things Happen to Good People?" In *Changing Conceptions of Conspiracy,* ed. C. F. Graumann and S. Moscovici, 1–14. New York: Springer.

Hanchard, Michael. 1999. "Afro-Modernity: Temporality, Politics, and the African Diaspora." *Public Culture* (special issue: "Alter/native Modernities") 11 (1): 245–68.

Hannerz, Ulf. 1996. *Transnational Connections: Culture, People, Places.* London: Routledge.

Heideking, Jürgen. 2000. "The Pattern of American Modernity from the Revolution to the Civil War." *Daedalus* (special issue: "Multiple Modernities") 129 (1): 219–47.

Hofstadter, Richard. 1965. *The Paranoid Style in American Politics and Other Essays.* Cambridge, Mass.: Harvard University Press.

Horton, Robin. 1970. "African Traditional Thought and Western Science." In *Rationality,* ed. B. Wilson, 131–71. Oxford: Blackwell.

Hutson, James H. 1984. "The Origins of 'the Paranoid Style in American Politics': Public Jealousy from the Age of Walpole to the Age of Jackson." In *Saints and Revolutionaries: Essays on Early American History,* ed. David D. Hall, John M. Murrin, and Thad W. Tate. New York: Norton.

Ingwerson, Marshall. 1990. "Bush Speech Calls for New World Order." *Christian Science Monitor,* 13 September, 7.

James, Nigel. 2001. "Militias, the Patriot Movement, and the Internet: The Ideology of Conspiracism." In *The Age of Anxiety: Conspiracy Theory and the Human Sciences,* ed. Jane Parish and Martin Parker. Oxford: Blackwell.

Kapferer, Bruce. 1997. *The Feast of the Sorcerer: Practices of Consciousness and Power.* Chicago: University of Chicago Press.

Kaviraj, Sudipta. 2000. "Modernity and Politics in India." *Daedalus* (special issue: "Multiple Modernities") 129 (1): 137–62.

Kearney, M. 1995. "The Local and the Global: The Anthropology of Globalization and Transnationalism." *Annual Review of Anthropology* 24:547–65.

Keeley, Brian L. 1999. "Of Conspiracy Theories." *Journal of Philosophy* 96 (3): 109–26.

Klass, Phillip J. 1983. *UFOs: The Public Deceived.* New York: Prometheus.

Klonoff, Elizabeth A., and Hope Landrine. 1999. "Do Blacks Believe That HIV/AIDS Is a Government Conspiracy against Them?" *Preventative Medicine* 28:451–57.

Knauft, Bruce M. 1997. "Theoretical Currents in Late Modern Cultural Anthropology." *Cultural Dynamics* 9 (3): 277–300.

Knight, P. 2001. *Conspiracy Culture: American Paranoia from Kennedy to the "X-Files."* New York: Routledge.

———, ed. 2002. *Conspiracy Nation: The Politics of Paranoia in Postwar America.* New York: New York University Press.

Kolakowski, Leszek. 1990. *Modernity on Endless Trial.* Chicago: Chicago University Press.

Kopits, George, and Jon Craig. 1998. *Transparency in Government Operations.* Washington, D.C.: International Monetary Fund.

La Fontaine, Jean S. 1998. *Speak of the Devil: Tales of Satanic Abuse in Contemporary England.* Cambridge: Cambridge University Press.

Lan, David. 1985. *Guns and Rain: Guerrillas and Spirit Mediums in Zimbabwe.* Berkeley and Los Angeles: University of California Press.

Larsson, Mats, and David Lundberg. 1998. *The Transparent Market.* London: Macmillan.

Lee, Leo Ou-fan. 1999. *Shanghai Modern: The Flowering of New Urban Culture in China, 1930–1945.* Cambridge, Mass.: Harvard University Press.

Lerner, Daniel. 1958. *The Passing of Traditional Society: Modernizing the Middle East.* New York: Free Press.

Lévy-Bruhl, Lucien. [1910] 1985. *How Natives Think.* Translated by Lilian A. Clare. Princeton, N.J.: Princeton University Press.

Limón, José. 1994. *Dancing with the Devil: Society and Cultural Poetics in Mexican-American South Texas.* Madison: University of Wisconsin Press.

Lynch, Caitrin. 1999. "The 'Good Girls' of Sri Lankan Modernity: Moral Orders of Nationalism and Capitalism." *Identities: Global Studies in Culture and Power* 6 (1): 55–90.

Marceau, Gabrielle, and Peter N. Pedersen. 1999. "Is the WTO Open and Transparent? A Discussion of the Relationship of the WTO with Non-Governmental Organisations and Civil Society's Claims for More Transparency and Public Participation." *Journal of World Trade* 33 (1): 5–49.

Marcus, George E., ed. 1999. *Paranoia within Reason: A Casebook on Conspiracy as Explanation.* Chicago: University of Chicago Press.

McLuhan, Marshall. 1964. *Understanding Media: The Extensions of Man.* New York: Mentor.

Melley, Timothy. 2000. *Empire of Conspiracy: The Culture of Paranoia in Postwar America.* Ithaca: Cornell University Press.

Mintz, S. 1985. *Sweetness and Power: The Place of Sugar in Modern History.* London: Penguin.

Morris, Rosalind C. 2000a. *In the Place of Origins: Modernity and Its Mediums in Northern Thailand*. Durham: Duke University Press.

———. 2000b. "Modernity's Media and the End of Mediumship? On the Aesthetic Economy of Transparency in Thailand." *Public Culture* (special issue: "Millennial Capitalism and the Culture of Neoliberalism") 12 (2): 457–75.

Nash, June. [1979] 1993. *We Eat the Mines and the Mines Eat Us: Dependency and Exploitation in Bolivian Tin Mines*. New York: Columbia University Press.

Ong, Aihwa. 1987. *Spirits of Resistance and Capitalist Discipline: Factory Women in Malaysia*. Albany: State University of New York Press.

Ortiz, Renato. 2000. "From Incomplete Modernity to World Modernity." *Daedalus* (special issue: "Multiple Modernities") 129 (1): 249–60.

Ortner, Sherry. 1995. "Resistance and the Problem of Ethnographic Refusal." *Comparative Studies in Society and History* 37:173–93.

Ostler, Jeffrey. 1995. "The Rhetoric of Conspiracy and the Formation of Kansas Populism." *Agricultural History* 69 (1): 1–27.

Parish, Jane, and Martin Parker, eds. 2001. *The Age of Anxiety: Conspiracy Theory and the Human Sciences*. Oxford: Blackwell.

Parsons, S., W. Simmons, F. Shinhoster, and J. Kilburn. 1999. "A Test of the Grapevine: An Empirical Examination of Conspiracy Theories among African Americans." *Sociological Spectrum* 19 (2): 201–22.

Phillips, Michael M. 1998. "IMF Makes a Push for Good Government: Developing Nations Chafe as Funds Are Held Back over Corruption, Rights." *Wall Street Journal*, 19 March, A2.

Pigden, Charles. 1993. "Popper Revisited; or, What Is Wrong with Conspiracy Theories?" *Philosophy of the Social Sciences* 25 (1): 3–34.

Piot, Charles. 1999. *Remotely Global: Village Modernity in West Africa*. Chicago: University of Chicago Press.

Pipes, Daniel. 1992. "Dealing with Middle Eastern Conspiracy Theories." *Orbis* 36 (1): 41–56.

———. 1996. *The Hidden Hand: Middle East Fears of Conspiracy*. New York: Macmillan.

Pitcavage, Mark. 2001. "Camouflage and Conspiracy: The Militia Movement from Ruby Ridge to Y2K." *American Behavioral Scientist* 44 (2): 957–81.

Popper, Karl. 1966. *The Open Society and Its Enemies*. Vol. 2, *The High Tide of Prophecy: Hegel, Marx, and the Aftermath*. London: Routledge and Kegan Paul.

Pye, Lucian W. 1966. *Aspects of Political Development: An Analytic Study*. Boston: Little, Brown.

Randle, Kevin D. 1998. *Project Moon Dust: Beyond Roswell—Exposing the Government's Continuing Covert UFO Investigations Cover-Ups*. New York: Avon.

Revkin, Andrew C. 1996. "Conspiracy Theories Rife on Demise of Flight 800." *New York Times*, 17 September, B5.

Robertson, F. 1971. "A Jacksonian Attack on Monopoly." In *The Fear of Conspiracy:*

Images of Un-American Subversion from the Revolution to the Present, ed. David Brion Davis, 69–73. Ithaca: Cornell University Press.

Robertson, Roland. 1995. "Globalization: Time-Space and Homogeneity-Heterogeneity." In *Global Modernities*, ed. M. Featherstone. Newbury Park, Calif.: Sage.

Robotham, Don. 1998. "Transnationalism in the Caribbean: Formal and Informal." *American Ethnologist* 25 (2): 307–21.

Rostow, W. W. 1960. *The Stages of Economic Growth*. Cambridge: Cambridge University Press.

Safire, William. 1995. "On Language: Conspiracy Theory." *New York Times Magazine*, 5 November, sec. 6, p. 24.

———. 1998. "Transparency, Totally." *New York Times Magazine*, 4 January, sec. 6, p. 4.

Sahlins, Marshall. 1976. *Culture and Practical Reason*. Chicago: University of Chicago Press.

———. 1993. "Goodbye to *Tristes Tropes:* Ethnography in the Context of Modern World History." *Journal of Modern History* 65:1–25.

Saler, Benson, Charles A. Ziegler, and Charles B. Moore. 1997. UFO *Crash at Roswell: The Genesis of a Modern Myth*. Washington, D.C.: Smithsonian Institution Press.

Sanders, Todd. 2001. "Save Our Skins: Structural Adjustment, Morality, and the Occult in Tanzania." In *Magical Interpretations, Material Realities: Modernity, Witchcraft, and the Occult in Postcolonial Africa*, ed. Henrietta L. Moore and Todd Sanders, 160–83. London: Routledge.

Sasson, T. 1995. "African-American Conspiracy Theories and the Social Construction of Crime." *Sociological Inquiry* 65 (3–4): 265–85.

Scheper-Hughes, Nancy. 1996. "Theft of Life: Organ Stealing Rumours." *Anthropology Today* 12 (3): 3–10.

———. 1998a. "Bodies of Apartheid: Witchcraft, Rumor, and Racism Confound South Africa's Organ Transplant Program." *Worldview* 11 (4): 47–53.

———. 1998b. "Truth and Rumor on the Organ Trail." *Natural History* 10 (October): 48–58.

———. 2000. "The Global Traffic in Human Organs." *Current Anthropology* 41 (2): 191–224.

Scholte, Jan Aart. 1998. "Globalization, Governance, and Democracy in Post-Communist Romania." *Democratization* 5 (4): 52–77.

Scott, James C. 1985. *Weapons of the Weak: Everyday Forms of Peasant Resistance*. New Haven: Yale University Press.

———. 1990. *Domination and the Art of Resistance: Hidden Transcripts*. New Haven: Yale University Press.

Shukla, S. N. 1998. "Good Governance: Need for Openness and Transparency." *Indian Journal of Public Administration* 44 (3): 398–406.

Smith, R. Jeffrey, and Bradley Graham. 1997. "Destroy Warheads? Is This the Start of Something New?" *Washington Post*, 22 March, A1.

Straus, Ira. 1996. "When Conspiracy Theory Replaces Thought." *Christian Science Monitor,* 13 May, 19.

Strieber, Whitley. 1987. *Communion: The True Story.* New York: Morrow.

Tapper, Richard. 1999. "The Enemies' Plots and the English Hand: Official Control and Popular Agency in Iran." Paper Presented at the workshop "Transparency and Conspiracy: Powers Revealed and Concealed in (the) Global Village(s)," London School of Economics and Political Science, London, 28–29 May.

Taussig, Michael T. 1980. *The Devil and Commodity Fetishism in South America.* Chapel Hill: University of North Carolina Press.

———. 1987. *Shamanism, Colonialism, and the Wild Man: A Study in Terror and Healing.* Chicago: University of Chicago Press.

Taylor, Charles. 1999. "Two Theories of Modernity." *Public Culture* (special issue: "Alter/native Modernities") 11 (1): 153–74.

Thomas, S. B., and S. C. Quinn. 1991. "The Tuskegee Syphilis Study, 1932–1972." *American Journal of Public Health* 60:1498–1505.

Turner, Patricia A. 1993. *I Heard It through the Grapevine: Rumor in African-American Culture.* Berkeley and Los Angeles: University of California Press.

Uhlenbrock, Tom. 1997a. "Fears of UN Takeover Find Audience in Laude." *St. Louis Post-Dispatch,* 9 April, B1.

———. 1997b. "Residents Fear Huge Government Land Grab: 'It's Not a Conspiracy Theory, It's All There.'" *St. Louis Post-Dispatch,* 6 April, A6.

United Nations. 1993. *Transparency in Armaments: The Mediterranean Region.* New York: United Nations.

———. 1994. *Transparency in Armaments: Regional Dialogue and Disarmament.* New York: United Nations.

Verdery, Katherine. 1996. *What Was Socialism and What Comes Next?* Princeton: Princeton University Press.

"A War on Global Corruption." 1993. *New York Times,* 11 May, D2.

Warner, L. 1987. "What's Good about Oklahoma?" *Free Inquiry in Creative Sociology* 15 (2): 221–24.

Waters, Anita M. 1997. "Conspiracy Theories as Ethnosociologies: Explanation and Intention in African American Political Culture." *Journal of Black Studies* 28 (1): 112–25.

Watts, Michael. 1996. "Islamic Modernities? Citizenship, Civil Society, and Islamism in a Nigerian City." *Public Culture* 8 (2): 251–90.

Webb, Gray. 1999. *Dark Alliance: The CIA, the Contras, and the Crack Cocaine Explosion.* New York: Seven Stories.

Weiming, Tu. 2000. "Implications of the Rise of 'Confucian' East Asia." *Daedalus* (special issue: "Multiple Modernities") 129 (1): 195–218.

West, Harry G. 2001. "Sorcery of Construction and Socialist Modernization: Ways of Understanding Power in Postcolonial Mozambique." *American Ethnologist* 28 (1): 119–50.

White, Luise. 1997. "The Traffic in Heads: Bodies, Borders, and the Articulation of Regional Histories." *Journal of Southern African Studies* 23 (2): 325–38.

Wittrock, Björn. 2000. "Modernity: One, None, or Many? European Origins and Modernity as a Global Condition." *Daedalus* (special issue: "Multiple Modernities") 129 (1): 31–60.

Wright, Robin. 1993. "Two Terms for the New Age." *Los Angeles Times,* 17 August, H5.

Yang, Mayfair Mei-hui. 2000. "Putting Global Capitalism in Its Place: Economic Hybridity, Bataille, and Ritual Expenditure." *Current Anthropology* 41 (4): 477–509.

Ziegler, Charles A. 1999. "UFOs and the US Intelligence Community." *Intelligence and National Security* 14 (2): 1–25.

Zonis, Marvin, and Craig M. Joseph. 1994. "Conspiracy Thinking in the Middle East." *Political Psychology* 15 (3): 443–59.

1

Gods, Markets, and the IMF in the Korean Spirit World

LAUREL KENDALL

The most comically outrageous gods in the Korean shamanic pantheon are the Officials and Spirit Warriors, the gods who bring the family
good harvests or business success but who, when ignored or vexed, cause all
manner of disasters, from a lack of customers to a theft or a loan default.
Shamans manifest these spirits as greedy beings of formidable appetite who
are initially contemptuous of the piles of meat, fruit, and rice cake that the
clients have piled up as offerings. The encounter between god and client is
predictable, a bargaining, bantering game. The spirits, through the person
of the shaman, disdain the heaps of offering food that the clients have provided, demand music and dancing partners, and wipe their rumps with the
ten-thousand-won notes that they are offered by way of appeasement. The
god asks, "How can you expect me to help you if this is all that you can provide for me?" And from the client, "First make me rich; then next time I'll
give you more. Next time I'll take you to a rib house." Gods demand, and
clients hold out, often with theatrical reticence, then slowly, playfully relin-
quish more cash until, eventually, a compromise is reached. In the spring
of 1998, after the collapse of the Korean market the previous fall, when the
supernatural Official began to complain, I heard a shaman shout from the
sidelines in her clients' defense, "It's all because of the IMF. We'll do better
next time." The line was repeated throughout the afternoon. It had become
her standard refrain.

Greedy gods and the IMF. One was an apt personification of the potent but volatile market, bestowing both largesse and ruin. The other, as it was invoked in that anxious spring of 1998, was not the international financial organization based in Washington, D.C., or even the list of stringent conditions that that body had imposed on Korea the previous December in exchange for financial aid to alleviate the collapsing market. IMF had become "a household word symbolizing economic difficulties and national disgrace" (Suh 1998: 34), a shorthand for a climate of despair, a climate in the sense of a force of nature, invisible in its onset but devastating in its consequences.

Shamanic rituals in Korea address ordinary crises, the day-to-day manifestations of modernity's malcontents (Comaroff and Comaroff 1993), what Todd Sanders and Harry West have described as the "fragmented, contradictory, and disquieting process that produces untenable situations and unfulfilled desires" (Sanders and West 1999). As instrumental acts, confrontations with gods and ancestors in playful and sometimes poignant rituals permit, if not a transparent aperture on the forces that drive Korean modernity, some critical lenses through which participants view the living out of modernity's consequences as they engage a capricious market. This essay is about the act of viewing the contemporary Korean moment through shamanic lenses. I shall also describe how, in the spring of 1998, the condition of "the IMF" was sometimes seen as beyond the reach of shamanic instrumentality. In a moment of touted "openness" and "accountability," the lens was opaque, and this, too, was a local vision of the contemporary moment.

Shamans and Their Clients within Korean Modernity

Fifty years ago, the Republic of Korea (hereafter "South Korea") was an impoverished agricultural country, liberated from the Japanese Empire in 1945 but simultaneously severed from its industrial north by Cold War fiat. Between 1950 and 1953, the entire peninsula would be ravaged by a fratricidal war, invaded, bombed, and occupied by foreign armies. From that vantage point, the present moment could not have been imagined. By the mid-1990s, the "miracle" of Korea's economic success was global knowledge. The Korean economy ranked eleventh in terms of size, with a GNP of $425 billion (current dollars, 1995). In 1995, more than three of four Koreans lived in cities with populations greater than fifty thousand, a far larger proportion than in the United States. Unrelieved rows of high-rise apartments sprang up, seemingly overnight, on a landscape that had once been rice fields and rural villages.[1]

The story of Korean development has been told and its lessons debated in both scholarly and popular accounts. For now, a capsule summary will suffice. In the 1960s, following Park Chung-hee's coup d'état, an interventionist state initiated a series of ambitious five-year plans for the development of an export-oriented economy, initially with light industry (textiles, wigs, plywood, clothing, footwear, and labor-intensive electronic assembly) and subsequently with high-tech, capital-intensive electronics and heavy industry (ships, cars, steel, and chemicals). Government policies favored large corporations with trade monopolies and easy access to credit and (for a time) effectively suppressed labor unrest among a first-generation workforce that was educated, disciplined, and motivated to work long days under harsh conditions (Amsden 1989; Eckert 1991; Haggard, Kim, and Moon 1991; Moskowitz 1982). But it is also a story of the intersection of interests between the government, the military, and monopoly capital, producing a powerful new elite (Cho 1987; Eckert 1993; Kim 1997), and a story of massive urban migration that left a radically depopulated countryside in its wake (Koo 1990). As told by nearly every Korean over the age of forty, it is a tale of a hard and threadbare life recollected from new circumstances replete with unimagined material comforts and expanded opportunities for one's children.[2] And, because this story is told as a national triumph of the will, a victory over past humiliations, the necessity of capitulating to the demands imposed by a foreign body, the IMF, was particularly galling.

Shamans do not appear as characters in the story of Korean modernity as it is usually told. For nearly a century, the dreamers of a modern Korea regarded shamans as artifacts of rural backwardness, destined to vanish from an educated and enlightened populace. Ironically, contemporary nationalists celebrate shamans as living artifacts of deep cultural traditions. The romantics, no less than the detractors, consign shamans to a time other than this time, situate them in the rural hinterland of the modern imagination, in de Certeau's (1984) terms. But the story of Korean modernity is also a story about tremendous risk, potential ruin, ambition, envy, and disappointment. The emotional consequences of this story are set at play in contemporary Korean shamanic rituals where healing takes place through a language of casting off ominous forces and bringing auspicious potential into the home.

I want to distinguish my argument from another, one that is often articulated in intellectual circles within Korea and must be given its due. The Popular Culture Movement (Minjung munhwa undong), which peaked during the prodemocracy protests of the 1980s, looks at the modernity process, not through rose-colored lenses, but through a glass darkly. The movement celebrates shamanic rituals as the religious expression of the oppressed and sees shamans as ministering to the victims of colonial exploitation, military dictatorship, and native and multinational capitalism (CTC-CCA 1981; Wells 1995). In the late 1980s, protest dramas were choreographed in the form of shamanic rituals intended to sooth the aggrieved souls of martyrs to democracy and labor rights, sometimes with the aid of practicing shamans (Choi 1993, 1995; Kim 1994; Kim 1989a).[3] The Popular Culture Movement's gloss is compelling because it places shamanic practices within contemporary socioeconomic processes, both local and global, and because it draws the Korean material toward an expanding and important literature that interprets witchcraft, spirit possession, devil pacts, and other popular religious forms as within the logic of a modern consciousness borne by those who have been most directly victimized by exploitative developmental processes or marginalized by their consequences.[4]

Appropriate cases have been analyzed in Korea (Kim 1989a, 1989b, 1992), and some of my own published material (e.g., Kendall 1977) could well be interpreted as following in this vein, but Korea also begs a broadening of the scope of affliction induced by modernity processes and salved by popular religion. In Korea, shamans and their clients emerge from a relatively prosperous society, a developmental "success story." The majority of clients whom I have encountered over the last decade or more are arguably "middle class." Far from resisting the deployment of wealth and power, they are struggling to stay in the game. Business concerns are often what bring them to visit shamans.

A "Then" and a "Now"

A number of recent studies have situated shamans within shifting historical contingencies (e.g., Roseman, in press; Taussig 1987; Thomas and Humphrey 1994). Let me describe the particular contingencies that bracket my own understanding of Korean shamans and their work. At the end of 1976, I began fieldwork with a shaman, her colleagues, and their clients in a rural village not far from Seoul. Although, by 1975, the majority of the Korean population was newly urban, and although, on the basis of a previous Peace Corps residence in Seoul, I knew very well that Korean cities were filled with shamans, I followed the implicit assumption of my generation that the real anthropology of Korea was to be pursued through fieldwork in rural villages. That experience did not equip me with a baseline understanding of "traditional" Korean shamanic practices, for what I saw was very much in flux and had likely always been in motion. What I did gain was an appreciation of the world in which many of the clients whom I encountered in the 1980s and 1990s grew up, the world their parents knew. It was a short but useful historical horizon on a rapidly changing society.

In the 1970s, I found a system of popular religious practices centered on the household with the physical house as its central symbol. Gods inhabited the house structure and protected the house site from malevolent incursions, dropping their guard when vexed or offended by neglect or pollution, and allowing the restless dead or baleful forces to enter the house, bringing sickness or other misfortune. Large sums of cash, new furniture, or, in the 1970s, significant new consumer goods such as televisions or hi-fi equipment would cause the gods to "open wide their eyes." Like extortionate flesh-and-blood officials, the House Site Official (T'ŏju taegam) would demand a cut from any windfall, and, in such cases, shamans would advise their clients to offer a cup of wine or make a minor offering (Kendall 1985).

It was a supernatural constellation appropriate to the worldview of small family farmers, households dependent on their own collective labor as family-centered enterprises, pooling common resources for children's education, for ceremonial expenses, for medical and other emergencies, and, increasingly, for the new consumer goods that were being produced for the domestic market. In the 1970s, rural development policies encouraged diversification, and several households had invested in vinyl greenhouses in which to grow marketable produce or were raising rabbits for pelts. With the village's close proximity to a growing town on the periphery of the capital city, fully half the village households were recorded in the census as no longer "agricultural." They retained a few dry fields for produce, and brought their seasonal surpluses to market, but derived their primary income from cottage industries, by driving taxicabs, or as hired labor in the nearby town (Kendall 1985: chap. 2). Many village children were, from their late teens, working in factories and sending money home, but only a few would return to rural life. This was no pristine preindustrial peasant society but rather the latest permutation of a plugged-in rural way of life that had included taxes, rents, investments, and market cognizance for a very long time.[5]

Common concerns brought to shamans in those years were illnesses, particularly sudden and intractable illnesses, and issues of family disharmony: delinquent children, adulterous spouses, inharmonious relationships between mothers-in-law and daughters-in-law. In Korean shamanic ritual, affliction is a family matter; individual illness is symptomatic of a fundamental misalignment in the family's relationship with its household gods and ancestors, a rupture that face-to-face encounters with these same spirits during a shaman's rituals are intended to heal. Then, as now, most shamans did not claim miraculous powers to heal biomedical illness per se so much as the ability to address an underlying crisis condition that not only threatened the family with persistent or serious ill health and medical bills but also indicated a generalized climate of misfortune, a misalignment between the family and its gods and ancestors. The decision to sponsor a *kut*—a major ritual intended to entertain the spirits—was then, as now, usually precipitated by more than one inauspicious condition affecting more than one family member.

When kut were performed in the rural farmhouses of the 1970s, the house became a significant backdrop to the process of healing, a material representation of the household as a social, economic, and ritual unit. Gods and ancestors were summoned outside the house gate and invited inside the walled courtyard. Although most of the kut was performed on the open veranda, with the arrival of the appropriate spirits the action shifted to the inner room, the storage platform, and the kitchen. The final segments marked a gradual progress away from the house, through the open courtyard, to a final expelling of malevolent and polluting forces beyond the house gate. House and household had been purified, secured, and reoriented toward a more auspicious future (Kendall 1985: chaps. 1, 5, 6).

But, even in this quasi-rural world of more than twenty years past, not all the shaman's clients were from farmers' households, and not all of them lived in rural villages. I attended kut in cramped rented rooms and in households along city lanes where issues of traffic flow and noise pollution made it impossible to perform critical segments outside the gate. Symbolically satisfactory spatial compromises were negotiated. Among the most ardent clients of the village shaman was a group of women engaged in small family businesses in the nearby town who were the children or the neighbors of children of village households. One woman, the robust proprietress of a rice shop, sponsored a kut in response to a combination of illness and theft and thereafter became an enthusiastic client, introducing her shopkeeping neighbors to this shaman, with the result that some of these women also sponsored rituals. Reviewing my notes from that earlier time, I find "bad business" listed as a common reason for such women to sponsor kut or smaller rituals. Taxi drivers' wives were also frequent clients, making offerings and purchasing talismans to avert the accident that could claim a husband's life or the family fortune that was riding on the wheels of his car. One woman, whose taxi-driving husband had been involved in a serious accident and had gone to prison on a manslaughter charge, became a client when her husband began a new career as a bus driver. She went back to her earlier practice of praying at Buddhist temples after the gas tank on his bus exploded. Households that had left the drudgery of rural life, enticed by the prospect of small but precarious financial endeavors, were seeking in popular religion a means of coming to terms with the "adventurous, aggressive, risk-taking, high-roller element" that Michael Taussig finds at the heart of cultural responses to capitalism (Taussig 1995: 394).

By the early 1990s, I realized that the perils of small enterprises had become a dominant theme in many of the rituals that I was attending, rituals sponsored by the owner of the failed small factory, by the bankrupt private contractor, by the couple who wondered whether the husband should quit his company job and join his wife in running a clothing shop. Some younger shamans were inclined to boast about the financial rewards that their clients gained by sponsoring rituals. Others offered wry comments on what they saw as their clients' preoccupations with wealth and advancement. Ms. Shin, an energetic young shaman of whom more later, spoke with great heat and humor about clients who would promptly sever their relationship with a shaman if the kut that they had sponsored did not bear fruit in the way of immediate financial gain. Yongsu's Mother, a longtime informant, offered the acerbic view that kut for good fortune (*chesu kut*) were popular because, "if this house has so much money, then that house will sponsor a kut to get more money," a supernatural currency for keeping up with the Joneses. She noted that, in the past, kut for good fortune were rare: "Who had the money for it? If someone was sick, then you would hold a healing kut [*uhwan kut*], even if you went into debt for it. You had to do it [in contrast with kut for good fortune]." She holds that kut to send the ancestors to paradise were more common in the past: "Nowadays, who concerns themselves with the ancestors? People only care about themselves. They don't take the trouble to send the ancestors off properly [with a special *chinogi kut* for this purpose]. They just have the shamans do a small send-off for the ancestors at the end of a kut that they have sponsored for their own good fortune."

Resisting the temptation of a simple comparison between the materialistic present and a purported better, simpler time when all of us were younger, I began to explore the prevalence of business concerns in contemporary shamanic practices. In the summer of 1994, I made random observations of eighteen kut and smaller rituals held in the public shrines where Seoul shamans do the ritual work that cannot be easily accommodated in small apartments.

I made a point of visiting both up-market and down-market shrines and met a range of shamans and clients previously unknown to me. The results appeared in an article facetiously titled "Korean Shamans and the Spirits of Capitalism" (Kendall 1996b). Fully fifteen of the eighteen sponsors of kut were engaged in some form of small business, although they ranged across a spectrum of wealth and opportunity from the proprietors of small factories (for stainless steel and for quilt stuffing), to owners of a mushroom-importing business, restaurants, and shops, to a freelance furniture mover, the proprietress of a hole-in-the-wall bar, and an electrician. Divinations revealed that, in addition to these enterprises, several of the female sponsors were also involved in various real estate ventures.

Petty entrepreneurs constitute an ill-defined but significant group, rarely mentioned in a scholarly literature that has thus far focused ethnographic attention on farmers, workers, and the white-collar middle class (Chang 1991: 107; Koo 1987: 379–80). Slightly less than one-third of all nonfarm workers are self-employed or work for family businesses (*Korea Statistical Yearbook* 1990: 75). Many of the small businesspeople whom I met, both men and women, had spent their childhood in rural villages and their early adulthood in factory jobs, turning to commerce as a cleaner, safer, potentially more lucrative means of making a living. While the government's development strategies have consistently favored monopolies at the expense of small businesses, and while white-collar company employment constitutes the middle-class ideal, most petty entrepreneurs would describe themselves as middle class and see themselves as capable of advancing through the system. This optimism, as well as a profound sense of risk, fuels the rituals that they enact with shamans.[6]

In the summer of 1994, far and away the most common reason for sponsoring a ritual was business anxiety, the central concern in all but five of the rituals in my sample of eighteen such events. Prognostications of wealth or good business were given in every single ritual. Several kut were held for clients in response to critical losses—two failing restaurants, a fraudulent claim on an order of mushrooms, responsibility for a debt fraudulently incurred by a son-in-law, and a flower shop without customers. Business concerns sometimes came bundled with other issues: physical aches and pains or financial anxieties that caused husbands to drink to excess, undermine their health, and abuse their wives (Kendall 1996b: 518).

The tongue clucking of my shaman friends aside, this mingling of gods and money does not represent a confrontation between "two radically distinct ways of apprehending or evaluating the world of persons and of things," between peasant morality and a capitalist system such as Michael Taussig (1980: 17) posited in his seminal *The Devil and Commodity Fetishism*. This reification of a pristine precapitalist tradition has been the most roundly critiqued element of Taussig's provocative work (Marcus and Fischer 1986: 185, n. 4; Sallinow 1989; Weller 1994: 142) and has been shed in his subsequent writing (see Taussig 1995). What we find in Korea is a smooth, near-seamless shaping of the popular religious practices of small family farmers, already in many senses "entrepreneurial," to the experiences of urban petty entrepreneurs, in many cases the children of rural households. My assumption is that shamanic rituals continue to address the needs and anxieties of clients in the 1990s, to construct dramas of ritual healing that are both insightful and emotionally compelling. The remainder of this essay is a discussion of how and why, into the time of the IMF.

Shamans and Cultural Production

In his survey of world "shamanisms," Piers Vitebsky describes shamanic practice as a quintessentially fluid and innovative "chameleon-like" phenomenon (Vitebsky 1995: 154). Wherever anthropologists feel justified in using the term *shaman*, individuals so described are persons empowered to report from "out there," either by recounting their adventures of magical flight or by invoking the spirits and manifesting them in their own bodies. Korean shamans—the *mudang, mansin,* or *posal*—transmit dreams, visions, and intuitions in the persona of gods and ancestors whose inspired words and formulaic phrases pour from their mouths. The shaman's power is twofold, both to *see* by divining and defining the will of the spirits and to *effect* by performing the ritual acts that will satisfy the spirits and bring an auspicious outcome to the ritual. Both attributes are realized in open, fluid performance. In an initial consultation, the mansin sizes up the client's situation and determines what hungry gods and restless ancestors are behind a particular run of misfortunes. If the mansin's assessment meshes well with the client's understanding of present circumstances and family history, the client might agree to sponsor the recommended ritual. During a kut or smaller offering, the presiding shaman and her associates also provide a steady flow of prognostications, delivered by each god in succession. The shaman is only one of several varieties of diviner in Korea, some inspirational and some relying on readings of the lunar horoscope or other mechanistic means.[7] Mansin see themselves as distinguished from other inspirational diviners, and from untrained initiates, by their mastery of the music, dances, chants, and ritual lore needed to serve the spirits, to please and entertain them by manifesting them in kut to secure an auspicious outcome for the client household.

To manifest a spirit, the shaman garbs herself in the appropriate costume, sometimes several layers of costumes in anticipation of a sequence of spirits, and gracefully dances. Drumbeats and clashing cymbals become rapid and intense as the shaman jumps and revolves on the balls of her feet until she is ready to speak and mime in the persona of the manifesting spirit. Mansin do not claim a one-on-one possession; they see visions, hear sounds, experience bodily sensations, and have strong intuitions that they must perform into a spiritual presence with more or less volition, depending on the strength of their inspiration (Kendall 1996a). This condition of nonfixate within a frame of reassuringly predictable ritual structure and standard performance business makes the shamanic world a particularly dynamic domain of popular religious expression that is open to the stuff of contemporary experience.

Among the hoards of unquiet dead chanted away at the end of a Korean shaman's kut, the murdered, diseased, and drowned souls who parade in shamanic visions, one finds as well the victims of twentieth-century technologies, those who died of carbon monoxide poisoning, in airplane crashes, or in traffic accidents (while riding in taxis and private cars or on motorcycles). Gods once associated with the prosperity of family farms and feted after the harvest are now solidly entrenched in the world of family enterprise. Through the mouths of shamans, they proclaim an active presence as "the Spirit Warrior of Business, the Spirit Warrior of Commerce, the Electrician's Spirit Warrior" (Changsa Sinjang, Yŏngŏp Sinjang, Chŏnŏpkisul Sinjang), "the Official of Commerce, the Official of the Automobile, the Commerce Official of the Flower Shop" (Sangŏp Taegam, Chagayung Taegam, Hwawŏn Sangŏp Taegam). For the proprietors of a faltering rib restaurant (*kalbijip*), a shaman proclaimed herself to be "the Official of the Kitchen, the Official of the Kitchen Knife [a particularly important piece of equipment in a rib house], and the Official of the Restaurant Counter" (Chubang Taegam, Chubang K'al Taegam, K'aunt'ŏ Taegam).

The shamans' songs and divinations package auspicious prognostications in the imagery of client enterprises. For a florist, "Bunches of flowers are going in (to fill a large order), whether sitting or standing you will hear the sound of the door (opening constantly for clients). . . . Those who come in will not leave empty-handed. The luck of the [flower shop] will open wide." For the electrician, "Though my client goes east, west, south, and north . . .

I will help so that there will be no power failure." For a family that runs a travel agency, the spirit Official of the Vehicle (Cha Taegam) will "seize the front tire and seize the back tire and move the vehicle to an auspicious place" (Kendall 1996b: 518).

The kings and generals, princesses, and buddhas who appear in antique dress inhabit a landscape where references to raising a multistory *pilding*—they have borrowed the English word—are hyperbolic prognostications of good fortune for more modest investments, such as my own household's successful purchase of a small co-op apartment in New York, a failed factory owner's financial recovery, and a bar girl's future prospects for a bar of her own. The spirits foretell, "I will give you other people's money; tomorrow you will receive a bank loan"; they promise customers who will pay "with cash and not credit" and tell a mother that her child will grow up to be rich, "maybe a company president."

The gods' greedy appetites, their *yoksim*, are a self-parody of client aspirations as when the shaman, in the persona of a demanding spirit, claims, "Your yoksim is even greater than my own." *Yoksim* is a word commonly used to describe the drive that propels people to succeed in the competitive marketplace (Abelmann 2001). It is not an admirable quality, but it is recognized as a necessary attribute of material success in the contemporary world. Potent gods have more yoksim, they are more bothersome and dangerous, but they also have more force of power. The gods' demands become a parody of client aspirations in a society that regards commerce with profound ambivalence as a rewarding but also a dirty and suspect enterprise (Eckert 1991: 225; Moon 1990).

The volatility of the market, the seeming arbitrariness of success or failure, is also personified in the behavior of spirits: do well by them, and they grant you good fortune; unwittingly offend them, and they harass you (Kendall 1985: chap. 6). Consider, for example, Mrs. Pok's story. She is the child of a shaman and has honored the spirits throughout her adult life. Her husband had worked for a major electronics firm but was forced into early retirement in his forties. Now it was Mrs. Pok who went into business. In 1994, she opened a florist shop in a neighborhood where there were several other similar shops.[8] She had been in business for only a short while when someone placed an order with her for 1.4 million won (U.S.$1,750). The shopkeepers in the neighborhood said that this was an unprecedented windfall for a new business. She began to dream of securing a major account from her husband's former company. Mrs. Pok, her shaman mother, and just possibly her neighbors attributed her early good fortune to the benevolence of the spirits that the shaman mother had zealously invoked and propitiated on Mrs. Pok's behalf.

But then, only a few months later, business was off. For three weeks, barely a customer a day visited her shop. Now the neighboring florists confirmed her dismay, telling her that this was not normal. This sudden falling off of business was ominous, suggestive of divine displeasure. Mrs. Pok began to suffer pains in her legs, a further confirmation that a kut was in order. The spirits that appeared at her kut affirmed that, yes, a ritual lapse had left her vulnerable to misfortune. They also suggested that her shopkeeping neighbors had taken ritual measures (*yebang*) to shore up their own good fortune at her expense.[9] She was told to perform ritual countermeasures, avoid any food bestowed by her neighbors, and cast salt in the wake of any rival shopkeeper who might drop by for a visit.[10]

Swings of good and bad fortune have a crushing immediacy for shopkeepers like Mrs. Pok. Because access to capital is restricted in Korea, small businesses have difficulty securing bank credit (Janelli with Yim 1993: 64). Consequently, they have been drawn into the informal curb market, where loans are more precarious and the interest high.[11] In the first five months of 1992, 3,646 companies—mostly small and medium-sized businesses—went bankrupt (*Korea Newsreview*, 1 August 1992: 15). More generally, by the 1990s, the fizz was disappearing from the Korean economy. World market conditions, which had been favorable to the products of cheap Korean labor in earlier decades, changed, becoming unfavorable at a time when prosperity at home had brought a higher cost of living, labor militancy won higher wages, and new markets for cheap labor in China and Southeast Asia opened to global capitalist enterprises. Korean factories were moving offshore, and the *chaebŏl* (monopoly corporations enjoying special government favor) that had once been seen as bastions of secure corporate employment began to trim their operations. Mrs. Pok's husband's early retirement was a symptom of the times (Lee 2001; Lett 1998; Moon 2001).[12]

But, in 1994, neither the shamans nor their clients, nor I, could have seen that the small personal crises so often precipitated by precarious credit were warning tremors. Although, by 1994, many were already experiencing the consequences of economic downturn, the expectation was that many others would get rich; the gods and good fortune could still smile. In the context of 1994, I had written of shamanic rituals as "one means by which some 'modern' and 'middle class' people both play and reflect upon a game whose odds are most likely stacked against them" (Kendall 1996b: 523). These may be the most sadly prophetic words that I shall ever write.

I had written from the vantage point of small shopkeepers and informal credit, but a high-risk game was also being played at the top. Korean banks had been receiving short-term foreign-currency loans at low rates. The Korean banks then loaned the borrowed funds at higher rates, valued in won. This arrangement was highly profitable so long as the won remained stable and the foreign-currency lenders remained willing to roll over the loans. In the fall of 1997, either spooked by sinking markets in Southeast Asia or simply in need of capital, lenders began to take money out of Korea, forcing the Korean banks to call in their loans. This betrayed the magnitude of debt within the overextended chaebŏl, where money had been lent and loans guaranteed between divisions in such a complex way that no one outside the structure knew the precise figures or the source of liability (Park and Rhee 1998; Root et al. 1999). Despite a campaign for financial reform initiated well before the crash, government oversight had been inadequate at best. The bankruptcy of the Hanbo Iron and Steel Company in early 1997, a harbinger of other bankruptcies to come, revealed that state-controlled banks, the major creditors of Korean chaebŏl, had extended loans to Hanbo well beyond the legally permissible limits (Pollack 1997).

With the flight of foreign credit in the fall, the Bank of Korea went through billions of dollars of its own reserves in a futile attempt to arrest the won's precipitous slide. It was not to be. Owing to the won's free fall, the foreign-debt load doubled in the space of a month. In December 1997, nearly depleted of reserves and facing default, the Bank of Korea requested financial aid from the International Monetary Fund. The government agreed to accept the IMF's conditions for stabilizing the economy. These measures were widely resented (Suh 1998). The regulation and tightening of credit limited flagging businesses' access to cash, causing further defaults along precariously balanced chains of credit (Strom 1998). Devaluation of the won brought inflation, particularly with respect to foreign commodities (Suh 1998). South Korea depends on imported petroleum for fuel. Grain (for food and animal feed), iron ore, and coking coal are also significant imports. The high cost of sugar was felt in every home, but poorer households, which devoted a larger proportion of their income to food and fuel, bore the brunt of devaluation (Lee and Lee 2000). The IMF's insistence on "labor market flexibility," combined with the business failures already precipitated by credit failures, increased the scope of layoffs and general unemployment.

Although the government had been urging labor market "rationalization" and "accountability" in market transactions for some time, capitulation to the IMF demands was widely viewed as an act of national humiliation, even as the citizenry had, in happier times, been encouraged to view South Korea's prosperity as their common triumph. In intellectual circles, there was talk of the IMF's attempt to establish a "trusteeship" over South Korea (Cho 1998: 1) and of the country's "annexation" by the IMF, of "living under IMF rule" (Park 1997), the bitter language of the colonial past. The pervasive sense of powerlessness that Koreans felt at that moment was effectively fetishized in small novelty dolls sold at rest stops along Korean highways, a little black figure, tightly bound and gagged, bearing the legend "IMF."

I returned to Korea in the spring of 1998, "the IMF era" (*IMF sidae*) as it was dubbed in promotions for "IMF bargain sales" and economy meals of "IMF burgers" and instant packaged noodles—attempts by struggling entre-preneurs to encourage consumption in the name of thrift. With rumors that the worst layoffs were still to come, everyone was waiting for the other shoe to fall. Like old ghosts from another time, images of unemployed men sleep-ing in public parks, abandoned children, and suicides haunted the media and nearly every conversation. While no precipitous disaster had as yet befallen my immediate contacts, everyone seemed to have been affected in at least some small way. The struggling shopkeeper or restaurant proprietor found it difficult to muster even a scrap of optimism for better times, the cab driver sat idle for hours in a queue of empty vehicles waiting for a fare, the dance instructor's long-standing classes for bank employees were canceled for lack of funds, the civil servant wondered whether he would still have a job after the next round of layoffs. While the reforms imposed by the IMF had been touted as ushering in a new era of transparency and accountability in the banking and corporate sectors (E. Kim 1998), for people on the street the future was illegible.

And things would get worse. Unemployment would peak at 8.4 percent in the first quarter of 1999, a three- to fourfold increase over immediate pre-crisis rates and significantly higher than rates for the early 1980s, before the Korean economy had achieved its globally recognized "miracle" status (OECD 2001; Lee and Rhee 2000).[13] Homelessness, all but nonexistent in precrisis Seoul, would rise precipitously by the fall of 1998. Into 1999, busi-nesses would continue to fail at three times precrisis rates. The demise of cer-tain chaebŏl would command press attention, but most bankruptcies would occur among small and medium-sized companies (Lee and Lee 2000). Local governments would trim civil service jobs by 12 percent (Lee and Lee 2000).

At the time of this writing, the crisis is officially "over." By 2000, Korea's

GDP already exceeded precrisis levels (Lee and Rhee 2000). But this model recovery has been won at some cost, particularly in the domain of employment. Manufacturing and construction have retrenched, and, with the "rationalization" of corporate and public-sector employment, college students who once anticipated professional careers and participation in a much-idealized middle-class lifestyle are claiming positions formerly held by high school graduates. The most marginalized members of the economy—female, less-educated, and less-experienced workers—are the most likely to be unemployed. Across a broader spectrum, economic restructuring means a notching down of the spectacular dreams of social and economic advancement that typified Korean life before the crisis (Lee and Rhee 2000; Lee and Lee 2000).

In the spring of 1998, the IMF era had hit the shamanic world as well. Shamans were seeing clients who had lost their jobs, clients at risk of losing their jobs, clients at risk of losing their businesses, clients at risk of losing their investments because they could not meet their payments, clients who had taken defaults on the credit that they had extended to family or friends, clients who were experiencing domestic violence and the suicides of family members as a consequence of economic stress.[14] In the words of one young shaman, "There isn't anything that doesn't come from the IMF." While few of these family crises were beyond the shamans' pre-IMF experience, they had become ubiquitous motifs. The precariousness of informal credit and the fragility of small enterprises were pervasive themes in my field notes from the early 1990s. The link between financial anxiety and economic stress was not new. I did hear, in several places, of kut held for the benefit of husbands whose jobs seemed precarious. Before the crash, I had remarked on the relative absence of white-collar households and corporate employees in general among the shaman's clients (Kendall 1996b). This made sense when kut spoke to chance, volatility, and risk and the corporate world promised jobs that were stable, relative to the precariousness of small businesses. As noted above, this had begun to change by the early 1990s, but what had been a subtle, gradual process became the order of the day in the time of the IMF. It is not surprising that employment anxieties were routinely articulated at kut in the spring of 1998.[15] The most profound difference wrought by the age of the IMF was the transformation of a climate of optimism—stoked by the palpable possibility of material advancement—into a pervasive ambience of blocked opportunity and declining fortune.

My longtime teacher, Yongsu's Mother, diagnosed within the logic of her own experience, offering rituals to purge the spirits of frustration and anger and bring the family to a more auspicious state. During one of my visits, a neighbor woman stopped by on her way home from the clinic, miserable with the aches, dizziness, and stomach pain that I would call *flu* but Koreans attribute to sheer exhaustion (*momsal*). I had first met this woman many years ago when she had sold cups of sweetened instant coffee in the market, a cheerful and energetic young vender equipped with a large red plastic thermos. From her perch, she had studied the market and dreamed of bigger things, possibly a shoe stall. Her husband was handicapped, and she was the primary breadwinner for her three-generation family. Against the shaman's advice (so Yongsu's Mother claimed in retrospect),[16] she had gone from her successful coffee enterprise to clothing and, when that failed, leaving her in debt, to vending the hearty soups that are said to be good for a hangover. She had recently entrusted the equivalent of several thousand U.S. dollars to a friend, but the friend had lost the money in some failed financial scheme. The betrayal was particularly galling because she had honored a second request for money from this same friend and given it in the firm belief that the entire debt would be honored. "These days, you can't trust anyone," she said. The loss was a cause of continuing upset, paired in her conversation with complaints of her aches and pains, and this was not her only problem. An attempt to repair the bathroom had gone awry, requiring yet more costly repairs and yet more debt. Her pained and weathered face carried no trace of the buoyant young woman I remembered.

Her case was like many that I had heard before the IMF era. Although acute physical illness had caused her to summon Yongsu's Mother a few nights previously and Yongsu's Mother had exorcised her with a pelting of millet, both shaman and client accepted that the client's aches and pains were somehow connected to her larger burden of anxiety. In Arthur Kleinman's (1980) terms, this is *somatization*, the experience of psychosocial stress as bodily pain that is at least tacitly recognized by a spectrum of sacred and secular medical practitioners in many Asian societies and more gradually in the West. The things that made this woman anxious were, in the shaman's view, a consequence of problematic relations between her family and their gods and ancestors, but she also saw her client's situation within the frame of bad times and limited options.

"Will they sponsor a kut?" I asked. "Don't be silly. With all that debt, where would they get the money for a kut? We'll just do a simple offering in the shrine." Shamans inevitably felt the economic crisis reverberate in their own practice when clients in need of kut could not afford them, even at reduced prices. The South Korean media did not hesitate to berate shamans for profiting from the economic crisis, but this was a predictable reaction (S. Kim 1998). The shamans, too, were taking a loss.

In some quarters, however, the shamans' ability to see the invisible was in great demand. Shaman initiates typically gain their first following through the astuteness of their visions but sustain successful careers through the mastery of ritual lore. Recently, however, I have encountered some urban shamans who seem content with careers as diviners, performing only simple prayers for their clients and disdaining a long and sometimes humiliating and exploitative tutelage with an exacting senior shaman. The media have given them a successful role model in celebrity shaman Sim Chin-song, whose astonishingly accurate prediction of the death of North Korean premier Kim Il-sung—told to an undercover newspaper reporter—created a media sensation. The subsequent publication of Sim's autobiography, *The Woman Chosen by the Spirits* (1995), boosted her to fame and fortune such that she is said to be booked for divination sessions with the rich and famous for the next several years.

In the spring of 1998, the IMF era was confounding two otherwise successful diviners of my acquaintance in unexpected ways, challenging them with the limitations of their own powers. I had met the Fairy Maid in 1994 when she was new to her practice. At the time, she had fairly bubbled with confidence in her abilities. Her divinations were always accurate, and her prayers always worked; children were born to barren couples, and businesses succeeded. She had mastered the technical knowledge of her practice in record time. Four years later, she was doing very well. Where I had last seen her in the rented room of a traditional Korean house, I met her again in a newly purchased apartment, crammed with appliances, imitation Louis XIV furniture, ornate knickknacks, and overbearing arrangements of artificial flowers.[17] But the Fairy Maid was troubled by the expectations of clients in desperate circumstances: "I do a great deal of praying for such people of course, but I can't solve all their problems. It's difficult for me because I can't satisfy them. I say to such people, 'I'm not a god. It's beyond my power. You need to cultivate your own strength. In today's language, it would be easier if you thought of this as *counseling* [she uses the English word].'" The Fairy Maid is cautious. She tells us that shamans have been sued by clients when a sponsored kut did not deliver the financial success that they had been promised. She tells us that her spirits have cautioned her to avoid performing kut in public shrines, to minister to clients quietly in her own household shrine, a view compatible with her own sense of her strengths as a diviner and performer of small but efficacious prayer rituals rather than as a skilled performer of the dances, songs, chants, mime, and feats of balance required to invoke and entertain the spirits during kut.

Ms. Shin is an articulate and thoughtful young shaman, active in seeking recognition and respect for her profession. In four years, her circumstances had also improved; she had relocated her family from a large apartment to a spacious two-story house. Like the Fairy Maid, but with more anguish than impatience, she expressed pain over her inability to help her clients:

> I tell them, "I'm not someone who has control over the economy." I tell them, "I don't even understand very much about the economy. I'm not connected to it." What I really want to do is help set their minds at ease, but in these troubled times it's almost impossible to do that. I tell them, "It will be better in a few days. If you can just get by until next month, it'll be all right, don't worry." I can't do much more than this for them. I don't have the power to get them a job in a company. Since it's the economy that weighs on their hearts, I can't possibly give them a satisfactory resolution. . . . There are people who have nothing. It hurts me deep in my heart. There are so many cases where I can't lift their spirits, and that hurts me too. I've been a shaman for fifteen years, and I've never felt so bad. . . .
>
> There are families in difficulties, families where they can't afford to send their children to school. . . . There are people who can't afford to go to a proper hospital. They could be crippled for life in some of those small clinics. . . . I don't want to take their money. . . . Even though I might have nice things to tell them from the spirits, who can resolve their situation? . . . I'm a human being, just like everyone else. I eat, I shit, I piss. What I know is what the spirits have given me to know. . . . If I call them and they don't come, then I can't do anything.[18]

She had told Professor C., long before the crisis, that some disaster would befall Korea in the fall of 1997, something on the magnitude of a war. Now, several months after the onset of the crisis, Professor C. asks, "Was this it? Was it the IMF?" "Because my grandfathers are spirits, I don't know whether they knew about the IMF or not. They didn't tell me. What I heard was only the constant sound of their mourning and weeping ringing in my ears." The wordless crying of her spirits is a fitting image of Ms. Shin's frustration.

Conclusion

We are no longer surprised when ethnographic accounts of witchcraft, spirit possession, or shamanic practices grapple with the ominous forces of a precarious market and with the risk attendant on the processes of modernity more generally (see, e.g., Comaroff and Comaroff 1993; Geschiere 1997; Meyer 1998; Moon 2001; Selim 1997; Weller 1994). The descriptions offered in this essay suggest that Korean popular religion articulates—or, better, dramatizes in the personae of spirits—the anxieties of petty entrepreneurs. This same frame of family and household gods accommodates the concerns of farming households and now, most recently, of employees where the unstable job market threatens family security. Here, as elsewhere, popular religious practices are not "false consciousness" in the sense that practitioners have a naive, innocent, or even "precapitalist" perception of how markets work. Rather, as in equivalent situations in other places, the shaman's clients understand full well that the market is fraught with risk, with dangerous but inevitable elements of unpredictability. The consultations and rituals that clients and shamans perform together articulate anxieties that are the very stuff of experience, no less global than local (Meyer 1998: 768; Weller 1994: 162). Warnings from a few farsighted financial pundits aside (Pollack 1997), how many experts really anticipated the Asian financial crisis of 1997? Even warnings aside, economists have suggested that it would have been impossible to predict the precise conjunction of influences that caused the Korean market to fall exactly when it did (Park with Rhee 1998). It was as illegible as the weeping of spirits.

As Evans-Pritchard (1976) recognized long ago, at the core of much popular religious practice are such questions as, Why me? Why now? Why not my neighbor? In Korea, such questions are posed and answered within the frame of family and household, where the consequences of economic and other crises are most directly experienced. This same domestic frame circumscribes the jurisdiction of gods and, by extension, the power of shamans.[19] The failure of my own business and my neighbor's run of good luck are both relative to a larger economic climate, over which gods, shamans, and small businesspeople have no control.[20] In the same sense, household gods can mediate the worst effects of a bad horoscope—an unfavorable orientation of person, time, and place—but they have no ultimate influence over the mechanistic forces that order the cosmos in which they and their human counterparts abide (Kendall 1985: 94–99). Indeed, the shamans' common expressions for an impasse of cosmological misfortune, *moga magida* (something is blocked) or *uni magida* (fortune is blocked), were apt characterizations of personal frustrations engendered by the IMF era.

A few celebrities aside, shamans are typically reluctant to divine beyond the particular fortunes of client families. In the summer of 1994, in the wake of reports that North Korea was stockpiling nuclear weapons, and when war talk was rife, one seasoned shaman chuckled over clients who wanted to know whether an attack was imminent, whether they should start stockpiling rice. She considered such questions as being well beyond the capability of her spirits. Shamanic voices from the IMF era indicate that there are moments when global politicoeconomic forces can be so well concealed in their onset and so all-pervasively devastating in their consequences as to render the spirits mute and impotent—at least for a time.

In the spring of 1998, the IMF claimed a force, a name, and a presence touching all lives, regardless of the temperament of one's own domestic spirits. The word had taken on a life of its own as something more mythically potent than a body of global financial regulators. It stood, not for transparency and fiscal accountability, but for a welter of concealed powers in distant places, both foreign and domestic, whose veiled operations had wreaked havoc, not only on the abstraction *nation*, but on many simple lives. The image of a silent and powerless spirit world in the face of this thing called the IMF was a fair reflection of what many Koreans were feeling in the spring of 1998.

But the shamans encountered in this essay are too articulate to be silenced for long. They are *experienced practitioners* in the Comaroffs' sense of the term, ritual specialists who are skilled in making universal signs speak to particular realities (Comaroff and Comaroff 1993: xxii). By the spring of 1998, they were drawing the dread IMF into the local logic of Korean shamanic practice as a force that must be recognized, even though it be beyond the reach of their ritual manipulation. I opened my discussion with a shaman's invocation of the IMF as a sufficient excuse for insufficient offerings. On another occasion, I heard a client ask a shaman to work some harm on the supervisor who had caused her husband to lose his job. "Don't worry," the young posal told her with a chuckle. "My spirits tell me that it will all be resolved by the fall. The IMF will take care of it."

Notes

The data used in this chapter were collected during several field trips financed by the Belo-Tanenbaum Fund of the American Museum of Natural History. I am grateful to Seung-ja Kim for her assistance and insight in 1994 and 1998. Homer Williams has continued to educate me regarding the Korean economy; he provided many facts, statistics, and critical sources for this chapter. Eun Mee Kim generously shared information regarding small businesses. I am grateful to Jean and John Comaroff for their comments as conference discussants and to Todd Sanders and Harry West and an anonymous reviewer for many helpful suggestions in the revision of this effort. I alone am responsible for its shortcomings.

1 In 1996, only 34.78 percent of the U.S. population lived in cities with populations of fifty thousand or more, compared with 78.5 percent for Korea. The contrast is even more striking for larger cities. Almost half of all Koreans (47.8 percent) live in cities of 1 million or more, while, in the United States, only 13.7 percent do. Even allowing for the slipperiness of the concept of *city* as a demographic unit, and allowing that large numbers of Americans leading essentially "urban" work lives reside in relatively small political units—suburbs, exurbs, unincorporated areas—the South Korean population is proportionately more urban than that of the United States. (Economic information has been taken from the *Statistical Abstract of the United States* [1998, table 1354]. Population data on Koreans in cities are from *Korean Census* [1995]. Corresponding data on the urban population in the United States are from table 47 of the *Statistical Abstract of the United States* [1995]. This information was compiled by Homer Williams.)

2 On the way in which middle-aged Korean women account for class mobility against a premise that, in the world of their youth, "we were all poor," see Abelmann (1997a, 1997b, 2001).

3 While sympathetic to the politics of the movement, Choi expresses profound discomfort with movement intellectuals' claims to represent and lead the cultural expression of the masses.

4 Seminal works would include Comaroff (1985), Comaroff and Comaroff (1992), Nash (1979), Ong (1987), and Taussig (1980).

5 The extent of Korea's commercialization before the twentieth century is much debated. Some claim that the commercialization of customary relationships in land and labor was already under way in some parts of Korea by the eighteenth century, while others chart significant developments from the end of the nineteenth century. The debate is summarized in Eckert (1991). The story of Korean agriculture under colonial rule (1910–45) is a tale of expanding markets, intense population pressure, increasing tenancy, and out-migration (Williams 1982). More recent decades brought intensive capitalization and mechanization as the rural population shrank (Sorensen 1988).

6 For a discussion of Korean economic policy, see Kim (1997). For discussions of class and perceptions of class, see Kim (1987) and Koo (1987).

7 For a description of the range of divination practices employed in Korea, see Young (1980).

8 Although she denied any prior business experience, we may assume that, like

many Korean housewives, Mrs. Pok had at least invested money in informal credit associations and may have been involved in more serious investments.

9 The term *yebang* means "prevention" or "prophylaxis." I had encountered it previously in ritual contexts as an exorcistic measure to prevent future misfortune, but here it was described in a manner suggestive of sorcery and countersorcery.

10 This story, and others like it, is also told in Kendall (1996b).

11 See stories in *Maeil kyŏngje sinmun*, 5 September 1985; and "Bankruptcies Highest since '87," *Korea Newsreview*, 1 August 1992: 15. In 1979, the government extended protection to small enterprises in certain areas of manufacture and, in 1985, simplified procedures for licensing businesses (*Maeil kyŏngje sinmun*, 10 December 1985; and Eun Mee Kim, personal communication, 24 June 1992). In 1992, protection extended to small businesses in certain areas of manufacture was lifted (Choi 1992: 14). Access to bank credit for certain categories of viable small businesses expanded after the financial crisis (Lee and Rhee 2000).

12 Writing of the salaried elite within a major South Korean conglomerate in the late 1980s, Roger Janelli and Dawnhee Yim describe a relatively stable pattern of employment, with most resignations occurring among more recent hires. Resignations were possible after an unfavorable transfer or when given pointed indications that one's performance was unsatisfactory (Janelli with Yim 1993: 152–55). By the time of Denise Lett's fieldwork among the white-collar middle class, only a few years later, the situation had altered, and many white-collar workers were either terminated at mid-career or given the incentive to resign through lack of promotion (Lett 1994: 109, 150–51; Lett 1998). By the late 1990s, there was significant evidence in the popular literature to suggest that many young Koreans were questioning the human costs of a corporate lifestyle (Moon 2001).

13 While even the peak rate might appear low in comparative perspective, it is generally regarded as an underestimate, particularly with respect to the informal sector. In relative terms, following on two decades of nearly stable, "virtually full" employment, it constituted a shock to the system (Lee and Rhee 2000: 17).

14 Suicides of men who had either lost their jobs or seen their businesses fail as a consequence of the economic crisis were widely reported in the media and frequently cited in conversations about the economic crisis. One of the shamans whom I interviewed had recently seen a client whose husband had committed suicide a few days previously.

15 I did not witness these myself but spoke with shamans who had participated in them.

16 In my experience, shamans and their spirits are fiscally conservative, taking a "wait-and-see" approach to bold financial ventures, but they do predict auspicious months for new activities.

17 Unlike many shamans, she also enjoys a stable marriage with a husband who works as a diviner. The ostentation of their surroundings is probably accomplished through their joint earnings.

18 Ms. Shin is also trained to divine according to the lunar calendar, using technique rather than divine inspiration. When the spirits fail to send appropriate visions, she resorts to this other skill, at which she is highly adept.

19 The notion of divine jurisdictions is pervasive in East Asian popular religion and is derived from the conceptualization of the Confucian polity as a nested hierarchy of administrative authority, the smallest unit of which is the small polity of the household (Wolf 1974).

20 Certain shamans stylized as "national shamans" (*nara mansin*) periodically perform large public kut as prayers for prosperity, for national reunification, or, in the drought year 1994, for rain. They do this on the authority of the tutelary spirits of a particular village or township or may even presume to draw on the authority of national founders and heroes. Although there is some precedent from dynastic times for communal kut, today such rituals are colorful but abbreviated media events, far removed from day-to-day popular religious practice.

References

Abelmann, Nancy. 1997a. "Narrating Selfhood and Personality in South Korea: Women and Social Mobility." *American Ethnologist* 24 (4): 786–812.

———. 1997b. "Women's Class Mobility and Identities in South Korea: A Gendered, Transnational, Narrative Approach." *Journal of Asian Studies* 56 (2): 398–420.

———. 2001. "Women, Mobility, and Desire: Narrating Class and Gender in South Korea." In *Under Construction: The Gendering of Modernity, Class, and Construction in the Republic of Korea,* ed. Laurel Kendall, 25–54. Honolulu: University of Hawaii Press.

Amsden, Alice H. 1989. *Asia's Next Giant: South Korea and Late Industrialization.* New York: Oxford University Press.

Chang, Yun-shik. 1991. The Personalist Ethic and the Market in Korea. *Comparative Studies in Society and History* 33:106–29.

Cho, Han Haejoang. 1998. "The Formation of Subjectivity within Uneven Development: 'You Exist within an Imaginary Well.'" Paper presented at the conference "Inter-Asia Cultural Studies Conference: Problematizing Asia," Center for Asia-Pacific/Cultural Studies, National Tsing Hua University, Taipei, Taiwan, 13–16 July.

Cho, Oakla. 1987. "Societal Resilience in the Korean Context." *Korea Journal* 27 (10): 28–34.

Choi, Chungmoo. 1993. "The Discourse of Decolonization and Popular Memory: South Korea." *Positions* 1 (1): 77–102.

———. 1995. "Minjung Culture Movement and the Construction of Popular Culture in Korea." In *South Korea's Minjung Movement: The Culture and Politics of Dissidence,* ed. Kenneth M. Wells, 105–18. Honolulu: University of Hawaii Press.

Choi, Sung-jn. 1992. "Will the Doomsday of Small Business Come?" *Korea Newsreview*, 1 August, 14.

Comaroff, Jean. 1985. *Body of Power, Spirit of Resistance: The Culture and History of a South African People*. Chicago: University of Chicago Press.

Comaroff, Jean, and John Comaroff, eds. 1993. *Modernity and Its Malcontents: Ritual and Power in Postcolonial Africa*. Chicago: University of Chicago Press.

Comaroff, John, and Jean Comaroff. 1992. *Ethnography and the Historical Imagination*. Boulder, Colo.: Westview.

CTC-CCA, ed. 1981. *Minjung Theology: People as the Subjects of History*. London: Zed.

de Certeau, Michel. 1984. *The Practice of Everyday Life*. Translated by Steven Rendall. Berkeley and Los Angeles: University of California Press.

Eckert, Carter J. 1991. *Offspring of Empire: The Koch'ang Kims and the Colonial Origins of Korean Capitalism, 1876–1945*. Seattle: University of Washington Press.

———. 1993. "The South Korean Bourgeoisie: A Class in Search of Hegemony." In *State and Society in Contemporary Korea*, ed. Hagen Koo, 95–103. Ithaca: Cornell University Press.

Evans-Pritchard, E. E. 1976. *Witchcraft, Oracles, and Magic among the Azande*. Oxford: Clarendon Press.

Geschiere, Peter. 1997. *The Modernity of Witchcraft: Politics and the Occult in Postcolonial Africa*. Charlottesville: University Press of Virginia.

Haggard, Stephan, Byung-kook Kim, and Chung-in Moon. 1991. "The Transition to Export-Led Growth in South Korea: 1954–1966." *Journal of Asian Studies* 50 (4): 850–69.

Janelli, Roger L., with Dawnhee Yim. 1993. *Making Capitalism: The Social and Cultural Construction of a South Korean Conglomerate*. Stanford: Stanford University Press.

Kendall, Laurel. 1977. "Caught between Ancestors and Spirits: A Field Report of a Korean Mansin's Healing *Kut*." *Korea Journal* 17 (8): 8–23.

———. 1985. *Shamans, Housewives, and Other Restless Spirits: Women in Korean Ritual Life*. Honolulu: University of Hawaii Press.

———. 1996a. "Initiating Performance: The Story of Chini, a Korean Shaman." In *The Performance of Healing*, ed. Carol Laderman and Marina Roseman, 17–58. New York: Routledge.

———. 1996b. "Korean Shamans and the Spirits of Capitalism." *American Anthropologist* 98 (3): 512–27.

Kim, E. Han. 1998. "The Korean Financial Crisis and the Future of Its Economy." *Korea Journal* 38 (2): 56–65.

Kim, Eun Mee. 1997. *Big Business, Strong State: Collusion and Conflict in South Korean Development, 1960–1990*. Albany: State University of New York Press.

Kim, Kwang-ok. 1994. "Rituals of Resistance: The Manipulation of Shamanism in Contemporary Korea." In *Asian Visions of Authority: Religion and the Modern*

States of East and Southeast Asia, ed. Charles F. Keyes, Laurel Kendall, and Helen Hardacre, 195–220. Honolulu: University of Hawaii Press.

Kim, Seong-nae. 1989a. "Chronicle of Violence, Ritual of Mourning: Cheju Shamanism in Korea." Ph.D. diss., University of Michigan.

———. 1989b. "Lamentations of the Dead: The Historical Imagery of Violence on Cheju Island, South Korea." *Journal of Ritual Studies* 3 (2): 252–86.

———. 1992. "Dances of *Toch'aebi* and Songs of Exorcism in Cheju Shamanism." *Diogenes* 158: 57–68.

———. 1998. "Economic Thought of Traditional Religion in Korea." Paper Delivered at the workshop "Religion and Economy in East Asia," Eberhard-Karls-University, Tübingen, Germany.

Kim, Seung-Kuk. 1987. "Class Formation and Labor Process in Korea: With Special Reference to Working Class Consciousness." In *Dependency Issues in Korean Development: Comparative Perspectives,* ed. Kyong-dong Kim, 398–415. Seoul: Seoul National University Press.

Kleinman, Arthur. 1980. *Patients and Healers in the Context of Culture.* Vol. 3. Berkeley and Los Angeles: University of California Press.

Koo, Hagen. 1987. "Dependency Issues, Class Inequality, and Social Conflict in Korean Development." In *Dependency Issues in Korean Development: Comparative Perspectives,* ed. Kyong-dong Kim, 375–97. Seoul: Seoul National University Press.

———. 1990. "From Farm to Factory." *American Sociological Review* 55:669–81.

Korea Statistical Yearbook. 1990. Seoul: Republic of Korea, Economic Planning Board, Bureau of Statistics.

Korean Census. 1995. Seoul: Republic of Korea, Economic Planning Board, Bureau of Statistics.

Lee, Jong-Wha, and Changyong Rhee. 2000. "Macroeconomic Impacts of the Korean Financial Crisis: Comparison with the Cross-Country Patterns." http://www.stern.nyu.edu/globalmacro/countries/korea.html. Accessed 10 November 2001.

Lee, June. 2001. "Discourses of Illness, Meanings of Modernity: A Gendered Construction of *Songinbyong.*" In *Under Construction: The Gendering of Modernity, Class, and Consumption in the Republic of Korea,* ed. Laurel Kendall, 79–113. Honolulu: University of Hawaii Press.

Lee, Young Youn, and Hyun-Hoon Lee. 2000. "Korea: Financial Crisis, Structural Reform, and Social Consequences. In *The Social Impact of the Asia Crisis,* ed. Tran Van Hoa, 57–84. New York: Palgrave.

Lett, Denise Potrzeba. 1994. "Family, Status, and Korea's New Urban Middle Class." Ph.D. diss., University of Washington.

———. 1998. *In Pursuit of Status: The Making of South Korea's "New" Urban Middle Class.* Cambridge, Mass.: Harvard University Asia Center.

Marcus, George E., and Michael M. J. Fischer. 1986. *Anthropology as Cultural Critique: An Experimental Moment in the Human Sciences*. Chicago: University of Chicago Press.

Meyer, Birgit. 1998. "Commodities and the Power of Prayer: Pentecostalist Attitudes towards Consumption in Contemporary Ghana." *Development and Change* 29:751–76.

Moon, Okpyo. 1990. "Urban Middle Class Wives in Contemporary Korea: Their Roles, Responsibilities and Dilemma." *Korea Journal* 30 (11): 30–43.

Moon, Seungsook. 2001. "The Production and Subversion of Hegemonic Masculinity: Reconfiguring Gender Hierarchy in Contemporary South Korea." In *Under Construction: The Gendering of Modernity, Class, and Consumption in the Republic of Korea,* ed. Laurel Kendall, 79–113. Honolulu: University of Hawaii Press.

Moskowitz, Carl. 1982. "Korean Development and Korean Studies—a Review Article." *Journal of Asian Studies* 42:63–90.

Nash, June. 1979. *We Eat the Mines and the Mines Eat Us: Dependency and Exploitation in Bolivian Tin Mines*. New York: Columbia University Press.

Ong, Aihwa. 1987. *Spirits of Resistance and Capitalist Discipline: Factory Women in Malaysia*. Albany: State University of New York Press.

Organization for Economic Cooperation and Development (OECD). 2001. *OECD Economic Survey: Korea*. Paris: OECD.

Park, Daekeun, and Changyong Rhee. 1998. "Currency Crisis in Korea: Could It Have Been Avoided?" http://www.stern.nyu.edu/-nroubini/asia/KoreaEcCrisis.html. Accessed 20 October 2001.

Park, Heh-Rahn. 1997. "Problematizing the Discursive Formation of the Asian Pacific at the Absence of Intra-Asian Multivocalities." Paper presented at the annual meeting of the Modern Language Association, December.

Pollack, Andrew. 1997. "South Korea: Despite World-Class Economy, Sense of Decline." *New York Times*, 4 February. http://www.stern.nyu.edu/-nroubini/asia/KoreaEcCrisisNYT297.html. Accessed 20 October 2001.

Root, Hilton L., et al. 1999. "The New Korea: Crisis Brings Opportunity." 7 September. http://www.milken-inst.org/mod23/korea.html. Accessed 10 November 2001.

Roseman, Marina. Forthcoming. *Colonizing the Imagination: Dreams, Songs, and Other Encounters of a Rainforest People*. Berkeley and Los Angeles: University of California Press.

Sallinow, M. J. 1989. "Precious Metals in the Andean Moral Economy." In *Money and the Morality of Exchange,* ed. Jonathan Parry and Maurice Bloch, 209–31. Cambridge: Cambridge University Press.

Sanders, Todd, and Harry West. 1999. "Transparency and Conspiracy: Power Revealed and Concealed in the Global Village." Conference call for papers. London: London School of Economics and Political Science.

Selim, Monique. 1997. "Les génies therapeutes du politique au service du marché." In *Essai d'anthropologie politique sur le Laos contemporaine: Marché, socialisme, et génies*, ed. Bernard Hours and Monique Selim, 299–352. Paris: L'Haramattan.

Sim, Chin-song. 1995. *Sini sŏnt'aekhan yŏja* (The woman chosen by the spirits). Seoul: Paeksong.

Sorensen, Clark. 1988. *Over the Mountains Are Mountains: Korean Peasant Households and Their Adaptations to Rapid Industrialization.* Seattle: University of Washington Press.

Statistical Abstract of the United States. 1995. Washington, D.C.: U.S. Census Bureau, Statistical Compendia Branch.

Statistical Abstract of the United States. 1998. Washington, D.C.: U.S. Census Bureau, Statistical Compendia Branch.

Strom, Stephanie. 1998. "In Korea, Domestic Loans Said to Be Serious Problem." *New York Times*, 10 February. http://www.nytimes.com/library/financial/021098korea-economy.html. Accessed 20 October 2001.

Suh, Sang-Mok. 1998. "The Korean Currency Crisis: What Can We Learn From It?" *Korea Journal* 38 (2): 34–44.

Taussig, Michael. 1980. *The Devil and Commodity Fetishism in South America.* Chapel Hill: University of North Carolina Press.

———. 1987. *Shamanism, Colonialism, and the Wild Man: A Study in Terror and Healing.* Chicago: University of Chicago Press.

———. 1995. "The Sun Gives without Receiving: An Old Story." *Comparative Studies in Society and History* 37:368–98.

Thomas, Nicholas, and Caroline Humphrey, eds. 1994. *Shamanism, History, and the State.* Ann Arbor: University of Michigan Press.

Vitebsky, Piers. 1995. *The Shaman: Voyages of the Soul, Trance, Ecstasy, and Healing from Siberia to the Amazon.* London: Macmillan.

Weller, Robert P. 1994. "Capitalism, Community, and the Rise of Amoral Cults in Taiwan." In *Asian Visions of Authority: Religion and the Modern States of East and Southeast Asia,* ed. Charles F. Keyes, Laurel Kendall, and Helen Hardacre, 141–64. Honolulu: University of Hawaii Press.

Wells, Kenneth M., ed. 1995. *South Korea's Minjung Movement: The Culture and Politics of Dissidence.* Honolulu: University of Hawaii Press.

Williams, Homer Farrand. 1982. "Rationalization and Impoverishment: Trends Affecting the Korean Peasant under Japanese Colonial Rule, 1918–1942." M.A. thesis, University of Hawaii.

Wolf, Arthur P. 1974. "Gods, Ghosts, and Ancestors." In *Religion and Ritual in Chinese Society,* ed. Arthur P. Wolf, 131–82. Stanford: Stanford University Press.

Young, Barbara. 1980. "Spirits and Other Signs: An Ethnography of Divination in Seoul, R.O.K." Ph.D. diss., University of Washington.

2

"Diabolic Realities": Narratives of Conspiracy, Transparency, and "Ritual Murder" in the Nigerian Popular Print and Electronic Media

MISTY L. BASTIAN

Consequently, the environment we found ourselves [has] now become filthy, insecured and insensitive. The truth is that Nigeria today is stinking with diabolic realities, of which if nothing is done, God will cast his anger upon this nation. Nigerians should arise to fight evils. First, we must look inwardly to identify the driving force behind these realities. Paradoxically, in my reflection, I seem to have identified the temptation for quick riches and inordinate love for power. This could be traced to our battered economy which has been aggravated by an act of mismanagement by those who happened to be on the seat of power. And because everybody wants to survive and accumulate wealth, all these vices are in the ascendancy almost at all levels [of] our society. People now look forward for money and nothing else. This has been the hypocrisy of a large proportion of our people—a hypocrisy that has percolated through the entire spectrum of the nation and is alienating many people from the nation's ideal value.
—Amaechi Ukor, "Our Time's Horrifying Realities"

On 22 September 1996, during the heyday of the now late Nigerian dictator General Sani Abacha, a murder mystery began to unfold in Owerri, the capital of Imo State. A young boy named Ikechukwu Okonkwo had disappeared three days before—one of a growing number of the city's children who had disappeared or been abducted since 1994—and suspicions were aroused throughout the town that members of Owerri's social elite were somehow involved. On this September day, after being sighted in a nearby rural area trying to wash blood from his clothes and body, an employee of the well-known Owerri Otokoto Hotel was caught by a police roadblock. The ironically named Innocent Ekeanyanwu was transporting the head of the missing boy, wrapped in plastic, in the trunk of his hired automobile.

At the request of Owerri's superintendent of police, Ekeanyanwu's image was subsequently broadcast on live television. In this powerful media image, the malefactor was shown holding what the press would call "his 'prize,'" Ikechukwu Okonkwo's still bleeding head. This televisual spectacle enflamed the Owerri populace, particularly its lower classes, who were weary both of strange disappearances and of the notion that their city had become a notorious center for wrongdoing. Hundreds of young men gathered at Owerri's central market, where they discussed the latest outrage and considered aloud what should be done to stop the supposedly bloodthirsty elites once and for all. The men in the marketplace soon turned from their orations and directed their attentions instead toward demolishing the houses, cars, and businesses of Owerri's parvenu millionaires, along with the palace of the chairman of the Imo State Council of Ndi-Eze (i.e., the council of "traditional kings") and three buildings that housed two "new-breed" evangelical churches and one ashram.

All the millionaires escaped with their lives. However, by the end of what became known as the "Otokoto Riots," the military had been called in to aid police in curbing further violence, and much of Owerri's prime real estate—along with the city's national reputation—was in ashes. Any trust remaining between Owerri's elite and its poorer populations was also ruined. By the first anniversary of the "riots," six of Owerri's most successful young businessmen would die by government firing squad for their part in the secret society blamed for the city's child abductions, two of Owerri's most prominent elders would be held in detention for conspiracy in the Ikechukwu Okonkwo killing, and one of the richest men in Nigeria would stand accused by the executed conspirators as the covert financier of all child abduction and ritual murder in Owerri. Three other alleged conspirators would be dead under unexplained circumstances in Owerri's town jail, before they could testify against any of those subsequently executed or held in custody. Even Eze Egwunwoke, the formerly respected "royal father" of Owerri (Osokoya 1997), was reviled in the streets for devaluing the title-taking system of Owerri by "selling" these status names and social positions to the city's suspiciously nouveaux riches.

The hallmark of the entire Otokoto affair—as represented in the Nigerian media and, hence, as now remembered by most literate Nigerians—was, not only the murder of a young boy and the subsequent destruction of wealthy men's property, but the supposed material proof of an elite conspiracy to garner riches at the expense of the ordinary Nigerian people. What was shocking was not so much the notion that the rich would exploit the poor but that it could be proved that Nigerian elites would go beyond well-known frauds and dabble in the killing of people for their body parts, used magically in "making money the easy way." Therefore, the events unfolding in Owerri during late 1996 were of intense interest to Nigerians across the country. The Owerri broadcast images of the head of young Ikechukwu Okonkwo in the hands of his accused murderer quickly became ubiquitous in the Nigerian media, not only shown on national television, but also captured as photographic stills and used as illustrations in magazines and newspapers. They also circulated informally in cheaply printed almanacs sold by streetcorner vendors and in markets throughout the nation.

Whether viewed momentarily on live television, perused in the press at a more leisurely pace, pinned to one's wall, or captured on videotape for a constant reappraisal, here was the proof of rumored conspiracies, a spectacular symptom—delivered by the media for Nigerian internal consumption—of the country's slide into social and economic anarchy. This nationally encompassing, Nigerian desire to see, capture, and, therefore, know the spectacular "truth" of conspiracy is similar to Chaney's (1993: 22) more general description of public spectacle in the late-modern period: "The spectacular as an invitation to interest and as a characterization is an opportunity to see something outside of the conventional constraints of everyday experience. It must therefore resemble its subject matter in a way that often runs counter to fantasy and which gives the yet-to-be-imagined concrete form. The spectacular is an opportunity to experience the transcendence of mundane availability, although in the looseness of popular associations we often describe the thrill of such experience as fantastic."[1]

Even the most skeptical Nigerians were convinced by the late 1990s that killing for body parts occurred as a part of urban "everyday experience," and many had claimed to have seen mutilated bodies that could only be the evidence of this trade. But nothing had quite the immediacy of this image of Innocent Ekeanyanwu and his "prize"; nothing else lent the horrific idea of "ritual murder" for personal profit such "concrete form." The image was fantastic in Chaney's sense as well as galvanizing; what it wrought in the Nigerian sociopolitical landscape—as well as in its "mediascape" (Appadurai 1998: 35)—was more than a nine days' wonder.[2] The very term *Otokoto* entered Nigerian speech in late 1996 as a shorthand for this type of behavior, and its constant usage reminded people again and again, by reference to the spectacular image and its connection to a conspiratorial narrative, of the reality of money magic.

In this essay, I will examine Nigerian popular press and other media narratives about the Otokoto affair, trying to understand exactly what sort of social "symptom" conspiracy theories and stories represent in Nigerian imaginaries at the end of the twentieth century. As we will see, the Otokoto story is actually a concatenation of several types of narratives: notably, stories about elite conspiracy against its own class (in kidnappings of valued children for ransoms to be paid in dollars) and against the poor (ritual murder of undervalued children for the purposes of money magic). Otokoto stories, in the press and elsewhere, also forced a reconsideration of competing narratives of official, government transparency in the case, notably through commissions of inquiry and the publication of two government-sanctioned "white papers."

These more official narratives of transparency and government rationality were subverted by the press's inclusion of printed and, outside Nigeria itself, Internet speculation about the principle actors and their connection to the Otokoto murder and ongoing disappearances in Owerri. The dramatis personae of Otokoto included government administrators of dubious probity, the leaders and members of evangelical churches offering avenues to quick wealth, and those church's most public patrons, the youthful Owerri millionaires whose automobiles, palatial homes, and luxury shops were destroyed on 24 September 1996. Otokoto narratives also eventually grew beyond local discourses of secret societies and "ritual murder" to encompass global issues like public resources being sold, for hard currency, on the black market to rapacious foreign companies.

While it was still not circumspect to point fingers directly toward General Abacha in 1996–97, Nigerian media narratives could make oblique reference to his regime's collusion in these conspiracies of wealth and power to rob the poorest Nigerians of everything, including their lives and their progeny. The final section of the essay will, therefore, discuss how one Nigerian media outlet, the Internet-based *Post Express Wired*, covertly used Otokoto to critique the federal military government (FMG) and what the *Post Express Wired*'s editorial "page" viewed as the FMG's endemic cronyism, corruption, and lack of any real commitment to political transparency or morality. Throughout the essay, I will also explore how categories like *conspiracy* and *transparency* are challenged by the events and media coverage of the Otokoto affair—particularly how the often-cited theoretical connection between conspiracy and "unreason" or transparency and the rationalization processes of late modernity may not really be as obvious as one might imagine.

"Criminal Tendencies" or "Jungle Justice"? Otokoto Backgrounds

CRIMINAL TENDENCIES: AIRPORTS, OVERCONSUMPTION,
AND "419 MEN" IN OWERRI

What brought this sadistic phenomenon [ritual murder] to the fore was the Owerri incident. A peaceful and serene town known more for its neatness and a generally accommodating disposition, the Imo State capital began to acquire a reputation for criminal tendencies in the early 90's. Inhabitants who spoke to *Theweek* linked the phenomenal transformation to the activities of "419" men and drug couriers.
—Taye Ige, "For the Love of Money"

When I last visited the small Igbo city of Owerri in late 1987, it was indeed a "peaceful and serene town." Northern Igbo speakers in Onitsha described Owerri to me as a big village when they were kind or simply as "bush" when they were not. Owerri's internal Igbo reputation was as a town that maintained its old ways and that had never quite recovered from the brutalities of the Biafran civil war. Outside the Igbo-speaking areas in Nigeria, Owerri was not as well-known as larger southeastern cities like Enugu or Port Harcourt, and, unlike those cities, it had no airport.

There was, before the implementation of Nigeria's structural adjustment program in 1987, much infrastructural work in the southeast, most of it funded by the government's 1970s and early 1980s petroleum bonanza. Enugu and Port Harcourt's airports were direct products of this pre–oil bust push for "development," and other airports were still under construction— if somewhat sporadically—during those later days of the bust. According to some of its Western-educated citizens, Owerri also needed to find a way to build an airport and fly trade and prosperity into the town. The hallmark of late-1980s Nigerian political, economic, and cultural discourse was a sincere belief in the power of individual and collective entrepreneurship (Bastian 1992, 1996). My Owerri friends were prepared in 1988 to raise money from individual donors as well as to convince businesses to contribute to a fund for their proposed airport. With a combination of government and private funding and seven years' hard work, the project was finally completed.

According to Taye Ige's report on Otokoto in *Theweek*, the building of the airport in 1994 did, indeed, bring wealth and increased entrepreneurship into Owerri. However, there were unintended consequences of the town's "opening up" to global markets and the new types of traders who were flourishing even under conditions of SAP (as structural adjustment was known in the country) during the early 1990s.[3] While there was a housing boom among the new elites and "imposing mansions, shops, supermarkets, high class hotels and restaurants began to spring up in many parts of the town" (Ige 1997: 17), the ordinary Owerri people saw few improvements in their everyday lives. These recently constructed urban amenities were all sites of elite privilege, where some Owerri indigenes might find employment, but to which very few could gain any more personal or pleasurable entrance.

Luxurious commodities also became available in Owerri during the early 1990s, but mostly through a set of exclusive shops. These shops catered to members of their owners' class: the newly affluent and generally youthful social elites of the town. Besides the arrival of airplanes in Owerri's skies for the first time since Federalist bombing attacks during the late 1960s, the town's bicycles and decrepit Peugeot 504 taxis now shared its potholed streets with the extraordinarily expensive automobiles and sports utility vehicles of the nouveaux riches. While the poorest Owerri indigenes listened to Igbo-language programs on their radios and visited more wealthy relatives to watch frequently disrupted local television programming or videos, the town's mansions were equipped with generators providing constant power, satellite dishes, videodiscs, and giant-screen televisions showing current international news, business reports, dramas, sitcoms, and music and movie programming from Great Britain and the United States.

By 1996, *ndi owerre* (Owerri indigenes) could, indeed, *see* what they had been missing before airport prosperity, but for most of them this was little more than a glimpse through the ornate gates of elite mansions or into shops whose goods had price tags the equivalent of several months' earnings. Since a number of the town's parvenu millionaires were not ndi owerre themselves (Ozurumba 1998), old ideals of reciprocity between wealthy and poorer clan members did not seem to apply under the new regime. This lack of reciprocity was especially felt as the young elites took titles and demonstrated their dollar/naira power at public, "cultural" events like masquerade outings, weddings, and funerals. Successful business entrepreneurship in 1990s

Owerri did not automatically "trickle down" to those without access to cash, elite networks, or new technologies.

Up to a point, the Owerri story of the ever-widening chasm between the rich minority and the poor majority was every Nigerian city's story in the 1990s. One might even go so far as to suggest that it is a more general story of the division between globalization's orphans and the new "information elite" all around the world (see Žižek 1997: 127). Although taking under consideration Appadurai's (1998: 189) point about the fragile construction of locality and local knowledges inside globalizing society, I would like to suggest that the Otokoto affair constitutes a peculiarly *local* response to this seemingly global fact of late-modern life. Most of the world's cities do not go up in flames over a televised image of a man holding a human head; our own televisions show scenes remarkably like this, or describe such scenes and worse, on almost an hourly basis.

In southeastern Nigeria, however, and particularly in the Owerri of 1996, this image managed to encapsulate a set of local anxieties or to manifest a set of local imaginaries that were too terrible to bear without direct action. The beginning of Otokoto was partially a Debordian spectacle: one that has a material reality and that (re)organizes the world and social relations in the world (Debord [1967] 1994: 14). But Owerri's response to this spectacle was quite the opposite of that envisioned by Debord in late-1960s Paris. People did not merely sit in their homes in "the empire of modern passivity" (Debord [1967] 1994: 15) and accept the new reality shown to them on their television screens. They took to the streets and expressed their outrage over what they had seen, using their words, hands, and bodies to tear down the things that stood for what they most feared and despised. The question for outsider analysis must be: What had they seen? To understand that, we must re-view the scene of wealthy young people and their expensive buildings and commodities, asking a question that was uppermost in the minds of many of Owerri's ordinary citizens during the 1990s: From where, in what was officially touted as an age of fiscal austerity, did the money for all this excess come?

There could be no doubt that some of the nouveaux riches were entrepreneurs in just the spirit claimed by my Igbo-speaking informants during the late 1980s. The Owerri elites did not only sit in their palatial houses and consume television and a range of other, modern commodities. They appeared around town, buying and selling these same commodities, driving in their "exotic automobiles" with trading partners, and boarding planes at the airport for the other Nigerian cities, where important business deals were made and elite wealth was generated in the 1990s. They were also seen at the most fashionable evangelical churches, where the "gospel of money"—which says that it is a sign of divine grace to prosper in difficult financial times—was preached by pastors from social backgrounds similar to their own or by former media celebrities who brought a special type of glitz and glamour to Christian services. Although the majority of Owerri's inhabitants were the products of mission Christian education, both Catholic and Protestant, these "new-breed" churches were generally distrusted by the lower classes. Indeed, churches in Owerri where millionaires congregated sported telling names like the Overcomers Christian Mission and the Winners' Chapel, names that pointed to the upwardly mobile ethos of the newly monied.

Ndi owerre also took notice that not all the town's arriviste elites espoused Pentecostal Christianity, that some were to be found at less mainstream religious locations like the Grail Message and Sat Guru Maharaj Ji's worship centers (Umunna 1996: 10). One or two wealthy Igbo speakers in Owerri even went so far in the 1990s as to convert to Islam, giving them religious ties with the northern military and business establishment that most southeasterners could not match.[4] There was already a well-developed set of rumors in circulation about some unsavory practices of the gospel-of-money evangelicals in Nigeria (Marshall 1993; Bastian 1998).[5] The fact that Owerri's millionaires also frequented ashrams and lodges, as well as mosques, caused the town's more orthodox Christians to wonder what other unusual rituals were taking place behind the locked gates and storefronts of those same elites.

In what originally appeared to be an unrelated phenomenon, the 1990s also saw a series of unresolved disappearances and kidnappings in Owerri. Although it is certain that people disappeared or were kidnapped from the city prior to 1990, Otokoto media narratives stress that, around 1994, ndi owerre became aware that there was an epidemic of child theft and kidnapping in their state. Rumors about the disappearance of children in the modern era are often moral tales about the disappearance of the safety of lineage, "the family," and locality, stories about anxieties over the future in uncertain times (Farge and Ravel 1991; Ginzberg 1991; Ivy 1995). Attempting to make their own moral interpretation of these disappearances and extortions, Owerri residents reinterpreted another, unusual development in the town— the sudden growth of a youthful, endogamous class with a good deal of leisure and ready cash.

These young elites had the freedom to travel (whether physically or virtually through media) and enough money to marry and take titles at an early age, build lavish houses, and flaunt their riches in the faces of their suffering neighbors. When the question was posed about the origins of such untoward wealth, two possibilities beyond legitimate entrepreneurship presented themselves to the Owerri imaginary. First, the money could be the ill-gotten gains of Nigeria's emerging culture of drug couriership and weapons sales. Second, and even more frighteningly, the money could be the product of the worst type of crime: the direct exploitation of children, whether as targets for parental extortion or as targets for money magic, a practice otherwise known in Nigerian Anglophone circles as *ritual murder*.[6]

"JUNGLE JUSTICE": RITUAL MURDER, MORAL INDIGNATION, AND POPULAR ACTION IN THE OTOKOTO AFFAIR

Members of the irate mob arrogated to themselves the power of the judge and jury. It was for them apparently, an opportunity for a putsch, for a cleansing of their once peaceful town. And they went about it with maddening fury. They pointed out magnificent buildings within the city suspected to belong to fraudsters and kidnappers. And once fingered, such buildings were marched upon and torched with exotic cars and other properties destroyed, their owners pronounced guilty by the mob. As the crowd moved from one part of the town to another, more people joined in the act of fury and more victims fell to its jungle justice. —Declan Okpalaeke, "Echoes of Otokoto"

Ritual murder as a category was introduced to Nigeria during the period of high colonialism, serving as a legalistic shorthand for a variety of activities that British administrators unhappily perceived all around them, most particularly in the southeastern part of the colony. These interdicted practices in Igbo-speaking areas included the sacrifice of domestic slaves at the funerals of important personages, the taking of heads in warfare, and the rumored existence of ritualized cannibalism.[7] In contemporary Nigeria, people are stilled charged by the police with the crime of ritual murder and can be tried by a court of law under statutes that remain unchanged since the colonial period. The Nigerian popular media have taken up this category and trumpet "Ritual Murder!" in thirty-point headlines or in electronic newscasts whenever there is any hint of sacrifice or the use of body parts for magical purposes in a local death. The domestic slave trade has been banned in Nigeria since 1915, with slave immolation unofficially banned at least ten years before that, and an allegation of cannibalism is so sensational that any reported instance receives front-page coverage in every nationally circulated tabloid.[8] Accusations of ritual murder are frequent in the Nigerian press, and people discussed it among themselves as a sad fact of life in the country during the

1990s, even while they roundly condemned it as a sign of the nation's ethical decay. It should come as little surprise, then, that the extraordinary level of child disappearance and kidnapping in Owerri in the 1990s would cause citizens of the town to believe that they were experiencing a wave of ritual murders for the purposes of money magic.

One thing was immediately clear when ritual murder reentered the popular Owerri imaginary during the mid-1990s: not all the children who disappeared remained in captivity or vanished forever, so ritual murder was not being practiced *tout court*. Those whose parents were wealthy enough to provide a ransom, preferably in U.S. dollars, were likely to be returned and to have the Owerri police actively investigate their removal from the family compound. The regime of the then–police commissioner David Abure was seen by ordinary ndi owerre as corrupt and clearly connected to the "419 men" (Onyla 1997: 18). There was also talk of a possible "syndicate" of wealthy men who extorted hard currency from other members of their own class through kidnapping their colleagues' children. One set of rumors about the wealthiest urban dwellers postulated that they were alumni of "secret cults" from their university days or members of exclusive, adult "secret societies" like the Ogboni. University cults in Nigeria attract their membership from among those who are already socially well connected and are associated with various forms of extortion on university campuses. Membership in them is perceived to be a precursor for elite membership in more national but nonetheless secret groups (Kalu, personal communication, 1999; Bastian 2001). In Nigerians' common knowledge of the dynamics and history of class secrecy in the country, there was a model already in place on which Owerri indigenes could mold new stories of conspiratorial elites.

After the traumatic kidnapping of the daughter of a prominent local physician, a Dr. Okoh, in May 1995, one of these secret elite cults came into better focus for ndi owerre. This group announced itself to Dr. Okoh as the Black Scorpions, informing him that a U.S.$12,000 ransom was required for the girl's safe return (Umunna 1997: 14–15). Dr. Okoh managed to convince local police authorities to help in pursuing the kidnappers. Under pressure from members of Owerri's elite to regain the girl and punish what seemed a particularly well-organized set of felons, the police finally discovered the hideout of the Black Scorpions and extracted information from them about their leadership. Some months elapsed before the police were ready to bring the wealthiest of the Black Scorpions' purported leaders, Obidiozor Duru and Amanze Onuoha, before the Imo State Robbery and Firearms Tribunal on charges of armed robbery, a capital offense in contemporary Nigeria.

Even then Duru and Onuoha were treated more like honored guests than prisoners on a potential death watch. They received liberal visiting privileges, they ate food from their own homes, and Duru (a Ph.D. in psychology from California State) even managed to impregnate one of his female jailers, celebrating a "traditional wedding" with her before his case was completed.

With the Black Scorpions incarcerated, the numbers of child kidnappings in Owerri dropped. However, the epidemic of lower-class child disappearances did not noticeably abate. None of the media sources that I consulted gives an exact figure for how many children disappeared before Ikechukwu Okonkwo, and it is entirely possible that any number given would be an exaggeration after the Otokoto fact. Ordinary Owerri people themselves were convinced that children continued to vanish mysteriously throughout the city. Here we are in a realm not unlike that which Brian Massumi (1993: 11) describes as the "general disaster that is already upon us, woven into the fabric of day-to-day life," deep in the mediascapes of late modernity. Owerri's citizens felt this overwhelming disaster of child loss and responded to it, even as they may have elaborated on its material reality, perhaps to give it a clearer, more defined face. It took only one documented case of child disappearance ending in ritual murder to extrapolate to wider conspiracies of money magicians or 419 men behind every locked gate in the town. And it took only one media-documented image to crystallize a desire to act out Owerri's moral repulsion into very specific (and transparent) action leveled against those who were deemed conspiratorial.

Although the young millionaires and their accomplices were in jail, rumor in Owerri had it that older, more important, and politically connected criminals were being treated as "sacred cows" by the police (Umunna 1996: 17). Distrust simmered among ndi owerre, and the more prudent nouveaux riches quietly developed escape strategies in case of trouble. One of the men under suspicion was Chief Vincent Duru, the father of Obidiozor Duru and the owner of an Owerri hotel known as the Otokoto. Duru's hotel was a fashionable location where youthful elites met, drank, and made assignations. Duru himself knew most of the imprisoned Black Scorpions and served as their patron, at the same time maintaining his ties to the police and local government. This brought surveillance on him and his associates—more, perhaps, by Owerri indigenes themselves than by the state police force.

The surveillance of the ndi owerre was rewarded when Ikechukwu Okonkwo's headless body was taken from the Otokoto Hotel to the local morgue. The movement of Ikechukwu's corpse brought people out of their houses and compounds and marked the beginning of Owerri residents' overt interest in the hotel premises. Some Owerri indigenes began to keep watch in front of the medical center at this time, waiting for official confirmation of "ritual murder." This confirmation was to come, not from a statement issued in front of the morgue or from police headquarters, but from the Imo State television station.

Although media reports are unclear why local television received permission to film Ekeanyanwu and his "prize," it is possible that the police wished to assure ndi owerre that local law enforcement was transparently and actively investigating such crimes. Besides suspicions already aroused about police competence in Owerri, this was a time of rampant official corruption in Nigeria. For instance, during the late 1990s Sani Abacha's entire family was implicated in blatant schemes to wring the country of its last petro dollar (see Anosa 1998). Owerri was administered by a group of men put into place by the Abacha regime, many of them outsiders to the city, and a number of them from ethnic/linguistic groups outside the southeast. They were, therefore, distrusted, and their financial dealings involving the state treasury were considered suspect.

Into this climate of distrust, anxiety, rumor, and scandal, the televised image of Innocent Ekeanyanwu holding his victim's head—meant to assuage public fear and demonstrate official transparency—burst like an incendiary bomb. As Wark (1994: 26) notes: "Images displaced around the media vector are weapons now, but of a different kind from the old fashioned warheads of the military vector proper. Like the weapons of the cold war, these can backfire." What is interesting for present purposes is the manner in which this particular image/weapon turned back against those who thought to profit by it.

On 24 September, when the image was first broadcast, ndi owerre congregated in the town's central marketplace. Markets in Igbo-speaking areas are locations where people are involved in much more than ordinary commerce (Bastian 1992). They are central places in every town where residents come to hear and exchange news, surveil their neighbors, and demonstrate their good fortune at important moments. Contemporary Igbo markets are places where news is constructed and disseminated, print and electronic media present in the market space adding to older forms of communication there. News of the "proof" that "headhunters" lived among ndi owerre therefore spread rapidly through the market, and newspapers printed photographs of the now ubiquitous televisual images as well as new pictures taken at the site of Ikechukwu's improper burial.

Young men were particularly agitated by the news and flooded the market, making speeches and threats against Owerri's millionaires. Young men are the best-represented demographic in southeastern Nigeria's marketplaces even at more ordinary times since they make up the majority of active traders and businessmen in the region. However, this was an extraordinary event, and young men who were unemployed or who worked in other businesses around town also came to the Owerri main market in order to participate in the protest. Under- and unemployed, often feeling themselves to be without future prospects, poorer young men in contemporary Nigeria represent a node of energetic discontent that has regularly exploded into violent action. When young men gathered in the public market space to critique the Owerri nouveaux riches and demand justice for Ikechukwu Okonkwo, it was, therefore, inevitable under the political and social conditions of 1990s Nigeria that they would take matters into their own hands.

The crowd from the market first went to the morgue, then rushed to the Otokoto Hotel and burned it, moving rapidly to Vincent Duru's nearby palatial home. Duru himself managed to escape. Once Duru's personal properties and automobiles were destroyed, the crowd dispersed in groups to various parts of the city and began to attack other sites of elite privilege. The Piano Stores were sacked, as were one other hotel and a number of businesses. Both the palace of Eze Egwunwoke and his petrol station were destroyed, along with one of his personal homes, fifteen air conditioners, and numerous cars (Osokoya 1997: 3). After taking on the millionaires and the air-conditioned king of Owerri, the rioters then moved to the homes of former Imo State officials. The administrators were targeted because of "their alleged unwillingness to properly tackle several cases of ritual murder, kidnapping and robbery while in office" (Ige 1997: 18). Finally, the "youths" were convinced by the military state administrator to stop their street action. The Otokoto rioters were assured that there would be a full, state-level investigation of the incident.

While Owerri continued to seethe, Innocent Ekeanyanwu died suddenly in his prison cell—before he could testify against his former employer or give a full statement to the police about his own actions. The Imo State police commissioner immediately issued a statement to the press, disclaiming any police responsibility in the thirty-two-year-old prisoner's death, and suggesting that there could have been no foul play. Unconvinced, and concerned that the killer had been murdered by mystical means while in the hands of the administration, Owerri's young men returned to the streets, determined to find their own evidence of ritual murder. They turned to the homes of "suspected dealers in human body parts," supposedly discovering some evidence of this trade in one house (Umunna 1996: 10). They also marched against several of the new-breed evangelical churches. A particular target was Overcomers Christian Mission, where it was rumored that the crowd discovered human skulls and other, non-Christian ritual paraphernalia. The police later made an official inventory of the mission contents, including a series of animal skulls, pots filled with vulture and other feathers, as well as chalk, red candles, books on "mystic" subjects, photographs, cowries, objects shaped like human beings, and bottles containing unidentified powders and herbal substances (Umunna 1996: 10). Encouraged by their success, the crowd marched on other churches, a lodge, and an ashram. Of the religious centers most popular with Owerri's millionaires, only Winners Chapel was saved because it was surrounded by police, who repelled the crowd.

By the time the riot was over on 27 September, twenty-six buildings and numerous vehicles were in ruins, "a veritable postscript to an innocent land turned upside-down by a despicable band of money worshippers" (Ige 1997: 18) or the sign of southeastern Nigeria's "backsliding into barbarity" (Adejare 1997). In the next section of the essay, I will consider how official and media discourses were constructed around these two discursive poles in the aftermath of the Otokoto affair, paying special attention to the way in which commentaries about General Abacha and his friends and appointees were inserted into a set of "think pieces" on the current state of Nigerian morals and immoralities. As the FMG tried to find a way to address the sentiments emerging after Otokoto while maintaining its control over a nervous and unfriendly southeastern population, Nigerians all over the globe wondered in print and on the Internet about their increasingly uncivil society. At the same time, they tried to dissect the causes of this incivility, using Otokoto as a potent metaphor for their plight, looking to avoid triggering censorship or too much notice from their military rulers.

"The Tip of the Iceberg" or a Move toward Transparency?
Commissions of Inquiry, Government White Papers, and Editorial
Responses to Otokoto

It's true, [DeLillo] suggests, that capitalism has penetrated everywhere, but its globalization has not resulted in global rationalization and Weber's iron cage. It seems instead to have sponsored a profound reversal: the emergence of zones and forces like those that

imperial expansion has erased: jungle-like techno-tangles; dangerous unknown "tribes"; secret cults with their own codes and ceremonies, vast conspiracies.
—George E. Marcus, "Introduction: The Paranoid Style Now"

In this section, I explore the fear, on the part of both journalists and ordinary Nigerians, that Marcus's globalized primitivism, dredged from colonialist imaginaries, has become a diabolic reality in their country. In editorials in the *Post Express Wired*, an Internet news medium meant to offer virtual Nigerians (Bastian 1999) an opportunity to read the latest news and commentary from their country, Nigeria was portrayed after Otokoto as a place plagued by the specter of its imperially imagined past and aspects of a premodern African social life perhaps best left behind. "Tribalism" is not so much the issue in these editorials as is "cultism" and "barbarism" among the superelites of the Nigerian state. This elite attitude led, according to the press, to political assassination, official and unofficial conspiracies among the powerful, and, finally, to ritual murder and money magic throughout Nigeria during the 1990s. These images were not all "techno-tangles," however, as they also enabled Nigerians to refract sensationalist stereotypes of African cannibalism and the uncontrolled supernaturalism of the "jungle" into a discourse about the production of immorality under late-modern conditions.[9]

READING THE WHITE PAPER

Although the *Post Express Wired* covered the Otokoto affair extensively in its news sections, its editorial staff did not comment on Owerri's difficulties until 11 March 1997, just after the first, abridged government White Paper on the "riots" was released (*Post Express Wired* 1997b). The White Paper was the product of a commission of inquiry, one of many convened during the twentieth century by colonial and postindependence Nigerian administrators. These Nigerian commissions of inquiry have become infamous for their irresolute conclusions as well as for their exoneration of powerful people, local governments, and whatever regime is in power at the time.[10] The Otokoto Commission, which met in early 1997 to hear testimony and develop a report, was no exception to the perceived elite and state manipulation of "facts." Not only was the ultimate verdict of the commission that "no person, persons or group is/are identifiable as being responsible for organising the destruction," but the White Paper further noted, using the words of one witness, that "no human being in Owerri or Imo State or anywhere else big or small instigated, motivated or organised the mayhem. No mortal creature could have organised or teleguided such [an] unprecedented mob in such colossal moving force. Only God could and He did to serve his purpose" (*Post Express Wired* 1997a).

This pious statement, in keeping with southern Nigerian evangelical Christian mores, was seen in the press and by many people around the nation as a cynical move on the part of the state to simulate ordinary people's values while masking its own immorality. One editorial (*Post Express Wired* 1997b) noted that it was not surprising that the first, abridged White Paper—which named elites and government functionaries as complicit in the numerous corruptions of 1990s Owerri life—was immediately withdrawn from public circulation, all copies destroyed, and the report completely redrafted. The Imo State administrator was reported to have pulled the first White Paper for fear that its conclusions would enflame the city's population into a second "Otokoto." Some of my Nigerian immigrant colleagues suggested privately, however, that what the administrator really feared was General Abacha using the Otokoto affair as an excuse to institute a stronger version of military rule in the city.

Since just such blatant militarization was taking place not far from Owerri in the Delta region, this was hardly idle speculation (Nixon 2000). The second White Paper invited an intensification of the military presence in Owerri, calling for closer scrutiny of Owerri by the National Drug Law Enforcement Agency (NDLEA), a tighter control over police activities by administrators, the institution of joint army-police patrols known as "Operation Storm," and the proliferation of police checkpoints all around the city (*Post Express Wired* 1997a). Each of these "recommendations" from the White Paper was accepted and immediately implemented by the Abacha administration.

One way in which the regime attempted to ingratiate itself with global powers after the 1995 execution of Ken Saro-Wiwa (Bastian 2000) was to agree to tighter liaisons with international law enforcement organizations, most especially with the Drug Enforcement Agency (DEA) of the United States.[11] This meant that DEA agents were allowed into the interior of Nigeria to "assist" NDLEA officers in their work. Putting Owerri's "419 men" under sophisticated drug law enforcement surveillance would not only give the government the illusion of official transparency in the eyes of the Owerri people but also strengthen ties with the West when Abacha needed them most. The local media showed little concern over the extension of the NDLEA's power and did not question Owerri's new status as a recognized locus for the international drug trade. Even if this modern reality meant the curtailment of certain liberties, it was one that ordinary Nigerians and journalists seemed quite content to live with.

While being told by the second White Paper to learn slogans like "Crime Does Not Pay," "Shun 419," "Study to Survive," and "Work Hard to Earn Income," after 1997 Owerri residents found that the demands of ordinary citizenship were more difficult than ever. Military transparency was more literalist than was its civilian counterpart. Ndi owerre were required to stand by their cars for physical inspections at some checkpoints and were subject to military search and seizure of their goods. This new, more panoptic Owerri intruded the discipline attendant on any militarized space directly onto the bodies of its civilian citizenry. The moralizing discourse of White Paper sloganeering also gave birth to other, more tangible inscriptions on Owerri's landscape. Otokoto-related buildings, tracks of land, and streets in the town were linguistically "cleansed" of their old names, if not of their wicked associations in the memories of ordinary Owerri people, and local landmarks with deep, Igbo cultural associations were dismantled and disappeared by military order.

Some Igbo speakers felt that this assault on the conceptual as well as material cityscape of Owerri represented an affront to Igbo political power, even going so far as to connect the historical defeat of Igbo nationalism during the early 1970s to the fallout from Otokoto in the late 1990s (Ilozue 1999). This is the sort of conspiratorial story that Kathleen Stewart (1999: 17) discusses: "a texting of everyday life where everything is connected and the connections are uncanny. There are moments of déjà vu, moments when the sense of overdetermination is palpable." Since the defeat of Igbo nationalism has been experienced in some quarters as a defeat of Igbo masculinity, the déjà vu in this instance was doubled.

Otokoto and Biafra were both moments when young Igbo men attempted to stand up to the power of a military with a political agenda and wealthy elders bent (as many young men saw it) on selling their patrimony. They were also moments when young men's emasculation in the face of foreign capital and external interests were made physically manifest. By linking Otokoto and Biafra, then, editorialists and immigrant critics were making a strong statement about their own felt powerlessness—and celebrating a moment when young men stood up against what threatened society at large. The editorials and discussions around Otokoto were, therefore, subtle but telling critiques of the conspiracies of the instruments of rationality—state-level bureaucracies, police, and military forces. True transparency was found in the

direct action of militant youths, however irrational and "mob-like" their behavior. During General Abacha's lifetime, such praise of popular disorder
had to be obscure. Its implications, however, would be debated more openly
when the dictator was dead.

READING ABOUT OTOKOTO ON THE
ELECTRONIC EDITORIAL "PAGE"

In 1997, before the Abacha regime ended in the general's death, even virtual
Nigerian media like the *Post Express Wired* needed to write in veiled terms
about the national ramifications of Otokoto. The *Post Express Wired*'s first
editorial on Otokoto, for instance, was careful to praise the Imo State administration, saying that "all hope is not lost in the fight against crime and
their perpetrators in our society" because of the government's commission
of inquiry (*Post Express Wired* 1997b). Nonetheless, the anonymous edito-
rialist warned that the public was in no mood to be denied full access to
the commission's report and suggested that information on Otokoto must
be understood as "public property." If the Imo State administration or the
larger government should be reticent in its treatment of the defendants or
reluctant to let "justice . . . be done, no matter whose ox is gored," then it
would be "inviting chaos and jungle justice." Ndi owerre had discovered the
truth for themselves through their actions during Otokoto and would not be
satisfied with the government doing any less or appearing to cover up the evidence. In the climate of enforced transparency, corrupt jurisprudence could
lead only to jungle justice, with all that term's symbolic baggage. This editorial was published simultaneously on the Web and in print at a moment
when General Abacha was retreating completely from public view, even as
his supporters were making noises about "self-succession" and "permanent
transition." No one expected the general to die, and a hopelessness took hold
of the Nigerian psyche, both at home and abroad. At such a moment, the
evocation of jungle justice and information as public property were heady
stuff.

Under the conditions of late modernity, representations of the political are
often hedged about or permeated by the personal. Debates about personal
responsibility in Otokoto were heated, not only between people in face-to-
face discussions, but also within the *Post Express Wired* website. The personality in question in these debates was not that of the Otokoto defendants,
however, but the Nigerian *national* personality, a personality that had been
"civilized" but was now in imminent danger of sliding down into "primitive
barbarity" (Adejare 1997). This regressivist view of society was, to those who

espoused it, the product of a residuum of "primitive belief" meeting global necessities of "material well-being or outright cash" (Adejare 1997).

In this formulation of Nigeria's Otokoto dilemma, the anachronistic unreason of the premodern world lingers on the edges of Nigeria's wildly capitalistic, wildly unreasonable modern culture, waiting for an opportunity to syncretize itself and return to the center. These barbaric peripheries of the Nigerian national persona subvert ordinary, Western-educated Nigerians' desires to take part in international economic and political affairs: "Of what use is the guarantee of fundamental human rights in our constitution if some of our compatriots are viewed as beings born to be sacrificed?" Even Christianity is tainted by its connections to money hunger and "the growing trend of satanism." The Christian moralists' solution to Otokoto is for southern Nigerians to look into their souls and rediscover their true African Christianity, repressing what "should be consigned to the shadowy corners of [their] past history," and bringing the national personality back to a spiritual "civilization" (Adejare 1997). One way in which this renewed Christian morality should be demonstrated is through a national commitment to official transparency—in the organized Christian churches and the Islamic Council of Nigeria as well as in political organizations like the office of the inspector general of police.

As the Otokoto trial dragged on into 1998 without appreciable resolution, *Post Express Wired* editorialists criticized the government more boldly—but remained circumspect in how they framed their criticism. Zebulon Agomuo's (1998) editorial "The Era of Killings" is a useful example of this type of journalistic narrative. Agomuo begins the short piece by conflating assassinations and ritual murders, which immediately enables him to make a subtle comparison between General Abacha's way of governing (through plausibly deniable state terrorism) and the Otokoto conspirators' alleged methods of disappearing and exploiting human beings for the purposes of money magic. The "Era of Killings" began, according to this journalist's version of the conspiratorial narrative, with the mysterious parcel bomb death of the journalist Dele Giwa in the 1980s.

Many Nigerians in the early twenty-first century consider Dele Giwa to be the first martyr under the developing military repression. Making an editorial connection between Dele Giwa and Ikechukwu Okonkwo is, then, a rhetorical move that enables the knowledgeable reader to see how far down the road of national tragedy the FMG had traveled by 1998. What begins with the "justifiable" (in Machiavellian terms) destruction of political enemies has degenerated into a wholesale slaughter of the innocent population.

Agomuo's (1998) language is graphic as he describes the condition of Lagos, the former capital of Nigeria:

> Our major expressways, within the city of Lagos, have become dumping grounds for corpses. It has become necessary to believe that most of the corpses on the expressways are not victims of automobiles [*sic*] accidents but clear victims of ritual killings. . . . It is a thing to lament about, over the rate at which human beings are missing in our cities today. People are being abducted to make money. While there is wailing and great sorrow in one home over a member of the family that is missing, there is joy and great gladness in some other because the missing man has become [a] money machine to enrich it. Man-hunt has assumed a worrisome proportion in this society of ours, so much so that many people are presently living in fears [*sic*]. . . .
>
> The truth is that the incidences of killings we do not see or hear about, far surpass the few ones we do see or hear about. We are all endangered. Living in Nigeria presently is just a matter of God's divine protection.

In the late 1980s, I read editorials in the Nigerian popular press suggesting that some politicians and town elders in the southeast were like witches, acting as predators to steal the lives of their constituents and juniors (see Bastian 1993). However, I rarely read anything suggesting that the entire population of the country was at risk. Local government elections were generating anxiety in 1988, but there was hope that a real transition toward civilian rule was under way. No one could then predict the horrific turn of events in the 1990s. A decade after Emma Agu's 1987 editorial on friendless, political bloodhounds, Agomuo portrays a much more desperate situation. When he writes of "man-hunt," he means not only the predatory and degrading hunt before ritual murder but also assassinations and other forms of political violence. He means the reader to think about the disappearances suffered by unknown numbers of activists, students, and others in the Delta and along the southeastern coast who, purposefully or by accident, ran afoul of the military and multinational oil companies during the mid- to late 1990s. Finally, he means the reader to meditate on the Abacha regime's escalating state security apparatus—or, more precisely, its simulacrum since it was difficult in the last, Kafkaesque year of Abacha's rule to tell whether the men who arrived at the door to carry people away were actually members of the secret police, agents of the NDLEA, unofficially hired thugs, or kidnappers with their own, entrepreneurial agenda.[12]

Whether any particular Nigerian would remain alive in 1998 was, in Agomuo's pessimistic view, strictly in the hands of God. Little surprise, then, that the general's sudden death was seen as providential. Indeed, this sense that something far worse was in store for the country, something that could still occur if the invisible hand of the deity should be withdrawn, continues to pervade the Nigerian imaginary. In late May 1999, for instance, rumors that President-Elect Obasanjo had been assassinated by the military electrified the southern half of the nation. Only his image on television, assuring the public that he was very much alive, well, and preparing to take office, was effective in calming the fear. This televised reassurance did not flash onto screens quickly enough in some areas, however, and a certain amount of elite property was destroyed before people returned to their homes (Naijabeat-News 1999).

Meanwhile, many of the Otokoto defendants continued to languish in an Imo State jail, neither convicted nor exonerated, adding to the general sense that things may not really have changed, and elevating the level of mediated anxiety. The impact of Otokoto has not, however, been uniformly negative—nor has Otokoto proved to be only an occult symptom of the larger Nigerian dis-ease of "an optimistic faith in free enterprise encounters" confronted with "the realities of neoliberal economics" (Comaroff and Comaroff 1999: 294). "Doing Otokoto" in twenty-first-century Nigeria has both positive and negative valances: it means rioting and lawlessness, certainly, but it also means violently uncovering a hidden truth, making plain what everyone suspects but no one dares see or say.

In a world where conspiratorial imaginings (and possibly conspiratorial actions) are pandemic, infecting our social relations with distrust and anxiety, there is something refreshing in a case where people understood themselves to have momentarily confronted a terrible truth—and to have ripped it out by its branches, even if not by its roots. In Otokoto, ndi owerre refused to sit, transfixed, in their living rooms as the spectacle played on their television screens. They went instead into the public spaces that had served their ancestors well, and they acted out a public, communal gesture of disgust. Otokoto was not a "figuration" of postmodern irony but a movement, however brief and fragmented, toward reestablishing a sense of *local* Owerri values and a local Owerri place at the heart of the globalized, surveilled, and modernized city. Such movements are well worth knowing about, wherever they occur.

Notes

I would like to thank various, anonymous members of the Nigerian community abroad who have shared their thoughts and materials on Otokoto and Nigerian politics with me. I would also like to thank Professor Ogbu Kalu of the McCormick Theological Seminary for our many discussions about Nigeria at Harvard's Center for the Study of World Religions in 1998–99, especially for his insights on and for sharing unpublished work relating to "cultism" in southern Nigerian universities. Professor Helen Henderson of the University of Arizona and Dr. Daniel J. Smith of Brown University have also been valuable resources. Thanks to all the participants in the 1999 London School of Economics Workshop on Transparency and Conspiracy, with special thanks to Jean Comaroff, Todd Sanders, and Harry West for their insightful and stimulating comments on an earlier version of this essay. Finally, I am indebted as well to one anonymous reviewer for thought-provoking comments on this manuscript.

1 To be more precise, this may have been a southern Nigerian desire to capture and know this spectacular truth. It is unclear from the media materials with which I am dealing in this essay how the Otokoto riots were received in the largely Muslim north of the country. However, the coverage did resonate in a manner that appeared to transcend ethnicity in the southern half of the nation. Words and images were part of this "capture," linking the virtual and actual participants into a (mediated) activity that enabled them all to enter into the reality of the spectacular. One is reminded of Lévi-Strauss's (1963: 174) discussion of a Native American witchcraft narrative and its representative power: "Witchcraft and the ideas associated with it cease to exist as a diffuse complex of poorly formulated sentiments and representations and become embodied in real experience."

2 According to Appadurai (1998: 35–36), "Mediascapes, whether produced by private or state interests, tend to be image-centered, narrative-based accounts of strips of reality, and what they offer to those who experience and transform them is a series of elements (such as characters, plots, and textual forms) out of which scripts can be formed of imagined lives, their own as well as those of others living in other places. These scripts can and do get disaggregated into complex sets of metaphors by which people live . . . as they help to constitute narratives of the Other and protonarratives of possible lives, fantasies that could become prolegomena to the desire for acquisition and movement."

3 Writing about the partial demise of air travel from the city after the Otokoto affair, Anokuru (1997) notes that Owerri indigenes and airline employees alike were suspicious of the sudden flurry of air traffic out of the Imo State Airport: "The patrons of these regular flights were middle class business people and suspected 419 operators who were said to have relocated their business bases to Owerri, when the heat which was turned on them in Lagos became unbearable. As a result, flights were usually fully booked by these 'traders' who were shuttling

between the Imo State capital and Lagos on [a] daily basis, hunting for 'deals.' "
On 419 and Otokoto in Owerri, see also Smith (2001).

4 Since the mid-nineteenth century and the early twentieth, intense missioniza-
tion secured most of Igboland for Christianity. During the Biafran civil war
in the late 1960s, e.g., most Igbo-speaking people constructed themselves not
only as Biafrans but also as Christians, in opposition to the northern Nigerian
(Hausa/Fulani) and southern Yoruba Muslims.

5 During the commission of inquiry called by the Imo State government to investigate the Otokoto affair, Rogers Uwadi, the Methodist bishop of Owerri, stigmatized these new-breed churches as the "toxic waste of America" and places
where people "practice pentecostal witchcraft" (quoted in Umunna 1996: 10).

6 In a nonfiction work intended for internal Nigerian consumption, one of the
country's most well-known novelists, Elechi Amadi (1982: 19–20), discusses
ritual murder as a social category as well as a material reality. He suggests that
its perpetrators are pursued most properly through the Nigerian courts of law.
He does, however, see the difficulty in eradicating such crimes: "Rituals are connected with religion, and religion cannot be eliminated, only modified."

7 I have no intention of entering the cannibalism debate—a vast literature war
begun by Arens (1979), carried forward by anthropologists like Sanday (1986),
and continuing with a certain virulence to the present day—with this assertion
but am perfectly willing to agree that most of the "cannibalism" that colonial-
ists feared took place in their own heads. Nonetheless, such was the power of
the colonial metaphor of cannibalism that all Igbo practices around the dead
were carefully scrutinized by colonial officials and the missionaries who preceded
them. The reality of human sacrifice among Igbo speakers *during the early colonial
period* can, however, be in no doubt. It was witnessed firsthand and recorded by a
number of missionaries (themselves of African origin) in Onitsha and elsewhere.
See, e.g., Buck (1872).

8 There was in February 1999 a sensational case of serial murder and "cannibalism" in Lagos that remained a tabloid, electronic, and "legitimate" press staple
throughout the first half of that year. The shack under a Lagos expressway fly-
over of Cyril Orji, the alleged murdered and cannibal, became a tourist attraction
and the cause of a daily traffic jam after his supposed deeds were made public in
the media.

9 For a similar analysis of "occult economies" in South Africa at the end of the
twentieth century, see Comaroff and Comaroff (1999).

10 For more on Nigerian commissions of inquiry, see Bastian (1992). For more on
this type of official inquiry in South Africa, see Ashforth (1990).

11 The similarity in the names of these two drug law enforcement offices is hardly
coincidental. The NDLEA was clearly modeled on the older and globally well-
recognized DEA and uses many of the DEA's most cherished tactics. Cooperation between the two organizations has included NDLEA agents training in the

United States with the DEA or in Nigeria in seminars under DEA auspices (see, e.g., Alabi 1998).

12 Baudrillard's (1988: 168) distinction between dissimulation and simulation is very useful here: "Feigning or dissimulating leaves the reality principle intact: the difference is always clear, it is only masked; whereas simulation threatens the difference between 'true' and 'false,' between 'real' and 'imaginary.'" The line between those who simulated government authority and those who actually had it in Nigeria was by 1998 so blurred that law-abiding citizens would often drive through "police" roadblocks rather than risk being robbed and killed by government-issued weapons.

References

Adejare, Oluwole. 1997. "Otokoto Saga: Back to Barbarity." Editorial. *Post Express Wired*, 15 March. http://www.postexpresswired.com/postexpress.nsf. Accessed July 1999.

Agomuo, Zebulon. 1998. "The Era of Killings." *Post Express Wired*. 1/25/98 (editorial). Editorial. *Post Express Wired*, 25 January. http://www.postexpresswired.com/postexpress.nsf. Accessed July 1999.

Agu, Emma. 1987. "Politics and the Witch's Malice." *Sunday Statesman*, 13 December, "Forum" column.

Alabi, Frank. 1998. "Workshop on Advance Fee Fraud Holds in Lagos." *Post Express Wired*, 31 July. http://www.postexpresswired.com/postexpress.nsf. Accessed July 1999.

Amadi, Elechi. 1982. *Ethics in Nigerian Culture*. Ibadan, Nigeria: Heinemann.

Anokuru, Emeka. 1997. "Owerri Airport Records Low Passenger Traffic." *Post Express Wired*, 18 August. http://www.postexpresswired.com/postexpress.nsf. Accessed July 1999.

Anosa, Victor. 1998. "Africa's Presidential Robbers." Editorial. *Post Express Wired*, 27 November. http://www.postexpresswired.com/postexpress.nsf. Accessed July 1999.

Appadurai, Arjun. 1998. *Modernity at Large: Cultural Dimensions of Globalization*. Minneapolis: University of Minnesota Press.

Arens, W. 1979. *The Man-Eating Myth: Anthropology and Anthropophagy*. New York: Oxford University Press.

Ashforth, Adam. 1990. *The Politics of Official Discourse in Twentieth-Century South Africa*. Oxford: Clarendon.

Bastian, Misty L. 1992. "The World as Marketplace: Historical, Cosmological and Popular Constructions of the Onitsha Market System." Ph.D. diss., Department of Anthropology, University of Chicago.

———. 1993. "'Bloodhounds Who Have No Friends': Witchcraft and Locality in the Nigerian Popular Press." In *Modernity and Its Malcontents: Ritual and Power in Postcolonial Africa,* ed. Jean Comaroff and John Comaroff, 129–66. Chicago: University of Chicago Press.

———. 1996. "Female 'Alhajis' and Entrepreneurial Fashions: Flexible Identities in Southeastern Nigerian Clothing Practice." In *Clothing and Difference: Embodied Identities in Colonial and Post-Colonial Africa,* ed. Hildi Hendrickson, 97–132. Durham: Duke University Press.

———. 1998. "Fires, Tricksters, and Poisoned Medicines: Popular Cultures of Rumor in Onitsha, Nigeria, and Its Markets." *Etnofoor* 11 (2): 111–32.

———. 1999. "Nationalism in a Virtual Space: Immigrant Nigerians on the Internet." *West Africa Review* 1 (1): n.p. http://www.africaresource.com/war/bastian.htlm.

———. 2000. " 'Buried Beneath Six Feet of Crude Oil': State-Sponsored Death and the Absent Body of Ken Saro-Wiwa." In *Ken Saro-Wiwa: Writer and Political Activist,* ed. Craig W. McLuckie and Aubrey McPhail, 127–52. Boulder, Colo.: Lynne Rienner.

———. 2001. "Vulture Men, Campus Cultists, and Teenaged Witches: Modern Magics in Nigerian Popular Media." In *Magical Interpretations, Material Realities: Modernity, Witchcraft, and the Occult in Postcolonial Africa,* ed. Henrietta L. Moore and Todd Sanders. London: Routledge.

Baudrillard, Jean. 1988. *Selected Writings.* Edited by Mark Poster. Stanford: Stanford University Press.

Buck, John, Rev. 1872. Second annual report. October. University of Birmingham, CMS Archives, C A3/09.

Chaney, David. 1993. *Fictions of Collective Life: Public Drama in Late Modern Culture.* New York: Routledge.

Comaroff, Jean, and John L. Comaroff. 1999. "Occult Economies and the Violence of Abstraction: Notes from the South African Postcolony." *American Ethnologist* 26 (2): 279–303.

Debord, Guy. [1967] 1994. *The Society of the Spectacle.* New York: Zone.

Farge, Arlette, and Jacques Ravel. 1991. *The Vanishing Children of Paris: Rumor and Politics before the French Revolution.* Cambridge, Mass.: Harvard University Press.

Ginzberg, Carlo. 1991. *Ecstasies: Deciphering the Witches' Sabbath.* New York: Pantheon.

Ige, Taye. 1997. "For the Love of Money." *Theweek* (Lagos), 14 October, 16–18.

Ilozue, Chukwujekwu. 1999. "Ikenga, Ofo Symbols in Owerri Removed." *Vanguard News* (Lagos, Web ed.), 26 April. http://www.vanguardngr.com. Accessed July 1999.

Ivy, Marilyn. 1995. "Have You Seen Me? Recovering the Inner Child in Late Twentieth Century America." In *Children and the Politics of Culture,* ed. Sharon Stephens, 79–104. Princeton: Princeton University Press.

Lévi-Strauss, Claude. 1963. *Structural Anthropology.* New York: Basic.

Marcus, George E. 1999. "Introduction: The Paranoid Style Now." In *Paranoia within*

Reason: A Casebook on Conspiracy as Explanation, ed. George E. Marcus, 1–11. Chicago: University of Chicago Press.

Marshall, Ruth. 1993. " 'Power in the Name of Jesus': Social Transformation and Pentecostalism in Western Nigeria 'Revisited.' " In *Legitimacy and the State in Twentieth-Century Africa,* ed. Terence Ranger and Olufemi Vaughan, 213–46. London: Macmillan.

Massumi, Brian. 1993. "Everywhere You Want to Be: Introduction to Fear." In *The Politics of Everyday Fear,* ed. Brian Massumi, 3–38. Minneapolis: University of Minnesota Press.

Naijabeat-News. 1999. "Obasanjo Is Dead Rumour Causes Chaos." Listserv posting, 15 May. This listserv is no longer active, but a copy of this item is available from the author on request.

Nixon, Rob. 2000. "Pipe Dreams: Ken Saro-Wiwa, Environmental Justice, and Microminority Rights." In *Ken Saro-Wiwa: Writer and Political Activist,* ed. Craig W. McLuckie and Aubrey McPhail, 109–26. Boulder: Lynne Rienner.

Okpalaeke, Declan. 1999. "Echoes of Otokoto." *Guardian* (Lagos, Web ed.), 23 January. http://www.ngrguardiannews.com/features/ft737706.htm. Accessed July 1999.

Onyla, Louis. 1997. "Ikechukwu's Spirit Marches On." *Theweek* (Lagos), 10 March, 18–20.

Osokoya, Jide. 1997. "Otokoto Murder Latest: Ritual Killings Haunt Owerri at Xmas." *Today's Choice* (Lagos), 1–21 January, 3.

Ozurumba, Davey. 1998. "Otokoto Revisited." Editorial. *Post Express Wired,* 4 May. http://www.postexpresswired.com/postexpress.nsf. Accessed July 1999.

Post Express Wired. 1997a. "Govt White Paper on the Otokoto Saga." Partial text of the second Government White Paper. 13 March. http://www.postexpresswired.com/postexpress.nsf. Accessed July 1999.

———. 1997b. "The Otokoto Verdicts." 3/11/97 (editorial, credited to "Staff"). Editorial. 11 March. http://www.postexpresswired.com/postexpress.nsf. Accessed July 1999.

Sanday, Peggy. 1986. *Divine Hunger: Cannibalism as a Cultural System.* Cambridge: Cambridge University Press.

Smith, Daniel J. 2001. "Ritual Killing, 419, and Rast Wealth: Inequality and the Popular Imagination in Southeastern Nigeria." *American Ethnologist* 28 (4): 803–26.

Stewart, Kathleen. 1999. "Conspiracy Theory's Worlds." In *Paranoia within Reason: A Casebook on Conspiracy as Explanation,* ed. George E. Marcus, 13–19. Chicago: University of Chicago Press.

Ukor, Amaechi. 1997. "Our Time's Horrifying Realities." Editorial. *Post Express Wired,* 30 December. http://www.postexpresswired.com/postexpress.nsf. Accessed July 1999.

Umunna, Isaac. 1996. "Just before the Crackdown." *Theweek* (Lagos), 9 December, 8–13.

———. 1997. "Time to Die." *Theweek* (Lagos), 11 August, 10–15.

Wark, Mackenzie. 1994. *Virtual Geography: Living with Global Media Events*. Bloomington: Indiana University Press.

Žižek, Slavoj. 1997. *The Plague of Fantasies*. London: Verso.

3

"Who Rules Us Now?" Identity Tokens, Sorcery, and Other Metaphors in the 1994 Mozambican Elections

HARRY G. WEST

"The elders refuse to have their photos taken," Elías told me from the passenger seat of my pickup truck as we bounced and squeaked along the dusty road leading from one village to the next somewhere on the Mueda Plateau in the dry season of 1994.[1] "In South Africa, they waited in lines overnight to vote,[2] but here, in Mozambique, we can't even get them to register."

I had met Elías for the first time only a few weeks before when I entered the headquarters of the Mozambican National Resistance (RENAMO, or Resistência Nacional Moçambicana) in the coastal provincial capital, Pemba, to request an interview with the Cabo Delgado party delegate.[3] The October 1992 peace accord between RENAMO rebels and the Front for the Liberation of Mozambique (FRELIMO, or Frente de Libertação de Moçambique) government and the subsequent buildup to October 1994 elections had made of political reform a vibrant local industry, creating lucrative jobs in institutions brokering the Mozambican peace process, including the United Nations Operation in Mozambique (UNOMOZ) and its component institution overseeing the electoral process, the United Nations Development Programme (UNDP) as well as the National Elections Commission (CNE, or Comissão Nacional de Eleições) and its executive organ, the Technical Secretariat for Electoral Administration (STAE, or Secretariado Técnico de Administração Eleitoral).[4] Barely twenty years of age, Elías had found his first industry niche campaigning for the former insurgents, just as others like him seized opportunities with smaller opposition parties or with the ruling FRELIMO party.[5]

A Makua speaker from southern Cabo Delgado, Elías now wandered hostile terrain in the north of the province, where local Makonde-speaking residents often reminded visitors of the role that they had played in giving birth to the anticolonial FRELIMO insurgency at a time before Elías (and his RENAMO party) had been born as well as of their continuing loyalty to FRELIMO in the context of the postindependence civil war.[6] Were it not for my passing and offering him a ride, Elías would have had to walk five kilometers or more to the next village as he had between dozens of other villages over the past several days. Elías, I learned, had found a second and more lucrative niche in the Mozambican peace industry, now working for STAE as a civic educator, explaining the registration and voting processes to rural Mozambicans.[7] With generous support from the United Nations and international donors and nongovernmental organizations, citizens throughout the largely rural nation were to be issued photo-identification voter-registration cards that they would be able to use months later to elect the president of Mozambique and representatives to the national assembly.[8] "Supporters of both parties [FRELIMO and RENAMO] must participate in this process everywhere so that, later, no one can claim the elections were fraudulent," Elías told me proudly.[9]

Even so, Elías found his job frustrating. "People out here don't understand these things," he lamented. "They are afraid to have their photos taken. They don't know what to do with the card. They are afraid they will lose it and then get in trouble. It's all so strange to people out here in the bush." I wondered whether Elías had given these ideas to or taken them from UN election monitors or other STAE officials, many of whom, in any case, shared his assumptions. My ethnohistorical research on the plateau over the past year had suggested otherwise, however. Not only, I had discovered, had most Muedans had substantial experience as bearers of identity cards and similar tokens of personal identification, but they were also adept at "reading" others' cards, even if they were illiterate.

On many occasions, when I first arrived in a village to initiate research, the elders assembled to receive me demanded that my Mozambican research collaborator, Marcos Mandumbwe, and I show identification. The most demanding crowds were not satisfied with my embossed letters of introduction from the district administrator, the provincial governor, the ministers of culture and of state administration, and the rector of the Eduardo Mondlane University in Maputo. They demanded that Marcos produce, one after another, his national identity card, his veteran's association membership card, and his FRELIMO party card.[10] They then demanded that I show my cards: my University of Wisconsin student-identity card, my passport, and my Mozambican resident's card usually sufficed. For good measure, I sometimes passed around my Pennsylvania drivers' license and my Visa credit card—each bearing holograms that were carefully studied—and my National Registry of Emergency Medical Technicians card, whose AMA symbol depicting a serpent coiled around a staff generally provoked lively discussion. When I later revisited an individual to whom I had already appropriately introduced myself, he or she would often retreat inside the house to retrieve the business card that I had left behind on my first visit. As we conversed, the person would hold my card respectfully.

Given this comfort with the idea of identity cards, why did Muedan elders remain reticent to accept voter cards in 1994? In this essay, I explore this question by examining the messages that these cards conveyed for Muedan elders in comparison with the messages that they conveyed for officials. Elías and his election-sponsoring colleagues conceived of voter-identity cards, first and foremost, as mere logistic devises—tickets permitting individuals to pass through election turnstiles, so to speak. If election officials thought that voter-identity cards, along with other artifacts of the electoral bureaucracy, "said something" to those who would use them, they believed that the message was a simple one, articulating the rationality of the electoral process that these devises enacted. I will argue that election officials thus presented the bureaucratic artifacts of democracy to Mozambicans as a metaphor for the individual privacy and, simultaneously, for the national transparency of the democratic political process.

The hesitancy to register that Elías witnessed among Muedan elders derived, I suggest, not from inexperience with identity cards and such things, or from an inability to "read" their metaphoric messages, but, rather, from a complexity of previous experience and a deeper reading that engendered ambivalence. I examine a variety of what I refer to as *identity tokens* with which Muedans have had experience—voter-registration cards, party-membership cards, military marching orders, tax receipts, labor passbooks, church-issued medallions, and, even, medicinal substances. In Muedans' experiences, identity tokens have operated sometimes in a realm visible to all and sometimes in a realm invisible at least to some. What is more, identity tokens have been used sometimes to render Muedans legible to power and sometimes to hide them from it.

In any case, with each of these kinds of identity tokens, Muedans have been marked in one way or another by either benevolent or maleficent actors, including precolonial settlement heads, the colonial state, Catholic missionaries, the FRELIMO guerrilla army, and the postindependence state. They have, thus, been situated within complex and, often, dangerous fields of power. One of these fields of power has been that of sorcery, a realm defined by ambivalent forces that has been interwoven with changing historical contexts over the past century.

For Muedans in 1994, voter cards echoed with messages embedded in identity tokens of the past, warning of the capriciousness of power, reminding them that power works in both visible and invisible realms and that it reveals itself and/or its subjects when this serves its purposes but conceals itself and/or its subjects when this serves its purposes better. In refusing to accept voter-identity cards, Muedan elders rejected the simple metaphor advanced by election organizers in favor of their own, more complex analogies rooted in historical experiences in which identity tokens were previously used. Among the richest of metaphoric associations made by Muedans were those invoking the realm of sorcery, highlighting the inevitable opacity of political process. Through the language of sorcery, Muedans expressed understandings of the 1994 peace process *that could not be expressed otherwise* (Favret-Saada 1980: 13), thereby accomplishing even better than election organizers *the mission of metaphor* (Fernandez 1986).

The Artifacts of Electoral Bureaucracy: A Material Metaphor for Political Transparency?

In his provocative analysis of art and anthropological theory, Alfred Gell (1998: 18) suggests that "social agency can be exercised relative to 'things' and social agency can be exercised by 'things.'" As an example, Gell tells us that a car owner may "regard a car as a body-part, a prosthesis, something invested with his (or her) own social agency vis-à-vis other social agents. . . . [A]n injury suffered by the car is a personal blow, an outrage, even though the damage can be made good and the insurance company will pay."

Gell's idea may be easily applied to tokens of personal identity—objects that may act, and be treated, as extensions of the person. In the Victorian era, for example, visitors left calling cards as traces of their presence when the person visited was not home to receive them, betraying an investment of personhood in the card itself. Japanese businessmen today invest even more of themselves in their business cards. If pause is not taken by a recipient, if the card is not viewed and fondled with appreciation, the giver is insulted; to write on a Japanese business card is tantamount to defacing the person.[11] The credit-card industry demonstrates keen awareness that a card may be recognized as an extension of the person. Preferred cards with high credit limits or without limits, such as American Express gold cards or Diner's Club cards, are all said to "command respect" for the bearer; in the language of the credit industry, it is difficult to distinguish whether it is the card or its bearer that is "honored where you see this sign."[12] When treated in such ways, cards take on the quality of material metonyms; as the card is treated, so is the person.

Sifting through my documents, then, Muedans subjected my person to intense scrutiny and discovered who I was by reading them as extensions of my person, as material metonyms. They went beyond this, however, discerning my "legitimacy" and determining how I should be treated. They were able to do this only because these documents provided a window on a larger field of power relations. Signatures of prominent officials or insignia of powerful institutions on my documents indicated my alliances (and implied my enmities). Muedans recognized that failure to cooperate with me might bring down on them the wrath of officials whose credentials I carried with me.[13] In this sense, Muedans studied my cards and letters as components to a bureaucratic system that metaphorically represented political relations between myself as holder of a document and others as signatories; my ties with national and local authority figures were analogous with the copresence of our names on the documents that I carried with me. The metaphoric and metonymic aspects of identity tokens are, in such cases, mutually dependent. For these bureaucratic artifacts to be treated as extensions of individual persons, they must stand in relation to a larger system of artifacts that operates as a metaphor for social relations among those identified, and vice versa.

In the process of registering the Mozambican populace for the 1994 elections and of staging those elections, election officials created a material metaphor of many components in the form of a system of electoral bureaucratic artifacts. Individual identity tokens in the form of voter cards (and, later, ballots) operated within the electoral bureaucracy as metonymic representations of each Mozambican of voting age. The political existence of each Mozambican was made manifest in a laminated voter card, replete with a photographic image of the individual, his or her signature and date and place of birth, and a voter-registration number, all on security paper with the seal of the Mozambican state in the background (Synge 1997: 122; African-European Institute/AWEPA 1995: 18); once the registration period concluded, Mozambicans without cards did not, for all intents and purposes, exist politically. The political will of each Mozambican was made manifest in an X marked on a ballot card. In the end, the political legitimacy of winning candidates was likened to the relative height of the stack of ballot cards with Xs marked beside their names and pictures as compared with the height of other stacks of ballot cards with Xs marked beside other candidates' names and pictures.

In the grand scheme of things, the movement of voter cards to the polls and ballot cards to tallying centers constituted a vast metaphor for the political process in postwar Mozambique. Not only did these gestures provide a logistic means of enacting democracy; they also represented the democratic process to both participants and observers in salient ways. As voter cards and ballots were standardized, the weight of each voter's preference was said to be equal. As each voter's X was concealed from the view of peers between the folds of the completed ballot card, the political allegiance of each voter was said to be secret. As the counting of votes was witnessed by representatives of diverse parties and by neutral bystanders, the political process was said to be "transparent."

These final two points warrant focused attention, for, more than anything else, the concern for secrecy at the individual level and for transparency at the national level motivated those who organized and monitored the Mozambican elections (Synge 1997: 115–16). The exercise or threat of coercion against the electorate by either political party or claims by the eventual losers that the elections were fraudulent could equally have contributed to a renewal of civil war, it was widely feared. The resources donated by the international community to the Mozambican peace process to forestall such a tragedy were small by international standards yet massive by Mozambican ones. On its own, Mozambique could never have produced an electoral register of such sophistication or issued such state-of-the-art identity cards to voters. What is more, the incapacity of the Mozambican state to sustain the electoral registration system bequeathed to it by the international community in 1994 was clearly recognized. "It's a one-shot deal," one election monitor told me, grinning cynically. "All this rigmarole for two days of theater. Next time around, half these people will have lost their cards, and the other half will be dead. In the meantime, those who come of age to vote won't be able to get cards because all the photo machines will have been broken or stolen." [14] Despite such gloomy prognostication, the initiative was deemed essential by nearly everyone involved. Why?

When the FRELIMO party organized village-level elections in years past to choose village presidents and representatives to district assemblies, mass meetings were called, and citizens were asked to raise their hands or to stand in a line behind their candidates to indicate their choices. At the village level, such techniques operate in full view of the assembled community; the results produced are witnessed as "valid" (nonfraudulent) even if everyone understands that they may be shaped significantly by popular respect for or fear of organizing and/or observing powers. To the absence of secrecy at the individual level in such elections is added a lack of transparency when the exercise is expanded to the national scale. The "national village" cannot witness itself directly, making such methods opaque, not only to international observers, but also to voters themselves. To ensure the credibility of electoral results to both participants and observers, election organizers attempted in 1994 to create a material metaphor more visible to the nation than the nation itself but one that, at the same time, demonstrated to participants that their votes would not render them individually accountable to the candidates.[15]

Election officials appear not to have considered that the material metaphor that they produced in 1994 could be read in any way but that which they intended. The error of this assumption was, in Mueda, linked to the misplaced belief that elders refusing to register were unfamiliar with things such as identity cards and that they were, consequently, afraid to accept cards in principle. As I discuss in the following section, the elder generation of Muedans has had considerable experience with cards and other such identity tokens. As a result, when presented as components to a material metaphor of political processes and relations of power, such *artifacts* carried multiple and, sometimes, contradictory messages. Beyond this, because the use of voter cards led Muedans to associate the current context of the 1994 elections with prior contexts in which identity tokens were used, these previous *situations* themselves served as metaphors for current experience. Cards, in other words, referred Muedans, not only to the international community's logic of democratic transparency, but also to logics of power that had saturated previous contexts in which identity tokens were used.[16] To understand the resultant polyvalence of identity tokens, I present, not a cultural biography of particular tokens, as Kopytoff (1986) might propose, but instead a cultural genealogy of the family of identity tokens.

Rendering Populations Legible to the State:
Tax Receipts and Passbooks

Only a few short years after the Mueda Plateau was "pacified" by the Portuguese, Muedans gained their first experiences with identity tokens, albeit rudimentary ones. Lacking the capital to invest directly in the Mozambican interior, the Portuguese had, in 1891, granted to the Nyassa Company a chartered territory corresponding to the present-day provinces of Niassa and Cabo Delgado (Neil-Tomlinson 1977; Vail 1976). Only after 1920 did the Nyassa Company establish administration over the populations of the plateau, which had been conquered ca. 1917 by a Portuguese army concerned with securing the Rovuma River border against the threat of German invasion during World War I (West 1997b: 75–79). Also undercapitalized and unable to invest in extracting natural resources, the Nyassa Company depended on a "hut tax" levied on local populations as its principal source of income.

Initially, company tax collectors were frustrated by the ability of men to flee the settlement on news of their approach, but, in time, the company modified its tactics, targeting women, instead of men, as tax subjects. An elder in the village of Namakandi described the company's new methods to me as follows:

> The company collected taxes in a very particular way. . . . They came to the settlement, and they grabbed the women. Not young girls, only women. They took them to jails and held them. To free them, men had to go there and pay two escudos for each woman.[17] We would get this money at a store in Muidumbe.[18] We carried sacks of groundnuts—heavy, one hundred kilos—and sold them for less than fifty centavos each.[19] In this way we collected the money. When a woman was freed, she was given a strip of cloth dyed green with the juice of tomato leaves.[20] This "receipt" was put in a glass flask that would be hung by a string around her neck. This meant that she had paid. It told everyone, "Don't take me again; I've already paid."

The accounts of European explorers traveling in the region at this time round out this elder's description. In 1924, the British consul reported "actual slavery under cruel and barbaric conditions" inside company territory (quoted in Vail 1976: 414). Captive women were forced to work until ransomed, were often denied sufficient food, and were sometimes beaten and/or raped; one report indicated two or three deaths per day of women held at a particular company post (see Neil-Tomlinson 1977: 125).

While the elder in Namikandi told me the story of life under Nyassa Company rule, his wife sat on a reed mat on the ground only a few feet away, shelling peanuts. When her husband mentioned the flask in which receipts were deposited, she arose and entered her house; when she came out again, she carried a small glass bottle, not unlike a vial from which serum might be drawn for a medical injection. She presented it to me solemnly. She did not tell me to whom it had belonged, but this memento of a forebear who had suffered under the economic regime made possible by the object had survived for at least sixty years, presumably over three or more generations. (That this object could be preserved for such a long time challenges the notion espoused by Elías and his colleagues that Muedans would be unable to avoid losing their 1994 voter cards.)

The Nyassa Company charter expired in 1929, whereupon the Portuguese took over direct administrative responsibility for company territories. Life under Portuguese rule was little different than before, however. Like the company, the Portuguese administration levied a hut tax, capturing women and issuing them a receipt once they had been "redeemed" by a family member. To raise tax money, Muedans cultivated cash crops such as groundnuts, cashew nuts, sesame seed, castor oil seed, or rice for sale to local merchants. A forty-kilogram sack of shelled groundnuts fetched twenty escudos (approximately $0.99), exactly the rate of individual tax first imposed by the colonial regime.[21]

In 1938, in an attempt to ensure cheap inputs for Portuguese metropolitan industries, a new labor practice was established whereby rural Mozambicans were required to cultivate specific cash crops on a locally determined area of their own land to be sold at prices set by the government. In Mueda, the chosen crop was cotton. Male heads of household and their first wives were required to cultivate one hectare. Junior wives and single women (including widows) were required to cultivate a half hectare each. All individuals between the ages of eighteen and fifty-five were issued a production card detailing name, age, place of residence, and information relevant to the cotton produced on their fields and brought to market (Isaacman 1996: 38–69). If Muedans failed to meet production requirements, they were considered to be less than fully employed in agriculture and were required to seek contract work on a colonial plantation or in public works projects.[22] Undertaking contract work exempted an individual from cotton-production requirements, and many men chose this option. They were issued *cadernetes* (passbooks) in which work status and completed contracts were recorded (Newitt 1995: 471). Muedans carried cotton-production cards or passbooks with them constantly, for, if they were questioned by police or *cipais* (native police officers) and could not show that they had completed (or were in the process of completing) their required labor, they might be press-ganged on the spot.[23] The colonial administration ensured that local chiefs assisted in policing labor requirements by paying these figures a commission on taxes collected and on laborers "recruited."

The tactics adopted by the Portuguese in their colonies were far from unusual. According to John Torpey (1998), the authority of modern states might be more accurately defined as resting, not on a monopoly over the means of violence, as Weber suggested, but, rather, on a monopoly over the right to authorize and regulate movement. States, Torpey tells us, seek, not simply to *penetrate*, but also to *embrace* subject societies.[24] Their ability to do so depends on what Gérard Noiriel has called the *revolution identificatoire* (cited in Torpey 1998: 242).[25] From revolutionary France to the Soviet Union to apartheid South Africa, as Torpey discusses, states have consolidated power by controlling the movements and economic activities of their populations through the use of internal passports, passbooks, and other forms of personal identification.[26] So central were the pass laws to the apartheid state in South Africa that antiapartheid protests (e.g., Sharpeville) often centered around the burning of passbooks (Garcelon and Torpey 1996: 29–30).[27]

James Scott has approached the issue of techniques of state consolidation through a different, but equally revealing, vocabulary that places the use of personal identification documents and other identity tokens in a broader perspective. States, he tells us, inevitably seek to render their subjects "legible." In doing so, states not only read their subject societies but also give shape to them at the same time, making possible specific relations of power within their domains (Scott 1998: 83). Scott writes: "Legibility is a condition of manipulation. Any substantial state intervention in society—to vaccinate a population, produce goods, mobilize labor, tax people and their property, conduct literacy campaigns, conscript soldiers, enforce sanitation standards, catch criminals, start universal schooling—requires the invention of units that are visible. The units in question might be citizens, villages, trees, fields, houses, or people grouped according to age, depending on the type of intervention. Whatever the units being manipulated, they must be organized in a manner that permits them to be identified, observed, recorded, counted, aggregated, and monitored" (1998: 183).

Through the issuance of tax receipts and passbooks, the Nyassa Company and the Portuguese administration, in succession, marked Mozambicans in order to render them legible and, consequently, amenable to "embrace" (to use Torpey's term) and "manipulation" (to use Scott's); in this case, their specific objectives were tax collection and labor mobilization. Most Muedans complied with and sometimes even assisted the state in its campaign to mark them, for the consequences of being caught outside the state "embrace" could be worse than state work requirements.

Muedans had two options available to them if they wished to escape the grasp of the state. The first of these was to flee the long arm of the Portuguese administration, taking up residence in remote areas or, more frequently, crossing the border into Tanganyika, where British colonial administration offered a more favorable labor regime. Substantial numbers of Muedans chose this path. Most found employment on sisal plantations, where they often worked for several years at a time before returning home, if at all.[28]

The second option was, initially, less apparent to most Muedans. In 1924, Montfortian missionaries had established the first Catholic mission to the Mueda Plateau.[29] For more than a decade, the mission struggled to attract converts, but, in time, it was discovered that work done at the mission qualified as contract work, exempting the laborer from forced cotton cultivation. In the early 1930s, a small group of Muedans took up residence beside the mission, working its agricultural fields and constructing its buildings. To this captive audience, the mission's Dutch padres offered classes in the catechism. Catechumens discovered, to their delight, that the Virgin Mary medallions given them by the padres identified them as mission adherents to a wide audience, including agents of the colonial administration and their police and cipais, all of whom treated "converts" with greater respect. As the church grew on the plateau, catechism classes were offered in settlements, sometimes at a considerable distance from the mission proper. Regardless of whether catechumens lived and worked at the mission, they found that the Virgin Mary medallions protected them from abusive treatment, if not from labor obligations altogether.[30]

Muedans fleeing Mozambique for Tanganyika responded to the colonial state's attempts to render them legible by escaping what Scott calls "state space" in favor of a "nonstate space" or, at least, the "state space" of a more tolerable state. By contrast, mission adherents created a "nonstate space" within the geographical boundaries of the Mozambican state. Ironically, to accomplish this, they turned the state's technique around on the state, donning identity tokens that marked them as church subjects.

Whereas, in the colonial period, personal identity tokens rendered individual Muedans visible to authority, the anticolonial movement would produce its own identity tokens and use them, not only to mark populations it sought to monitor and control, but also to cloak these same people from the eyes of the state. In doing so, Mozambican nationalists responded to the exigencies presented them by the historical context in which they operated.

FRELIMO was born in exile of numerous ethnic-based parties formed of migrant worker communities in neighboring countries (see Opello 1975; Munslow 1983; West 1997b: 145–51). Among these parties was MANU (at first, the Makonde African National Union and, later, the Mozambique African National Union), founded in Dar es Salaam, Tanzania, and comprising primarily Makonde speakers. In June 1960, MANU leaders organized a public demonstration at the district colonial office in Mueda, precipitating a showdown with the Portuguese administration that resulted in violence—an event called the *Mueda Massacre* by nationalists—after the demonstrators were arrested and their supporters protested.[31]

MANU was reorganized under the leadership of Mateu Mmole, a son of migrant sisal plantation workers from a village in the lowlands southeast of Mueda who had attended university in Uganda and, later, in England. Under Mmole's leadership, MANU's membership base expanded. In Tanzania, new members paid a fee and were issued membership cards. The Mueda Massacre had suggested to Mozambican nationalists like Mmole that future political activities "in the interior" would have to be undertaken in secret. Initially, MANU representatives traveling inside Mozambique were instructed to deposit their membership cards with MANU officers in Tanzania and to pick them up again on crossing back out of Mozambique. Over time, these mobilizers developed clandestine links in the Mueda region by tapping into networks of returning migrant workers and of members of the mission community. Eventually, MANU began selling party membership cards in the interior as well.

On 25 June 1962, FRELIMO was formed in Dar es Salaam. Although MANU leaders including Mmole were quickly marginalized within the new leadership structure, the network of mobilizers created by MANU was absorbed into FRELIMO. FRELIMO cards were sold for fifteen escudos (approximately $0.52) or three shillings. Mobilizers inscribed the names of new members on their cards and recorded their names in a register. The description given me by a tailor named Agostinho Mandumbwe of the work that he did as a FRELIMO mobilizer testifies to the dangers that these figures faced:

> I did this work in the wee hours of the morning. Soon, almost everyone in my settlement had a card. But Adriano Makajojo, who was working with the PIDE [the Portuguese secret police], suspected me. He worked closely with the *régulo*,[32] Ambrosio Naengo. One day, Ambrosio came to see my uncle, and he said that he would catch me selling cards and he would cut my head off. Then he would have my body buried here but take my head to the administrator in Mueda [town]. . . . Adriano informed the Portuguese in Mueda about me, and one day the troops came to my home. I was working at my sewing machine, sitting on my sewing bench. I got up and greeted them and asked them to sit down. One of them sat on the bench. They asked me why I was selling FRELIMO cards, and I said I wasn't. I told them that only the poor do that. I told them that I had work. I didn't need to get involved with such confusion. All the while, the soldier was sitting on my bench, looking around suspiciously. The cards were right under his ass! There was a secret compartment in the bench where I kept them hidden.

Mobilizers had to take great caution in choosing those to whom they would sell membership cards. Without betraying their motives to a larger community that might include individuals collaborating with the Portuguese secret police, mobilizers had to observe the political behavior of and positions taken by potential candidates carefully. Jacinto Omar traveled from settlement to settlement as a member of a ceremonial dance society, working, all the while, as a FRELIMO mobilizer:

> I used these occasions to get to know people and to decide who was trustworthy. Normally, a *mapiko*[33] dancer was respected when he danced in another settlement,[34] and it was easy to make friends. Everyone wanted to get to know me. Some people already knew that I was FRELIMO, but others did not. I spoke a special language on these occasions. I would say to someone I knew about another person I had observed, "I would like this one to be our friend. What is he like?" and my friend might tell me, "He's OK; he's fine." So I would begin to chat with this person. After three or four conversations, I would say, "I have something to tell you," and I would talk about FRELIMO. Most people told me that they had been waiting a long time for someone to approach them.

Elders who served the Portuguese as administrative intermediaries presented FRELIMO mobilizers with special problems. These men could be persuasive allies within their communities, but, as they profited personally from colonial rule, they were trusted only reluctantly. Alexio Timbanga, who worked for FRELIMO in the régulo Nkwemba's region, described to me his strategy there:

> Nkwemba knew that there was a movement and that cards were being sold, and he thought that I knew about it. He resented the fact that FRELIMO would work through me and not through him, the régulo. He asked me, and I said I knew nothing. So Nkwemba said, "We are going to find out together, you and me, and we are going to buy cards." I told him I didn't want one. Of course, I already had one, and I could get him one, but only trustworthy people could be given one, and it was too dangerous to let Nkwemba have one so easily. So I tested him. I had a letter delivered to him telling him he had three days to buy a card or else he should slaughter all his ducks and eat well because he was going to die. After he got the letter, he said he still wanted the card, so I said I would see if I could find out about it. I returned and told him it would cost twenty-five escudos (approximately $0.86). But he was willing to pay, so I decided he was serious. I gave him a card but told him it came from Namaua.[35]

In time, the FRELIMO campaign to mobilize support on the Mueda Plateau intensified. Influential figures collaborating with the Portuguese secret police were assassinated, and death threats were issued to those refusing to buy FRELIMO cards. In many cases, those who resisted the FRELIMO membership drive awoke at night to find their houses on fire. As in the past, Muedans were being marked with identity tokens that they could forgo only at great personal risk. Those who refused to buy cards would not be "recognized" by FRELIMO and might very well be killed by the nationalists.

These marking cards, however, were meant to be visible, not to the state, but, rather, to an antistate insurgency. In fact, FRELIMO cards were intended to be *invisible* to the state, as were those who carried them. In the crucial months between FRELIMO's formation and the initiation of its armed campaign, the organization's only tangible activity in the interior was the sale of membership cards. The card was not used for identification within the organization, nor was it used to gain entry to meetings of any sort. Once purchased, in fact, it was best for the member and for the organization that the card never again be seen by anyone, including fellow FRELIMO members.

The party card was, quite simply, a liability to all concerned. Since the sale of cards did not generate substantial revenues for FRELIMO, the principal purpose served was to place members in a situation of shared risk, creating complicity among them. Individuals who refused to purchase cards took no risk and, therefore, demonstrated no commitment to FRELIMO. Those who bought cards crossed over into a world of collective conspiracy, effectively hiding themselves as they hid away the card they had bought.[36]

For most of the colonial period, Muedans contended with a singular power that openly marked them, rendering them legible for the purpose of manipulating their labor power. In the context of anticolonial insurgency, Muedans found themselves between two competing forces. Identity tokens in this new field of power both revealed and concealed; those whom FRELIMO struggled to hide, the Portuguese sought to expose. The occasional successes of the Portuguese highlighted the potentially lethal ambivalence of the marks that Muedans bore. When, in late 1963, two FRELIMO mobilizers at the top of the clandestine hierarchy were captured, the Portuguese came into possession of their party registers as well. A few fortunate members got word and fled across the border to Tanzania, but many were rounded up, imprisoned, and tortured by Portuguese secret police agents hoping to obtain the names of their fellow party members and, thus, look even deeper into the hidden realm that FRELIMO had started to build through the sale of party membership cards. Some captured FRELIMO members died in prison, while many others were held for the duration of the independence war (1964–74). The only "crime" committed by most had been accepting a FRELIMO card.

For its part, FRELIMO continued the use of personalized documents in its *zonas libertadas* (liberated zones)—a nonstate space opened up in the midst of the anticolonial insurgency.[37] The party membership card was replaced, however, by a document more suitable to the context: the *guia de marcha* (marching order). FRELIMO militants moving about in the interior carried with them these papers, detailing their assigned task. Those unable to present this document to guerrilla commanders whom they encountered might easily be accused of collaboration with the Portuguese and executed. One ex-guerrilla, who moved widely among civilian populations in the liberated zones as a superintendent in the FRELIMO education system, told me: "Your mother wouldn't receive you and cook your dinner if you did not have marching orders signed by a FRELIMO commander." Even after independence, as FRELIMO fought to suppress the spread of RENAMO, the guia de marcha was used to monitor and control the movements of Mozambicans traveling to destinations as close as a neighboring village. Ironically, FRELIMO now marked its populations much as the colonial state that it had defeated had.[38]

Keys to an Invisible Realm: The Substances of Sorcery

I have suggested that the experience that Muedans already had with identity cards and other identity tokens provided meaningful references for them in interpreting the potential significance of voter-identity cards in the novel historical context of the 1994 elections. Before further exploring this issue, I wish to look one layer deeper. In the midst of their experiences with colonial tax collectors and labor recruiters, with Catholic missionaries, with guerrilla mobilizers and colonial secret police, and with postindependence village officials, Muedans drew yet other analogies. In salient ways, their experiences with and beliefs in sorcery provided them with lenses through which to view the diverse historical events and processes of the twentieth century.

Even before colonial officials sought to mark them so as to render them legible to the state, Muedans appreciated the importance of vision to the exercise of power. From the precolonial period, residents of the Mueda Plateau region recognized the operation of power in two realms. In a realm visible to the ordinary person, power derived from one's control over labor and the goods produced by one's subordinates. Settlement heads consolidated power by attracting sister's sons and their brides (for whom the settlement head had arranged bridewealth) to live in the settlement, by raiding neighbors to take captives, and by organizing trade caravans.[39] In a parallel realm, invisible to the ordinary person, power obeyed a different logic. Through the use of a medicinal substance called *shikupi*, sorcerers could render themselves invisible and attack their rivals, consuming their wealth and feeding on their flesh.[40]

To preserve the continuity of his power in the visible realm, the successful settlement head had to protect the prosperity and well-being of his people lest they abandon his settlement. This entailed not only defending the settlement militarily but also quashing the nefarious activities of sorcerers in the invisible realm. The settlement head combated sorcery in two principle ways. The first of these was to practice what was referred to as a "sorcery of construction" (*uwavi wa kudenga*). Vicente Anawena, an elder living in the village of Matambalale when I interviewed him in 1994, provides a poignant description of this technique:

If someone in the settlement fell ill or died, the *nang'olo mwene kaya* [settlement head] would go out into the *shitala* [men's meeting house in the settlement center] in the wee hours of the morning, just before sunrise, and he would stand and speak out loud at the top of his voice: "I see you! I know who you are! You are killing us, the people of this settlement! You are killing us with your *uwavi* [sorcery]! We don't want your uwavi here! If you do not stop, I will drive you from this settlement! I see you! I know who you are!"

When I asked Vicente how the settlement head could see sorcerers, I was told, "He was himself a sorcerer. He had to be in order to know who the others were, to monitor and control them." Other elders with whom I spoke were in complete agreement with this interpretation. Settlement heads, like menacing sorcerers, were believed to possess shikupi and to use it to enter into the hidden realm of sorcery.[41] Unlike those whose activities they combated, however, these authority figures were understood to be "cured" or "reformed" sorcerers who used the power of sorcery to socially constructive ends.

The second way in which settlement heads and other elders of responsibility combated sorcery was through treating the settlement or its individual inhabitants with medicinal substances to prevent or combat unseen destructive forces. *Vantela* (medicinal healers), also said to be "cured" or "reformed" sorcerers, gave sorcery victims medicinal substances to turn sorcery back on its sender. Those treated in this way were instructed to hide the medicines given them for reasons of personal security (much as recipients of FRELIMO cards were told to hide these objects). If seen, medicinal substances could be rendered inefficacious or even attract sorcerers anxious to see whether they might overcome them. Settlement heads also combated sorcery with medicinal substances. By burying countersorcery substances in the ground beneath the pathways leading to and from the settlement, these elders marked their territory against the invasion of contesting powers. They also marked individual bodies by anointing settlement residents with *ing'opedi* (a white powder made of sorghum flour and various medicinal substances). In this way, they indicated to sorcerers (who would see these marks long after they disappeared from the view of the ordinary person) that these bodies were under the protective custody of an authority figure who would defend them against aggression.

Like the Virgin Mary medallions worn by mission adherents in the colonial period, or like FRELIMO party membership cards in the period of the independence war, ing'opedi constituted a means by which a protective authority marked its subjects. This mark defined the position of the individual in a complex field of power relations, defending him or her against potential aggressors but also making him or her beholden to the marking authority. Whereas the FRELIMO party card, a dangerously visible identity token, rendered the individual who hid it invisible to menacing power, however, ing'opedi, a mark invisible to most after a short time, offered a visible signal to sorcerers, protecting the individual from predation.

Sorcery and Metaphor: Saying That Which Cannot Be Said Otherwise

James Fernandez has written, "However men may analyze their experiences in any domain, they inevitably know and understand them best by referring them to other domains for elucidation" (1986: 25). The more novel an experience, the greater the need to seek meaning in terms of the already familiar. According to Fernandez, people say what cannot otherwise be said—understand that which cannot otherwise be understood—through metaphoric reference, an act of predication on an inchoate situation. This predication, he writes, "says that something much more concrete and graspable—a rolling stone, a bird in the hand—is equivalent to the essential elements in another situation we have difficulty grasping" (Fernandez 1986: 8).

In 1994, the people of Mozambique were presented with a novel situation—nationwide, multiparty general elections in which they were not only permitted but actively encouraged to vote by party-neutral organizing institutions and aggressively courted by competing political parties. To aid Mozambicans in making sense of this unfamiliar experience, election organizers presented them with a material metaphor, as I have argued. The democratic political process, it was suggested, is like the regularized movement of cards into and out of polling stations. Identifiable voter cards enter, unidentifiable ballot cards exit. The marking of cards remains invisible, the counting of cards visible. The metaphor provided by the bureaucratic artifacts of the vote was intended to help Muedans understand that the process itself was at once secret on the individual level and transparent on the national level.[42]

As strange as this new phenomenon was for them, Muedans nonetheless understood that neither metaphors nor political processes are ever so simple. To begin with the metaphor, Muedans "read" identity cards in far more probing ways than issuing institutions might have expected. Where election organizers invoked a simple metaphor (in the form of the bureaucratic artifacts of the electoral process) with the objective of clarifying the meaning of a strange new experience, Muedans extended the metaphor by associating identity tokens with previously experienced examples and even went beyond the metaphor to posit analogies of their own. The concrete domain of cards, intended to lend clarity to the obscure domain of elections, itself conveyed complexity deriving from past experiences in which identity tokens had been used. Muedans easily associated voter cards with colonial tax receipts and passbooks, with Virgin Mary medallions, with FRELIMO party cards, and even with the medicinal substances of sorcery and, hence, with dangerous games of hide and seek played with capricious forms of power. These experiential domains themselves became metaphors for the operation of power in the current context. The domain of sorcery served Muedans as a particularly rich interpretive resource—a "root metaphor" (to use the term that Sherry Ortner borrows from Stephen Pepper) that "provide[d] a set of categories for conceptualizing other aspects of experience" (Ortner 1973: 1340). Like the French peasants in the Bocage region described in Jeanne Favret-Saada's ethnography (1980), who express in the language of witchcraft *that which cannot be said otherwise*, Muedans, in 1994, explained to themselves in the language of sorcery *that which could not be understood otherwise*, just as they had done in previous historical contexts.

Muedans remained wary of the novel powers with which they came into contact in 1994, notwithstanding civic educators telling them that elections would rationalize power in postwar Mozambique. As Muedans articulated their own metaphors, the authority figures participating in and organizing the 1994 elections were held up against figures of authority previously experienced, and likenesses were explored. Past experiences warned Muedans that the powerful sometimes protect their charges, creating a secure and prosperous environment well defended against the lethal surveillance of potential enemies but that they also, sometimes, mark their subjects to render them legible and manipulable to their own ends.

As I sat conversing with Muedans in plateau villages throughout the dry season of 1994, UN helicopters shuttled overhead, carrying arms collected from demobilized government troops stationed in the town of Mueda to the provincial UN command in Pemba, and carrying elections materials from Pemba into Mueda. The civil war had brought chaos into the lives of all Mozambicans. Estimates of casualties vary widely, but tens of thousands lost their lives in the fighting, and hundreds of thousands died as a result of famine and disease exacerbated by the war (Human Rights Watch 1992: 41). More than a million were forced to take refuge across Mozambique's borders, and several million more were displaced internally. Although Muedans had been largely spared direct exposure to RENAMO,[43] they suffered from the generalized economic crisis brought on by the war, which paralyzed social services, trade, and communication. During the eleven months that I spent in Mueda in 1994, I met no one who was not relieved, even elated, by the peace, even if many feared that it would not last.

Some Muedans embraced institutions brokering the Mozambican peace, becoming vocal and sincere advocates of democratic process; the eventual success of the 1994 elections was in large measure a result of the work of such individuals.[44] Just like Elías, many young people found jobs in the peace process, often reaping substantial personal benefit as clients of new forms of power. Far larger numbers simply registered for the vote and, later, cast their ballots; by the end of the electoral registration campaign, nearly all Muedans—including large numbers of initially skeptical elders—had, indeed, joined this category.[45]

Others, however, continued to hold these novel institutions and their simple metaphors at arm's length. Muedans with whom I was meeting often looked to the UN helicopters in the sky and shook their heads with a mixture of suspicion and contempt. They complained that reckless drivers of UN vehicles injured and sometimes killed villagers.[46] They bemoaned liaisons between UN peacekeeping troops and the young women they took as prostitutes. They resented the arrogance shown them by young Mozambican men and women such as Elías who had found wealth unprecedented serving as agents of the peace process.

"Who controls these people?" asked Faustino Vanomba (the leader of the 1960 demonstration that resulted in the Mueda Massacre). Like many Muedans (who pride themselves on having been the last Mozambican people to succumb to colonial overrule and the first to liberate themselves), Vanomba looked on the UN arrival as a return of colonial authority. "Didn't we fight the *luta armada* [the independence war against the Portuguese] so that Mozambique would be ruled by Mozambicans?" he asked me. "Who rules us now?"

Because the UN demobilization center in the town of Mueda hosted only FRELIMO troops, Vanomba, like other Muedans, saw firsthand only FRELIMO troops being disarmed. Complicating this image, there were a number of Portuguese nationals among the ranks of UN personnel;[47] rumors circulated on the plateau that the Portuguese district administrator presiding over Mueda at the time of the Mueda Massacre was among UN troops in Cabo Delgado. What is more, UN soldiers moved about in helicopters just as the Portuguese army had during the independence war.

When I asked elders the reasons behind their refusals to have their photos taken for voter-identity cards, many betrayed the feeling that no incentives existed to cooperate and that those working for electoral institutions alone stood to gain by popular compliance (just as chiefs serving the Portuguese as administrative intermediaries had alone profited by colonial rule). One man told me, defiantly, "If it's so important to the UN that we have these cards, then let them pay us to get them!"[48] Such expressions were founded in a historically steeped understanding that those who issue identity tokens are empowered in some way by thus marking populations but that benefits to those populations may or may not be forthcoming. Another man told me, "I got a FRELIMO card, and I fought in the luta; what did it get me? I have nothing!"

Still others betrayed a fear that cooperation might place them in a dangerous position within a complex field of power wherein the relative capacities of actors known and unknown remained uncertain. Some, for example, expressed reservations about "joining a party" other than FRELIMO, meaning the UN party or the CNE party, that wished to issue them a "membership card" (African-European Institute/AWEPA 1995: 52). As the United Nations did not coerce compliance, many saw no reason to take the risk of procuring yet another identity token.

In speaking of the UN presence, many Muedans made explicit reference to sorcery. Muedan sorcerers have long been known to make lions that prowl the land and devour victims at their command (West 1997b: 60–72). During the independence war, it was believed that sorcerers could make helicopters and other vehicles in which they could ride in search of victims, allowing them to extend the range over which they could operate. In 1994, Muedans turned a suspicious eye on UN vehicles and aircraft. I was told numerous times the story of a "one-hundred-seat" UN helicopter that had crashed in the middle of the night outside the village of Lilondo. No physical remains were found, I was told, but the crash site was marked by flattened brush in a wide circle.[49] "Sorcery!" was the simple explanation given by most second-hand witnesses to this and other "strange" events happening in and around UN installations. Others reluctant to register feared more familiar sorcerers. Many remained certain that their votes would, in fact, be seen (by means of sorcery) by those who might take offense (most likely FRELIMO), despite provisions for a "secret ballot" (see also Synge 1997: 129; African-European Institute/AWEPA 1995: 42).

Bridging Domains, Semantic and Experiential

The ambivalence that Muedans showed toward electoral institutions and processes derived, I suggest, in large measure from the ambivalence saturating their points of reference. If, however, we are to accept as metaphor the references to past experience made by Muedans in their attempts to get a grasp on the meaning of the 1994 elections, we must refine our account of the workings of metaphor. Fernandez tells us that we best understand experience in one domain by making reference to another. The most celebrated examples of metaphor are ones in which it is clear to all concerned that the metaphoric predicate and the target subject inhabit distinct domains. An active person is not actually a rolling stone, nor is an immediate opportunity actually a bird in a hand. Such metaphors work, as David Sapir explains, by making us "aware of the simultaneous likeness and unlikeness of the two terms" and then asking us to imagine, *knowing it to be untrue*, that the two terms are alike in more ways than immediately apparent. In the case of "George is a lion," Sapir tells us, metaphor "allows us . . . to assume for a moment that although George is 'really' like a lion only in certain specific ways [both are mammals, e.g.], he might be a lot more like a lion than in just those ways [George is fierce, e.g.]" (Sapir and Crocker 1977: 9). Where calling George a lion links two distinct semantic domains, the metaphor works, in part, by calling attention to the depth of the chasm between the domains that it bridges. George's lion-like fierceness makes him an *unusual* human.

This is not necessarily so when Muedans associate voter-identity cards with passbooks, or with FRELIMO party cards, or with ing'opedi or when they draw analogies to encounters with the colonial state, or with the FRELIMO guerrilla, or with sorcerers of construction or of ruin to make sense of current political reforms. For Muedans, the semantic domains in question often rest on the foundation of a singular, continuous experiential domain. The following example is illustrative. As described above, during the independence war FRELIMO leaders required Muedans to carry with them personal documents in the form of marching orders, thereby allowing individual movements to be monitored and controlled in an environment where the infiltration of counterinsurgents posed an immediate threat. Muedans reckoned that these documents marked them as subjects of protective FRELIMO authorities much like ing'opedi marked residents of colonial-era settlements as subjects of protective settlement heads. At the same time, however, many Muedans suspected that FRELIMO security operatives actually made use of the substances of sorcery to maintain surveillance over the activities of (enemy) sorcerers in the invisible realm inside FRELIMO liberated zones. During the war, I was told, FRELIMO security operatives would come into camp and line people up, look into their eyes, and select a few of them to take away for internment or for execution as traitors. How did they know? Not only did they *act* like sorcerers of construction, I was told; they *were* sorcerers.

In the context of the 1994 elections, analogies and straight identities overlapped in similar ways. When the United Nations agreed to broker the Mozambican peace process by overseeing the demobilization of combatant armies and the staging of elections, the Mozambican government agreed to provide UNOMOZ with the residential accommodations, office spaces, and warehouses needed by the UN mission. As UN personnel arrived in Mozambique, however, they were frequently told by government officials that such installations were available only through the private rental market. The landlords to whom the United Nations wound up paying rents were, most often, none other than ranking government officials who, in recent months, had "privatized" government properties and infrastructural assets to themselves. Muedan elders with whom I spoke often pointed out that, in the post-peace-accord scramble, political party leaders (whether FRELIMO or RENAMO), government officials, and individuals in the employ of the United Nations were "eating well," "eating more than their share," or even "eating everything." Those familiar with African political discourse will recognize that this language metaphorically links the behavior that it describes to actions in the realm of witchcraft and/or sorcery in which individuals feed their insatiable appetites by consuming others (Bayart 1993; Schatzberg 1993; Geschiere 1997). For many Muedans, however, the powerful (often the same people who led FRELIMO in the independence war) *acted* like sorcerers, again, because they *were* sorcerers, as they had long been. What is more, in the current context, Muedan observers were inclined to characterize the acts of the powerful as sorcery of ruin (*uwavi wa lwanongo*) rather than as sorcery of construction (*uwavi wa kudenga*).

Transparency and Conspiracy: Metaphors, Unmasking, and Masking

Accepting Muedan associations between past and present political contexts as examples of metaphor requires another fundamental refinement to our understanding of metaphor. Fernandez tells us that "the semantic movement accomplished by metaphor is from the abstract and inchoate in the subject to the more concrete, ostensive, and easily graspable in the metaphoric predicate" (1986: 38). Through reference to past experiences, including colonialism, guerrilla warfare, and sorcery, Muedans did not, however, merely "clarify" the meaning of contemporary political processes. In the contexts to which they turned for meaning, power was, as often as not, experienced and remembered as opaque and capricious (cf. Kendall, chapter 1 in this volume). The colonial era was no less chaotic and confusing for Muedans than the post-peace-accord period. The same can be said of the period of the war for independence. And, as I have argued elsewhere (West 1997a, 2001), a defining characteristic of sorcery as a cultural schema for the understanding of social relations is its inherent ambiguity and ambivalence. Not being possessors of shikupi themselves—not being able to see into the hidden realm where sorcery is practiced—few Muedans actually claim to know much about sorcery's logic and operation. Reference to any of these contexts in the present day, then, may actually render interpretation more ambiguous.

Where political processes are concerned, clarifying statements may be more dangerous words to utter than are obscuring innuendos. Through cautious and subtle reference to sorcery—a discourse much larger than any individual speaker—Muedans can posit vague associations between power and predation in specific contexts, knowing that the images that they produce in small gatherings will be reproduced and broadly disseminated even without their continued individual commentary. Should trouble arise, one can deny responsibility for having initiated critique.

What is more, Muedans seem to understand, simple analogies simply do not suffice to capture the complexity of political process. The powerful do not always allow events to follow the logic of "rationalized" and "transparent" proscriptions without a fight. Consequently, there are always veiled interests and hidden agendas at work, notwithstanding official political rhetoric. A complex and ambivalent metaphor like sorcery thus serves Muedans well as they seek to make sense of local and national politics.

Ann Game and Andrew Metcalfe suggest, contrary to Fernandez's definition, that it is in the nature of metaphor to preserve ambiguity. They write, "Metaphor works with indeterminacy to keep meaning safe from the final clarification that is its obituary" (1996: 50). I conclude that metaphor may both *unmask* that to which it refers, as Fernandez suggests, and *adorn it with a mask* of its own making, as Game and Metcalfe suggest; metaphor may conceal as well as reveal.[50] Elsewhere, Fernandez admits as much, suggesting that symbolic productions "edify . . . by puzzlement" (1986: 222). He writes: "Symbolic productions speak to that inchoate condition, at once providing us with images which we can perform so as to act our way through those intense moments in life (the sacred ones—in which dilemmas, ambiguities and problems ultimately unresolvable threaten to overwhelm us); while at the same time they expand our awareness and temper our intolerance for such incongruities and incompatibilities" (Fernandez 1986: 223).

Given this, we must reconsider the simple metaphor presented by officials organizing the 1994 election in Mozambique. This metaphor did not so much reveal the "rationality" of a "transparent" political process as adorn that process with a mask suggesting that what lay beneath it was transparent.[51] In countering this representation, Muedan elders replaced that mask with one of their own, portraying beneath it conspiring powers lingering within political processes in post-peace-accord Mozambique.

George Lakoff and Mark Johnson (1980) tell us that the conceptual systems that structure our thoughts, actions, and communications are laced with metaphoric references, referring us to other domains. Because these domains, too, are shot through with metaphor, references beget still more references—metaphors upon metaphors (cf. Schrauwers, chapter 4 in this volume; and Harding and Stewart, chapter 9 in this volume). Where election organizers asked Mozambicans to explore the first layer of metaphoric reference, Muedans followed the infinite recess of meaning deeper, allowing them to see conspiring forces that harbingers of a brave new "transparent" world did not.

Notes

I wish to acknowledge the constructive commentary provided on this essay by participants in the Transparency and Conspiracy workshop, including, especially, Todd Sanders, John Comaroff, and Jean Comaroff, as well as by an anonymous reviewer for Duke University Press.

1 I have used a pseudonym to protect the identity of my informant.
2 Elías refers here to the South African elections held 26–28 April 1994, which offered the first opportunity for that nation's African population to vote (see *Economist* 1994).
3 The highest-ranking RENAMO party official at the provincial level is called the provincial *delegate*.
4 The Rome peace accord called for the United Nations to play a role in monitoring the cease-fire and subsequent elections (Alden 1998: 68). According to the UN Blue Book on its operation in Mozambique, "The CNE and its executive secretariat were responsible for the conduct, preparation and organization of the elections. The United Nations Development Programme coordinated interna-

tional financial and material support and provided technical assistance through-out the entire electoral process in the areas of organization, training, civic education, jurisprudence, social communication and financial management" (United Nations 1995: 56). See also Alden (1998: 77) and Synge (1997: 116–17, 121). Both the CNE and STAE were newly created party-neutral organs of the Mozambican government.

5 Trust funds were established to finance fledgling parties, including RENAMO. The amount given to RENAMO totaled $17.6 million (Synge 1997: 119). Sixteen other parties were given an initial sum of $50,000 each and were promised another $50,000 if they could provide accounting for the first installment, but few succeeded in doing so (United Nations 1995: 59; Synge 1997: 118).

6 The FRELIMO guerrilla insurgency against the Portuguese began in the Mueda Plateau region in 1964. FRELIMO maintained its central base throughout the war (which lasted until 1974) on the Mueda Plateau among sympathetic Makonde-speaking communities. See West (1997b).

   The Mozambican civil war began in 1977 when Rhodesian security forces trained and financed a small group of Mozambican dissidents and deployed them to attack Zimbabwean nationalists camped on the Mozambican side of the border. The insurgents—who came to be called RENAMO—were adopted by the South African military when Zimbabwean nationalists took power over the former Rhodesia, and they were used to "destabilize" a FRELIMO government hostile to Pretoria. Between 1977 and 1992, RENAMO expanded in the Mozambican interior, becoming increasingly (although never completely) self-sufficient. See Vines (1991).

7 Between 1 June and 2 September 1994, eight thousand Mozambicans were employed to register the population for the vote. Additionally, sixteen hundred teams of five Mozambicans were engaged as civic educators. The United Nations used a fleet of twenty-six helicopters to ensure access to remote regions for registration and civic education teams (United Nations 1995: 57; Synge 1997: 121–22). In the end, 6,363,311 of an estimated 7,894,850 eligible voters were registered (United Nations 1995: 58; Synge 1997: 122).

8 Seventeen nations and international institutions contributed $64.5 million to this effort (United Nations 1995: 56; Synge 1997: 117). The European Union provided the funds that were used specifically to pay for voter-identity cards (Synge 1997: 121).

9 Elías paid no heed to other, smaller opposition parties in his comments.

10 Many veterans of FRELIMO's war against the Portuguese belong to the Associação dos Combatentes de Luta de Libertação Nacional (ACLLN).

   As Mueda is a region in which the population overwhelmingly supports FRELIMO, Marcos would have been suspect if not in possession of an ACLLN card and a FRELIMO party card.

11 I have been unable to locate any anthropological account dealing with Japanese

business cards, but most travel guides and travel dictionaries make mention of the requisite ceremoniousness of business-card exchanges in Japan.

12 Feinberg, Westgate, and Burroughs (1992) suggest that people may pay more for such cards even when they present no tangible consumer advantages because they wish to be perceived according to characteristics associated with the card by advertisers and consumers.

Visa advertisements in the United States portray celebrities whom knowing store clerks refuse to "recognize" without a Visa card, e.g. For a sociological analysis of the credit card in general, see Ritzer (1995).

13 My passport might have served this same function where people recognized the power of its signatories. From the outset, passports have carried the message (articulated explicitly) that host governments are requested to respect the rights of the expatriates traveling within their territory and render assistance when necessary as an expression of respect toward the issuing nation. Over time, it has become impossible to cross international borders without a passport. Within this context, to deny a passport to a citizen is to deny that citizen the right to travel. In the United States, debate over the right to a passport has generally focused around cases involving individuals traveling to countries with which the United States has strained relations or cases involving individuals with Socialist or Communist affiliations (see Lansing 1981; Jaffe 1956; and Fanelli 1955). Cases in which the individual's travel is said to undermine national interests are rare, however. Near universal issuance of passports, in any case, has diluted the message that these documents convey.

14 In preparation for the 1999 national elections, the CNE and STAE indeed found it necessary to reregister all Mozambican voters (Hanlon 1999). This necessity derived in part from the fact that the 1994 registration process was not computerized.

15 It warrants pointing out that the dilemma remained largely unresolved. Most villagers failed to see the dramatic televised images of votes being counted at tallying stations and, hence, saw only a part of the metaphor. Their consequent distrust produced, paradoxically, the need for election officials to make even more assertive proclamations regarding the transparency of the process.

16 Muedans would most likely have made such associations even if cards were not used, for, in interpreting the meaning of novel situations, they could not have avoided turning to past experiences. The use of identity tokens, however, brought such associations into sharper focus.

17 This would have been approximately $0.60 in 1920 and $0.10 in 1925.

18 The Nyassa Company maintained an administrative post at Muidumbe, on the southeastern edge of the plateau.

19 One escudo is equivalent to one hundred centavos.

20 It is doubtful that this cloth was actually dyed in the juice of tomato leaves. Tomatoes were introduced on the plateau with the arrival of the Nyassa Company, but

people might have easily "forged" tax receipts had this method been used. It is likely that the dye used was the color of tomato leaves and that my informant, or those who told him of these things, assumed that the dye was actually the juice of tomato leaves.

21 Beginning in 1943, men were required to pay 50 escudos (approximately $1.81) and women 25 escudos (approximately $0.90) per year. By 1947, these rates had risen to 90 escudos (approximately $3.61) and 50 escudos (approximately $2.00), respectively, at which time women were exempted from the payment of taxes. Rates for men rose to as high as 120 escudos (approximately $4.15) by 1957.

22 The largest contract employer in the region was the Mocímboa Sisal Syndicate, referred to locally as *mpanga* (West 1997b: 101–2). The most common form of public works was the construction of roadways, referred to locally as *mwangani*.

23 This sometimes happened in any case.

24 Torpey notes that the German word for embrace, *erfassen*, "means to 'grasp' or to 'lay hold of' in the sense of 'register'" (1998: 244).

25 Torpey's treatment of identity documents supports my notion that identity tokens stand in metonymic relation to the individuals they represent and, in combination with other bureaucratic artifacts, in metaphoric relation to social relations. He writes, "The document held by the individual as 'ID' thus corresponds to an entire series of files chronicling movements, economic transactions, familial ties, illnesses, and much else besides—the power/knowledge grid in which individuals are processed and constituted as administrative subjects of states" (1998: 248).

26 In cases like South Africa and the Soviet Union, personal identity documents have also been used to control access to residential areas. For an in-depth case history of the uses of such identity documents in Russia and the Soviet Union, see Matthews (1993); on South Africa, see Hindson (1987), Savage (1986), and Kahn (1949). Such documents have never been used in the United States (although, in the wake of the events of 11 September 2001, this policy has been debated); instead, drivers' licenses and social security cards are often required as means of identification, particularly in securing social benefits. The under-twenty-one female college students studied by Scheibel (1992) attest to this in a low-stakes example when they express the need to procure "fake IDs" in order to gain access to bars where their social cohorts gather. The experiences of undocumented immigrants described by Chavez (1992) testify, in a much higher-stakes context, to the monopoly maintained by the American state over the right to authorize and control movement within its borders even in the absence of mandatory identification for its citizens.

27 I thank Jean Comaroff for calling my attention to this point. Along the same lines, MacPhail (1997) provides an account of references to the pass laws in South African poetry. One poignant example, written by Oswald Mbuyiseni Mtshali, includes the following passage: "Without it I'm lost, with it I'm lost, a cipher in Albert Street. I hate it. I nurse it, my pass, my everything" (38).

28 As many as 27,000 Makonde may have been working in Tanganyika around 1950, at which time 136,000 Makonde (living on and around the Mueda Plateau) were registered by Mozambican census takers. Most elder men I interviewed spent some time on the sisal plantations of colonial Tanganyika, while a small number of elder women I encountered had undertaken such migratory work. See West (1997b: 103–6).

29 For a historical account of the Montfortian missions in the Mueda Plateau region, see West (1997b: 112–28).

30 In the late colonial period, Muedans also discovered that membership in state-sanctioned agricultural cooperatives could shield them, in similar fashion, from the abuse of colonial officials and agents and from other labor requirements. Cooperatives operated in the Mueda region for only a short time, however. See Isaacman (1982: 13–14) and West (1997b: 132).

31 At this time, members of this organization may not yet have referred to themselves as MANU (West 1997b: 145–51). The number of casualties is disputed. Nationalists suggested that as many as six hundred were killed, while Portuguese accounts sometimes place the number of casualties in the single digits.

32 A régulo was a chief who served as a colonial administrative intermediary.

33 *Mapiko* refers to a ceremonial dance performed at initiation rites and other occasions.

34 Mapiko dancers had, for some time, used the ceremony as a way of expressing a veiled critique of colonialism. Masks worn by the dancers sometimes caricatured colonial officials (Alpers 1983: 149).

35 Namaua is a nearby, but not neighboring, village.

36 Party cards sold to Zimbabwean nationalists served similar functions by presenting members with similar dilemmas, although in that case the funds generated by the sale of cards were used to support further recruitment activities (Jocelyn Alexander, personal communication, 28 April 1999). According to Karen McCarthy Brown (personal communication, 28 May 1999), Haitian secret societies have made similar use of society passports.

37 FRELIMO controlled most of the Mueda Plateau region during the war.

38 As described above, most states mark their populations in one way or another to control their movements. The irony, in this case, lies in the fact that the antistate insurgency severely criticized the colonial state's policies but was forced to adopt similar tactics on coming to power over the state. In the same way, the Bolshevik Party criticized tsarist policies but ultimately instituted even more far-reaching controls through issuing internal passports (Matthews 1993).

39 Muedans traded india rubber, bee's wax, and oil seeds at the coast for cloth, iron, and firearms.

40 For a detailed account of this, see West (1997b: 60–72).

41 If questioned directly about this, most who had been settlements heads (such

as Vicente) would grant themselves an exemption to this rule, explaining that in their case it was a confidant working with them who saw into the realm of sorcery.

42 As the vote drew near, RENAMO president Afonso Dhlakama nonetheless declared that he would view anything less than a RENAMO victory as evidence of fraud (Alden 1998: 92). The day before voting began, Dhlakama announced a RENAMO boycott. Dhlakama's withdrawal was based on his suspicion that surplus voter-registration material (peopleless cards) would be used to rig the elections. Dhlakama's party rejoined the elections only at the end of the first day of voting after considerable international pressure was applied and assurances provided that the issue would be investigated thoroughly (Synge 1997: 130–34).

43 RENAMO established small bases in the lowlands to the southeast and southwest of the plateau late in the war and even attacked plateau villages on a few occasions but never consolidated a presence on the plateau.

44 By any reasonable account, the 1994 Mozambican elections were an overwhelming success on their own terms. More than two-thirds of all Mozambicans of voting age participated, according to the United Nations, "patiently, seriously and with great dignity" (United Nations 1995: 63). There were no major irregularities, and all parties ultimately accepted the results, bringing an era of national upheaval to a definitive end. See also Synge (1997: 134) and African-European Institute/AWEPA (1995).

45 Many elders were, ultimately, persuaded to register because the process provided them with a personal photo, free of charge. Personal photos are rare and treasured commodities among elder Muedan villagers. Many, indeed, approached me in the months after election registration had ended, asking if I could use my camera to produce identity cards with personal photos. (I thank Richard Tapper for stimulating commentary on this point.)

46 I am aware of at least one such incident that occurred on the plateau and of several others in Cabo Delgado Province.

47 This was inevitable given that the United Nations relied on a contingent of Portuguese-language speakers to ensure direct communication with Mozambicans.

48 Even polling monitors asked what was in it for them, seizing on the extension of the vote to a third day to threaten a walkout if not paid more for their work (Synge 1997: 134–35; African-European Institute/AWEPA 1995: 58–61).

49 The scene described to me was reminiscent of crop circles found in the English countryside.

50 For this very reason, Aristotle categorized metaphor as a rhetorical devise rather than as an instrument of logic (Tilley 1999: 9).

51 I am reminded of T-shirts that I have seen depicting the spinal column and rib cage or of *carnaval* customs with images of the human skeleton.

References

African-European Institute/AWEPA. 1995. *Report of AWEPA's Observation of the Mozambican Electoral Process, 1992–1994.* Amsterdam: African-European Institute/AWEPA.

Alden, Chris. 1998. "The United Nations, Elections, and the Resolution of Conflict in Mozambique." In *War and Peace in Mozambique,* ed. Stephen Chan and Moisés Venâncio Houndmills, 67–97. London: Macmillan.

Alpers, Edward. 1983. "The Role of Culture in the Liberation of Mozambique." *Ufahamu* 12 (3): 143–89.

Bayart, Jean-François. 1993. *The State in Africa: The Politics of the Belly.* London: Longman.

Chavez, Leo R. 1992. *Shadowed Lives: Undocumented Immigrants in American Society.* Fort Worth, Tex.: Harcourt Brace Jovanovich College.

Economist. 1994. "At Last." 30 April, 65–66.

Fanelli, Joseph A. 1955. "Passport—Right or Privilege?" *Annals of the American Academy of Political and Social Science* 300:36–40.

Favret-Saada, Jeanne. 1980. *Deadly Words: Witchcraft in the Bocage.* Cambridge: Cambridge University Press.

Feinberg, Richard A., Lori S. Westgate, and W. Jeffrey Burroughs. 1992. "Credit Cards and Social Identity." *Semiotica* 91 (1/2): 99–108.

Fernandez, James. 1986. *Persuasions and Performances: The Play of Tropes in Culture.* Bloomington: Indiana University Press.

Game, Ann, and Andrew Metcalfe. 1996. *Passionate Sociology.* Thousand Oaks, Calif.: Sage.

Garcelon, Marc, and John Torpey. 1996. "Internal Colonialism and Document-Based Labor Control in the Soviet Union and South Africa." Paper presented at the annual meeting of the American Sociological Association, New York, August.

Gell, Alfred. 1998. *Art and Agency: An Anthropological Theory.* Oxford: Oxford University Press.

Geschiere, Peter. 1997. *The Modernity of Witchcraft: Politics and the Occult in Postcolonial Africa.* Charlottesville: University Press of Virginia.

Hanlon, Joseph. 1999. *Mozambique Peace Process Bulletin.* No. 22. Amsterdam: AWEPA (The European Parliamentarians for Africa).

Hindson, Doug. 1987. *Pass Controls and the Urban African Proletariat.* Johannesburg: Ravan.

Human Rights Watch. 1992. *Conspicuous Destruction: War, Famine, and the Reform Process in Mozambique.* New York: Human Rights Watch.

Isaacman, Allen. 1982. "The Mozambique Cotton Cooperative: The Creation of a Grassroots Alternative to Forced Commodity Relations." *African Studies Review* 25 (2–3): 5–25.

————. 1996. *Cotton Is the Mother of Poverty: Peasants, Work, and the Rural Struggle in Colonial Mozambique, 1938–1961.* Portsmouth: Heinemann.

Jaffe, Louis L. 1956. "The Right to Travel: The Passport Problem." *Foreign Affairs* 35 (1): 17–28.

Kahn, Ellison. 1949. "The Pass Laws." In *Handbook of Race Relations in South Africa,* ed. Ellen Hellmann, 275–91. Capetown: Oxford University Press.

Kopytoff, Igor. 1986. "The Cultural Biography of Things: Commoditization as Process." In *The Social Life of Things: Commodities in Cultural Perspective,* ed. Arjun Appadurai, 64–91. Cambridge: Cambridge University Press.

Lakoff, George, and Mark Johnson. 1980. *Metaphors We Live By.* Chicago: University of Chicago Press.

Lansing, Paul. 1981. "Freedom to Travel: Is the Issuance of a Passport an Individual Right or a Government Prerogative?" *Denver Journal of International Law and Policy* 11 (15): 15–35.

MacPhail, C. L. 1997. "Poetry and Pass Laws: Humanistic Geography in Urban South Africa." *South African Geographical Journal* 79 (1): 35–42.

Matthews, Mervyn. 1993. *The Passport Society: Controlling Movement in Russia and the USSR.* Boulder, Colo.: Westview.

Munslow, Barry. 1983. *Mozambique: The Revolution and Its Origins.* London: Longman.

Neil-Tomlinson, Barry. 1977. "The Nyassa Chartered Company: 1891–1929." *Journal of African History* 18 (1): 109–28.

Newitt, Malyn. 1995. *A History of Mozambique.* Bloomington: Indiana University Press.

Opello, Walter. 1975. "Pluralism and Elite Conflict in an Independence Movement: FRELIMO in the 1960s." *Journal of Southern African Studies* 2 (1): 66–82.

Ortner, Sherry. 1973. "On Key Symbols." *American Anthropologist* 75 (5): 1338–46.

Ritzer, George. 1995. *Expressing America: A Critique of the Global Credit Card Society.* Thousand Oaks, Calif.: Pine Forge.

Sapir, J. David, and Christopher Crocker, eds. 1977. *The Social Use of Metaphor.* Philadelphia: University of Pennsylvania Press.

Savage, Michael. 1986. "The Imposition of Pass Laws on the African Population in South Africa, 1916–1984." *African Affairs* 85 (339): 181–205.

Schatzberg, Michael. 1993. "Power, Legitimacy, and 'Democratization' in Africa." *Africa* 63 (4): 445–61.

Scheibel, Dean. 1992. "Faking Identity in Clubland: The Communicative Performance of 'Fake ID.'" *Text and Performance Quarterly* 12: 160–75.

Scott, James C. 1998. *Seeing Like a State: How Certain Schemes to Improve the Human Condition Have Failed.* New Haven: Yale University Press.

Synge, Richard. 1997. *Mozambique: UN Peacekeeping in Action, 1992–94.* Washington, D.C.: United States Institute of Peace Press.

Tilley, Christopher. 1999. *Metaphor and Material Culture*. Oxford: Blackwell.

Torpey, John. 1998. "Coming and Going: On the State Monopolization of the Legitimate 'Means of Movement.' " *Sociological Theory* 16 (3): 239–59.

United Nations. 1995. *The United Nations and Mozambique, 1992–1995*. New York: United Nations.

Vail, Leroy. 1976. "Mozambique's Chartered Companies: The Rule of the Feeble." *Journal of African History* 17 (3): 389–416.

Vines, Alex. 1991. RENAMO: *Terrorism in Mozambique*. London: James Currey.

West, Harry G. 1997a. "Creative Destruction and Sorcery of Construction: Power, Hope, and Suspicion in Post-War Mozambique." *Cahiers d'études africaines* 147 (xxxvii-3): 675–98. Reprinted in *Political and Legal Anthropology Review* 20, no. 1 (1997): 13–31.

———. 1997b. "Sorcery of Construction and Sorcery of Ruin: Power and Ambivalence on the Mueda Plateau, Mozambique (1882–1994)." Ph.D. diss., Department of Anthropology, University of Wisconsin, Madison.

———. 2001. "Sorcery of Construction and Socialist Modernization: Ways of Understanding Power in Postcolonial Mozambique." *American Ethnologist* 28 (1): 119–50.

4

Through a Glass Darkly: Charity, Conspiracy, and Power in New Order Indonesia

ALBERT SCHRAUWERS

Charity never faileth: but whether there be prophecies, they shall fail; whether there be tongues, they shall cease; whether there be knowledge, it shall vanish away. For we know in part, and we prophesy in part. But when that which is perfect is come, then that which is in part shall be done away. When I was a child, I spake as a child, I understood as a child, I thought as a child: but when I became a man, I put away childish things. For now we see through a glass, darkly; but then face to face: now I know in part; but then shall I know even as also I am known. And now abideth faith, hope, charity, these three; but the greatest of these is charity.
—1 Cor. 13:8–13

The antithesis of Suharto's "New Order" state (*Orde Baru*) is, not the implied "Old Order," but, rather, "disorder." The New Order state emerged, phoenix-like, out of a collapsed economy, regional rebellions, and an aborted "Communist coup." Military discipline combined with a technocratic style of management directly imported from the Berkeley Department of Economics has kept these forces at bay through a carefully crafted mixture of "development," "modernization," and "Pancasila democracy." During its thirty-odd years of bureaucratic rationalization, the New Order state has sought to tie the hundreds of islands, languages, and ethnic and religious groups that compose this *tanah air*—this "sea-land"—into a united whole. The disorder of diversity has been governmentalized and regularized, subjected to state tutelage (*pembinaan*) and enforced homogenization and modernization. This tutelage aims to create a vigilant citizenry, a citizenry attuned to the continuing danger that threatens this hard-won order: the conspiratorial specter of Communist infiltration and regional separatism. Order, as a legitimation for government intervention in civil society, makes sense only against this background peril.

Yet the hard-won order so vigorously defended by the state is less than transparent to those at the periphery of power. In the relatively underpopulated, rural districts of the Outer Islands, in areas like Lake Poso in Central Sulawesi, state-imposed "order" has disrupted the well-worn ruts of daily life and imposed new and frequently contradictory demands on locals' time and resources. The neat chains of bureaucratic competence and control are the means by which power has been centralized in Jakarta, but they paradoxically make executing even the simplest of regulations a complex minefield, a paper trail traversed only with the aid of bribes and extrabureaucratic connections. When all roads lead to Rome, the quickest route home is "corruption." Such corruption is viewed as a necessary evil, as systematically administered in some departments as the bureaucracy that it circumvents. Such corruption tests the state's claims of "order"; the means-ends rationality of government, its discourses of "open and transparent" bureaucratic process, can easily be reinterpreted as the multiplication of rules for the personal enrichment of those with "connections."

There is, however, a thin, easily traversed line between corruption and conspiracy theory. Corruption, the accumulation of personal wealth through the manipulation of bureaucratic office, would seem to secularized Westerners to be nothing more than opportunism, a sad and lamentable comment on human nature. Yet, to locals, the obscure processes through which open and transparent government works often seem to perpetuate larger agendas reflecting the ethnic and religious fault lines of the district. The "rules" of corruption, always implied and never stated, are interpreted as signs of a larger project of enforced state Islamicization of this largely Christian enclave. Bureaucratic processes that work to undermine the Christian school system or the church-run hospital or prevent Christians from obtaining government posts all seem to point to the dominant role of a Muslim elite with a cabalistic plan for enforced conversion. Such fears reflect the history of the region, recalling the *Darul Islam* (Islamic state) rebellions to the south in the late 1950s during which Christians were slaughtered or forced to convert to Islam (Harvey 1977: 17–40). Islam continues to provide the only viable alternative to the secular constitutional ideology enforced on all groups by the New Order in 1984 (Hefner 1997). For this Christian minority, then, the state's mythic threat, Communism, has less palpable salience than their own conspiratorial fears of the all-powerful, but unseen, workings of Islam lying behind the impartial secular facade of the New Order.

This conspiracy should not be read, however, as a simple struggle to control the secular terrain of the state; the ultimate prize is of greater worth. While Islam has challenged the hegemony of the state and provided its own alternate model of governmentality, it does not do so within the limited, mechanistic vocabulary of secular instrumentalism. Rather, as I have already suggested, the alternative hegemony provided by Islam is predicated on issues of faith in things unseen, in powers that transcend the impoverished "disenchanted world" of the bureaucrats. Pemberton describes how the unseen workings of such power escape the New Order's tutelage in Java: "To counter the dominant claims of cultural orderliness . . . I consider events known to Javanese as *rebutan,* struggles among rivals fighting over power-laden objects, contestations of desire whose points of intense focus range from the charged remnants of an offering given a tutelary spirit to, in the context of Javanese historical chronicles, the king's throne itself. . . . In practice, acts of *rebutan* appear as disruptive events, incidents of sheer conflict (*konflik*) ultimately intolerable for New Order security, unrecognizable as 'tradition'" (1994: 18). Perceived by the New Order as an absence of order, the reordering potential of *rebutan* is dismissed. They do not fit within dominant models of "tradition," and, hence, the alternate models of power, the "occult cosmologies" that they disclose, remain unseen by the state. But faith in such powers can, it is argued, move mountains—and now, apparently, even remove despots like Suharto. In this essay, then, I wish to focus on this half-hidden occult power, the kinds of conspiratorial events through which it is known, and the ritual technologies by which it is tapped.

The conspiratorial fears of Christians in the highlands of Central Sulawesi are, thus, more than a reaction to an Islamic political ideology; conspiracy theories play themselves out in a realm of unseen powers that exceed both formal politics and the state bureaucracies. Ironically, these Christians have their own, similar political ideology and political party as adjuncts to their own faith. The church provides an institutional home for Christian models of governmentality inherited from Dutch Calvinist missionaries (Schrauwers 2000). In the Netherlands, Christian political parties have maintained a parliamentary majority for much of this century (Stuurman 1983). This combination of rational bureaucratization and religious faith challenges the post-

Enlightenment assumption that the specific "ethic" of Protestantism was a cultural predisposition toward ascetic accumulation, an enlargement of the space of civil society, a fostering of the growth of the capitalist market, and a resulting "disenchantment" with the world as things "religious" were increasingly separated from the mechanistic workings of the natural world. As a product of Dutch Calvinism, the extensive bureaucracy of the Christian Church of Central Sulawesi has inculcated its own discourse on power—a power rooted in "Allah," a political terrain shared but also contested with Islam. The conspiratorial fears of Christians and Muslims in Central Sulawesi thus reinterpret the mundane bureaucratic landscape, the transparent "order" of the New Order state, as but one arena within which their battle of faith in unseen powers is waged. Conspiracy theories contest the state's claims to ultimate power and sketch out an alternate, unseen terrain whose reality makes sense of, and transcends, the obscure workings of corruption.

I would, however, like to dwell on the irony that I have just noted—that Christians, like Muslims, have constructed extensive bureaucratic organizations of their own, bureaucracies no different in structure or function from those of the state in their claims of open and transparent governance. The Christian Church of Central Sulawesi manages some 350 congregations, a Christian school system, a hospital, and a variety of development and training projects that parallel the operations of the state system. But, in practice, the operations of the church polity are no more transparent than are those of the state, and accusations of corruption by church officials are frequent. Church officials—who are usually kinsmen—are accused of transgressing the "axiom of amity" (Fortes 1969: 235–37) by which kinship in this community is defined; these corrupt "misers" are accused of being deficient in "charity." Rather than acting like beneficent elder siblings as they should, these officials make use of the power that their kinship status lends them to enrich themselves (Schrauwers 2002). Their dispossessed kin, deprived of a voice in either church or state bureaucracies, have few resources with which to contest their lot; their resort to yet another occult cosmology, the idiom of witchcraft and sorcery, is one means by which battles in the unseen realm are waged, won, and lost. My point, then, is to underscore that the politics of this unseen realm always exceeds the structural determinacies of these open and transparent bureaucracies. The Weberian process of bureaucratic rationalization seems, rather than "disenchanting" the world and creating an "iron cage," rather to provoke a renewed turn to rebutan, to disruptive events that exceed the carefully calculated orders of either the New Order or the church.

By focusing on the Russian doll-within-a-doll-like aspect of these nested bureaucracies and conspiracy theories, I hope to emphasize the political dynamics of these occult cosmologies. Occult cosmologies, whether "religious" or "magical," offer important conceptual tools to people confronted with the obscure workings of open government. Such occult cosmologies allow for the local redefinition of political ideologies by translating mundane occurrences to another, "more real" plane. But, by opening up open government and revealing the unseen workings of power, such cosmologies also allow individuals to introduce more personal forms of agency into the omnipresent, impersonal government structures that regulate their world; their competing discourses of power highlight the Achilles heel of the otherwise invincible leviathan of the state. Occult cosmologies offer "occult technologies" by which the larger, unseen powers that be can be manipulated and corruption transcended. To substantiate these general arguments, I will in the remainder of this essay open up one particular set of dolls within dolls in the village of Tentena on the shores of Lake Poso in Central Sulawesi, Indonesia.

Order and Disorder

These various strands of governmentality were brought together for me quite clearly on a sunny morning, 10 January 1997, when two turboprop helicopters bearing the minister of interior affairs and the minister of defense landed on the grass runway of the Missionary Aviation Fellowship airstrip near the Lake Poso Festival site in Tentena, an isolated village in Central Sulawesi. They were greeted by Soerjadi, the government-sponsored head of the Partai Demokrasi Indonesia (PDI), the Indonesian Democratic Party, the state-engineered amalgam of the Nationalist Party and Parkindo, the Indonesian Protestant Party, who had arrived the day before. Come to celebrate the twenty-fourth anniversary of the founding of the party, this convoy of dignitaries proceeded to temporary open-air shelters erected at the festival grounds. After their short speeches, the ministers promptly returned to Jakarta. Short sound bites of their speeches (but not Soerjadi's) were duly televised that evening on the national news.

This apparently pedestrian occurrence—the normal and open proceedings of political parties, the electioneering, the sound bites on the evening news—was the end product of a series of remarkable events related to me with a conspiratorial air. The Indonesian Democratic Party was approaching the 1997 elections handicapped by an internal leadership struggle between Soerjadi, a Suharto-sponsored candidate, and Megawati Sukarnoputri, the daughter of past president Sukarno and an advocate of democratic reform. The New Order military regime had, it was said, fostered this internal power struggle in its political rival to undermine Megawati's growing popularity among the Indonesian middle class. This internecine struggle erupted in widespread riots in Jakarta and at the previous party convention in Sumatra. Indeed, it was the fear of further riots that had pushed Soerjadi to search for a safe haven for this party convention, the isolated village of Tentena in the highlands of Central Sulawesi. Amid ministers of state and numerous squads of well-armed soldiers, an affable Soerjadi, an "opposition" party leader, calmly electioneered, safe in the knowledge of government support against his political rival.

It is not, however, to the irregular workings of the political machinery that I would like to draw attention. I turn, rather, to the portentous signs that abounded in the run-up to the convention by which the operation of the hidden powers underlying such corruption were revealed. Local pranksters had discovered the value of the newly installed telephone system; an anonymous call to the minister in the dead of night threatened to firebomb the largest church in Tentena, evoking a reaction that threatened to overwhelm the preparations for the PDI convention. Word-of-mouth reports of a series of church burnings in Java and Kalimantan had just begun to circulate; hence, the prank was treated with great seriousness. Similar church burnings had occurred in the recent past in Palu, the provincial capital, and Ujung Pandang to the south. A night watch was instituted at the church, with a minimum of twenty men standing guard. The district head imposed a similar night watch throughout the area in anticipation of PDI partisans from the south; nighttime patrols of villagers armed with machetes maintained the tense peace until the convention was over. This apparently fortuitous overlap of open political process and religious and political tensions was very much heightened by perceived threats and escalating ripostes: "Of course the threat came from some hot-headed Muslim youths! But let them actually try something. We will be ready. We control both ends of the valley. We will sweep them before us!" What had begun as a national "secular" political process (a "Festival of Democracy," *Pesta Demokrasi* [Pemberton 1994: 4]) ended in conspiracies of religiously motivated conflict, rebutan, that disclosed the occult cosmology by which locals interpret politics.

These complex events need to be unpacked and carefully examined from the perspective of each of the participants; each interprets the events within his or her own political framework and definitions of how power works. It is acute social tensions between religious and ethnic groups such as this

that are used by the New Order as legitimation for its intrusion in the political process. At its crudest, such intervention may take the form of depos-
ing Megawati as head of the PDI and supporting the candidacy of Soerjadi.
More frequently, state policy has greater subtlety. Two of the most perti-
nent policies revealed in this particular episode are the state's management
of "primordial" ethnic and religious identities through the enforced secularization of the opposition political parties such as the PDI (Hefner 1997) and
the careful management of cultural "traditions" in theme parks like the Lake
Poso Festival Grounds, site of the PDI conference (Pemberton 1994: 152–61).
Since 1984, all organizations, including religiously oriented ones, were forced
to acknowledge the *Pancasila,* the ideological basis of New Order rule, as
their *asas tunggal,* the sole basis of their ideology. This subsumption of the
Qur'an, the word of God, to the word of man evoked widespread but ineffec-
tive resistance from many Muslim organizations, including the Muslim political party, the United Development Party (Partai Persatuan Pembangunan)
(Ramage 1995: 35–39). The Christian political parties had all been amalga-
mated under the domination of the secular Nationalist Party and, thus, had
similarly been "disenchanted" on the enforced trek to secular modernity.

Similar policies for the management of "tradition" (*adat*) attempt to pull
the teeth of "primordial" ethnic identities and shape a unified national identity. The staging of the PDI conference at the Lake Poso Festival Grounds was
no accident but itself a commitment to the national motto of "unity in diversity." With twenty-five distinct languages spoken in the province of Central
Sulawesi alone, achieving unity out of diversity is no easy task. Current state
cultural policy limits the expression of ethnic identities as only local manifestations of "shared" pan-Indonesian ideals (Kipp 1993). The state's assumption that the local and particular can be translated into core national values
at once defines the content of local "cultures" and the role of "culture" in
the production of social order. The representations created through cultural
centralization in Jakarta have now been reexported to their original sites to
redefine, not only their content, but also their function. This amounts to a redefinition of ethnicity in Indonesia in terms of "part cultures," as "folk" traditions that can be understood only in relation to the new "great" tradition
defined by the Indonesian state (cf. Redfield 1960). The cultural representations perpetuated through state-sponsored sites like the Lake Poso Festival
Grounds thus define previously diverse groups in terms of their place within a
larger Indonesian cultural mosaic composed of similarly shaped and colored
tiles (cf. Pemberton 1994: 152–61; Hutajulu 1995; Daniels 1999).

However, this simple delineation of pragmatic government policy ignores local conceptions of how hidden power works. The instrumentality of social-scientific analysis of this sort shares state assumptions about power and bureaucracies. The ideology of open and transparent government would insist that "policies" are developed by those in power at the center and then passed along bureaucratic chains that implement perfectly these policy decisions on subject populations in the periphery. Such a construction accepts state presuppositions of the primordial nature of ethnic and religious groups as well as of the instrumental nature of bureaucratic power. To locals, well versed in the arts of corruption, bureaucracies are not the perfect conduits of centralized power that the regime might hope. The state is not perceived as a uniform whole. Such bureaucracies may be totalizing in scope, but they are not centralized; they may intrude in all aspects of daily life, but different bureaucracies may make different and contradictory demands. There is an ambiguity about state intentions that leaves them open to interpretation. These contradictory bureaucratic demands feed local conspiratorial fears of the all-powerful, but unseen, workings of Islam lying behind the impartial secular facade of the New Order. The implementation of state policies aimed at secularizing politics and civil society is interpreted locally as anti-Christian and, hence, as part of a larger Islamic agenda.

It is important to underscore that this alternate idiom of power, this occult cosmology, maps the same political terrain as the state's modernist instrumentality—just in a different way. The conspiratorial fears of local Christians are not simply about rival religious groups attempting to assume control over the state bureaucracy. Rather, they are about a battle of faith, part of which is played out through instrumental politics, but much of which is carried out through unseen forces, by means of occult technologies. Christians do not fear simply the Islamicization of the state; they fear for their souls. That the fear of church burnings should assume such monumental proportions at precisely the moment of the PDI conference, surrounded as it was with all the trappings of state (including well-armed special forces troops), is itself an indication that such worldly power is no counter to the real power driving the day-to-day world, largely hidden from view. I turn, then, from the conspiratorial fears of these Christians to the occult cosmologies within which such battles of faith are played out.

I was first introduced to the significance of such hidden powers in this local Christian occult cosmology a few years before, when I first arrived in the area to conduct my doctoral research. I was roused from my room early one evening to join a family prayer group. The situation was unusual. Earlier in the day, my landlady's older sister and her husband had arrived from Poso, the regency capital, where they lived. They had come to gather family support in a time of crisis; their daughter Pada had been kidnapped.

I was confused. Their daughter had been kidnapped, and their response was to flee the city, seek out their kin, and hold a prayer meeting? What about the police?

But the situation was unusual. Pada's father, Papa Pada, had been born a Muslim. When he married Mama Pada, he had converted to Christianity over the objections of the uncle who had raised him. This uncle swore that he would exact his revenge, and now was the time. Since Islam had lost a soul, a soul had to be paid in return. Papa Pada's daughter had been kidnapped, and she was to be married to a distant cousin in the Islamic manner.

In this scenario, Pada, whom I knew to be a willful young woman, seemed entirely too passive. She has been bewitched with love magic, was the reply. She was drawn into their house and drugged and is now guarded around the clock.

Mama and Papa Pada had fled to their kin seeking their aid. Ngkai Tua, the patriarch of the clan, immediately called a prayer meeting, and I was called to participate. The eight brothers and sisters, and their families, crowded into the main room of the house for what was a surprisingly short vigil. Papa Tua, an elder in the church and the husband of the oldest sibling, did most of the speaking. He prayed for God's help in revealing a path out of this quandary and expressed the family's faith that God's plan would no doubt soon become clear to them as well. I was to find that the invocation of God's plan was no empty formality but the lens through which these events were to be interpreted.

The most touching moment occurred when Papa Pada himself stood and publicly prayed for the release of his daughter. His words were simple but eloquent. After the service was over, a friend explained the true significance of his prayer.

Although a convert to Christianity, Papa Pada had never before prayed in public. It was a significant step that, in his time of greatest need, he would turn so publicly to God and express his faith. The entire family had been touched.

It was decided that the next day, Friday, the two oldest sisters would go to the regency capital and attempt to see Pada. They would try to enter the house during Friday prayers at the mosque, when most of the men of the uncle's household would be gone. No one would attempt to harm women, it was thought, especially these two, who were Pada's "mothers."

The women returned that evening with a miraculous tale. They had entered the house as planned, surprised to find the door unguarded and the house empty—with the exception of Pada, whom they found crying in an upper-floor room. Pada related how she had been shocked awake the previous night with the sudden realization that she had been bewitched; this had miraculously occurred at precisely the moment that her father had stood in public prayer and displayed his faith in the power of the Christian God. The three women fled to safety.

While such "miraculous" occurrences are hardly commonplace, they clearly reveal to locals, even if momentarily, the unseen power that orders the day-to-day world to meet God's own purposes. In this battle for souls, any weapon may be seized on: church burnings to test Christian faith; Muslim professors who hinder Christian students from obtaining their degrees in state universities; the pulling of state funding from the Christian hospital; the use of love magic to entrap an unwary young woman into an Islamic union; and a kidnapping to strengthen a father's faith. This is not simply a political battle to acquire the trappings of secular power but an epic battle played out on a different plane, a reality that is glimpsed only partially but that operates on faith. And, as this brief anecdote makes clear, religious faith is intimately tied to the kinship groups that it makes possible.

That Papa and Mama Pada would turn to her extended sibling group for aid, and that their response would be to hold a prayer meeting, is, thus, typical of the way in which Christianity has been "enculturated" in the Christian Church of Central Sulawesi. The occult cosmology of these highland Christians cannot be understood in abstract theological terms alone; the church itself underplays the importance of theology and, instead, ensures the "truth" of sermons by ensuring that only authorized individuals may preach (for any other to *naik mimbar*, "to preach," would be *puloru*, "subject to divine retribution"). These individuals, like Papa Tua, stand at the center of extended kin groups that are simultaneously economic, religious, and political networks. To understand the larger battle of occult cosmologies, the political struggle between Islam and Christianity, it is crucial, first, to understand the manner in which kinship and Christianity have been bound together in the highlands through acts of charity.

Kinship and "Charity"

To understand the relation between kinship, religious faith, and the political ramifications of these hidden powers, it is essential to trace the manner in which Dutch missionaries inculcated Christianity in the area. The Christian Church of Central Sulawesi (hereafter GKST) was formed in 1947 and is headquartered in the village of Tentena on the shores of Lake Poso (Kruyt 1970). Its impressive new synod buildings as well as many of its health and development programs were funded by the Dutch Reformed Church out of whose mission it grew (Schrauwers 2000). The GKST was the initial proving ground for what became an important missiological innovation in Dutch Protestant missions in Indonesia: the "sociological mission method" as developed by the missionary-ethnographer Albert C. Kruyt at the turn of the century (Randwijck 1981: 2:410–15). Kruyt was deeply affected by the reforms in colonial administration taking place as the Dutch "rounded off" their empire in Indonesia by solidifying their control over peripheral areas like Central Sulawesi. These areas were to be ruled indirectly through customary law (*adat*), which necessitated that anthropological studies be made. Kruyt married such anthropological study with his own mission goals; after more than a decade of unsuccessful preaching in the highlands, he had come to the conclusion that Christian piety could never be inculcated where Christianity was perceived as a foreign imposition. He thus engaged in a thorough study of local adat so as selectively to rework indigenous beliefs and rituals within a Christian framework. The enculturation of Christianity called for a transformation in the subject of conversion; culture rather than the individual was to be Christianized.

One of the primary means by which Kruyt accomplished this goal was to incorporate *monuntu*, an indigenous political process associated with ritualized feasting, within the church as the primary means of Christian preaching. Feasts (*polimbu*) are easily improvised because they are an extension of everyday practices that simultaneously constitute hierarchy and dependency, through sharing, production, and reproduction. Feasting is common to the most basic of productive activities as well as the largest rituals of social reproduction because it is an implicit, practical "strategy," a set of situationally effective schemes and tactics for accomplishing specific practical objectives as varied as planting, marrying, or honoring the dead (cf. Bourdieu 1977:

79). The hierarchy that is created through the feast thus has its roots in the daily inculcation of politeness behaviors and the coercive power of parents shared by both daily and communal meals. No one was allowed to leave a feast until the most senior member was finished eating and had taken the opportunity to monuntu (advise) his juniors on matters of communal concern such as the next day's farming. Kruyt ([1912] 1950: 1:196–98) emphasizes that monuntu was the primary "legal" process (i.e., means of dispute settlement) of traditional villages.

Kruyt's success in incorporating this political process as preaching within the church tied the church's basic administrative and worship unit, the evangelization group, to both feasting and kinship. Every congregation is subdivided into a number of evangelization groups, which meet alternately in members' homes for a worship service on Saturday (i.e., in addition to communal worship on Sunday). Each evangelization group is led by a church elder, linking this particular constituency to the governing body of the congregation. This elder is responsible for preaching (monuntu) to the evangelization group on the occasion of its weekly meetings, each of which assumes the form of a "feast." The elder's sermon is supposed to be contextually related to the circumstances of the host and, hence, has a great deal of disciplinary potential; elders are able to preach on the "sins" of their constituents and point them on the road to redemption. Given that the evangelization group is largely composed of closely related families and that the church elder is also a kinship elder, the Saturday worship service encapsulates kinship relations within the polity of the church.

Worship in the evangelization group has, thus, come to reflect the cultural idioms through which kinship is expressed. A key cultural concept is *sintuwu maroso* (a strong sense of communal aid) and its material manifestation, *posintuwu* (the gift). These concepts lie at the root of a kinship ideology that emphasizes sharing: *be maya mombereke*, kin should not mutually calculate costs and benefits. This noncalculative injunction in the kinship sphere has assumed increasing importance as the local economy has been commodified, and it establishes the kinship sphere in opposition to the market. The oppositional character of the kinship vocabulary was necessitated by the Dutch appropriation of the word *oli* as "price"; this word also lies at the root of bridewealth (*oli mporongo*) and, hence, inflects on the way in which this bridewealth (frequently money) is collected through gifts (*posintuwu*) from kin. In other words, the noncalculative series of posintuwu exchanges between kin is one means by which the special "sharing" characteristics of kinship are highlighted and distinguished from the market economy

(Schrauwers 1999). Posintuwu exchange has become a key symbol of this kinship sphere.

Posintuwu exchanges provide the crucial material support needed to hold the feasts now associated with the Protestant worship service. At its simplest, the "feast" at an evangelization group meeting may consist of nothing but several kinds of cookies or cakes. But even this simple feast can be a major burden as the largest evangelization groups have sixty members. The rotating hosts of these worship services may frequently decide to "praise God" for some blessing by holding a more lavish affair. They may butcher a pig, for example, in celebration of a birthday. The more lavish the feast, the greater the status of the host. Such large feasts can succeed only with the extensive material assistance of kin through gifts of posintuwu. The status of the host is garnered through the generosity of their gift giving in the past in relation to the return gifts that make the lavish feast possible, despite an ideology emphasizing that they are "pure gifts" given with no expectation of return. Each return gift solidifies the kinship relationship but also establishes the return giver as an equal. The gift giving during an evangelization group feast thus consists of a series of dyadic status competitions.

It is generosity in gift giving that is the mark of a leader within the kinship sphere. The elders of evangelization groups are, thus, noted for their generosity, a generosity that is explicitly contrasted with the kinds of calculation for profit typical of the market. And, as the local economy has become increasingly embedded in the market and more and more aspects of social reproduction commodified, this kin ideology has been increasingly stressed through the holding of more and larger feasts. The feasts associated with the Protestant worship services are also political occasions, a means of extending the disciplinary power of the church; hence, they have been encouraged by the church. The expansion of the noncalculative gift-giving ideology of posintuwu exchange, feasting, and church power is, thus, the end product of Kruyt's mission project to enculturate Christianity, that is, to create a local Christian culture. This enculturated Christianity has been increasingly bureaucratized and regulated within the GKST as the pattern originating in the evangelization groups has been applied to other constituencies, such as the women's, men's, and youth groups, all under the hierarchical control of elders and the church synod.

Faced with a crisis of faith, it was, thus, natural for Papa Pada to turn to his brother-in-law, Papa Tua (the husband of Papa Pada's eldest sibling), for help. Since this was perceived as a crisis of faith, Papa Tua led a prayer meeting asking for God's guidance. Such meetings are, as I just outlined, the primary "ritual technology" of highland Christianity, a general format for approaching and influencing the sacred. But Papa Tua also generously lent his car for, and sent his wife on, the next day's expedition to free Pada. Thus, what I had initially thought of as an odd reaction to a kidnapping I eventually understood to be a culturally appropriate utilization of concrete kinship and sacred resources.

Church elders such as Papa Tua are, thus, noted for both their knowledge of the occult cosmology of Protestantism as well as their generosity within the kinship sphere; faith and kinship are inextricably intertwined. The commodification of the local economy has made the church the defender of an idealized kinship sphere characterized by generosity. Yet, as I will argue, this kinship sphere and posintuwu gift exchange are essential for capitalist agricultural production and, hence, have expanded with the introduction of a market economy. Balancing the two sides of the system, generosity and the market, has proved difficult and gives rise to occult conspiracy theories of a different kind.

Misers, the Church, and Kinship

Church elders like Papa Tua link the basic kin groups through which local religious politics is played out with the extensive Dutch-funded bureaucracy of the Christian Church of Central Sulawesi and its development projects, school system, and hospital. Church elders are pivotal power brokers in numerous social fields. But the linkage of kinship, generosity, and spiritual guidance in the role of elder creates an ideal that is difficult to live up to. Before turning to the ways in which this failure is interpreted locally (in the idioms of "corruption" and "witchcraft"), I would like to underscore the structural paradoxes of the local economy that make such failure endemic, to explain, in other words, why the idealized "charitable" elder is so frequently held up to be "miserly." The primary means by which these generous familial patrons gain the wealth to which they owe their position is an initial act of greed by which they monopolize family resources. The role of elder is, thus, an ambiguous one, at once a source of patronage and a figure of resentment.

The ideal of generosity has proved difficult to isolate from a commodified local economy. It is important to emphasize, therefore, that the opposition between a kinship sphere characterized by generosity and a profit-motivated market sphere is largely ideological; kinship and the market are also intimately intertwined (Schrauwers 1999). Posintuwu exchange serves the role of institutionalizing the particular "altruistic" character of local kinship ideology: a prohibition on calculation and an injunction to be generous. But, as I have argued elsewhere, the institutional ideology surrounding gift giving cannot be automatically assumed to motivate individual participants (Schrauwers 2000: 145–52). All gift givers find it to their advantage to emphasize the posintuwu ideal of the "free gift," but it is careful calculation that now leads to the decision whether to be generous. To the generous gift givers eager to maintain their reputation, the ideal of the free gift underscores their magnanimity. To the calculating feast giver attempting to benefit from the generosity of others, the ideal of the free gift limits their obligation to repay an equal amount.

The kinship sphere is, thus, ideologically characterized in terms of the altruistic generosity of siblings—a category that extends laterally to third cousins. It is to those who have the ability to hold lavish feasts, to those who are elders, that the poorer members of the community turn for aid. Since the local economy has been increasingly commodified with the introduction of Green Revolution technologies, even "subsistence production" now requires cash inputs. As Kahn (1993: 65) characterizes this process of "peasantization," a continuum of peasant economic behaviors emerges. On the one hand is the "traditional" peasant, whose activities are made possible only through commoditized inputs; on the other is the "capitalist" peasant, whose success is owed to maximizing the exploitation of traditional resources such as family land and labor. In each case, both commoditized and "free traditional" inputs are necessary for the reproduction of household production. Yet all these peasant forms of production depend on the maximization of free inputs (i.e., inputs not acquired through market mechanisms). These free traditional inputs all fall within the kinship sphere, where, ideologically, they are not to be maximized but shared altruistically with poorer siblings. In practice, however, the general poverty of the area necessitates the careful calculation of these generous acts; because even the capitalist peasant depends on the kinship sphere to ensure his profitability, generosity may be selectively dispensed to maximize his own gains from the kinship sphere. I have elsewhere described how the labor and land made available within the kinship sphere form a "moral economy" distinguished ideologically through its borrowing of the language of the gift, of posintuwu exchange, and how this moral economy makes commodity production feasible (Schrauwers 1995, 1999, 2000).

It is this increasing tendency to manipulate the supposedly altruistic bonds of kin generosity for material gain that has resulted in the frequently muttered accusations of corruption made against elders and church officials. On the one hand, these greedy misers (*bagagu*) take advantage of their positions in the church for personal gain. Church vehicles, for example, would be brought for repair to independent mechanics when the church had its own well-equipped garage and mechanics; the independent mechanics would inflate the bill and pay off the church employee who brought the vehicle in. Papa Tua, an elder and onetime synod commission member, was said to have pulled strings to get a Dutch-funded scholarship redirected to his own son. On the other hand, these accusations of corruption in the church simply point to what is accepted as a characteristic of these individuals within their kin groups; their willingness to exploit the church for personal gain is an indication that they are equally prone to abusing their own kin. Papa Tua was the subject of many muttered accusations of being a bagagu by his poorer kin; they pointed out how their own impoverishment was itself the product of his greed. When he had first married the eldest sibling in the family, he had pressed his father-in-law to divide the family resources. In the division, he appropriated the lion's share, as his immediate needs took priority over the still hypothetical needs of the younger children. My own research assistant, Papa Atin, claims to have been disinherited: "But I was only ten. What could I do?"

The generosity of elders and their ability to share the wealth may originate in an initial act of greed such as this, and their continued viability as kin patrons may further depend on their manipulation of the ideology of the gift and of church office. Hence, whispered accusations of being a bagagu may ironically follow from the very acts of generosity for which elders should gain renown. My research assistant, for example, asked Papa Tua for permission to farm peanuts on a half-hectare parcel of land that had lain fallow for fifteen years. The permission was granted, but on the condition that, one year after the heavy work of clearing the land was done, Papa Atin was to plant chocolate trees—which were to belong entirely to Papa Tua—between the peanut plants. Papa Atin was enraged by this abuse of what he considered family land, but, since Papa Tua had officially registered the property in his own name, he was powerless and had to acquiesce to the demand. Papa Tua's behavior contrasted sharply with that of a more distant sibling who owned the adjacent half-hectare piece of land; not only did he grant Papa Atin permission to farm the land, but he even plowed it for him!

The ambiguity in the role of elder is not limited to the mundane, economic exchanges by which kinship is defined. The elder's role links economy and kinship with the ritual technology of the church. It is elders who provide the definitive interpretation of God's word in their sermons and make evident the otherwise hidden actions of God's hand. The elders' ability to misuse the altruistic language of posintuwu ideology for personal gain means that they are also potentially capable of misusing their position in the church. To whom, or what, then, do the dispossessed turn for protection when faced with the combined might of religious, kinship, and economic authority? I argued earlier that the church's appeal to hidden powers, and its use of conspiracy theory in relation to the state, was a means of introducing agency into the omnipresent, impersonal government structures that regulated their world. Similarly, when faced with the abuses of an omnipotent church, locals turn to an alternate set of hidden powers to combat it: sorcery, or *doti*. Such occult powers have no official place within Christian cosmology; they appear as rebutan, disorderly or disruptive events that lie outside the scope of sermons and theology.

When I returned to Central Sulawesi two years after the kidnapping of Pada, I arrived just in time to take part in the large feast marking the forty-day anniversary of the death of Papa Pada. Papa Pada had died unexpectedly of a heart attack and was sincerely mourned by his wife's family. Yet the depth of their feelings was not revealed until I was almost ready to return home a few months later. Relations within the family had seemed particularly strained, largely, I felt, because of the financial pressure that Papa Tua was experiencing funding his son's university expenses in Jakarta. The strain was taking its toll on his health, and, one afternoon, he experienced what seemed an angina attack. Some accusing glares were directed at me by his brother, Papa Obi, who claimed that I could have resolved the stress with a generous gift of my own, were I not too close to my research assistant, Papa Atin, whom I "was paying too much." The atmosphere in the house was oppressive for both myself and my research assistant, so we left for a walk. This early evening walk took us past the cemetery, a site usually avoided after dark for fear of the potentially malevolent spirits of the dead. I was abruptly taken by surprise when Papa Atin suggested that we visit the grave of Papa Pada.

The graveyard was on a small hill overlooking the village, dark but dimly illuminated by the moon. Papa Atin led me between the densely packed graves, each capped with a small, roofed, open structure. Papa Atin located the grave of his brother-in-law, the member of the family whom he said he missed the most. He climbed inside the small open structure and lit a cigarette, which he placed on the gravestone. He explained that Papa Pada had been truly generous, that he was the only member of the family into whose pocket Papa Atin felt he could reach for a cigarette. Now that he was dead, he had come to share a cigarette with him. He mourned, he said, because the truly generous die and the misers live on. He invited me inside the structure and then suggested that we could go "ecstasy" and speak directly with Papa Pada.[1] He sat silently for a few minutes, rocking back and forth, but finally stopped. It wasn't working, he said, because I lacked faith. As quickly as we had decided to come, we left. But, at the edge of the cemetery, Papa Atin needed to throw up. And then, further down the road, it happened again. He had been poisoned (with doti), he said, by Papa Tua's brother.

This was only the second time that I had visited the graveyard at night. Several years before, I had been investigating this magical substance, doti, of the sort that Papa Atin claimed was used to poison him. Doti are potent substances whose power largely seems to originate in the spells uttered over them. I had sought the most innocuous of mystical knowledge, love magic, as an inroad to the subject. Over drinks one night, I broached the subject with an acknowledged expert, Papa Cerli. As much for the others with us as for me, he dismissed the subject of love magic and insisted that, if I was serious about doti, I must follow him to the graveyard now. The challenge drew the immediate attention of everyone, as was, I think, its intent. Even then I knew that no one visited the graveyard at night, and someone had been buried there only the day before. The newly dead are frequently troublesome and dangerous spirits. Filled with the bravery of the nonbeliever, I agreed to go.

Papa Cerli muttered a few words into his hands as we walked to the graveyard and insisted that I hold his hand. We walked to the new grave and, like Papa Atin, "spoke" with the spirit of the dead young man before entering the small hut over his grave. Papa Cerli asked permission and then took a small piece of the crepe paper decorating the new grave. This, he said, is our proof. We returned to the house, and along the way I tried to quiz him about doti and what the point of the visit to the graveyard had been. He fended the questions off until just outside the door, when he turned and said, somewhat cynically, "We must make much of what we have seen." The grave decoration was produced for our waiting friends, whose reaction was less laudatory than circumspect. The next morning, I was questioned by a number of villagers who had not been present the previous evening but who had quickly learned of my trip to the graveyard. Was it true? I misinterpreted their intent. I was quick to proclaim that I had intended no offense and had not known that we were going to "desecrate" a grave by stealing part of the grave decorations. But they seemed unconcerned and simply wanted to know what I had learned. For, as Papa Cerli had made clear, such trips to the graveyard, the interchanges with the spirits of the dead, are a path by which one seeks knowledge of doti.

Such a path is dangerous—not only because of the precocious nature of these spirits, but also because of the long-term effects of the use of doti. While doti offers the power to control others, its continued use over time increasingly makes its material aspects unnecessary. The evil substance thought to grant it power is slowly incorporated into the user, who then makes the transition from being a mere sorcerer to being a werewolf (*pongko*). Such werewolves are able to transform their shape into that of animals. And, at night, their heads separate from their bodies, with entrails dragging below, as they use their flapping ears to fly to their enemies. They eat the livers of their victims, leaving them alive but without a soul, to die slowly over the following days.

Papa Cerli's own quest to master doti was, thus, viewed with a great deal of suspicion and fear. The werewolf disease was also thought to be inherited, and the last werewolf in the village had been Papa Cerli's grandfather. Papa Cerli's grandfather had been an elder in the church, yet, at the end of his life (about twenty years ago), he stood accused of being a werewolf by none other than Papa Cerli himself. As a child, Papa Cerli had related stories of his grandfather's nightly transformations to others. These accusations were widely taken up, leading to panic in the village, a surprise given the grandfather's status as an elder. But, as I pointed out earlier, the role is by its very nature ambiguous; the elder is, ideally, generous and altruistic yet, in practice, greedy and grasping.

These two aspects of the occult, doti and werewolves, are connected yet distinct. Most, like Papa Cerli and Papa Atin, turn to doti in quest of protective magic, not in the quest to harm others as werewolves. Becoming a werewolf is the result of the misuse of doti. Those in quest of protective magic are, rather, seeking protection from the bagagu, the misers who would exploit them. They seek a special class of doti, *opu-opu*, which can protect them from various kinds of harm. Theirs is a tricky path that, because of its ambiguous nature, is full of pitfalls; it can lead to a slide into evil and, thus, to accusations against themselves. But, as Papa Cerli's cynical comment as we emerged from the graveyard indicated, the *reputation* for bravery, for consorting with spirits, for having opu-opu, can be just as important as actually having this magical power: "We must make much of what we have seen." Papa Cerli and Papa Atin both turned to these extratheological powers in an effort to counter the misuse of secular and religious bureaucracies. This was their last-ditch attempt to gain agency in the face of an increasingly governmentalized and "orderly" world where the economic, religious, and political odds were stacked against them. It was only by being "disorderly," by dragging these contests into the realm of occult cosmologies that lie outside the scope of the regimented bureaucracies, that they can use the power of conspiracy to challenge their oppressors.

Papa Atin's graveside quest had failed, and so, too, he had acquiesced to the demands of his familial bagagu/elder. However, Papa Cerli's more successful quests made him a figure of fear and, hence, local power. He was then locked in a hostile dispute with his uncle, a church elder, who was attempting to steal a part of his house lot and demanding that he demolish his kitchen so that the uncle could build his own house there. The uncle was married to the village mayor, so Papa Cerli faced the combined pressures of both church and state. But Papa Cerli was unbowed; fear of his mystic potency served as an effective counter to his apparent weak position in local power relations. Despite the prominence of his opponents, potential corruption was overcome, and Papa Cerli won his case.

Conclusion

By moving from hegemonic state discourses on order, to religious discourses on charity, to occult discourses on power, I hope to have provided a view, "through a glass darkly," of the "occult economy" of Central Sulawesi (Comaroff and Comaroff 1999). This occult landscape is revealed to the uninitiated in moments of conflict, of rebutan, when struggles for an obscurely perceived power assume central stage. Because these battles are fought on the occult plane and offer an alternate view of how the world works, they are cast in dominant discourses as conspiratorial. Here, I have tried to demonstrate how the conspiratorial fears of the people of Central Sulawesi are based in an occult cosmology that links an enculturated Protestantism with an indigenous set of magic and witchcraft beliefs. We should not expect this occult cosmology to have a great deal of internal coherence since it is only ever glimpsed "in part" and revealed through conspiratorial intrigue. I have nonetheless tried to disentangle the multiple layers of these intrigues, to move from the static structures, the rationalized bureaucracies of church and state, to the realm of culture that they seek to order and control. And, like Pemberton, I have tried to show how the disruptive events of rebutan fall outside the incorporated culture (*adat*) regulated by church and state. These events introduce more personal forms of agency by which individuals seek to overcome the corruption that lies at the heart of order.

At one level, conspiratorial fears of Islamic domination of the New Order serve to demonize the state, uncovering its "Festivals of Democracy" as thinly veiled attacks on the church and, hence, on kinship and the ideal of charity. New Order attempts to secularize politics and defuse ethnic tensions are themselves reconstrued as Islamic attacks on the enculturated Christianity through which local ethnic identity manifests itself. The linkage of feasting and preaching within the rational bureaucracy of the church makes it the defender of a kinship sphere made necessary by the commodification of the local economy. This kinship sphere and posintuwu gift exchange are essential for capitalist agricultural production and, hence, have expanded with the introduction of a market economy. Any attack on the church and its feasting tradition thus endangers local livelihoods. But the centralization of power within the bureaucracy of the church and its particular cultural cast both challenge the New Order's own attempts to monopolize power and co-opt culture. The success with which the church has enculturated itself largely defines local ethnicity in religious terms. State attempts to manage ethnicity to fend off ethnic separatism thus impinge on the local power relations holding the church together. New Order attempts to centralize the provision of local services such as education and health under its direct control further impinge on the modernist bureaucracy of the church supported with Dutch mission funds. There is, thus, a real conflict of interest between the church and the state that largely accounts for why the state is the object of local conspiracy theories.

I have also pointed out, however, that the ideal terms in which the kinship sphere has been defined are impossible to live up to. The ideological division of gift and market economies, of the motives of generosity and greed, cannot be so clearly demarcated in practice. Elder siblings are in a unique structural position, one that allows them to be miserly (bagagu), to hoard familial resources; this initial act of greed allows them to practice a family politics of charity while exploiting their kin for unpaid labor and other resources. And these patronage networks serve to entrench them within the church as the elders of the evangelization groups through which much of the feasting is conducted. The ambiguity in the role of elder, at once miserly (bagagu) and yet measured against the kinship ideal of charity, can lead to their potential demonization as pongko, as werewolves. Local discourses on doti and pongko are a means by which the dispossessed may conspiratorially interpret the actions of corrupt church leaders. But, as the case of Papa Cerli made clear, these accusations can easily run both ways. Papa Cerli himself pursued protective doti, spells that would fend off the acquisitive advances of his uncle, the elder; but his own pursuit of doti was feared by others as the slippery path to ultimate evil. The agency that he gained, his ability to fight both church and state, thus comes at a price that he may yet have to pay. And, as my research assistant found that one late night, these occult forces are not always predictable and may choose to remain hidden.

Note

1   *Ecstasy*, the English word used by Papa Atin, was a reference to an altered state of consciousness, but one induced by drugs; the Indonesian news was generally filled with reports of the abuse of Ecstasy tablets in the Jakarta clubs.

References

Bourdieu, Pierre. 1977. *Outline of a Theory of Practice*. Translated by Richard Nice. Cambridge: Cambridge University Press.

Comaroff, Jean, and John L. Comaroff. 1999. "Occult Economies and the Violence of Abstraction: Notes from the South African Postcolony." *American Ethnologist* 26 (2): 279–303.

Daniels, Timothy. 1999. "Imagining Selves and Inventing Festival Srivijaya." *Journal of Southeast Asian Studies* 30 (1): 38–53.

Fortes, Meyer. 1969. *Kinship and the Social Order: The Legacy of Lewis Henry Morgan*. Chicago: Aldine.

Harvey, Barbara S. 1977. *Permesta: Half a Rebellion*. Monograph Series no. 57. Ithaca: Cornell Modern Indonesia Project.

Hefner, Robert W. 1997. "Islamization and Democratization in Indonesia." In *Islam in an Era of Nation-States*, ed. Robert W. Hefner and Patricia Horvatich, 75–127. Honolulu: University of Hawaii Press.

Hutajulu, Rithaony. 1995. "Tourism's Impact on Toba Batak Ceremony." *Bijdragen* (Royal Dutch Anthropological Institute) 151 (4): 639–55.

Kahn, Joel S. 1993. *Constituting the Minangkabau: Peasants, Culture, and Modernity in Colonial Indonesia*. Providence, R.I.: Berg.

Kipp, Rita. 1993. *Dissociated Identities: Ethnicity, Religion, and Class in an Indonesia Society*. Ann Arbor: University of Michigan Press.

Kruyt, Albert C. [1912] 1950. *De Bare'e Sprekende Toradjas van Midden Celebes (de Oost Toradjas).* 3 vols. 2d ed. Verhandelingen der Koninklijke Nederlandse Akademie van Wetenschappen, Afdeling Letterkunde, n.s., vol. 54. Amsterdam: Noord Hollandsche Uitgevers Maatschappij.

Kruyt, Jan. 1970. *Het Zendingsveld Poso: Geschiedenis van Een Konfrontatie.* Kampen: Uitgeversmij J.H. Kok N.V.

Pemberton, John. 1994. *On the Subject of "Java."* Ithaca: Cornell University Press.

Ramage, Douglas E. 1995. *Politics in Indonesia: Democracy, Islam, and the Ideology of Tolerance.* London: Routledge.

Randwijck, S. C. G. van. 1981. *Handelen en Denken in Dienst der Zending: Oegstgeest, 1897-1942.* 's-Gravenhage: Uitgeverij Boekencentrum bv.

Redfield, Robert. 1960. *The Little Community/Peasant Society and Culture.* Chicago: University of Chicago Press.

Schrauwers, Albert. 1995. "The Household and Shared Poverty in the Highlands of Central Sulawesi." *Journal of the Royal Anthropological Institute,* n.s., 1 (2): 337–57.

———. 1999. " 'It's Not Economical': The Market Roots of a Moral Economy." In *Transforming the Indonesian Uplands: Marginality, Power, and Production,* ed. Tania Li, 105-29. London: Harwood Academic.

———. 2000. *Colonial "Reformation" in the Highlands of Central Sulawesi, Indonesia, 1892-1995.* Toronto: University of Toronto Press.

———. 2002. "The Miser's Store: Property and Traditional Law in the Governance of the Economy." *Journal of Peasant Studies* 29 (2): 24-46.

Stuurman, Siep. 1983. *Verzuiling, Kapitalisme en Patriarchaat: Aspecten van de ontwikkeling van den moderne staat in Nederland.* Nijmegen: Socialistiese Uitgeverij Nijmegen.

5

Invisible Hands and Visible Goods: Revealed and Concealed Economies in Millennial Tanzania

TODD SANDERS

[African leaders] must become more accountable to their peoples. Transactions must become more transparent, and funds must be seen to be properly administered, with audit reports made public and procurement procedures overhauled.

—World Bank, *Sub-Saharan Africa* (1989)

The capacity to govern well in Africa is developing but still limited. Technical capacity is weak. Accountability and transparency are lacking.

—World Bank, *Adjustment in Africa* (1994)

Transparency is a major watchword—if not *the* major watchword—for policymakers, politicians, and other proponents of "modernity" at this *début de siècle*. In the United States today, this observation is as patent as it is pedestrian. Discourses of transparency permeate an array of American political arenas ranging from the Freedom of Information Act to the periodic unfolding of various presidential "-gates": Nixon's Watergate, Reagan's Irangate, Clinton's Zippergate. "We have the right to know," or so the public and media often proclaim. From this vantage point, openness is desirable, while things hidden from view are morally untenable. For only when political doings (and, naturally, their *un*doings) are revealed in full can people be held accountable for their actions.[1]

Nor is this solely an American preoccupation. All across the globe, modernity's mouthpieces place a heavy emphasis on, for instance, transparency in democratic processes, free elections in which all dealings are open to scrutiny, and the importance of such public visibility for legitimating those processes (e.g., Dundas 1994; Koffi 1993; Scholte 1998; Shukla 1998). The notion of transparency similarly lies central to the everyday operation of myriad transnational institutions like the United Nations, the European Union, the World Bank, the World Trade Organization, the International Monetary Fund, and various nongovernmental organizations (Clamers 1997; Kopits and Craig 1998; Kratz 1999; Marceau and Pedersen 1999). Whether uncovering covert weapons of mass destruction, monitoring electoral processes in far-flung locales, or revealing hidden (and sometimes hideous) realities through truth and reconciliation commissions or war tribunals, such institutions frequently operate on the assumption that obscurity and the New World Order are fundamentally at odds. A modern world must be a transparent world.

This desire to unveil the hidden, to disclose the closed, to reveal the concealed—in short, to make transparent that which is out of sight—is as central to economic processes as it is to political ones (Larsson and Lundberg 1998). Hardly surprising, really, given the popular Western view that political and economic liberalization are mutually intertwined (see Callaghy 1993). To provide but one example, the IMF has, in the interests of promoting democracy, continually insisted on radical economic restructuring across the globe, calling for the decentralization and privatization of state-run enterprises. In persistently asking probing questions about who controls what economic resources, to what ends, and for whose benefit, developers aim to make visible an underlying market-run rationality, to make transparent the everyday workings of local and global economies.

This is as true for Africa as elsewhere, as the epigraphs to this essay suggest: there can be no "development," no "modernization," until economic transactions are laid bare, until they are rendered "transparent" for all to see. To be truly modern, so the reasoning goes, our world simply *must* be transparent. Where it is not, we must make it so. In this respect, transparency is both a process and an outcome—it is modernity's moral compulsion as well as its characteristic feature, at once its motor and its message.

Yet, if modernity is characterized by "intensive reflexivity" (Eisenstadt 2000: 3; Giddens 1990: 36ff.), as Max Weber long ago assured us it was (see Faubion 1993: 113–15), it is somewhat surprising that *transparency,* one of the most conspicuous of modernity's current tropes, has received so little sustained analytical attention. All the more so when we notice that, in the real world, modernity and transparency rarely march hand-in-hand.

Take Tanzania. Many Tanzanians are today skeptical that modernity, in any form, necessarily coincides with transparency and accountability, as many Western proponents claim it should. This skepticism is multifaceted but results in part from their historical experiences with their northern neighbors in Kenya.

On the face of it, postcolonial Kenya has been one of the most enthusiastic supporters of the ideology of transparent political and economic processes. They have held elections. They have encouraged free enterprise. And they have fostered the private ownership of land. Perhaps unremarkably, given the Kenyan government's seeming modern line, Western developers have believed and encouraged their efforts in the form of massive amounts of economic capital that have flowed, and continue to flow, into the country.

Yet what seems to capture many Tanzanians' imaginations is, not these lofty ideals of transparency, but rather the "politics of the belly" (Bayart 1993) evident in the workings of the modern Kenyan system. For simmering beneath the surface of claims to transparency and rationality lurks the seedy underside of modern African governmentality: obscure but determining political intrigues from the lowest to the highest levels; elites who publicly espouse openness and fair competition but offstage accumulate staggering amounts of personal wealth—houses and automobiles, livestock and land—often through shadowy dealings with fellow "tribesmen," friends, and colleagues. As a result, many Tanzanians see the Kenyan model of modernity, *not* as a model of clarity or rationality, but as the very epitome of obscurity and ill-understood processes.[2] Modernity, from this perspective, breeds ambiguity not transparency.

This is certainly the view held by the Ihanzu of northern Tanzania, with whom I have lived and carried out fieldwork since the early 1990s. For these people—and the Ihanzu are scarcely alone here—modernity as locally envisaged and experienced is not about revealing but about concealing the powers that animate their world. As the Ihanzu are increasingly drawn into broader regional, national, and international markets and political structures, a process that has been ongoing for well over a century, the operation of powers in their world has been made not more rational, clear, or comprehensible but less so. This is an obfuscating process: a movement from relative understanding to virtual incomprehension, a subtle but certain undoing of all that is done. The irony, of course, is that Ihanzu experiences with modernity have proved precisely the opposite to what Western liberal visions would predict.

Today, we find, somewhat unexpectedly, one of the clearest Ihanzu statements on modernity in local discourses on witchcraft. But why witchcraft? As people modernize, shouldn't witchcraft and other "traditions" fade into oblivion, as Marx, Durkheim, and Weber each in his own way assured us they would? Hardly. African witchcraft has, it turns out, proved engagingly flexible and inflexibly engaged with novel postcolonial realities (Ashforth 1996; Auslander 1993; Comaroff and Comaroff 1993, in press; Geschiere 1997). Witchcraft is a discourse of the moment, speaking, in so many ways, to the conundrums of our contemporary world. It provides a particular sort of social diagnostic (Moore and Sanders 2001). How, exactly, this is so for the Ihanzu is the principal focus of this essay.

My argument runs as follows. In the Ihanzu cultural imagination, modernity is, above all, a world of modern material goods. Such modern goods circulate differently than what they call *traditional* goods do. While both modern and traditional goods are reputedly moved through the economy by the unseen powers of witchcraft, the powers that animate traditional transactions can be *seen*—by diviners and by the zero-sum logic made manifest in such processes. And, because they are seen, they are also understood. The powers that ensure the circulation of modern goods remain, in contrast, entirely hidden from view. The circulation, accumulation, and destruction of modern goods do not betray the powers of the hidden logics that drive such processes. Nor can such obscure logics be uncovered through divination. It therefore remains unclear whether accumulating modern goods necessarily implies, as it does with traditional goods, destroying the wealth of others. This has ensured that Ihanzu encounters with modernity remain, above all, deeply ambivalent.

To begin, we need to paint, with broad brushstrokes, a picture of Tanzania today and situate Ihanzu on this canvas. Only then can we begin to appreciate the extent to which Ihanzu witchcraft single-mindedly seeks out the sense—and the senselessness—of a rapidly changing postcolonial world.

Millennial Moments in the Tanzanian Postcolony

In recent years, the contours of Tanzania's postcolonial landscape have changed in remarkable ways. So much so, in fact, that the term *postcolonial* itself has little meaning, given the homogenizing demands that it makes on a nation that has continually transformed itself since independence in 1961. The advent of these changes, changes that would forever alter the nascent nation's cultural, political, and economic landscapes, can be traced to President Julius Nyerere's renowned program of African Socialism. *Ujamaa,* as it was known, was arguably the grandest social experiment ever attempted in Tanzania. Its avowed aim was to transform Tanzania into a modern nation-state, its populace into modern citizens. Crucially, this would be a "meaningful modernity," a modernity on Tanzanians' own terms, the parameters of which would not be dictated by the West.

Ujamaa had broad philosophical underpinnings. In theory, it was a "non-Marxist socialism" (Tripp 1997: 62) that many saw as uniquely African, at least insofar as it was informed by notions of unity (*umoja*) and self-reliance (*kujitegemea*) within the world system (see Nyerere 1968). In practice, ujamaa followed a Chinese model of state centralization, whereby administrative powers were highly concentrated in the central government and delegated to local-level authorities in diminishing amounts. Following the famous 1967 Arusha Declaration, in particular, the state's involvement in the economy grew dramatically, leading to the nationalization of major commercial, financial, and manufacturing institutions.[3] Borders with neighboring countries were closed; severe import restrictions on foreign goods and currencies were imposed; emphasis was placed on production within the nation, for the nation—a nation of citizens toiling for the good of all Tanzanians. For a number of complex reasons, ujamaa did not survive over the long run.

By the time I arrived in Tanzania in the early 1990s, the draconian Socialist edifice called *ujamaa* was on its last leg. The gradual yet irreversible withering of the omnipresent state had been under way for some years. And now, in the 1990s, a number of factors coalesced that would transform Tanzania's political and economic landscapes forever.

Central to these changes was the Zanzibar Declaration of 1991, as it later came to be known, which boldly challenged the 1967 Arusha Declaration and led to a number of consequential "amendments" to it, amendments that, in reality, radically undermined rather than updated the Arusha Declaration's original vision. "The symbolic importance of these changes," notes Tripp, "cannot be emphasized strongly enough, for the Arusha Declaration was the central document in establishing the egalitarian, self-reliant, and socialist orientation that Tanzania adopted" (1997: 171). A new "open" Tanzania now sat tantalizingly on the horizon. And this novel vision permeated every imaginable domain.

By 1992, Tanzania's ruling Revolutionary Party, the Chama Cha Mapinduzi (CCM), had allowed independent political parties to register. Within a few years, Tanzania's first ever multiparty elections were held. The party has since surrendered its stranglehold over the media. The three officially sanctioned, government-owned newspapers now circulate alongside a multitude of locally produced newspapers, tabloids, and magazines, not to mention any number of international news sources. The single state radio station has, of late, been joined by manifold others from near and far, and listeners tune in to listen to news, soccer matches, and other items of interest. Additionally, mainland Tanzania saw its first ever television broadcast in 1994. Today, urban and some rural citizens can watch the private network ITV, which broadcasts local and foreign serials and newscasts as well as many American sitcoms, soaps, and action movies. Furthermore, many urbanites in Dar es Salaam, Arusha, and other bustling centers now have regular access to cable and satellite systems that offer programming from around the globe.

Coinciding with these far-reaching political changes has been economic liberalization. In the early 1990s, the second president of the United Republic of Tanzania, Ali Hassan Mwinyi, opted publicly and categorically for the wholesale adoption of the IMF's structural adjustment program in a bid to transform Tanzania into a viable post-Socialist state. Several international banks like Standard Charter and Barclay's have, following their postindependence expulsions, reestablished themselves or are actively taking steps to do so. No longer do foreign-exchange restrictions apply; U.S. dollars and other foreign currencies can now be readily—and legally—exchanged at any number of *bureaux de change*. Formerly tightly controlled or closed terrestrial borders with neighboring countries have all been reopened, and everyday and luxury consumer goods (formerly controlled by the state) today flow en masse across them.

It is in the cities that these dramatic changes have most radically reconfigured people's life worlds. Privately owned shops are filled with consumer goods of every type imaginable. The informal economy is booming (Tripp 1997). Street markets bustle with urbanites, young and old, buying imported radios and CD players, designer-label jeans and other clothing. Following decades of shortages under ujamaa, enterprising Tanzanians have today filled their country with a plethora of new consumer goods—and dreams for a better future. "Ujamaa is dead," one Dar es Salaam street vendor enthusiastically told me in 1999. "Today, if we try, we can have anything we want!"

But such dreams are not always good ones and can just as easily become nightmares. For, as wealth in the shops and among an elite class of individuals increases, so, too, across a much broader segment of the population do relative poverty, envy, and untenable and unobtainable dreams of a vastly better future. On this score, ordinary Tanzanians recognize full well that economic liberalization has come with devastating costs (Kaiser 1996; Lugalla 1995, 1997; Ponte 1998).

As this suggests, there is a certain "millennial capitalism" (Comaroff and Comaroff 1999) in the air that appears to have affected—or, more correctly, *infected*—many Tanzanians. By *millennial capitalism,* I mean, not simply "capitalism at the millennium," but, more fundamentally, "capitalism invested with salvific force[,] with intense faith in its capacity, if rightly harnessed, wholly to transform the universe of the marginalized and disempowered" (Comaroff and Comaroff, in press). Indeed, while such millennial capitalism has recently reared its head across the globe, it has done so most spectacularly in postrevolutionary places like Eastern Europe, the former Soviet Union, and Tanzania, "where there has been an abrupt conversion to laissez-faire capitalism from tightly regulated material and moral economies; where evocative calls for entrepreneurialism confront the realities of marginalization in the planetary distribution of resources; where totalizing ideologies have suddenly given way to a spirit of deregulation, with its taunting mix of desire and disappointment, liberation and limitation" (Comaroff and Comaroff, in press). In such overdetermined circumstances, many Tanzanians feel, paradoxically, that they can do anything, and nothing at all, to better their situation.

No Tanzanian is today unaware of the country's recent, monumental transformations. The extent to which they have participated in them is, however, quite another matter. For, even as new idioms of *demokrasia* and "the free market" (*soko huria*) have taken hold and blazed, like wildfires, across the land, they have done so in a jerky and irregular manner. Economic liberalization has, on the whole, been an uneven process. The people of Ihanzu, like Tanzanians everywhere, are eager to come to terms with the sweeping changes that have recently arrived—if only piecemeal—on their doorstep.

The Ihanzu live over some six hundred square miles in north-central Tanzania, in the northernmost part of Iramba District.[4] This semiarid, relatively remote region is poorly connected to Tanzania's major urban centers: it is a ten-hour drive from Arusha, most of this on irregular, unpaved roads; it is even further from Dar es Salaam. The Ihanzu are predominantly agriculturalists and subsist in their precarious environment on sorghum, millet, and maize. These grains are used to make *ūgalī,* a stiff porridge that forms the basis of all meals. Sorghum also forms an important source of cash income when made into beer. Grain is rarely sold since there are no local markets for the sale of foodstuffs. Nor, given the often-unforgiving climate, is there ever much excess grain that could be sold anyway. Rainfall in this region is far from certain. Droughts and famines are common.

These harsh realities notwithstanding, of late, at this particular millennial moment, Ihanzu has experienced a veritable flood of modern consumer wares—or at least this is true for the better-connected parts of Ihanzu. One such place is the village of Ibaga.

Ibaga is located in western Ihanzu. While the village first appeared on the map in the early 1960s, it was only with the demise of ujamaa policies and the increased opening up of the economy through the 1990s that business interests skyrocketed. Today, Ibaga is home to five guest houses, a small restaurant, a high proportion of zinc-roofed homes, eight reasonably large, well-stocked shops, two petrol-powered grinding machines, and three fairly regular bus services that connect what has now become a regional economic trading center with the larger town of Singida and the city of Arusha. One particularly enterprising shopkeeper even has a generator that powers the only television and video player for hundreds of miles. It is here, too, in Ibaga, that people from all over Ihanzu come to purchase Tanzanian-made and imported products at a thriving monthly market. In comparison with the rest of Ihanzu, Ibaga has an abundance of modern material goods and goodies, all of which have provided fodder for imagining what a "modern" Ihanzu might look like and the powers that might make such a possibility into a reality.

One of the most intractable problems that villagers face has been coming to terms with the production, circulation, and consumption of these newly arrived modern goods—establishing, in other words, a meaningful relation between distant sites of production and local sites of consumption. How, exactly, do local shopkeepers, businesspersons, and others attract and amass modern wealth (cf. Bastian, chapter 2 in this volume)? It is at this juncture that witchcraft enters the picture. To see how and why, we must first consider Ihanzu notions of modernity and tradition and the colonial context from which they sprang.

"Modernity," "Tradition," and the Ihanzu Historical Experience

The aim of this section is to outline the role that German and British colonial powers played in Ihanzu, first, in reifying the categories *tradition* and *modernity* and, second, in filling these categories with meaning. There are three principle points that I wish to make. First, colonial and postcolonial administrators envisage(d) a world sharply divided between tradition and modernity.

Second, in these imaginings, tradition is about "things local," while modernity is about "things distant." And, finally, the Ihanzu today largely subscribe to this historically prevailing discourse on tradition and modernity, in terms of both the categories and the contents (see also Sanders, in press). In the sections that follow, I turn more directly to the role that witchcraft plays in imagining modernity today.

German and British colonial officials never found Ihanzu an easy place to deal with. In fact, from the first—and bloody—colonial encounter with the Ihanzu in 1893, European colonial powers considered the Ihanzu "primitive," "superstitious," and "tradition-bound."[5] Of course, these views were commonly held by colonials almost everywhere they landed, given the at-the-time-prevailing social evolutionary paradigm through which they saw the world. Yet Ihanzu's distant location and harsh climate nurtured these images to a greater degree than might otherwise have been possible.

As far as colonial power centers were concerned, Ihanzu remained well off the beaten track. The German-built fort at the Ihanzu village of Mkalama was one of the most remote and undesirable postings in the whole of Deutsch Ost Afrika. At least one German officer died and was buried there. When British forces took over the fort following the First World War, they fared little better. By 1919, only a year or so later, no fewer than nine British political officers had come and gone owing to the "notoriously unhealthy climate" (TNA 1919–20: 2, 22). In most British administrators' minds, Ihanzu truly was "the back of beyond" (RH ca. 1928).

Given the ever-present uncertainties of the climate and Ihanzu's relatively distant location, German and British administrators alike considered Ihanzu an improbable site for large-scale, intensive cash cropping.[6] Accordingly, throughout the colonial era, comparatively few efforts were made to improve local infrastructures. The "primitive" people of Ihanzu were instead looked on more as a labor reserve for other, more fertile parts of the country. If these people were to be "developed" or "modernized," they would have to enter the modern sphere, not at home as producers, but in distant locations as migrant laborers. The Ihanzu, like their neighbors, have, thus, been forced to trek long distances in search of labor—to urban centers like Singida and Arusha—since the Germans first imposed taxes in the area around the turn of the last century (Adam 1963a; Iliffe 1979: 161; TNA 1924: 2; TNA 1957).

British administrators posted in Ihanzu never entirely abandoned hope that these "tradition-bound" people might one day become "modern," however, even in the villages. Consider one district commissioner's comments in the 1920s concerning a recently inaugurated Ihanzu chief:

The authority, Asmani, comes of a line of rainmakers, but having spent the last seven years in the K[ings] A[frican] R[ifles] [in Dar es Salaam] prior to succeeding to the chiefship this year on the death of his uncle, Kali, it is more than probable that he does not know much about the art which was always jealously guarded by old Kali [the previous "chief"]. As far as can be ascertained, Asmani has not been initiated in accordance with tribal custom. It is anticipated therefore that rainmaking will not play such a prominent part in the tribal life as hitherto.

Asmani is a self-confident, large moustached, pushing native, addicted to European silk suiting and Panama hats. The Assistant District Officer informs me that he feels quite ashamed of his own poor khaki when Asmani strolls in to give him good-day.

. . . When he has become used to the change from private in the K.A.R. to leader of a tribe he will probably be quite a useful man. (TNA 1927: 12)

Among other things, these remarks show, first, how some colonial administrators serving in Ihanzu sharply differentiated between "traditional" things like rainmaking and more "modern" things like European silk suits and Panama hats and, second, how the former would eventually, it was hoped, be overcome by the latter. Additionally, they point up a particular colonial spatial imagining: distant is to modern as local is to traditional. The fact that Chief Asmani had lived far away from Ihanzu during his military service and donned European garments made him more progressive and modern in colonial eyes. It was, thus, thought that he would prove "quite a useful man," as chief, in wrenching the Ihanzu people from the traditional, locally focused world that they reputedly inhabited.

Colonial administrators' beliefs that the Ihanzu were traditional, combined with their policies on migrant labor and local (non)development, largely account for the situation in Ihanzu today. The few roads are unsealed and rarely graded. There is no electricity, no telephone access, and few working water pumps. The few government dispensaries are poorly stocked and often have no medicines at all. Even though Ihanzu has long been enmeshed in the modern world system, it bears few material markers that might underscore this point.

Today, postcolonial administrators continue to discuss the people of Ihanzu—if they discuss them at all—as an archetypal tradition-minded people. In a decidedly uncomfortable encounter with the district commissioner in 1995, I was told:

Well, you know, the chiefs here in Tanzania for a long time stopped modernity [*maendeleo*]. They kept people from becoming modern [*watu wa kisasa*]. They were against education, against good roads, against business, and against change. They only wanted old customs [*mila za zamani*], not modernity. Perhaps it's better that the chief stays there in Kirumi with his rainshrine. He had many years to send modernity backwards [*kurudisha nyuma maendeleo*]. Now they're gone, and the government's here. We will develop these people! Eh, I have yet to receive any of your reports from your work here. . . . I'd be very interested to read them. I think there might even be some cultural factors that are stopping these people from becoming modern, something I don't know about.

Anthropologists are not the only ones subjected to such unfortunate views. Worse still, the men and women of Ihanzu are regularly chastised for their alleged offense, as I discovered at many public, government meetings in the 1990s. "You should build modern houses with large windows, cement floors, and tin roofs, not miserable *matembe* like your grandparents built," demanded the district commissioner on one such occasion. The implication of such patronizing harangues, both today and in the past, is that the Ihanzu and the things they do are traditional and backward and that things modern are found elsewhere, usually in distant, urban places.[7] These discourses, their origins far from innocent, have given definitive shape to villagers' own conceptions of the categories *tradition* and *modernity* (see Sanders, in press).

In Ihanzu eyes, the categories of tradition (*jadi* or *mila*) and modernity (*maendeleo*) are conceptually and practically distinct. Everything in their cultural universe can, so I was told, be fitted into one of these two diametrically opposed categories. When Ihanzu men and women discuss tradition, they often imply that it is made up of timeless, unchanging artifacts and behaviors. This is the expressed ideal. Nevertheless, practices can and do belie these ideals since what counts as tradition—take annual rainmaking rites (cf. Adam 1963b; and Sanders 1998)—has sometimes changed dramatically over the years. Moreover, some things that are today considered traditional have been outright invented in recent years. For instance, in a 1986 battle over cattle between the Ihanzu, Iramba, and Sukuma, on the one hand, and the pastoral Datooga and Maasai, on the other, a Sukuma vigilante organization known as Sungusungu was used to great effect against the pastoralists.[8] The Ihanzu created their own version of this organization, which they call Nkili. It has since been expanded to include, not only cases of cattle theft, but theft of all sorts as well as some witchcraft cases. Nkili, people say, deals with things traditional and is therefore itself traditional. Other things are considered appropriate for their inclusion in the category *tradition* because of their apparent longevity.

Starting fires with sticks, for example, rather than with matches is said to be traditional since "this is how the ancestors did it." Other activities are similarly said to be traditional and, in theory, unchanging: all rainmaking rites; rain witchcraft; building mud and stick houses; cultivating sorghum and millet; brewing beer; hunting with bows and arrows; and herding. By extension, certain things are considered "traditional wealth": royal rainstones; rainmaking medicines; grain crops; livestock; mud and stick homes; and children, among other things. Note that "things traditional" are all thought to come from home. It is here, in the villages, that such traditional things are normally produced, exchanged, and consumed. "Things modern" (*mambo a kisasa*), to the contrary, are invariably produced in and linked to faraway places—the cities of Arusha and Singida or, better still, Europe, America, and (given Tanzania's postindependence ujamaa polices) China.

Although modernity means many things to many people—Christianity, sealed roads, street lamps, and well-stocked hospitals—modernity's overriding feature for most Ihanzu is its blatant and unrelenting materiality. More than anything else, the Ihanzu imagine modernity as a "world of goods," to borrow Douglas and Isherwood's (1979) phrase. But not any goods will do. More precisely, it is manufactured material goods that are not—and cannot—be produced at home in the villages. Bicycles, radios, plastic pitchers, tinned food, motorized transport, and zinc-roofed houses are the stuff of modernity for most Ihanzu today. The origins, the movements, and, frequently, the consumption of such modern goods are translocal in nature.

In the light of the Ihanzu's colonial and postcolonial experiences and their current understandings of modernity and tradition, it is wholly unremarkable that they see modernity as something possessed by other peoples in other places, something experienced briefly in the cities during wage labor and left behind when returning home. For this reason, modernity is something that by definition lies beyond their grasp, almost. This is also why Ibaga village—the only plausible local example of modernity in the making—has recently proved the site of such avid speculation.

"Traditional" and "modern" wealth are thought to move differently through the economy (see also Sanders 1999). What I hope to show in what follows—and this is the crux of my argument—is that the powers that ensure the circulation of traditional wealth can be rendered visible and, thus, comprehensible while those concerning the circulation of modern wealth cannot and, thus, remain, all told, mystified and mystifying.

Seen and Unseen Realms, Witchcraft and "Traditional" Wealth

The Ihanzu divide their world into two distinct realms. The first is the manifest world, the world that is visible and "obvious" to all. Herein lies the stuff of people's everyday existence: farming; herding; political dealings; economic exchanges; and so on.

The second world is unseen and runs parallel to the first. This is the realm of witches (*alogi*), ancestral spirits (*alũngũ*), and God (*itunda*). There is nothing particularly "wondrous" or "awe-inspiring" (Murphy 1998) about this invisible realm or the powers that operate within it. I would for this reason be reluctant to label it *supernatural* since such labels risk exoticization. Rather, this realm and its powers are very much a part of the Ihanzu lived-in world—albeit an invisible part of that world—and can more accurately be understood as "public secrets" (Ashforth 1996: 1194) that are both everyday and commonplace. People sometimes talk about the inner workings of this second realm as a "true secret" (*sili tai*) since such processes are, given their invisibility, poorly understood. Be that as it may, as we shall see momentarily, seers, as well as the visible effects of at least some types of witchcraft, provide enough clues for people to have a fairly good idea of how these hidden powers operate.

These visible and invisible realms are thought to be causally linked in that power originates in the unseen realm and has visible effects in the everyday world. That is, the world that the Ihanzu inhabit in their day-to-day lives is animated by unseen forces from another realm, the ultimate source of all cosmic power.[9] Hidden powers determine public outcomes. Thus, as with the logic of conspiracy theories, most everyday activities in Ihanzu—be they politics, economic transactions, or whatever—are thought to be guided and shaped in fundamental ways by invisible powers. Our everyday world is simply a facade that masks a deeper, more important and "real reality," one that lies beyond our immediate comprehension (Ashforth 1996: 1220; Douglas 1970: xvi).

Obscure though this second realm may be, not everyone is excluded from it. Ihanzu seers (*aganga;* sing. *mũganga*), in particular, are precariously poised between visible and invisible worlds. And they allegedly move freely between them. I use the term *seer*—rather than, say, *diviner, healer,* or anything else—

intentionally, to emphasize the visual nature of their perceptual powers. Seers allegedly experience the unseen realm of power firsthand, usually at night, by smearing special medicines (*makota*) just above their eyes. This enables them "to see" (*kūona*) witches in action (cf. Goody 1970: 227). Witches, for their part, are said to use similar medicines smeared above their eyes to make themselves invisible to mere mortals.

If seers participate in and, thus, understand the invisible realm of power, they can also access that world through divination sessions. Seers *see* clearly the determining powers of events in this world, past, present, and future, as inscribed on their chicken oracles. Seers and others sometimes described such oracles (*nzelya*) to me as "traditional X-rays" (*X-ray za kinyeji*), once again underscoring the visual nature of such perceptual powers. During divination sessions, seers are said *to see* witches, spirits, problems, and answers while reading (*kūsoma*) their X-ray chickens' entrails. With their in*sights* into the invisible realm of witches, seers can reputedly understand the truth (*tai*) about witches—who they are, what they do, and how they do it.

Traditionally, one of witches' favorite ploys has been to destroy other people's wealth in order to amass it for themselves. Grain in particular, usually sorghum, seems to be the type of wealth most coveted by witches. Sometimes they are said to use their powers to amass livestock too. When it comes to accumulating so-called traditional wealth through witchcraft, all methods imply an economy of limited good or a zero-sum game economy. In other words, traditional wealth exists, in Ihanzu eyes, "in finite quantity and is always in short supply" (Foster 1965: 296). What the witch takes others lose. Seers see this only too well—in the invisible realm and in their chickens' entrails. They can see clearly, so I was told, which witch has stolen what from whom. The operation of so-called traditional power is transparent, not only to the seer, but to ordinary villagers too. This is due to the visible traces that such hidden powers leave in the everyday world, including, as we shall see, wealth differentials generated between haves and have-nots.

There are a few methods that witches reputedly use to accumulate so-called traditional goods. The first is to suck the sorghum from fellow villagers' plots and onto their own with the aid of certain medicines. Men and women commonly claim that a witch often farms a small parcel of land but reaps an unusually large harvest. For this reason, many of those who regularly obtain large harvests are rumored to have dabbled in the diabolical to acquire their goods, implying that other villagers have been robbed. When it comes to traditional wealth like grain, Ihanzu witches can, therefore, rightly be considered mystical thieves (cf. Heald 1986). I know of several villagers who, having rapidly acquired unusual amounts of grain, are rumored to have done so at other villagers' immediate expense. As one woman told me, "You go out to your field and find that your sorghum has ripened but that it is all rubbish. There's nothing [no grain] there. It has been sucked to some witch's plot." It may not be obvious who, exactly, got what from whom. Or at least not obvious to ordinary villagers. But there is no doubt that one farmer's gain is another's loss.

A second method that witches allegedly use to amass traditional wealth is medicinally to attack and kill people in order to appropriate their labor. The following story, one that virtually anyone in Ihanzu could provide, tells of how this is supposedly done:

> Witches ride their hyenas through the night to find people and bewitch them. They are invisible, you know, because they put medicines on like this [indicating smearing just above the eyes] . . . . That person dies later, maybe in a week or a year. The witch then goes to the grave and pulls the corpse from the ground with medicines like this [indicating touching a medicinally covered index finger on the ground]. The witch takes this corpse home, puts medicine on its eyes so you can't see it, and makes it work on his fields at night. Sometimes these zombies [atumbūka] brew beer too and cook for the witch.

In this particular vision, the ever-consuming witch does nothing whatsoever except eat—quite literally—the fruits of the exploited zombie labor force in the form of stiff porridge, beer, and human labor.[10] In a similar but less extreme vein, witches sometimes steal peoples' souls at night but return them by morning; these souls are made to assist the witch in farming and other domestic duties. The hapless victim is said to wake with an aching and exhausted body. As with stolen grain from a neighbor's field, both these nefarious methods of obtaining labor imply an economy of limited good. In terms of traditional wealth like sorghum, a witch gains only what others lose, something of which all villagers are ruefully aware.

Another means that witches reputedly use to gain traditional wealth is to make a "pact with a seer" (ndagū). A witch-to-be may visit a seer with the aim of accumulating extraordinary amounts of traditional wealth. This wealth may be in the form of children, livestock, or grain, although the latter two are more common.[11] The seer, who knows about such matters from his participation in the invisible world, is said to provide the necessary medicine to make such things happen. But accumulating wealth in this way comes only at a cost, and a high one: the party in question must forgo one form of wealth—frequently childbearing capabilities—to amass another like grain or livestock. Consider the following case, itself iconic of many others.

There is a well-known middle-aged couple who live in the village of Matongo. This couple, it is rumored, are witches. Msa, as I will call him, is a reasonably well-to-do Christian man. He and his wife, Maria, also a Christian, own and farm unusually large tracts of land: three acres near their home, one acre in Maria's father's village, and another thirteen acres in a third village. In their house they have three large grain stores that provide ample grain for them and their two adopted children even in the worst famine years. This, together with nineteen cows, twenty-six goats, five sheep, and thirtysome chickens, makes them one of the wealthiest families in the area, at least in terms of "traditional" measures of wealth.

The fact that their children are adopted is not, villagers claim, incidental. Maria is infertile. Their children are in reality those of Msa's sister, a fact that everyone (except Msa and Maria) was eager to make apparent to me. But most are unsympathetic, for Msa has allegedly made a pact with a seer in which he willingly exchanged his wife's childbearing capabilities for a guarantee of copious quantities of livestock and grain. As such, it is said that the couple will be wealthy for life in terms of livestock and grain, though decidedly and irrevocably impoverished when it comes to children.

There are additional factors in this case worth noting. First, several villagers told me that Maria's breasts fluctuate in size inversely with the amount of grain in their grain stores. Thus, before the harvest, when grain stores are at their lowest levels, Maria's breasts are said to swell to considerable proportions. Conversely, when grain stores are filled to the hilt, just after the harvest, her breasts are virtually nonexistent.[12] This seasonal waxing and waning of breasts and crops points up in a somewhat conspicuous manner the direct trade-off imagined between different types of wealth and fertility, in this case, crops versus childbearing capabilities.

The foregoing should make it abundantly clear that those goods considered traditional—namely, grain, livestock, and progeny—are thought to circulate, one against the other, in what amounts to a zero-sum economy (cf. Meyer 1995; Gable 1997). Witches benefit only by depriving other villagers (or, with the ndagū pact, themselves) of their wealth. Whether sorghum is sucked directly from one plot to another or acquired less directly by killing and then appropriating the deceased's labor power, the witch's gain is the moral man's loss. Within this discourse, the traditional Ihanzu witch is simultaneously the prime accumulator *and* the consumer of material wealth. Witches' powers over the circulation of traditional wealth operate within a conceptually and geographically closed universe. For traditional wealth, the sites of production and consumption are virtually the same.

Seers know this. They can "see" the operation of invisible powers in their X-ray chickens. And they can even enter the invisible world of witches, if and when necessary, to get a better look. All other villagers know that so-called traditional goods circulate in this way too. Such goods are locally produced and are always in limited supply. They cannot be created from thin air. Thus, although the invisible realm of power is not open to inspection by ordinary villagers under ordinary circumstances, the modus operandi of those powers is plain enough. Witches must destroy to accumulate. The everyday effects of witchcraft involving traditional goods render its operational logic transparent—or at least transparent enough for people to make sense of the relation between occult power and traditional wealth. This is manifestly *not* the case when it comes to so-called modern economic processes.

Witchcraft and the Circulation of "Modern" Wealth

If witchcraft is often evoked in Ihanzu to understand the circulation of traditional goods, this is also the case with modern goods. Not unexpectedly, the powers of this (im)moral economy operate in roughly the same way. Invisible powers continue to determine the visible world. And witches, so people claim, continue doggedly to accumulate and destroy things. Yet there is at least one crucial difference between economies of traditional and modern goods that should give us pause: the workings of witches' powers in "modern" contexts are no longer obvious. Diviners claim not to be able to see them (cf. Kendall, chapter 1 in this volume). Ordinary people claim no longer to understand them. These invisible powers thus remain deeply ambivalent. To show why, I must provide further details.

On witches destroying modern wealth, the Ihanzu Lutheran preacher had this to say: "If a witch were clever perhaps they would use hyenas to carry sorghum home from their fields! But that would be progress/modernity [*maendeleo*], and the witch is against that. Instead they ride aimlessly through the night . . . to bewitch their own clanmates and children. This is the work of the witch in Ihanzu, stupidity taken to an extreme. Witches destroy—that's their job—people and progress."

In Ihanzu, such views are common. Witches, all seem to agree, intensely dislike development, modernity, or progress, all terms glossed as *maendeleo*. In this sense, Ihanzu witches, ever envious of their better-off neighbors, reinforce the familiar ethos of "keeping-behind-the-Joneses" or "nightmare egalitarianism" (Gable 1997) commonly found across Africa (Gluckman 1956: 96; Winter 1956: 147; Ardener 1970: 147–48; Fisiy and Geschiere 1991: 253). One shopkeeper in Ibaga village put it like this: "Most Ihanzu don't do business because they're afraid of their neighbors [i.e., witches], who won't allow them to get ahead [*kuendelea*]."

Another Ibaga shop owner I knew well, a Sukuma man by birth, told me the following: "There is something you must understand. Sukuma witches are ruthless, their medicines more powerful than those of the Ihanzu [witches]. The difference, though, is that Sukuma witches are not jealous [*wivu*] and so don't care if individuals prosper. . . . Ihanzu witches are different; they don't want people to modernize [*kuendelea*]; if they see someone is getting ahead, he gets bewitched."

Over the course of my fieldwork, I recorded many cases where unspecified witches allegedly destroyed modern goods in Ihanzu: ripping zinc roofs from people's homes with their medicines; compelling buses to crash into rocks, trees, and ditches or simply to stop dead in their tracks; stealing and joyriding on buses on nocturnal forays at ridiculous speeds through the bush; ruining petrol-powered grinding machines by causing snakes, hyraxes, and other small animals to enter and jam their inner gears. All such stories suggest that the Ihanzu witch and modernity cannot peacefully coexist. It comes as no surprise, then, to discover that men and women regularly evoke witchcraft to explain what they see as the failure of modernity in Ihanzu. Witches have always destroyed wealth. They continue to do so in its more modern forms.

But this is not the whole story. For, tellingly, people are not certain that witches attack modern wealth in order to accumulate it for themselves, as they supposedly do with "traditional" wealth. Their stories instead suggest that antimodern witches are more ridiculous than scheming and may gain nothing themselves for their dubious destructive efforts. Accumulation and destruction of so-called modern wealth appear *not* to be directly linked, a fact evident in what people say about local shopkeepers, their wealth, and the occult powers that they supposedly deploy to acquire it.

It was noted that, today, in the wake of Tanzania's recent liberalization of its economy, Ibaga village provides many Ihanzu with a convenient local example of modernity in the making. This village, and, more specifically, those who do business there, are often the subject of intense speculation and suspicion of witchcraft. No one else in Ihanzu has so much and does, so it seems, so little to get it. Shop shelves are piled high with seemingly endless supplies of modern consumer goods—pots and pans in all imaginable and unimaginable shapes and sizes; cloth; oil; mosquito nets; nail polish with sparkles;

plastic jewelry; tennis balls; thread; combs with pictures of Rambo on them; knives; clothes pins; candies and candles; transistor radios; and even Pepsi. It would be strange if villagers did not speculate about the sources of such goods. And speculate they do. From whence come these wares?

Many I spoke with in private voiced their concerns that such businesspersons used witchcraft to acquire their wares since it is common knowledge that no one gets rich by accident. Rather, accumulation of any sort requires determined efforts and frequently demands the exploitation of unseen powers of witchcraft. Yet, particularly with modern wealth, one central conceptual dilemma remains: since ordinary villagers in Ihanzu do not themselves possess many modern material goods, it is not conceivable that Ibaga shopkeepers acquire their wealth by depriving nearby residents. When it comes to modern wealth, there can be no locally based finite economy. It would be quite impossible, after all, to steal in a mystical manner goods from locals who do not possess such goods to begin with. As one elderly woman succinctly noted: "All those shopkeepers [in Ibaga village] are witches. How else do you think they fill their shops with those things they sell? Witchcraft, of course. . . . I don't know how they do it—who really knows the work of witches but witches?—but I do know one thing: they didn't get all those things from me!"

And here, at last, we come to the crux of the matter. When it comes to modern material goods, it is no longer reasonable to assume that Ihanzu witchcraft works in a zero-sum fashion as it does with more "traditional" forms of wealth (Foster 1964). Of course it might. It is just conceivable that the global movement of goods—translocal transactions between Ibaga shopkeepers, Arusha, Dar es Salaam, Kenya, Europe, and America—might be a conceptually closed, if vastly expanded, economy of goods. If so, then local shopkeepers are depriving others in far-flung locations, but not local villagers, of their modern wares. If not, these business witches are simply amassing modern material wealth from a distant and unlimited store of goods. In either case, modern economic processes have, by spanning vast distances, become virtually unintelligible. Unlike the powers that drive traditional goods through local economies, the movements of modern goods cannot be monitored—they cannot be "seen" through divination and through their transactional zero-sum logics. The logic of translocal transactions thus remains elusive. Myriad questions remain for the Ihanzu concerning the movements of modern wealth through the economy: Do modern witches really accumulate without depriving others? Are the distant economies of goods in which some locals now participate limited or limitless in supply?

Furthermore, why do some witches continue to destroy modern wealth if not to benefit themselves? Or do they benefit but in ways we have yet to understand? The distances between modern sites of production and local sites of consumption are simply too great, the paths between them too Byzantine, to know for certain the mechanism at work. In short, the driving mechanism of modernity, its *motor spiritus*, remains a topic of ongoing, anxious deliberation. And a good deal of such deliberation is done through an idiom of witchcraft (also Sanders 2001). Drawing meaningful links between distant "modern" sites of production and local "traditional" sites of consumption is, and will no doubt remain, an unfinished project.

Conclusion

I have argued that Ihanzu witchcraft involving what locals see as traditional wealth operates within a conceptually closed universe: it requires mystical predation where witches gain only at the expense of others. Thus, although the precise workings of "traditional" witchcraft are hidden from view, the operating logic can be inferred from its visible manifestations and from what diviners say. In contrast, where notions of witchcraft meet more "modern" forms of wealth, the nature of the links between wealth and invisible powers becomes much less obvious. Somewhat inexplicably, witches destroy wealth with seemingly no desire to appropriate it for themselves. Still other witches gain wealth, but apparently at no one's immediate expense, or at least no local's expense. The fact that these two discourses on modern witchcraft remain distinct suggests that Ihanzu experiences with modernity at home have been, at the very least, ambivalent. While encounters with modern materiality seem, on the surface, to offer the promise of amassing wealth at no one's expense, everyone suspects, on another level, that wealth must come from somewhere and someone. No one gets something for nothing. These competing notions of modern witchcraft appear to express people's hopes of actively participating in a world of material plenty while at the same time acknowledging their apprehensions about the vast inequalities—and, thus, grave moral quandaries—that such material accumulation implies.

But allow me to be entirely clear, lest my argument be misunderstood. By no means do I wish to impute to the Ihanzu some prelogical *mentalité primitif* that, muddled in a mystical fog, is incapable of grasping, let alone coping with, the ambivalences of our contemporary world. Quite the contrary. The Ihanzu may, in fact, possess better, not worse, insights into the conceptual quagmires of modernity. They may be better situated than many in the West to engage with the vagaries and uncertainties that frequently, if not always, accompany modern markets and novel regimes of production and consumption.

Recall, from the outset, that Western discourses of "modernity" and "transparency" go hand-in-hand, stressing, as they do, clarity, openness, and rationality of process. What is more, Western economics has guns and butter graphs, supply and demand curves that flaunt, in a most visible way, this apparent rationality. But we also have our "invisible hands" that move economies in mysterious and inexplicable ways. And, when our models of *homo oeconomicus* fail us altogether, in an effort to rescue them we cry, "Market failure!" to indicate that our market-model oracle has itself been bewitched. Rather than downplaying or ignoring such magicalities of modernity (Comaroff and Comaroff 1993)—the patently odd fact that hidden hands and other enigmatic economic processes drive, in some unspecified manner, our everyday world—the Ihanzu dwell on such absurdities. Indeed, for the Ihanzu, quite unlike many Western champions of modernity, these ambivalences are integral to modernity's makeup. Seen in this light, the Ihanzu hold what is perhaps a more nuanced view of "the modern." They recognize and confront head-on its deep-seated ambivalences. Not for a moment do they pretend, for convenience's sake, that our world can ever be rendered entirely transparent. From their perspective, it cannot. The world just doesn't work that way. The point, rather, is to try to make sense of modernity's seeming insensibilities, however fleeting that sense may be.

Notes

This essay is based on fieldwork carried out in Ihanzu, Tanzania, between August 1993–May 1995 and June–September 1999. I acknowledge the generous support of the U.K. Economic and Social Research Council, the U.S. National Institute of Health, the Royal Anthropological Institute, and the London School of Economics for funding different portions of this research and the Tanzania Commission for Science and Technology (COSTECH) for granting me research clearances. I am grateful to Jean Comaroff, Harry West, and an anonymous reviewer for their constructive comments and especially to the men and women of Ihanzu who have graciously allowed me to trespass in their lives.

1 The fact that modernization theory was largely an American creation (e.g., Rostow 1960), and that its advent coincided with postwar tensions on the international political scene, is not coincidental. At least according to official discourses, modernity meant freedom to choose, whether political parties or economic goods. It meant, above all, an open society, the workings of which were transpar-

ent and readily obvious to all. In this sense, to be modern was to be American. Naturally, this model made most sense when anchored firmly in its Cold War context, contrasted as it was with the "closed" and "unfree" Soviet Union.

2 Of course, with its postcolonial history of Socialist *ujamaa* policies, Tanzania was for many years seen by Kenyans and Westerners as the epitome of the closed society. Yet, ironically, ujamaa aimed to promote the very transparency that it was criticized for ignoring and that was seen to be lacking in Kenya. In theory, all Tanzanians were meant to participate in clearly identifiable chains of command that linked the most distant villager with the highest government official in Dar es Salaam. The economy, similarly, would operate as an open book, being collectively owned and run by the people for the people. Whether any of this happened in practice is a topic for another time.

3 Writings on the ujamaa period are voluminous. See, e.g., Hyden (1980), Shivji (1995), Stoger-Eising (2000), and, on the ujamaa villagization program, Ergas (1980) and Scott (1998: chap. 7).

4 The people refer to themselves as *Anyīhanzu*—"the people of Ihanzu." The land they call *Ihanzu*.

5 Such terms appear time and again in early written sources. The Germans were the first to enter the area. For some of their views on this point, see Werther (1894, 1898) and Kohl-Larsen (1939, 1943). For later British perspectives, see TNA (1920: 13), TNA (1920–21: 16), TNA (1927: 8), and RH (ca. 1928).

6 The only early attempt of which I am aware—a rubber plantation set up by Herr Bell near Mkalama village—failed miserably immediately after the First World War (see TNA 1919–20: 21).

7 Owing to the spottiness of historical documentation, the extent to which notions of modernity and tradition have changed from the colonial period to the contemporary period remains an open question, but this is no doubt a question that merits further investigation.

8 For more on Sukuma Sungusungu vigilante groups, see Bukurura (1994), Abrahams (1987), Mwaikusa (1994), and Fleisher (2000).

9 In this respect, Simmel was surely correct in noting that the "secret offers, so to speak, the possibility of a second world alongside the manifest world; and the latter is decisively influenced by the former" (Simmel [1906] 1950: 330).

10 Other Tanzanian groups like the Sukuma (Mesaki 1994: 49), Iramba (Lindström 1988: 183, n. 7), Fipa (Willis 1968: 4), and Kaguru (Beidelman 1963: 66, 93) appear to hold similar beliefs about nocturnal zombie laborers. None of the information that I collected on Ihanzu zombie laborers suggests any link with the slave trade, which probably tangentially affected Ihanzu in the late 1800s (cf. Shaw 1997, 2002), or with local imaginings of migrant labor (Comaroff and Comaroff, in press).

11 Other types of pacts are theoretically possible but less likely. For example, a couple may choose to forgo large harvests and all livestock in order to bear many

children. However, many suggest that such choices are uncommon and probably foolish since too many children without the means to care for them properly is a sure recipe—and in this case, an everlasting recipe—for personal disaster.

12 For the record, she reputedly makes up for the difference in the off-season by stuffing old clothes in her blouse.

References

Abrahams, Ray G. 1987. "*Sungusungu:* Village Vigilante Groups in Tanzania." *African Affairs* 86:179–96.

Adam, Virginia. 1963a. "Migrant Labour from Ihanzu." In *Conference Proceedings from the East African Institute of Social Research*. Kampala: Makerere College.

———. 1963b. "Rain Making Rites in Ihanzu." In *Conference Proceedings from the East African Institute of Social Research*. Kampala: Makerere College.

Ardener, Edwin. 1970. "Witchcraft, Economics, and the Continuity of Belief." In *Witchcraft Confessions and Accusations,* ed. Mary Douglas, 141–60. London: Tavistock.

Ashforth, Adam. 1996. "Of Secrecy and the Commonplace: Witchcraft and Power in Soweto." *Social Research* 63 (4): 1183–1234.

Auslander, Mark. 1993. "'Open the Wombs!': The Symbolic Politics of Modern Ngoni Witchfinding." In *Modernity and Its Malcontents: Ritual and Power in Postcolonial Africa,* ed. Jean Comaroff and John Comaroff, 167–92. Chicago: University of Chicago Press.

Bayart, J.-F. 1993. *The State in Africa: Politics of the Belly.* New York: Longman.

Beidelman, Thomas O. 1963. "Witchcraft in Ukaguru." In *Witchcraft and Sorcery in East Africa,* ed. John Middleton and E. Winter, 57–98. London: Routledge and Kegan Paul.

Bukurura, Sufian H. 1994. "*Sungusungu:* Vigilantes in West-Central Tanzania." Ph.D. thesis, Department of Anthropology, University of Cambridge.

Callaghy, Thomas M. 1993. "Vision and Politics in the Transformation of the Global Political Economy: Lessons from the Second and Third Worlds." In *Global Transformation and the Third World,* ed. Robert O. Slater, Barry M. Schutz, and Steven R. Dorr, 161–257. Boulder, Colo.: Lynne Rienner.

Clamers, Malcolm, ed. 1997. *Developing Arms Transparency.* Bradford, U.K.: Bradford University Press.

Comaroff, Jean, and John L. Comaroff. 1993. Introduction to *Modernity and Its Malcontents: Ritual and Power in Postcolonial Africa,* ed. Jean Comaroff and John Comaroff, xi–xxxvii. Chicago: University of Chicago Press.

———. 1999. "Occult Economies and the Violence of Abstraction: Notes from the South African Postcolony." *American Ethnologist* 26 (2): 279–303.

———. In press. "Alien-Nation: Zombies, Immigrants, and Millennial Capitalism."

In *Forces of Globalization*, ed. Gabriele Schwab. New York: Columbia University Press.

Douglas, Mary. 1970. "Thirty Years after *Witchcraft, Oracles, and Magic*." In *Witchcraft Confessions and Accusations*, ed. Mary Douglas, xiii–xxxviii. London: Tavistock.

Douglas, Mary, and Brian Isherwood. 1979. *The World of Goods: Towards an Anthropology of Consumption*. New York: Norton.

Dundas, C. W. 1994. "Transparency in Organizing Elections." *Round Table* 329:61–76.

Eisenstadt, S. N. 2000. "Multiple Modernities." *Daedalus* (special issue: "Multiple Modernities") 129 (1): 1–29.

Ergas, Z. 1980. "Why Did the *Ujamaa* Village Policy Fail? Towards a Global Analysis." *Journal of Modern African Studies* 18 (3): 387–410.

Faubion, James D. 1993. *Modern Greek Lessons: A Primer in Historical Constructivism.* Princeton: Princeton University Press.

Fisiy, Cyprian F., and Peter Geschiere. 1991. "Sorcery, Witchcraft, and Accumulation: Regional Variations in South and West Cameroon." *Critique of Anthropology* 11 (3): 251–78.

Fleisher, Michael L. 2000. "Sungusungu: State-Sponsored Village Vigilante Groups among the Kuria of Tanzania." *Africa* 70 (2): 209–28.

Foster, George M. 1964. "Treasure, Tales, and the Image of the Static Economy in a Mexican Peasant Community." *Journal of American Folklore* 77:39–44.

———. 1965. "Peasant Society and the Image of Limited Good." *American Anthropologist* 67:293–315.

Gable, Eric. 1997. "A Secret Shared: Fieldwork and the Sinister in a West African Village." *Cultural Anthropology* 12 (2): 213–33.

Geschiere, Peter. 1997. *The Modernity of Witchcraft: Politics and the Occult in Postcolonial Africa.* Charlottesville: University Press of Virginia.

Giddens, Anthony. 1990. *The Consequences of Modernity.* Stanford: Stanford University Press.

Gluckman, Max. 1956. *Custom and Conflict in Africa.* Oxford: Basil Blackwell.

Goody, Esther. 1970. "Legitimate and Illegitimate Aggression in a West African State." In *Witchcraft Confessions and Accusations*, ed. Mary Douglas, 207–44. London: Tavistock.

Heald, Suzette. 1986. "Witches and Thieves: Deviant Motivations in Gisu Society." *Man* 21:65–78.

Hyden, Goran. 1980. *Beyond Ujamaa in Tanzania: Underdevelopment and an Uncaptured Peasantry.* London: Heinemann.

Iliffe, John. 1979. *A Modern History of Tanganyika.* Cambridge: Cambridge University Press.

Kaiser, Paul J. 1996. "Structural Adjustment and the Fragile Nation: The Demise of Social Unity in Tanzania." *Journal of Modern African Studies* 34 (2): 227–37.

Koffi, N. 1993. "L'ideologie de la transparence et la democratie contemporaire." *Quest* 12 (1): 289–92.

Kohl-Larsen, Ludwig. 1939. *Simbo Janira: Kleiner Grosser Schwarzer Mann.* Kassel: Im Erich Röth.

———. 1943. *Auf Den Spuren Des Vormenschen (Deutsche Afrika-Expedition 1934–1936 und 1937–1939).* Stuttgart: Strecher und Schröder.

Kopits, George, and Jon Craig. 1998. *Transparency in Government Operations.* Washington, D.C.: International Monetary Fund.

Kratz, Catherine. 1999. "Transparency and the European Union." *Cultural Values* 3 (4): 387–92.

Larsson, Mats, and David Lundberg. 1998. *The Transparent Market.* London: Macmillan.

Lindström, Jan. 1988. "The Monopolization of a Spirit: Livestock Prestations during an Iramba Funeral." In *On the Meaning of Death: Essays on Mortuary Rituals and Eschatological Beliefs,* ed. S. Cederroth, C. Corlin, and J. Lindström, 169–83. Uppsala: Acta Universitatis Upsaliensis.

Lugalla, Joe L. P. 1995. "The Impact of Structural Adjustment Policies on Women's and Children's Health in Tanzania." *Review of African Political Economy* 63: 43–53.

———. 1997. "Development, Change, and Poverty in the Informal Sector during the Era of Structural Adjustment in Tanzania." *Canadian Journal of African Studies* 31 (3): 424–51.

Marceau, Gabrielle, and Peter N. Pedersen. 1999. "Is the WTO Open and Transparent? A Discussion of the Relationship of the WTO with Non-Governmental Organisations and Civil Society's Claims for More Transparency and Public Participation." *Journal of World Trade* 33 (1): 5–49.

Mesaki, Simeon. 1994. "Witch-Killing in Sukumaland." In *Witchcraft in Contemporary Tanzania,* ed. R. Abrahams, 47–60. Cambridge: African Studies Centre.

Meyer, Birgit. 1995. " 'Delivered from the Power of Darkness': Confessions of Satanic Riches in Christian Ghana." *Africa* 65 (2): 236–55.

Moore, Henrietta L., and Todd Sanders. 2001. "Magical Interpretations and Material Realities: An Introduction." In *Magical Interpretations, Material Realities: Modernity, Witchcraft, and the Occult in Postcolonial Africa,* ed. Henrietta L. Moore and Todd Sanders, 1–27. London: Routledge.

Murphy, William P. 1998. "The Sublime Dance of Mende Politics: An African Aesthetic of Charismatic Power." *American Ethnologist* 25 (4): 563–82.

Mwaikusa, J. T. 1994. "Maintaining Law and Order in Tanzania: The Role of *Sungusungu* Defence Groups." In *State, NGOs, and People's Organizations in the Provision of Services in East Africa,* ed. J. Semboja and O. Therkildsen. Copenhagen: Centre for Development Research.

Nyerere, Julius K. 1968. *Ujamaa: Essays on Socialism.* Dar es Salaam: Oxford University Press.

Ponte, Stefano. 1998. "Fast Crops, Fast Cash: Market Liberalization and Rural Livelihoods in Songea and Morogoro Districts, Tanzania." *Canadian Journal of African Studies* 32 (2): 316–48.

Rhodes House (RH). ca. 1928. "Mkalama: The Back of Beyond." By A. W. Wyatt, Acting District Officer. File MSS Afr. s. 272. Rhodes House, Oxford.

Rostow, W. W. 1960. *The Stages of Economic Growth*. Cambridge: Cambridge University Press.

Sanders, Todd. 1998. "Making Children, Making Chiefs: Gender, Power, and Ritual Legitimacy." *Africa* 68 (2): 238–62.

———. 1999. "Modernity, Wealth, and Witchcraft in Tanzania." *Research in Economic Anthropology* 20:117–31.

———. 2001. "Save Our Skins: Structural Adjustment, Morality, and the Occult in Tanzania." In *Magical Interpretations, Material Realities: Modernity, Witchcraft, and the Occult in Postcolonial Africa*, ed. Henrietta L. Moore and Todd Sanders, 160–83. London: Routledge.

———. In press. "Reconsidering Witchcraft: Postcolonial Africa and Analytic (Un)certainties." *American Anthropologist*.

Scholte, Jan Aart. 1998. "Globalization, Governance, and Democracy in Post-Communist Romania." *Democratization* 5 (4): 52–77.

Scott, James C. 1998. *Seeing Like the State: How Certain Schemes to Improve the Human Condition Have Failed*. New Haven: Yale University Press.

Shaw, Rosiland. 1997. "The Production of Witchcraft/Witchcraft as Production: Memory, Modernity, and the Slave Trade in Sierra Leone." *American Ethnologist* 24 (4): 856–76.

———. 2002. *Memories of the Slave Trade: Ritual and the Historical Imagination in Sierra Leone*. Chicago: University of Chicago Press.

Shivji, Issa G. 1995. "The Rule of Law and *Ujamaa* in the Ideological Formation of Tanzania." *Social and Legal Studies* 4 (2): 147–74.

Shukla, S. N. 1998. "Good Governance: Need for Openness and Transparency." *Indian Journal of Public Administration* 44 (3): 398–406.

Simmel, Georg. [1906] 1950. "The Secret and the Secret Society." In *The Sociology of Georg Simmel*, ed. Kurt H. Wolff, 307–76. Glencoe, Ill.: Free Press.

Stoger-Eising, V. 2000. "*Ujamaa* Revisited: Indigenous and European Influences in Nyerere's Social and Political Thought." *Africa* 70 (1): 118–43.

Tanzania National Archives (TNA). 1919–1920. "Mkalama Annual Report 1919–1920." File 1733/1. Tanzania National Archives, Dar es Salaam.

———. 1920. "Kondoa-Irangi Annual Report, 14 April 1920." File 1733/1. Tanzania National Archives, Dar es Salaam.

———. 1920–21. "Kondoa-Irangi Annual Report 1920–1921." File 1733:5. Tanzania National Archives, Dar es Salaam.

———. 1924. "Mkalama Annual Report, 1924." By J. F. Kenny-Dillon, Administrative Officer in Charge. File 1733/14: 91. Tanzania National Archives, Dar es Salaam.

———. 1927. "Singida District Annual Report 1927." File 967:823. Tanzania National Archives, Dar es Salaam.

———. 1957. "Local Courts, Iramba Division." By the Assistant Probation Officer. File 68/L4/2. Tanzania National Archives, Dar es Salaam.

Tripp, Aili Mari. 1997. *Changing the Rules: The Politics of Liberalization and the Urban Informal Economy in Tanzania.* Berkeley and Los Angeles: University of California Press.

Werther, C. W. 1894. *Zum Victoria Nyanza: Eine Antisklaverei-Expedition Und Forschungsreise.* Berlin: Gergonne.

———. 1898. *Die Mittleren Hochländer Des Nördlichen Deutsch-Ost-Afrika.* Berlin: Hermann Paetel.

Willis, Roy G. 1968. "Kamcape: An Anti-Sorcery Movement in South-West Tanzania." *Africa* 38:1–15.

Winter, E. H. 1956. *Bwamba: A Structural-Functional Analysis of a Patrilineal Society.* Cambridge: W. Heffer and Sons.

World Bank. 1989. *Sub-Saharan Africa: From Crisis to Sustainable Growth.* Washington, D.C.: World Bank.

———. 1994. *Adjustment in Africa: Reforms, Results, and the Road Ahead.* New York: Oxford University Press (for the World Bank).

6

Stalin and the Blue Elephant: Paranoia
and Complicity in Post-Communist
Metahistories

CAROLINE HUMPHREY

This essay draws attention to the hauntingly allegorical character
of certain responses to Communist repression. I analyze contemporary interpretations given to ancient stories by Buddhists in Russia and China, attempting, first, to understand this elliptical mode of explaining the recent
past and, then, to situate this idiom in the context of other kinds of response
now being revealed in the post-Soviet literature. At issue is the nature of responsibility for the campaigns of terror, in particular the devastation of the
Buddhist church in Russia in the 1930s. Stalin, for example, is said by Buryat
villagers to have been the reincarnation of the Blue Elephant, which, according to legend, lived in ancient times in India. The Blue Elephant labored all
its life to build a great Buddhist pagoda, but, when its efforts were ignored
by the high lama, it flew into a rage and committed a sin—it vowed to destroy Buddhism three times in its future rebirths. Stalin, people now say,
was the third and last of these reincarnations, and, therefore, he was destined by a fate beyond his control to unleash terrible events. I examine discussions around such stories to suggest that, having been caught up in the
seemingly objective and transparent, yet deeply irrational, accounts of the
Party-state, the narrators do not (at any rate at present) confront actions in
which they were both perpetrators and victims "matter-of-factly." Rather,
they reproblematize through metaphor and allegory the issue of what it is to
be an actor in history understood metahistorically.

It will be argued that, having been a particular target of the Stalinist pervasive discourse of suspicion and punishment—in other words, having been the object of paranoia in the common sense of the word—some Buryat Buddhists today are creating what can be seen as paranoic narratives of their own to explain the repressions. For the Buryat case, the term *paranoia* will be used, not in the everyday sense of being "pathological" or "malign," but as an analytical description for a particular kind of narrative, one of displacement, in which the actions attributed to an Other (in this case Stalin) are in some way "about" oneself. I argue that the reincarnation stories in some ways metaphorically mirror the paranoid discourse generated by Stalinism but that they also fundamentally challenge it by pointing up the crucial ethical issue erased by Socialist metahistory, the problem of individual accountability. These narratives are, I suggest, at some level "about" complicity and guilt, and the discussions that they evoke even perhaps reveal an uneasy identification with Stalin.

Why should such elliptical explanations appear, and why *today* in post-Soviet times, when one might have expected a more straightforward "telling the truth about Stalinism" to come to the fore? Later in the essay I discuss this question by contrasting the way in which Buryats and Mongols in Russia and China interpret the repressions with the far more open kinds of argument about the same fatal period now going on in the independent country of Mongolia. In both cases, there is a response to the Socialist-era discourse about the "objective," and thus "transparent," nature of history. It is the configurations of contemporary political landscapes that make the difference, for, in provincial Russia and China, the subject positions of Buryats and Mongols are still subordinated within political structures that close off space for open public discussion.

Any ethnic group may be conceived as having a repertoire of oral and written genres to which people may have recourse. The post-Soviet literature has already brought to our attention those genres in particular that seem "private," that appear to reveal people's inner thoughts and true understandings of painful times. There are, for example, the oral litanies and laments of Russians described by Nancy Ries (1997), the diaries of Russians and Ukrainians documented by Garros, Korenevskaya, and Lahusen (1995) and by Hellbeck (2000), or the biographical narratives of Latvians told to Skultans (1998). In their own ways, each of these genres implies a certain disposition of thoughts and experiences, characteristic revelations, concealments and lacunae, and references to other possible modes of expression.

If post-Socialist research has only fairly recently drawn attention to the implications of there being different modes of articulation of memory, there is a literature in anthropology and history that has explored this issue (Guha 1988; Connerton 1989; Lass 1994; Daniel 1996). The general tendency here has been to examine shifts between intimate (even unspoken) recollections and more public and "distanced" accounts. In such a construction of the problem, "distancing" appears as the effect of a variety of shifts away from individual subjectivity, for example, from the embodiment of pain to its articulation in speech, from oral to later written accounts, or from scrappy idiosyncratic discussions of events to their historicization and rationalization by intellectuals. In this way, what is individual appears as the more "close" and more "genuine."

Yet, to name but two writers, Das (1995), leaning on Koselleck (1985), and Skultans (1998) have in different ways challenged the assumption that experiential intensity necessarily implicates only "the individual." In Das (1995: 194), the institutions of society appropriate not only the body of the victim but also her silences and her speech, such that even physical pain cannot be treated as a purely private experience. In Skultans (1998: 22–25), intimate recollections of repression are frequently shaped in reference to themes from Latvian literature and cultural archetypes.[1]

It seems to me that the Buryat reincarnation narratives also suggest that there may be a shared or collective character to the experience of violent repression. And, unlike in a discourse that insists on direct personal experience as the only grounds for what is "really true," here the truth value is held to rest in the way the character of human action (in the abstract, understood philosophically) can be inferred from didactic legends. The issue of individual accountability thus appears as a matter of principle, of concern to Buddhist society at large. Distancing in this case occurs, not so much through a shift from the singular to the general or public, but from transferring shared, almost unspoken experience onto the template of a cultural narrative that mirrors the dilemma of this experience. In fact, even such narratives, like the particular variant of the Blue Elephant story used to explain Stalin, have never reached the wider public sphere. Political interpretations are discussed only in the most confidential circumstances, and I am sure that, as a foreign anthropologist, I would not have heard of them were it not that they were revealed to my Inner Mongolian graduate student when he described to Russian Buryats similar reincarnation accounts in China.[2]

Absolutely nonmodern in feel, these stories are instructive of values similar to those in the Jataka tales of ancient India (indeed, elaborate versions of them circulate like the Jataka stories as sacred texts among lamas). Ordinary Buryat believers have not only come to revere the parts of the (textually much longer) stories that they know but also made them their secret companions—secret if only for the reason that the truth that they conceal might well be stigmatized in the context of Russian and Chinese modernity. It is the choice of such means for talking about the terrible events of recent history that I attempt to explain in terms of paranoic discourse.

Accounting for Purges

With the publication of Arch Getty's and Oleg Nauman's excellent *The Road to Terror* (1999), based on archives of the Central Committee of the Soviet Communist Party, we at last have access to the ways of thinking of the architects of the purges. For most Party members, the Stalinist discourse of the victory of the proletariat was simply a self-apparent, political "universal truth" (Getty and Nauman 1999: 19). It rested on a Marxist philosophy of "objective stages of development," similar to the "laws" of material nature, resurrected by Stalin after the more opportunist strategy of Lenin.[3] The very term *chistka* (cleansing or purge) evokes the climate of infallible right-mindedness in which retrograde social forms were simply to be got rid of.

Yet their belief in the inevitability of success in the struggle against class enemies did not convince the Stalinists that they need not be afraid: "This was a political system in which even Politburo members carried revolvers. Recalling in the 1930s their formative experiences in the civil war, the Stalinists always believed themselves figuratively surrounded, constantly at war with powerful and conniving opponents." Collectively, these people were frightened of their surroundings: "Most of them were as afraid of political and social groups below them as of authorities on high" (Getty and Nauman 1999: 16). The dynamics of shifting alignments between Stalin at the summit, other Party circles, and the Party rank and file had the effect that the discourse and processes of terror reached everyone, right down into the most obscure of provinces. As Žižek points out (1999: 44), the fact that Stalinist irrationality pervaded the entire social body differentiated it from Nazism, which was "condensed" in anti-Semitism. If the Nazi investigators of non-Jews continued to look for proof of actual activity against the regime, the Stalinists were engaged in evident fabrications, invented plots, and so on— in other words, they generated paranoid accounts in the everyday sense of the word.

Buryats and other Asian peoples of Russia were as knitted into this situation as any Soviet citizens; and perhaps, as described later, they were entrapped even more than most in the duality of "historically necessary" yet arbitrary onslaughts. Only in the last few years have they begun to talk publicly about such matters, which they still call "closed themes" (*zakrytiye temy*). The particular genre discussed here erects its own explanatory metahistory (of reincarnation) as a counter to that of the earlier Party-state. Yet the two accounts are connected in that one, the Stalinist metahistory, has been a trigger for the reinterpretation of the other. The important point is that the displacement effected in the local narratives points to a tragic quandary at the heart of Communism, one that is entirely absent from the "transparent" Socialist discourse itself. In this sense, the stories undermine the assumptions of all official rationalities, even those of post-Socialist times, which continue to use expressions like *mistakes* and *excesses*. The reincarnation narratives work, not by opposing local realism to a political ideology full of symbolism, but by erecting their own cross-cutting, even more fantastic accounts. Yet these stories are in a sense true to lived experience in that, unlike the public discourse, they disclose the social predicament of personal accountability.

Recasting the great Communist leaders as "reincarnations" (*xubilgan*)[4] of legendary figures from ancient times, such accounts employ the metahistory of the destined rise and fall of time epochs (Sanskrit *kalpa*, Mongolian *galab*), within which, amid the constant cycle of rebirths, certain enlightened souls are incarnated in "lines" of exceptional people. The shift of such a religious discourse, mostly Buddhist in source, onto great secular leaders reveals to us a popular problematizing of political action. For in this contemporary genre it is the ethical weight of the acts (*üilin ür*, "the fruits of sin, karma") of previous lives that ultimately determines actions in the present one. As the people put it, there is a cause (*shaltgaan*) lying in ancient times that compels the leader to act the way he does. Thus, in effect, to say that a political leader is "really" the reincarnation of someone else is to raise the issue of the relation between personal intention and the metahistorical inevitability of an act.

With a quite different content, we can yet see that exactly this is also an unacknowledged quandary at the heart of the Stalinist project, as revealed in the trials of purged people. The "objective laws" of Marxist history proposed a necessary progress of stages, in which the proletarian revolution succeeded the democratic bourgeois one by virtue of eliminating all elements of the old society (aristocrats, priests, landowners, and so forth). From the mid-1930s on, when this transformation of society had already to all intents and purposes been accomplished, the continued invocation of the metahistorical laws became an elevation of the plane of "what must happen" above any mundane factuality and also, crucially, beyond the personal intentions of actors. This is why the trials could employ ludicrous charges and dismiss detailed counterevidence while simultaneously blotting out the very validity of subjective motivation. As Žižek writes in his illuminating discussion of the analogy between the Communist construct and the Christian notion of "objective" salvation:

> Do we not encounter another version of this same objectivisation in the Stalinist show trial? I can be subjectively honest, but if I am not touched by the Grace of the insight into the necessity of Communism, all my ethical integrity will make me no more than an honest, petty-bourgeois humanitarian opposed to the Communist cause, and in spite of my subjective honesty, I will remain forever "objectively guilty." These paradoxes cannot be dismissed as the simple machinations of the "totalitarian" power—they harbour a genuine tragic dimension overlooked by the standard liberal diatribes against "totalitarianism." (Žižek 1999: 30)

In this situation, Bukharin's emotional pleas at his trial that he was personally devoted to Stalin and was prepared to die for the cause could provoke only an uncanny laughter or shouted insults. The "properly perverse" attitude was to adopt the position of a pure instrument: "It's not me who is effectively doing it, I am merely the instrument of the higher historical necessity" (Žižek 1999: 30–32).

By an analogous displacement of the meaning of action—being both caused "previously" and seen as necessary in the broad religious diapason of time epochs—the idea of reincarnation has something of the same structure and erects a similar tragic impasse for individuals. Yet at the same time it proposes an utterly different central value to that of Communism—an ethics of dispassionate benevolence toward all living beings as opposed to ruthless devotion to winning the class struggle—and a quite different ontology of power. I shall, therefore, argue that the relation between reincarnation narratives and Communist metahistories is one of metaphor (or allegory), not one of mimicry, and that this distinction enables us to explore an important difference between Communist/post-Communist and colonial/postcolonial subjecthood. However, before moving on to this point, let me describe the wider context of the reincarnation stories.

Mongols living in China share the idiom of interpreting important political leaders as reincarnations. It is secretly said, for example, that Yuan Shikai, Mao Zedong, Jiang Jieshi, Jiang Qing, Liu Shaoqi, Hua Guofeng, and Hu Yaobang were all rebirths of legendary animals appearing in the tale *Journey to the West*,[5] which has enormous popularity in storybooks, comics, block prints, and television serials. The Blue Elephant story (in Inner Mongolia usually known as the Blue Bull)[6] also circulates and likewise is used as an allegory for talking about the actions of recent leaders. For example, in the Jirim region, where almost all the Buddhist monasteries were destroyed immediately after the Communist takeover, it is the Blue Bull that appears as fated to accomplish this annihilation of religion. Here, interestingly, joint responsibility makes its appearance, for Mao is said to have been reincarnated as the head of the bull, Liu Shaoqi as its chest, and Ulaanhüü (the Mongolian Communist leader during the 1950s and 1960s) as its buttocks.

We should note that, in all these interpretations, whether in Russia or China, it is the great leaders who figure. The identification of Stalin as the Blue Elephant is, I suggest, not simply "a case"; rather, it should be seen as more thoroughly exemplary, as an icon of the problem of personal accountability. I have argued elsewhere (Humphrey 1997a) that the exemplar is particularly salient as a mode of moral discourse in Sino-Mongolian cultures. Comparison of this cultural construction with the different ways in which Russians have conceptualized political leaders (Tumarkin 1983; Verdery 1999; Davies 2000: 50–51) would be a fruitful topic of further research. Suffice it to say here that, in the Mongolian variant, the leader-exemplar figures as the template for a pattern that the ordinary subject may, and, indeed, should, attempt to follow in herself.

The cognitive shock of hearing that Yuan Shikai, say, was the reincarnation of a turtle[7] is only strange and funny to an outsider, for, in these regions, in both cities and villages, the idiom of rebirth is prevalent in everyday life. Exceptional people all around are frequently said to "be" (or to have the souls of) previous beings, usually of deceased relatives. At the same time, there is an expectancy in the air that certain mighty historical figures like Chinggis Khan might be reborn, even in a neighborhood child. The reincarnation idea is not limited to Asian figures. Buryats say that, "because he is a friend of the Dalai Lama and Buddhism," Bill Clinton is a reincarnation of the Günchin Lama of Lhabrang Monastery in Gansu Province of China,[8] and several high Tibetan and Mongolian lamas are said to have been reborn as Russians. Nor is the idiom limited to Buddhist originals, for Kalmyks also said (at least they did in the early to mid-1990s [Stroganova 1999]) that the contemporary Kalmyk president, Kirsan Ilyumzhinov, is the reincarnation of the warrior hero from the epic *Janggar.*

Of course, such ideas would be contested by those of a sternly atheist cast of mind. But, in the 1990s, the deflation of the Communist hegemonic discourse threw the certainty of atheism into question. Now, if we think of Russia as a whole, there is what one might call a crisis of representational over-abundance, a plethora of possible explanations of the past, some of which are borrowed from Western accounts. In the distant Inner Asian provinces, however, a persisting cautiousness and epistemological unfamiliarity limit access to boldly debunking or liberal-analytical critiques. Instead, there is a kind of historiographical involution, a recourse to interpretations that make sense from a stance of subjective rumination, and this links the specific, long-silenced experientiality of the "great acts of terror" to customary sayings about the underlying causality of strange eventualities in everyday life. In short, the observations about reincarnations are the product of one kind of conviction about the nature of human life in time in these cultures. Reincarnation idioms have been employed for centuries in this region. But I shall argue that the contemporary stories, emerging out of the context of the heavy omnipresence of Communist dogmatic history, bring to the fore the element of personal responsibility by reconfiguring political power as predestined yet the outcome of ethically judged action. This is quite different, as discussed at the end of this essay, from the way in which the reincarnation idiom was used in earlier periods, when it was a means of magical reinforcement of cultural types of leadership.

An analysis in the conventional terms of *resistance* would be misplaced. For, here, the reincarnation idea acts precisely to affirm a kind of *identification* or *empathy* of ordinary Soviet citizen-perpetrators with Stalin and other leaders, stemming, I shall suggest, from their own complicity in terrible acts. This identification is, therefore, different from the "mimicry" discussed by Bhabha (1997) in the colonial situation. Bhabha (1997: 155) sees mimicry as a relation with an Other, as the repetition of partial presence, that articulates disturbances of cultural, racial, and historical difference that menace the narcissistic demand of colonial authority. His argument is complex but concludes, citing Lacan, that mimicry is essentially metonymic. Crossing the boundaries of the culture of enunciation, it produces, like camouflage, "a difference that is almost the same but not quite" (1997: 157). In our case, I argue, the Buryats are not engaged in mimicry of an authoritative Other. Rather, even if they differentiate themselves ethnically from Russians, they nevertheless see themselves as having been fully integrated in *the Soviet order*, that is, as engaged (complicit) in the practice of authority, both as subjects and as objects. Their narratives are, therefore, metaphoric rather than metonymic, in the sense that they reproduce in their own images the psychology of repression/silence and substitution found also in the Stalinist master narrative. To analyze this situation, I extract from psychoanalytical theory a particular version of the term *paranoia* in order to explore the dimension of the compulsive, enclosed quality of these narratives, both those of the Communist states themselves and those of the people living in their shadow.

Metahistory and Paranoia

The initial inspiration for using the terms *metahistory* and *paranoia* came from the volume edited by George Marcus, *Paranoia within Reason* (1999), which explores the plausibility of paranoid narratives in diverse sites in the post–Cold War world. *Metahistory*, taken from Hayden White (1973), seems a useful concept for a Communist/post-Communist environment in which Marxist ideologies themselves have taken the form of teleological philosophies of history. Marcus (1999: 4) sees a parallel between the situation today and that at the end of the nineteenth century discussed by Hayden White. That period, to paraphrase, was a time of a surfeit of descriptions and diagnoses of social change; there were numerous equally comprehensive and plausible yet apparently mutually exclusive conceptions of the same events.[9] It is the situation of diagnostic oversaturation, together with the collapse of the Cold War certainties, that provides the global context for what Marcus calls a contemporary "paranoid style," ranging from extreme responses to the professionalized rhetorics of "paranoia within reason" (1999: 8).

To explain the Buryat narratives, however, we need to construct a more specific notion of *paranoia* operating at a social level than that found in Marcus's (1999) introduction or in Stewart and Harding's (1999) discussion of the literature on contemporary apocalypse and millennialism. These authors use *paranoia* as a style and thereby direct attention to idioms of risk, trauma, catastrophe, victimization, surveillance, etc. prevalent in everyday discourses in our time. But such a blanket, aesthetic approach blots out both the creating subject and its particular experiential context. Anthropology also needs a concept of paranoia capable of penetrating the worlds of exceptional political terrorization. To this end, I return to Freud and the post-Freudian literature. This is not to repeat the mistake of viewing a socially generated narrative as a collective version of an individual neurosis (cf. Weiner 1999: 252); rather, it is to abstract out certain features of the paranoid complex in order to generate a concept that can work for an individual and in a shared way between people.[10] I leave aside, therefore, Freud's speculations on the causes of paranoic neuroses arising within clinical life histories, for example, that paranoia is a regression, a fixation at the stage of narcissism, and often a symptom of repressed homosexuality (Freud 1979: 206–

11). The focus here is, rather, on the features of paranoid thinking generated by subjects, in particular (especially political) contexts, and I suggest that three interlinked features are most important: the displacement onto the mental life of other people of "robbed" experience that is nevertheless subconsciously still present; the creation of a closed world of explanation of real people and events; and the sense of being tied up in an inexorable, externally determined process in which the future is preset.

Let me explain further. Freud notes that the paranoic's apprehension that what other people do is full of significance and interpretable[11] is in a sense justified, for the paranoic recognizes something that escapes normal people; he sees more clearly, but the displacement onto other people of a state of affairs really concerning himself renders this knowledge useless. In this kind of misrecognition, the paranoic is like the superstitious person. To explain this, Freud writes that he himself believes in the reality of external change and accident but not in the idea of internal, mental accidents, whereas, with the superstitious person, it is the other way around: he projects outward onto others meanings that I (Freud) look for within. The meaning of, for example, omens to the superstitious person corresponds to what is for Freud unconscious, but "the compulsion not to let chance count as chance, but to interpret it, is common to both of us" (Freud [1901] 1960: 257–58). If the superstitious person is one who does not understand the motivation of his own actions and reallocates it to the external world in terms of events rather than thoughts, with the paranoic this projection onto the external world amounts to the construction of a predetermined supernatural reality (Freud [1901] 1960: 258–59; see also the discussion of the case of Schreber in Freud [1979]). The task of psychoanalysis is to change this external reality back into a psychology of the unconscious. John Forrester therefore likens psychoanalysis to the undoing of a Laplacean determinism (the view that, given knowledge of initial conditions, the entire history of a system can be predicted, both forward and backward). It tries to undo identifications and "unwrite the future which the neurotic patient lives as already written, structured by the words and deeds of those he or she has identified with, whether they be those of mother, father, Marilyn Monroe, or Sigmund Freud" (Forrester 1990: 95).

To summarize, the features of paranoic thought that I identify here are the displacement onto other people and external events of internally generated, unconscious quandaries, the creation thereby of a "slanted" or supernatural reality, the view that this reality is determined and does not occur by chance, and, therefore, the view that this reality can and must be interpreted. The paranoic projections and identifications are closed, that is, resistant to un-raveling, in that they rest on a sense of conviction, and this, Freud writes, is because *there is in fact a certain truth to them*. From a psychoanalytical point of view, the conviction is justified in that there is a psychological origin of the idea that nothing is done by chance, and the paranoid subject then extends this outward to the rest of the context (Freud [1901] 1960: 256).

In the sociopolitical context we are considering here, I suggest, for people whose traumatic reality has been "stolen" by its unspeakableness in the hege-monic discourse of the Party-state, it is that unsymbolized experience that is nevertheless productive of the sense of conviction to which Freud refers, even while people's cultural narratives "displace" explanation into mythic and paradigmatic accounts.

Subjects of Repression

The reaction of Inner Asian people—"It is not by chance that we have been persecuted"—is a denial of the *actual* random quality of the purges when they reached their apogee in 1937. As Getty and Nauman (1999: 471–80) document, the strictly secret NKVD (Interior Ministry) operational order of 30 July 1937 prescribed the summary execution of more than 72,000 people under the blanket charge of being "anti-Soviet elements" and gave numerical quotas for each region of the country. The Buryat ASSR was to sentence 1,850 people under this order as well as carrying out punishments of certain cate-gories of their families. There was a surreal dissonance between this *secret* order and the public proclamation of the new constitution, adopted a year earlier in 1936, which had proposed contested elections and the enfranchise-ment of the entire population, including the very "anti-Soviet" categories like *former White officers* or *kulaks* now being hastily killed. "The same day that the press published the regulations on the upcoming contested elections, Stalin sent a telegram to all party organizations calling for mass executions" (Getty and Nauman 1999: 469).

But, if in reality they were attacked on the same arbitrary basis as every-one else, the Buryats and other Inner Asian peoples could still feel specially singled out because there were threads in the public master discourse that "justified" special measures in their case. One such rationale concerned fron-tiers. This was a lateral, geographical imaginary, later elaborated during the Cold War as "spheres of interest," "domino effects," and so forth, but its first and most intense image was that of the virtuous enclosed society, beyond which lay enemies liable to infiltrate or entice. Both the Buryats in Russia and the Mongols in China fell victim to this image, as they live in designated border zones that were subject to special and strict restrictions throughout the Socialist period (in China, some of the restrictions are still in place). These peoples were suspected of disloyal cross-border links, of having "pan-Mongolian" sympathies, of being spies for the Japanese in the Manchukuo period—indeed, of having relations with one another.

From this, we can perceive another dimension of mistrust, "nationalism" stemming from ethnic difference from the dominant populations of Russians in the Soviet Union and Han in China. True, the ethnic dimension was slightly differently structured in the two countries: in China, it was framed as a relation between a majority and "minorities." Government policies in the twentieth century have struggled to reconcile the principles of empire (multiplicity) and nation-state (oneness) exemplified in the phrase *minzu tuanje,* which means both "unity of all nationalities" and "national unity" (Bulag 2002). In the Soviet Union, diverse ethnicities were recognized as equally legitimate subjects, but they were hierarchicized administratively, and the explicit goal was for differences gradually to be erased with development toward the higher common plateau of the Soviet people (*Sovetskii narod*). In both countries, government structures expressed ways of handling, not only difference, but also developmental progress, as a process of radical modernization.

For peoples like the Buryats and the Mongols, the onslaught of the discourses of ethnic otherness and frontier disloyalty was undergirded by yet another, and equally disabling, element in the metahistory, that of their ignorance and superstitiousness, placing them and other peoples in earlier stages of social development. The master account of enlightenment and science, building a Marxist determinism onto earlier Russian ideas, not only was put into practice (universal education, including for adults, accompanied by the execution, imprisonment, exile, and intimidation of "backward" Buddhist lamas and shamans), but also appeared as an imaginative projection, lasting until the very end of the Soviet era in the late 1980s, in which religion figured as a lurking and dangerous subversion belonging to a past era. Thus, the metahistory of Socialist progress was imbued with a paranoic chiaroscuro, for only the future was "bright," whereas the past and its primitive recesses were shadowy and "dark" (in Russian, the phrase *temnyye lyudy,* lit. "dark people," meant also the blemished, shady, suspicious, ignorant, benighted people). Such people *could not be* in the vanguard of the Revolution.

The intersection of these "reasons," sometimes together and sometimes separately, and interwoven with the irrationality of numerical quotas, impelled harsh government actions against the Buryats and Mongols. They included the destruction of Buddhism in both countries, the relocation of communities, the purging of almost the entire Buryat Party leadership in 1937, the administrative cutting up and isolating of Buryat and Mongol populations, the physical elimination of around a quarter of Buryat intellectuals in the 1930s and 1940s, and the genocidal violence against Mongolians in China during the Cultural Revolution. The trauma of these punishments was doubly repressed—by the harsh, public, yet surreal certainty of the Party-state orders that people did get to hear about and by the silence surrounding the secret orders that left victims guessing why they had been singled out. At the same time, all public information and education was, not just strictly censored, but maintained in a limited, standardized, and quasi-ritualized language. The proscribing and prescribing of terminology and phraseology (for China, see Schoenhals [1992]; for the Soviet Union, see Yurchak [in press]) admitted of no extraneous, spontaneous elements—as in the characteristic closure of the paranoid narrative. If they were not to be taken at face value, public texts could be read only "between the lines" (Humphrey 1994). It is in this context that we can say the victims were "robbed" and disabled of speech. Accused people became at their trials discursively "Other," likened to "loathsome reptiles and repulsive filth."[12] The obsessive focus of the investigations—on details of whom the accused had met, a word that they had spoken—served to elaborate the fabrications of "the Japanese spy" or "the pan-Mongolian sympathizer," yet, at the same time, these details pointed, like symptoms, to a hidden content in Communism itself.

What I have tried to do in this section from a theoretical point of view is to point to the relatedness of what are often seen as distinct analytical concerns: the structure of the Communist administrative-territorial regimes; the appreciation that state historiography is a political force (on Foucault's lectures on state racism, see Stoler [1995: 62]); and the creation of experiential subject positions within empires and nation-states. Substantively, I have sketched out various sociopolitical dimensions combining to delineate a particular locus of regime-manufactured victimhood, a state that was denied public expression until recently. It is in the overall context of continued fear above all, but also of textual *interpretation* ("reading beyond"), common to the experience of all Soviet citizens even in recent times, that we must understand the stories of reincarnation.

The following story was told on several occasions in Buryatia in 1999.[13] These were private conversations in people's homes, using the Buryat language.[14] It was during discussions of national history that the story came up. Buryats in general are now actively reconfirming their adherence to religions of various kinds. They are rebuilding temples and monasteries, receiving Tibetan lamas, and sending students to study the religion in Mongolia and India, and, in this situation, many people identify strongly with Buddhism, seeing attacks on it as onslaughts on their own culture.[15]

> In India in ancient times there was a rich patron who had a Blue Elephant. He decided on the meritorious act of using his elephant to build a great temple-pagoda, the Jarang Hashir. Years went by, during which the temple was slowly constructed. The elephant spent so much energy that all his inner organs became visible through his skin. Because he used so much energy to good purpose, the elephant worked off all his previous sins; he became enlightened and could understand human words and minds. At last the high lama arrived to consecrate ("enliven," *rabnaila-*) the pagoda, and at this time he gave a blessing to all the people who contributed to its construction. Many people gathered together and listened to the blessing from the high lama. The patron got the best blessing of all. The Blue Elephant was standing there listening and thinking: "What kind of blessing will he give to me?" But the people had forgotten; the lama forgot, and he was not mentioned. The elephant gored the earth three times with a terrible roaring sound. And then he died. Then the high lama realized that the elephant had made a wrong vow (*boroo yorool talbijee*),[16] and he spoke it aloud as follows: "Because you have forgotten about me, I will destroy your Buddhism three times in my next births." So the lama pointed to the master of the elephant and said, "Now you also should make a vow, and it should say, 'I will kill you three times when you try to destroy Buddhism three times.'" The master agreed. We do not know about the first destruction; the second rebirth of the elephant was Langdarma, the king of Tibet who persecuted Buddhists, and the third was Stalin. The reincarnation of the patron was called Lhalung-baldorji.

Explaining this story, people say that it was predestined both that Stalin should hate Buddhism and that he had the power to destroy it. The execution of the will of the Blue Elephant had to happen because "even the Buddha and the deities" could not stop the working out of results of karmic action. Interestingly, the virtuous patron's rebirth to defend Buddhism is now entirely forgotten. The entire focus is on the tragic fate of the Blue Elephant.

The story is inserted in a wider metahistory. According to this, Stalin's "damaging" of Buddhism will not be repeated.[17] Throughout the Mongol-speaking world, there is an accepted vision of the future: from now on, no power will hurt Buddhism again until the end of Shakyamuni Buddha's *kalpa* (epoch). Buddhism will continue in its present state, not so prosperous, but at least not completely annihilated, until the advent of the religious war against infidels called Shambalyn Dain,[18] which will happen about 250 years from now. After twelve years of war, the religion will flourish in the whole world for five hundred years, and then it will decline for another three hundred years. People will gradually lose their faith. Thus, Buddhism will disappear after eight hundred years until the new epoch of the next buddha, Maitreya, starts.

Stalin is, thus, embedded in a vast, yet precisely delineated, metahistory. He acquires his own characteristics within this rationale. Buryats say he was one of the most powerful military and political leaders that the world has ever seen, and he achieved this pinnacle of power *because* he had accumulated great merit during his previous birth when he was the Blue Elephant. It is interesting that Stalin is referred to as *Stalin Bagshi* (Stalin Teacher), a term that simultaneously alludes to the Soviet representation of Stalin as Leader and Teacher and to the Mongolian connotations of *bagshi* as "exemplary teacher" or "guru." People say that, although Stalin damaged Buddhism as a result of making a "wrong" vow when he was distressed and offended (*gomdood*), at some deeper level he was also fond of Buddhism because in his previous birth (as the Blue Elephant) he had respected it and spent his whole life serving it. This is why Stalin gave permission for two monasteries to be reopened in the 1940s, and it also means that Stalin, as the Blue Elephant, was satisfied with the partial realization of his vow. In this whole explanation, Stalin as a historical individual, as the Communist leader executing intentional policy, is generally not conceptualized at all. Instead, he appears like a phantom of destiny, fated to destroy what he "really" loved.

Let us consider this further. Buddhist ethics in general does allow for the reversal of previous negative karmic determination by means of compensating good action. In the Mongolian view, this can happen with a revelatory change of heart, the advent of enlightened compassion (*bodi setgel*) in the individual, perhaps through meditation or the wise counsel of a guru. But the message of the Blue Elephant story is that this *did not* happen to Stalin.

In discussions around this theme, we can begin to see evidence of an unconscious displacement onto Stalin of people's own feelings of religious guilt. Some people in Alhana village, for example, picked up on the fact that Stalin had briefly studied at an Orthodox Christian seminary early in his life and claimed that this showed he was truly a religious person. His attack on Buddhism happened despite himself because he was the reincarnation of the Blue Elephant and was subject to the karma of ancient times. The attack was successful, they continued, because our Buryat people were due for persecution, and this was because of the accumulation of bad karma that had built up *among them* over a long time (*zonai üiliin ür*). The attacks of the previous two reincarnations of the Blue Elephant had not succeeded in damaging Buddhism because, in those times, the merit of the people was high. The Stalinist period, on the other hand, was a "living hell" (*amidu-yin tamu*), and such times occur when the sinful action of the people in general is very heavy.

The Present Political Context

Some readers might react by thinking that such a narrative is simply a strategic Buddhist interpretation of history, a prudent retreat into myth, entirely "reasonable" in the circumstances. Statements by some Buryats give a certain support to such an interpretation. For example, one man in his thirties said to me:

> You might think that there are just a few people left from those times, the veterans of the Great Patriotic War, whom we all regard as heroes. But . . . you avoid thinking about what they really did. And, in fact, there are also the thousands and thousands of police and informers and camp guards. They are still living next-door. They think what they did is right, I suppose. That is why no one blames anyone [*nikto nikogo ne osuzhdaet*]. That is why no publicity is given to lists of the repressed here. People still do not talk about the "closed themes." It comes from fear of punishment [*strakh nakazaniya*]. I think that is a good feeling. Why good? Because maybe nothing has changed very much [*malo chto izmenilos'*].

The pervasive social practices and institutions of Stalinism (accusations, secret denunciations, "criticism," dossiers on individuals) lasted long after Stalin's death and well into the experience of anyone but the very young today. The very fact that control waxed and waned, with periods of openness being followed by renewed prosecutions, has made people constantly wary. As this man continued, "You could say something when your guard was down and then be picked up for it years later because someone was listening and remembering. Silence is in our blood."

The fact is that, in Buryatia, the current president is a man of Communist hue who has been in power on and off since the 1970s. He maintains an authoritarian rule that has clashed with Buddhists in recent years.[19] In China, meanwhile, the political regime is, of course, still a Communist one. In Mongolia, on the other hand, social democratic governments have been in power through most of the 1990s,[20] the parliament has a human rights subcommittee, a monument has been erected to the victims of the purges, and a national memorial day for the victims is observed (Kaplonski 1999: 94–98). The reincarnation stories about political leaders are found in Russia and China but not, as far as I know, in present-day Mongolia. There, by contrast, we find a heated public debate about accountability both in parliament and in the press. The issue is whether the Party was really responsible for the purges or was just subject to overwhelming Soviet pressure, as its present members claim. As Kaplonski argues in his illuminating article, present transparency claims (that the truth is finally being told etc.) do not actually result in historical facticity being the point for most Mongolians. Rather, they are concerned with identity and the search for their heritage, that is, the question of whether the Socialist period was "Mongol" at all (Kaplonski 1999: 108). Be this as it may, the implication is that radically religious explanations like the reincarnation stories are the recourse of people who still cannot debate history openly.

Yet the interpretation of "reasonable caution" in Russia and China does not do justice to the ethnography, which points to a far more complex and agonized situation. One of the people who told the Blue Elephant story was a venerable woman in her nineties, who also treated the ethnographer to a rendition of an old song lauding Stalin Teacher to the skies.[21] At the lines:

Stalin Bagshin hainaar
hanaa hetgelee haijarab

By Stalin Teacher's goodness
Our ideas and disposition changed

her nephew, who was also in the room, became deeply angry and would not let her finish. He then described, perhaps for the first time to a stranger, how his uncle (the old woman's husband) had been arrested and exiled and died in great suffering. We see from this that the reincarnation narrative, which exculpates Stalin Teacher of personal blame, runs in people's minds along-side—and can evoke—another suppressed realm of knowledge and feeling. The story can, thus, act like a signal (of something else). In this way, it is similar to physical objects in the landscape, themselves silent, of course, but nevertheless potent reminders.

An example of this is the following account also told by Buryats in 1999:

> There was a great willow tree, over thirty meters high, with two tall branches pointing toward the two hills. This tree was the master-guardian spirit of the hills, and special offerings were made to it. Just before they began the mining of the east hill, eleven Russians came and started to cut down the willow. The local elders tried to stop them. But the men said, "It is not us who are cutting it; Stalin Teacher ordered us to do it." They began to cut the big branches, but that night several of them fell ill with a serious, unrecognizable disease. They stopped, but all of them fell victim to various illnesses, and all died within a month. The willow tree is still there, decaying slowly.

Although this story attributes the tree cutting to "eleven Russians," everyone knows that most of the local repressions were carried out by Buryat activists themselves.[22] During the conversations arising with the Blue Elephant story, other maimed objects were mentioned. These were sacred Buddhist ruins, darkened by memories of their bloody, sacrilegious use in Soviet times. People pointed out that Anan Monastery had been used as a slaughterhouse, that the Tsüügül and Egetüi Monasteries had been military bases,[23] and that Aga Monastery was used as a center for rehabilitating alcoholics. It cannot have been by accident that religious buildings were used for such purposes: the Soviets were "teaching a lesson," inscribing another contemptuous meaning onto hitherto sacred objects.

We should note that the sacred trees and monasteries were emblems of collective suffering, and I suggest that the self-attribution to the Buryat people collectively of sins and delusions is part of the same structure of ideas. The idea of time, or more specifically "a time" within history, is crucial to the understanding of the relation between individual and collective. Stalin could achieve his destructive goal because "the time" was right for that, and this was due to the sins and delusions built up collectively by the Buryat people just previously. Not only tragedies but also good fortune is explained in the same way. Thus, when an earthquake devastated areas of Inner Mongolia in the mid-1990s, Mongols said that the city of Huhhot was spared because the great Ulaan Gegeen Lama was there and his presence was efficacious because in their earlier lives the citizens collectively had provided meritoriously for his incarnation. In the case of Stalin, a lama explained that "we" (the Buryat people) must have done things to deserve his purges: we are like people crowded on a boat in a storm, our past misdeeds have built up to a heavy weight, and the ship must founder.

When contemporary people are surrounded by the mute split meanings of histories, the reincarnation narratives should not be understood simply as naive or as prudent alternatives to silence. They are possible interpretations in a situation where other histories could also be created (for, after all, the lists of victims do exist and their stories could be told privately in a matter-of-fact manner). But the complex moral relation with the leader that I have just tried to describe also exists as a cultural resource. With Stalin, it is almost as if Buryats are protecting his image from mundane explanations and accusations. The people who tell these stories know that they are saying something that others would regard as weird, but they do it, perhaps, because this is the language in which they can intimate that the issue is one of accountability for evil acts.

Ethicalization of Power

There is one last feature of these narratives that I should discuss before bringing this essay to a close. This is the issue of the specifically Socialist and post-Socialist conceptualization of political power. After all, could it not be argued that the Buryats have "always" retold ancient legends and held ideas of reincarnation and, therefore, that my interpretation in terms of the paranoia and complicity specific to Communist society is misplaced? It is not possible to do more than touch on this complex subject here, but, in brief, I argue that a shift occurred in popular conceptualizations of power with the experience of Communist totalizing relations. Before the Socialist revolutions, great political leaders were attributed with "power" (erx) as might, will, and superhuman domination, all unified in the one person. Ordinary people were in a relation of subject to master with such rulers. The king-like figure exercised his superhuman power in a universe pervaded by other supernatural beings and was often held to be the stronger. Sometimes the kingly power was aligned with religion (e.g., Buddhism, Orthodoxy) and sometimes not, but, in any case, the leader's *will* was indivisible from himself and his actions. This was true even if he was said to be a reincarnation, for that idea was treated like an extra, legitimizing addition to his powers.

It is with the totalizing social revolution of Communism that this changes, for, as mentioned earlier, in this new world no one could see herself as a nonparticipant in relations of domination. Fractally repeated at each level in society, Communist mastership and its "necessity" before history was inescapable; there were almost no subject positions beyond its reach, and virtually everyone at some stage in her life had the experience of being both a subordinate and a superior (Humphrey 1994). In this situation, I suggest, the Communist subject cannot see herself as essentially different from the leader, and neither of them can escape the quandary of responsibility. When we encounter the idea of reincarnation here, it has a new import, for it now serves to introduce the notion of karmic fate, and what this does is to crack open the relation between action and personal will. Below, I briefly substantiate these arguments.

The kinds of power wielded by secular leaders and religious reincarnations (*xubilgan*) were regarded as essentially different in Mongolian political theory.[24] But, among the folk, it was felt that the everyday "magical" power of the reincarnation was often also a key attribute of the kingly or military leader. It is documented, for example, that in the eighteenth century many Buryats regarded their sovereigns, the empresses of the Romanov dynasty, as reincarnations of Chinggis Khan's wayward daughter. She was said to have run away from her father, taking an army and a battle standard with her, to found the line of Russian "White Emperors" (*Tsagaan Khaad*). This daughter was herself held to be a reincarnation of the militant White Tara goddess of Buddhism, Tsagaan Dara-Eke (Potanin 1883: 868). The identification of the Russian White Emperors with a woman continued through the nineteenth and the twentieth centuries, that is, even when the tsar was a man. "The real [*chuxam*] White Tara is with you in Russia," a Mongol told the Russian geographer Potanin in 1879 (Potanin 1883: 320).

The important point to note here is that karma (*üiliin ür*, "the fruits of sin") is never mentioned in folk accounts at this period as an element of reincarnation. Rather, the idea is one of magical reinvigoration of each rebirth with the quality of the original—in this case, a rebellious militancy, notable in legends both of the White Tara and of Chinggis Khan's daughter (Humphrey 1997b). The same point applies to the eighteenth- and nineteenth-century identification of the Manchu emperor as a reincarnation of Manjushiri. The quality of wisdom, for which Manjushiri stands, is replicated in the emperor and demonstrated by his acts. In other words, I suggest, the idea of reincarnation served to reinforce the character of a given kingship but without compromising the view that any given ruler acts according to his or her own volition.

With Socialism, however, not only is rule secularized in the public master account, but also religion, and with it the whole discourse of reincarnation, becomes oppositional to state power. Simultaneously, and perhaps not by accident, reincarnation as pertaining to political leaders is ethicalized (i.e., seen as subject to karma by ordinary people).[25] We now have some autobiographies of Mongolian reincarnate lamas (Lattimore and Isono 1982: 142–43; Hyer and Jagchid 1983: 158–59) that make clear that twentieth-century xubilgans did, indeed, ruminate on the outcome of karma built up in previous incarnations and present actions. The Dilowa Xutagt pondered why it was that a profligate lama like his neighbor the Narvanchin Lama was able to work wonderful miracles. He observed, furthermore, that it was not only the trajectory of an individual soul that was at issue, for the collective sins of the population at large also affected their religious leader. He brought up the case of the difference between the body of his own last incarnation, a dissolute man, and that of the preceding one, who was a learned and pious lama. "To speak of 'good' and 'bad' incarnations is a very gross way of speaking," he wrote. "It may be that in my incarnation of two generations ago religious merit was accumulating elsewhere, . . . [but] ignorance and error [were] accumulating in the monastery territory itself, and therefore, as far as our moral eyes can see, the vehicle of my next incarnation was inferior to the one that had gone just before." "We are made aware that there are mysterious things," he concluded (Lattimore and Isono 1982: 142, 143).

This account is strikingly similar to the Buryats' attribution of the "living hell" of the Stalinist era to their own faults. Thus, by the early to mid-twentieth century, there was a wider context of popular rethinking of reincarnation that helps us understand the interpretations of the Blue Elephant narrative, where a karmic concept of reincarnation is shifted onto the political leader. In both cases, the lama pondering about his previous births and the Buryats thinking about Stalin as a reincarnation, actions are interpreted not only as ethical but also as caught up in skeins of relations beyond individual control or even comprehension. With this new understanding, it seems that the earlier magical power of the ruler-cum-reincarnation becomes qualified. Because of his inner, unacknowledged faith, Stalin only partially accomplished the vow to destroy Buddhism. A similar thought seems to lie behind an Inner Mongolian version of the Blue Bull story mentioned earlier, according to which it took three leaders (Mao Zedong as the head, Liu Shaoqi as the chest, and Ulaanhüü as the buttocks) to accomplish the destruction of Buddhism. In such ways, the leader's power is relegated (to a time period or to partial capability) and becomes encompassed within the long-term karma of the reincarnation—and, perhaps we could extrapolate to say, within the inexorable working out of Buddhist metahistory.

More generally, the difference between the nineteenth century and today is that, in the former period, differing metahistories could be made isomorphic with one another, producing an enriched, mutually reinforcing account of the convergence of different kinds of power, whereby it appeared as one and essentially free of Buddhist morality. In contemporary times, decades of confrontation between the religious and the secular, between the radically different ethics of Buddhism and Communism (not to speak of the Cold War discourse of "rightful" and "wrongful" power), have already rendered a single amoral vision of power impossible. The old simple acknowledgment "There is power" is no longer compelling for Buryats (just as for anthropologists certain Foucaldian-type general statements about power seem inadequate to account for ethnographic complexity).

Conclusion

This essay has been concerned with certain political perspectives of subjects earlier classified as "dark people" (in Russian, *temnyye lyudy*) and later as backward and superstitious latecomers to the grand project of progress. Understanding this enables us to see that paranoia and its aftermath in the post-Communist situation are situated first and foremost within particular structures of nationhood and statecraft. My account therefore tries to bring together two bodies of analysis, that is, to relate discussion of paranoic styles of thought (and responses to it) with accounts of how particular government systems produce citizens of various standings. The stories of reincarnation provide a window into this large theme since they are being produced among peoples that have been paradigmatic targets of Communist accusations.

At one level, the narrative of Stalin as the Blue Elephant might perhaps be understood as what the Russians call *inoskazaniye*, which is a kind of indirect hinting, often accusatory in tone. We could, thus, perhaps read into the theme of the ignoring of the elephant's labors in building the temple (also the forgetting of the turtle's merit; see n. 7 above) a parallel feeling of aggrieved neglect on the part of Buryat and Mongolian Communists. This would seem to be a logical inference from the subordinate, needing-to-be-led status accorded "backward" minorities in state politics.

It is significant, however, that this interpretation is not given by Buryat and Mongolian people and is, therefore, ethnographically inadequate. Rather, the implication of their discussions of the Blue Elephant story is an identification with the predicament of the leader, not because he had been ignored, but because he had to act as he did, against his better self. At the same time, there is a complete silence in this context about local participation in the repressions, which certainly took place even if the orders came from above. Specificities are occluded altogether by the cloudy idea of collective sins and delusions. It is for these reasons that I feel justified in using a particular idea of paranoia to analyze the narrative. Let me reiterate here the particular and abstracted sense in which the idea is applied. One may find in the literature examples of straightforward applications of paranoia to political situations, such as Gravers's discussion of nationalism in Burma. Gravers ([1993] 1999: 80–81), citing Foucault, describes as paranoic a structure of political action brought to bear on possible actions, in this case involving xenophobia in practically every political situation. There is a total blocking of alternative political practice, with the result that the subject's fear is invoked at a mere signal from the rulers. The Stalinist regime can be said to have been paranoid in this sense, and I suggest that the elliptical response of the Buryats is paranoic too, yet in a different way.

As I argued earlier, the Buryats do not create a metonymic simulacrum of the master narrative. Their sense of being integral actors within the Soviet order made it impossible for them to conceptualize it as something "Other" to be imitated, for in their own way they *were* it. Instead, their recourse has been to produce a particular kind of poetically metaphoric narrative. This is paranoic by virtue of its being self-enclosed, displaced from the self, and felt to be true and, therefore, not susceptible to disproof. Applying a discourse of the "fruits of sin" to Stalin, Mao, and Ulaanhüü, are people not displacing onto the mental life of other people what is suppressed in their own (Freud), and do they not thereby create a predetermined supernatural reality where nothing happens by accident? The notion of paranoia might still seem inappropriate here were it not that these local narratives re-create in mythic, Buddhist guise the anxious preoccupations of the Stalinists. That account proposed the transparent objectivity of the historical process. Yet, at the same time, it presupposed the existence of conspiracies and hidden enemies, the dark forces against which the light of progress was to prevail. The tragedy of the Buryats and Mongolians is that they existed in the Communist world as embodiments of *both* the dark and the light. For decades, the terrible events that they experienced as victims and perpetrators could not be spoken about. Even now, hidden behind literal statements such as, "They took the lamas behind the hill and shot them," lies the question of our political relation to (even our identification with) that *they*.

In such circumstances, the factual statement as a genre of speaking cannot be meaningful enough; it cannot suggest what we know. Rather, it seems that many people turn to allegory, the narrative that *demands* interpretation. These stories exemplifying the grand metaphor of fate in history, by attributing the cause of destined acts to the accumulated fruits of sin, point obliquely to the need to think about the "absent presence" at the heart of Communism, to what was laughed out of court in the show trials, the unresolved issue of personal intention and its political results.

Notes

A shorter version of this essay appeared in *Diogène*, no. 194 (spring 2002). I am very grateful to Bruce Grant, Martin Holbraad, Christos Lynteris, Yael Navaro-Yashin, Morten Pedersen, U. E. Bulag, the editors of the volume, and an anonymous reviewer for helpful comments made on an earlier version of this essay.

1. "In some narratives there is little sense of historical time. Rather the action oscillates between a contingent world of happenings, both terrible and lucky, and a world of unchanging repetitions in which archetypal selves are set in mythical time" (Skultans 1998: 25).

2. A. Hürelbaatar carried out fieldwork on Buryat Buddhism in both Russia and China during 1998–99. I am very grateful to him for first bringing the interpretations of reincarnation stories to my attention. Subsequently, on joint fieldwork in Inner Mongolia in the summer of 2000, we encountered further examples of this idiom, although local explanations were extremely circumspect owing to political circumstances.

3. As noted by Žižek (1999: 37–38), the ideology of Stalinism marked a return to the "objectivist" logic of necessary stages, in distinction from the Leninist position, which was to *intervene* in history. Žižek argues that Lenin even rejected the reified logic altogether, on the grounds that the complexity of concrete situations as well as the unexpected "subjective" actions always dislocate the straight line of the class struggle.

4. The Mongolian word *xubilgan* means "transformation" or "metamorphosis," from the verb *xubila-*, "to change," and it refers to the transitory body-vessel taken by a spiritual entity through time. The term is normally applied to the series of highly respected lamas embodying reincarnation lines of bodhisattvas or other saintly figures in Mongol regions (Hyer and Jagchid 1983: 14).

5. Chinese *Xi You Ji*. This was translated into Mongolian at least as early as the eighteenth century as the literary work *Baruunchi Jorchigsan Temdeglel*. Popularly, the story is known as "The Story of Tangsad Lama" ("Tangsad Lama-in Ülger"). Yuan Shikai, it is said, was the reincarnation of the Turtle, Jiang Jieshi of the

Black Dog of Heaven, Mao Zedong of the Pig Deity, Jiang Qing of the White Bone Devil (also the Pipa Devil), Hua Guofeng of Sha Seng, and Hu Yaobang of the Monkey.

6 Buryats of Alhana village in Aga Okrug (Russia) also said that "Stalin had the soul of the Blue Bull of India." The bull in Mongolian, and particularly Buryat, myth appears as a clan ancestor and is associated with autochthonous origin and the earth. The epithet *blue* has no symbolic significance that people remember today and is said to be simply descriptive.

7 The story of the turtle (Chinese *wang-ba*, Mongolian *yastan melxii*) has a somewhat similar structure to that of the Blue Elephant. The turtle accumulated merit by carrying Tangsad Lama and his disciples across the great river. He took them across on his back and, on reaching the other side safely, requested them to ask Buddha when his salvation would come. But they forgot. When they were returning home, now carrying the holy books from India, the turtle again obliged as carrier. Halfway across the river, he asked, "What is my fate?" They replied, "We forgot to ask." So the turtle turned over, and they all fell in the river. The Jirim Mongolian explanation of this story is that Yuan announced himself president and wanted to be emperor but that after this announcement he suddenly died. So Yuan is seen to have failed the Qing dynasty (analogously to the turtle suddenly turning over). Yet the idea is that Yuan also has merit and was badly treated.

8 This idea was expressed by Buryat Buddhist lamas from both Russia and China in 1999.

9 A broadly parallel account to that in Marcus could be given of the Russian and Chinese historiographical situations in the twentieth century. The beginning of the century, with the demise of the Manchu dynasty in China and Mongolia and the revolutionary attempts in Russia, was a time of heterogeneous and opposed descriptions and prognoses; this was succeeded by the period of modernist-Socialist certainty, which was followed by the present era of anxious attempts to explain rapid changes.

10 This possibility, of parallels in the "psychical products" of individuals and cultures, was suggested by Freud (1979: 220–23) in his postscript to his analysis of paranoia (the case of Schreber) and was later followed up in his *Totem and Taboo* and other works. Among anthropological discussions of issues involved are those of Faubion (1993: 391–92), who sees the social and the psychological as two modalities of experience implicating one another, and Weiner (1999: 252–54), who cites Ricoeur's notion of a dialectic between individual symbolic creations and "the symbols in use . . . which service in the clockwork of a given society."

11 "A striking and generally observed feature of the behaviour of paranoics is that they attach the greatest significance to the minor details of other people's behaviour which we ordinarily neglect, interpret them and make them the basis of far-reaching conclusions" (Freud [1901] 1960: 255).

12 Marginal note made by V. I. Yegorov on the Politburo's decree of 4 December 1937, cited in Getty and Nauman (1999: 466–67).

13 The storytellers included a Buddhist lama, an old women in her nineties, and villagers from Alhana in the Aga District, Chita Oblast, Russian Federation. Several younger people from the capital city of Ulan-Ude also knew this story.

14 The fact that the conversations were in Buryat is significant. A considerable proportion of Buryats do not know Buryat and use only Russian (a result of the Russian-only education policies in the 1970s and late 1980s). It is possible that these reincarnation stories are not known among Russian-only speakers.

15 Buddhism was strong among the Buryats living to the south and east of Lake Baikal from the early nineteenth century. "Western Buryats" living northwest of the lake were, however, shamanists and also experienced considerable Orthodox Christian missionary activity. The more Russified "western Buryats" have greater political prominence to this day. Buddhism has nevertheless acquired a strong position as a quasi-national religion in the 1990s, albeit with an uneasy relation to the government, which is dominated by Russians (Namsaraeva 1998).

16 *Yorool* (Mongolian written *irugal*) means "foundation," "deep cause," "portent," or "curse." In this context, the Buryat speakers were using the term to mean an oral will or vow given at death.

17 Buryats do not like using unlucky words like *ebderekh* (destruction, ruin) when discussing their religion; instead, they say *sübtekh* (damage, hurt, harm).

18 For an account of Mongolian legends associated with the mythic land of Shambala, see Damdinsüren (1977).

19 One violent example of such a clash occurred in 1998 when the president of Buryatia encouraged the loan of a Buddhist treasure (an old and valuable illustrated atlas of Tibetan medicine) to the United States for an exhibition. This was interpreted by many Buddhists as selling their birthright. Lamas blockaded the museum where the atlas was held and were beaten up when soldiers came to take it away. The use of physical violence was specifically authorized by the president (Zhukovskaya 1998).

20 The situation in Mongolia may change since the Mongolian People's Revolutionary Party (the equivalent of the Communist Party) was reelected in July 2000 in a landslide.

21 It seems that this song may have been composed specially for people subject to exile and punishment.

22 In Inner Mongolia, this fact is more explicitly recognized by local people, and those who feel guilty for participating in attacks on monasteries during the Cultural Revolution carry out various rituals of expiation (Humphrey and Hürelbaatar, fieldwork in Mergen Sum, 1998).

23 In 1990, when I visited the Tsüügül Monastery, it was in a ruinous state and covered with soldiers' graffiti. It has since been restored.

24 They embodied two laws or "principles of rule," the *yirtincu-yin yoson* (the law of the world) and the *nom-un yoson* (the law of the [sacred] book) (Popova 1987: 66).

25 Some degree of "ethicalization" of the idea of reincarnation probably preceded the establishment of the Socialist state in Mongolia. The nature of good rule was debated earlier during the "theocratic" period (1911–21), when a reincarnation, the Jebtsundamba Xutagt, was also head of state. Already in 1914 Mongolians were discussing how it was that a wise and good-hearted ruler could nevertheless preside over a weak government and increasingly poverty-stricken population. The conclusion of some influential writers was to lead in a different direction from religious ethics, however: Mongolia should abandon the tradition of the all-powerful single leader and follow the example of advanced countries where the people also have power and are consulted about what laws to follow (Popova 1987: 94). Such ideas were expressed in the journal *Shine Toli* (1914–16), which was edited by intellectuals influenced by debates proceeding in China and Russia.

References

Bhabha, Homi. 1997. "Of Mimicry and Man: The Ambivalence of Colonial Discourse." In *Tensions of Empire: Colonial Cultures in a Bourgeois World*, ed. Frederick Cooper and Ann L. Stoler, 152–60. Berkeley and Los Angeles: University of California Press.

Bulag, Uradyn E. 2002. *The Mongols at China's Edge: History and the Politics of National Unity*. New York: Rowman and Littlefield.

Connerton, Paul. 1989. *How Societies Remember*. Cambridge: Cambridge University Press.

Damdinsüren, Ts. 1977. "Ülger domgiin jargalt oron Shambal." *Zentralasiatische Studien* 11:351–88.

Daniel, E. Valentine. 1996. *Charred Lullabies: Chapters in an Ethnography of Violence*. Princeton: Princeton University Press.

Das, Veena. 1995. *Critical Events: An Anthropological Perspective on Contemporary India*. Delhi: Oxford University Press.

Davies, Sarah. 2000. "'Us against Them': Social Identity in Soviet Russia, 1934–41." In *Stalinism: New Directions*, ed. Sheila Fitzpatrick, 47–70. London: Routledge.

Faubion, James D. 1993. *Modern Greek Lessons: A Primer in Historical Constructivism*. Princeton: Princeton University Press.

Forrester, John. 1990. *The Seductions of Psychoanalysis: Freud, Lacan, and Derrida*. Cambridge: Cambridge University Press.

Freud, Sigmund. [1901] 1960. *The Psychopathology of Everyday Life*. Translated by J. Strachey with A. Freud. In *The Standard Edition of the Complete Psychological Works of Sigmund Freud*, vol. 6, ed. James Strachey. London: Hogarth.

———. 1979. *Case Histories II*. New York: Penguin.

Garros, Véronique, Natalia Korenevskaya, and Thomas Lahusen, eds. 1995. *Intimacy and Terror.* Translated by C. A. Flath. New York: New Press.

Getty, J. Arch, and Oleg V. Nauman. 1999. *The Road to Terror: Stalin and the Self-Destruction of the Bolsheviks, 1932–1939.* New Haven: Yale University Press.

Gravers, Mikael. [1993] 1999. *Nationalism as Political Paranoia in Burma: An Essay on the Historical Practice of Power.* Richmond, Va.: Nordic Institute of Asian Studies, Curzon.

Guha, Ranajit. 1988. "The Prose of Counter-Insurgency." In *Selected Subaltern Studies,* ed. Ranajit Guha and Gayatri Spivak, 45–88. New York: Oxford University Press.

Hellbeck, Jochen. 2000. "Fashioning the Stalinist Soul: The Diary of Stepan Podlubnyi, 1931–39." In *Stalinism: New Directions,* ed. Sheila Fitzpatrick, 77–116. New York: Routledge.

Humphrey, Caroline. 1994. "Remembering an Enemy: The Bogd Khaan in Twentieth Century Mongolia." In *Memory, History, and Opposition under State Socialism,* ed. R. Watson, 21–44. Santa Fé: School of American Research.

———. 1997a. "Exemplars and Rules: Aspects of the Discourse of Moralities in Mongolia." In *The Ethnography of Moralities,* ed. Signe Howell, 25–47. London: Routledge.

———. 1997b. "Genres and Diversity in Cultural Politics: On Representations of the Goddess Tara in Mongolia." *Inner Asia: Occasional Papers* 2 (1): 24–47.

Hyer, Paul, and Sechin Jagchid. 1983. *A Mongolian Living Buddha: Biography of the Kanjurwa Khutughtu.* Albany: State University of New York Press.

Kaplonski, Christopher. 1999. "Blame, Guilt, and Avoidance: The Struggle to Control the Past in Post-Socialist Mongolia." *History and Memory* 11 (2): 94–114.

Koselleck, Arthur. 1985. *Futures Past: On the Semantics of Historical Time.* Translated by Keith Tribe. Cambridge, Mass.: MIT Press.

Lass, Andrew. 1994. "From Memory to History: The Events of November 17 Dis/membered." In *Memory, History, and Opposition under State Socialism,* ed. Rubie S. Watson, 87–104. Santa Fé: School of American Research.

Lattimore, Owen, and Fujiko Isono. 1982. *The Diluv Khatagt: Memoirs and Autobiography of a Mongol Buddhist Reincarnation in Religion and Revolution.* Wiesbaden: Otto Harrassowitz.

Marcus, George E., ed. 1999. *Paranoia within Reason: A Casebook on Conspiracy as Explanation.* Chicago: University of Chicago Press.

Namsaraeva, Sayana. 1998. "Khambo-lama: Karma Rossii—v postoyannom bespo-koistve." *Kommersant-Vlast* 7 (259): 50–52.

Popova, Lidiya Pavlovana. 1987. *Obshchestvennaya mysl' Mongolii v epokhu 'probuzh-deniya Azii.'* Moscow: Nauka.

Potanin, G. N. 1883. *Ocherki Severo-Zapadnoi Mongolii.* Vol. 4. Materialy Etnografi-cheskiye. St. Petersburg: Kirshbaum, for Imp. Russk. Geog. Obshchestva.

Ries, Nancy. 1997. *Russian Talk: Culture and Conversation during Perestroika*. Ithaca: Cornell University Press.

Schoenhals, Michael. 1992. *Doing Things with Words in Chinese Politics: Five Studies*. China Research Monograph 41. Berkeley and Los Angeles: University of California Press.

Skultans, Vieda. 1998. *The Testimony of Lives: Narrative and Memory in Post-Soviet Latvia*. London: Routledge.

Stewart, Kathleen, and Susan Harding. 1999. "Bad Endings: American Apocalypsis." *Annual Reviews of Anthropology* 28:285–310.

Stoler, Ann Laura. 1995. *Race and Education of Desire: Foucault's History of Sexuality and the Colonial Order of Things*. Durham: Duke University Press.

Stroganova, Elena. 1999. "Millenarian Representations of the Contemporary Buryats." *Inner Asia* 1 (1): 111–20.

Tumarkin, Nina. 1983. *Lenin Lives! The Lenin Cult in Soviet Russia*. Cambridge, Mass.: Harvard University Press.

Verdery, Katherine. 1999. *The Political Lives of Dead Bodies: Reburial and Postsocialist Change*. New York: Columbia University Press.

Weiner, James. 1999. "Psychoanalysis and Anthropology: On the Temporality of Analysis." In *Anthropological Theory Today*, ed. Henrietta L. Moore, 234–57. Cambridge: Polity.

White, Hayden. 1973. *Metahistory*. Baltimore: Johns Hopkins University Press.

Yurchak, Akexei. In press. "Hegemony of Form: The Unexpected Outcome of the Soviet Linguistic Project."

Zhukovskaya, Nataliya L'vovna. 1998. "Atlas Tibetskoi meditsiny: Na perekrestke religii i politiki." *Etnos i Religiya* (Institut Etnologii i Antropologii) 45 (2): 227–42.

Žižek, Slavoj. 1999. "When the Party Commits Suicide." *New Left Review* 238:26–47.

7

Paranoia, Conspiracy, and Hegemony
in American Politics

DANIEL HELLINGER

Several controversial conspiracy theories ranging from plausible to preposterous have had a remarkable staying power in American political culture. Consider the following examples: Right-wing officials of the national security state assassinated Kennedy to prolong the Cold War. Bolshevism gave rise to a tightly controlled international organization dedicated to Communist world domination. M. L. King Jr. and Malcolm X were assassinated to sap the civil rights movement of its revolutionary potential. A shadowy international group, the Illuminati, is behind the unpatriotic surrender of sovereign power to an international financial elite. Preferring to keep the public ignorant of the presence of aliens, the government is covering up knowledge of a landing of extraterrestrials at Roswell, New Mexico.

Within a political culture that is chauvinistic and militant in its claim to constitute the world's greatest democratic experiment, what explains the widespread conviction that more sinister, conspiratorial forces control the government (or lurk behind it)? Richard Hofstadter (1965) provided the most influential attempt to answer this question in arguing that an underlying "paranoid style in American politics" periodically manifests itself in the history of the United States. Hofstadter laid the groundwork for dismissing conspiracy theory as pathology, as the title of his book entered the lexicon of the political culture. Less remembered is that Hofstadter also contended that conspiracy theories arise from the mass sentiment that popular sovereignty and republican principles are threatened by concentrated economic power and the exercise of American imperial power in world affairs.

Rather than dismiss all conspiracy theory as a form of pathology, this essay treats conspiracy itself as a form of collective, subjective behavior that deserves to be integrated into, not marginalized from, explanations of a structural and historical character. Positivist intellectual paradigms that dominate social science militate against adequate theorizing of this sort and serve to reinforce hegemony by diminishing the importance of agency and abuses of power in systems of domination. Against the claim that they are always disempowering, I argue that conspiracy theories sometimes serve popular resistance and empowerment because they cast suspicion on the transparency and legitimacy of actions undertaken by the police, military, and intelligence agencies, whose missions include actually undertaking conspiracies.

Hegemony refers here, following Gramsci (1971), to the ability of a ruling class to induce mass acceptance of prevailing social, cultural, and moral values. Hegemony is maintained by a complex and multifaceted process that cannot be reduced to conspiracy or to propaganda, especially in republican polities, which aim to decentralize power and render it more transparent. Insofar as certain features of power are not generally understood or visible to the public, political scientists would explain the apparently hidden character of influence in terms of social structures and processes that they would reveal with the tools of social science. Subjectivity and agency are relegated to narrative accounts of what happened; they are rarely incorporated into social-scientific explanation. Radical critiques that veer away from structural and toward instrumental views of power are subject to dismissal as "conspiracy theory." Not surprisingly, most radical critics flee the sobriquet, fearing to be tarred as paranoid.

In this essay, I contend that conspiracy theories are not uniformly pathological and disempowering. In a world where international elites promote pluralist democracy and market transparency, American foreign policy continues to be conducted through opaque processes that bear the hallmarks of conspiracy (see Hellinger and Judd 1994). The post–World War II era has been characterized by repeated scandals involving intelligence agencies, whose mission includes covert operations that thrive in a seamy social sphere that Peter Dale Scott (1996) calls *deep politics*. The suspicion of American expansionism that generated conspiracy theories in the populist era (1890–1930) finds its contemporary equivalent in suspicions that democratic sovereignty is being sacrificed on the altar of economic globalization. Conspiracy theories challenge elites to explain why they have contradicted republican ideals. Those elites' response is typically to dismiss the charges themselves as paranoid, but suspicion persists. We see this process operating in three cases examined in this chapter: The Iran-Contra scandal of 1986 and a related drug-trafficking scandal; conspiracy theories surrounding the assassination of President Kennedy; and mass suspicion of economic globalization.

The Unwelcome Place of Conspiracy in Social Science

For Hofstadter, the "paranoid style" is a distinctive American response to concentrated economic power in American society, characterized by "the qualities of heated exaggeration, suspiciousness, and conspiratorial fantasy" (1965: 3). His book draws on case studies of turn-of-the-century conspiratorial views of banking and monetary policy, visceral anti-British sentiments, and McCarthyism. He contends that genuine economic grievances underlay the conspiracy theories of populist movements between 1880 and 1930, but he views believers as pathologically deluded and hopelessly mired in their own ignorance (1965: 238–315).

This attitude prevails among the few researchers who take conspiracy seriously as a subject for study. A collaborative study of conspiracy by a psychiatrist and a political scientist concludes, "The most powerful value of conspiracy thinking is to remove responsibility from the person or group believing itself to be the victim of the conspiracy" (Robins and Post 1997: 55). The leftist journalist Michael Albert warns, "Conspiracy theorizing, even at its best, detracts from the difficult but worthy task of trying to understand society in order to change it" (1992). Chip Berlet, a freelance researcher specializing in the tracking of right-wing extremists, conceives of conspiracy theory as "a narrative that blames societal or individual problems on a scapegoat. . . . Conspiracism is a parody of institutional analysis" (Berlet 1997). Berlet warns that believers in conspiracy are susceptible to the disempowering appeal of cynical leaders with a cult-like appeal. He advises opponents of U.S. foreign policy to avoid "the problem of conflating documented facts with analysis and conclusions and then merging them with unsubstantiated conspiracy theories popular on the far right" (Berlet 1997).

Daniel Pipes, an academic and the editor of the *Middle East Quarterly*, is outright contemptuous in casting all revisionist historiography and radical thought as "conspiracy theory." "Much conspiracism in the United States is modish, reflecting a taste for puzzles and puzzlement," says Pipes. "While polite society derides the rude notions of true believers, it also stylishly accepts some of their premises. . . . Those who know better are lured by the very outlandishness and disrepute of conspiracy theories" (Pipes 1997: 14). Pipes includes within this fringe element anyone who entertains the thought that conspiracies played a role in the major political scandals and assassinations that rocked American politics in the Vietnam era. He sees the paranoid style in almost any critical historical or social-scientific analysis of oppression.

Little work in the political-science literature treats conspiracy as anything but a pathological political phenomenon.[1] With the exception of a few revisionist historians (e.g., Charles Beard, William A. Williams), most examinations of American foreign policy treat hegemony with what Michael Parenti calls the "stuff happens" approach to history and politics (Parenti 1994: 160–62). The rise of the United States to global hegemony is typically depicted as an unsought, unplanned movement of world history, culminating after World War II with American acceptance of global responsibility. In reality, teams of intellectuals, corporate executives, and diplomats mapped out a grand strategy for American interests after the war. Their planning included recognition of the need to have institutions, like the Central Intelligence Agency, capable of executing operations behind a screen of secrecy and deception (Parenti 1994; Hellinger and Judd 1994: 250). Revisionist historians and critical social scientists (e.g., Sklar 1980) who integrate such planning into their analysis of international affairs are usually dismissed as conspiracy theorists.

Realist and neorealist literature in political science tends to attribute important changes in international political regimes to global economic changes and shifts in the balance of power among great powers (Morgenthau 1948; Keohane 1980; Kennedy 1987). Marxists differ mainly in asking for whom this stability or change works. Consider, for example, William Robinson's recent, influential examination of U.S. hegemony in the post–Cold War world. Robinson insists that American promotion of democracy masks efforts to maintain global capitalism; he goes to considerable length to show that policymakers are conscious of this goal. Despite the conspiratorial overtones of such a theory, Robinson concludes, "Foreign policy flows from the historical and structural conditions under which individual policy makers and governments operate. The whole point of theory, of social science, is to uncover the forces and processes at work in the social universe which lie beneath—indeed, epistemologically speaking, out of the range of— sensory perceptions" (1996: 5).

But conspiracy theorists are also about the business of uncovering forces and processes lying beyond sensory perception. Conspiracies are not just for kooks; they feature centrally and broadly in the American popular imagination, as a glance at any number of popular novels, films, and television shows reveals. They comment on and provoke thought about the real contradictions between republican ideals, such as the degree of openness and transparency in democratic processes, and the actual practices of American hegemony played out on the global stage and at home. Conspiracy theories might be compared to hypernationalism or religious fundamentalism, or, as Benjamin Barber (1996) put it, "*jihad* against McWorld." They introduce subjectivity and individualized forms of accountability into the otherwise impersonal, structural forces that, according to social scientists, journalists, and historians, move our world. Dieter Groh, a social psychologist, sees conspiracy theory as a mass response of ordinary people to impersonal forces that they cannot control and do not understand (Schrauwers, chapter 4 in this volume). Despite attempts by ordinary people to live "in an upright, just manner, go to the right church, belong to a superior culture," says Groh, "they feel that this suffering is undeserved." So it is logical, he says, for them to search for a cause. "Thus the world around them is no longer as it should be. It becomes more and more an illusion, a semblance, while at the same time the evil that has occurred, or is occurring and is becoming more and more essential, takes place *behind* reality" (Groh 1987: 1). For Groh, conspiracy theory is more a coping mechanism than a pathology.

Anita Waters (1987) recommends that we reserve judgment on the truth of conspiracy theories and employ an ethnosociological approach. "Contrary to a psychopathology perspective that treats conspiracy theories as delusions," says Waters, "an ethnosociology approach expects that believers will be better acquainted with the social facts that are explained by conspiracy theories" (1987: 112). In this volume, we too deemphasize psychosociological approaches and entertain the reasonability of many conspiracy theories as ways of explaining events that are disturbing and unexpected to particular groups (see also Davis 1969). To move beyond the "paranoid-style thesis" in understanding conspiracy theory requires identification of the group(s) who hold the belief, attention to the events and circumstances that give rise to the conspiracy, and serious consideration of the credibility from the *point of view of the believers*. This latter strategy makes the most sense, I would contend, when we think about conspiracies as a form of collective political behavior, just as we do coups, political campaigns, or battles. Just as major political tendencies are not explained by these activities alone, so also they cannot be left out of any fully satisfactory explanation.

Theorizing Conspiracy

Conspiracy is subjective, group behavior involving three analytically distinct but interrelated characteristics: secrecy; vulnerability to defeat by exposure; and one or a combination of illegality, deception, betrayal of legitimate purposes of an authorized activity, and contradiction of generally accepted moral codes of behavior. The third criterion distinguishes conspiracies from other kinds of secret collaboration. Analogous to the latter are the huddles preceding each down in American football, where the players gather out of earshot of their opponents to plan their next play. A huddle becomes a conspiracy, for example, when players, induced by bribes from gamblers, use it to plan to lose the game deliberately or to "shave points" off the score. This would be illegal and/or a betrayal of the authorized purpose of the huddle—to plan tactics for winning the game.

Secrecy may be authorized in sensitive police matters or military operations, such as criminal investigations, diplomatic negotiations, or the formation of an order of battle. Intelligence agencies may be authorized to gather data or conduct covert activities within the bounds of international and national law for the purpose of defending the security of the state and its citizens. Governments may authorize diplomats to negotiate in secrecy to allow frank and confidential discussion of issues out of the glare of media. Such actions become conspiratorial only when actors violate international law, exceed mandates, protect or advance their own interests, harass or target political opponents, or plan a military coup. Conspiracy also arises when authorized representatives, officials of international organizations, and economic elites meet in secret, not to advance negotiations, but to avoid democratic procedures and deprive opponents of reasonable opportunities to subject treaties and agreements to debate.

Pipes usefully distinguishes, not only between real conspiracies and "fear of a nonexistent conspiracy," but also between *petty conspiracies* of limited ambition (regardless of their consequences) and *world conspiracies* (Pipes 1997: 20–21).[2] World conspiracy theories describe a "powerful, evil, and clandestine group that aspires to global hegemony; dupes and agents who extend the group's influence around the world so it is on the verge of succeeding; and a valiant but embattled group that urgently needs to help stave off catastrophe" (Pipes 1997: 21–22). I contend that elite conspiracies are not normally either world or petty in nature. They fit a third category that Pipes (1997: 20–21) mentions in little more than passing: "operational conspiracies."

Operational conspiracies seek to prevent or encourage a political out-come promoting or discouraging a significant shift in power among political actors—individuals, groups, or states. They involve a secret combination of political operatives or officials pursuing their goals through illegal or covert means (usually both). They seek to hide such outcomes and the means to achieve them from public view for fear of widespread reproach, defeat in constitutional or democratic arenas, or political (possibly criminal) sanction (Hellinger and Judd 1994: 4). Operational conspiracies are too commonly treated as world conspiracies. As the latter usually stretch the bounds of plausibility and are not regarded by believers as falsifiable, conflating the two makes it easy for analysts, such as Pipes, to dismiss the relevance and truth value of explanations incorporating conspiracy of any sort. However, operational conspiracy is intrinsic to covert actions undertaken by intelli-gence agencies, and exposure of covert actions has almost always proved embarrassing. The repeated recourse to operational conspiracies by elites re-inforces the credibility of broader conspiracy theories and undermines demo-cratic legitimacy.

Drugs, Covert Operations, and Conspiracy

Some conspiracy theorists contend that the U.S. intelligence apparatus has given birth to a group of rogue agents who constitute a shadow government, a "Secret Team" that has usurped power from constitutional authorities and has been repeatedly involved in scandals such as Watergate and Iran-Contra. In this section, I look at claims regarding the connected scandals of Iran-Contra and allegations that the CIA and other members of the Secret Team have complicity in introducing crack cocaine into American cities in the 1980s. Some conspiracy theorists see a seamless connection between these scandals and the assassination of Kennedy, which I take up in the next sec-tion.

Iran-Contra erupted when Reagan administration officials were caught illegally funneling funds from the sale of weapons to Iran and from other sources to the Nicaraguan Contras, who were organized by Washington to overthrow a government challenging U.S. hegemony. Policymakers believed it necessary to conceal their support (active or tacit) for fear of sanction under international and national law. Conspiracy was essential to the policy because the operation was in violation of restrictions imposed by the U.S. Congress. The need for secrecy was reinforced because, by the criteria of many human rights groups and international jurists, the Contras used terrorism in their struggle with the Sandinistas.[3]

Several conspiracies associated with Iran-Contra were arguably of treasonous proportions. The most notorious was revealed in a 1987 story distributed by the Knight-Ridder Newspaper wire service, which reported that Lt. Col. Oliver North "helped draft a plan in 1984 to impose martial law in the United States in case of an emergency." The martial law plan was designed to deal with anticipated domestic protest organized by opponents of the Reagan administration's policy toward Central America. "The secret plan called for the suspension of the Constitution, the transfer of governmental control to the little-known Federal Emergency Management Agency [FEMA], and the appointment of military commanders to run state and local governments. It also called for the declaration of martial law in the event of a crisis such as nuclear war, violent and widespread internal dissent, or national opposition to a U.S. invasion abroad" (*St. Louis Post-Dispatch,* 5 July 1987, 1). Opponents of the administration's policies demanded that the joint congressional committee investigating Iran-Contra in 1986 look into the North conspiracy, but the committee invoked national security grounds and rejected attempts by Representative Henry Gonzalez, a Democrat from Texas, to hold public hearings. It heard testimony on the FEMA matter only behind closed doors.

One organization that sought to unmask the Secret Team was the Left-Christian-oriented Christic Institute. In a case made famous by the movie *Silkwood,* the Christic Institute had gained credibility with the public for exposing crimes involving a corporate conspiracy in the nuclear power industry. Christic sought to replicate that success through a high-profile civil suit, ultimately dismissed, on behalf of American journalists injured in a bombing allegedly carried out by the Contras at La Penca, Costa Rica. The institute filed charges alleging that various members of the Secret Team violated the Neutrality Act and sought to invoke provisions of the Racketeering Influence and Corrupt Organization Act (RICO), which had been passed as a tool to prosecute the Mafia for criminal conspiracy. Christic's executive director, Michael Sheehan, detailed his case in a videotaped speech shown in thousands of house meetings organized by opponents of U.S. policy in Central America in which he denounced the conspirators as a rogue government within the government. According to Sheehan, "It is the American people who these people fear. They are afraid because [of] the program of assassination, the horribly dark secrets that they know" (Sheehan 1986).

Critics of Sheehan feared the lawsuit would distract attention from the historical and structural roots of the U.S.-orchestrated "low-intensity wars" in Central America. Berlet, for example, acknowledged that Christic had exposed many unsavory aspects of U.S. policy, but he charged the institute, and Sheehan in particular, with using tactics that illustrate "the problem of conflating documentable facts with analysis and conclusions and then merging them with unsubstantiated conspiracy theories popular on the far right [that have] plagued progressive foreign policy critiques for years" (Berlet 1997: no. 10, no. 11).

Indeed, the fate of North's conspiracy to impose martial law illustrates how the theory spun by Sheehan fails to capture the complexity of forces driving U.S. foreign policy. On learning of North's plan, Attorney General William French Smith protested to Robert C. MacFarlane, the president's national security adviser, who put an end to it. Clearly, North, CIA director William Casey, and other members of the so-called Secret Team did not possess the kind of power attributed to them by Sheehan, who elevated the operational conspiracies uncovered by Christic to the level of a world conspiracy. However, to ignore the conspiratorial aspects is to deny the powerful counterhegemonic potential of revealing plans laid by North and his associates. Secret operations bearing hallmarks of a coup d'état were hatched illegally at the highest levels of the world's most powerful state. North and other officials at the National Security Council shredded incriminating notes and documents and falsified others to provide cover. The revelation of these activities (in which Christic played a small but significant part) inflicted a serious propaganda setback on the media-savvy Reagan administration. Sheehan failed to understand the constraints that institutions and structures impose on conspirators; Berlet failed to appreciate their counterhegemonic potential.

The Secret Team story would arise again with a vengeance ten years later. On 18–20 August 1996, the *San Jose Mercury News* published a series of articles by the investigative journalist Gary Webb. The lead of the first story alleged that a San Francisco area "drug ring sold tons of cocaine to . . . street gangs of Los Angeles and funneled millions in drug profits to a Latin American guerrilla army [the Contras] run by the U.S. Central Intelligence Agency." Webb claimed that it was this "dark alliance" that "opened the first pipeline between Colombia's cocaine cartels and the black neighborhoods of Los Angeles, a city now known as the 'crack' capital of the world. The cocaine that flooded in helped spark a crack explosion in urban America and provided the cash and connections needed for L.A.'s gangs to buy automatic weapons." He described the network as "one of the most bizarre alliances in modern history: the union of a U.S. backed army attempting to overthrow a revolutionary Socialist government and the Uzi-toting 'gangstas' of Compton and South-Central Los Angeles." The series was later expanded into a book, *Dark Alliance* (Webb 1998).

Most mainstream media ignored Webb's story until African American political leaders began to use his work to demand accountability and an investigation of the charges (Overbeck 1996; Peterson 1997; Golden 1996a). Instead of pursuing additional leads, however, coverage emphasized shortcomings in Webb's reporting, disparaged its diffusion on the Internet and "call-in" radio shows, and alleged that believers were more gullible than most other Americans. Webb's professionalism came under attack in the *New York Times*, the *Washington Post*, and the *Los Angeles Times* (Adkins 1996; FAIR 1996; Solomon 1996, 1997; Overbeck 1996; Parry 1998); eventually the reporter was forced to resign from the *Mercury News*. Explaining the credibility of the story took precedence over investigating the facts.

Reporters looked for an explanation of the popular credibility of the story in the minds of the affected community. Although acknowledging that African Americans had good reason to be suspicious of government conspiracy, Tim Golden of the *New York Times* concluded, "The force of the *Mercury News* account appears to have relatively little to do with the quality of the evidence that it marshals to its case" (1996b). Adopting the detached and objective discursive style required by the professional norms of American journalism, Golden cited several African American intellectuals to buttress the claim that African Americans are more susceptible to conspiracy theory because they harbor "an endless supply of suspicion" (Golden 1996b). His lead for the story was an anecdote about a black woman in South-Central who "has seen crack cocaine rage through her neighborhood like a violent storm" and "found what she took to be proof of an unseen force behind the devastation." Golden chose not to present the woman's voice as authoritative but instead to evoke our pity for her supposedly irrational perspective.

The *Boston Globe*, in a front-page story, "True or False, Rumors Spread" (Haygood 1996), quoted Paul Young, the director of the Paul Robeson Cultural Center at Penn State University, in a way that seemed to validate African American suspicions. "Within the white community you need a scientific method for everything. You have to prove it scientifically. In order to prove the crack connection in Los Angeles to whites, you have to have proof of a CIA agent with drugs on his back dropping off the drugs in the community," said Young. The story cited other conspiracy theories said to be popular among African Americans, for example, claims that fried chicken restaurant chains and soft drink companies are deliberately poisoning blacks. The "dark alliance" story was equated with some conspiracy myths held by the far Right, such as the notion that black helicopters carrying UN troops will invade America. Presented in such a context, Young's words seemed to validate the idea that African Americans had deluded themselves about the source of crack. Journalists seemed committed a priori to discrediting Webb's story, and social science helped them explain it away as conspiracy theory.

An editorial in the *Tampa Tribune* (23 December 1996) attributed the hostile and skeptical reception that greeted CIA director John Deutsch when he appeared before a South-Central audience (to deny CIA complicity in drug trade) to the prejudices of the residents and to political opportunism. "Obviously there is more political capital in assigning blame than stressing personal responsibility," said the *Tribune*. In his book, Pipes excoriates black journalists and political leaders, including Jesse Jackson and Representative Maxine Waters, for putting any stock in the notion that the government was "complicit in the spread of crack." Even after the *Mercury News* backed off the story, this "had little impact on black opinion . . . which widely accepted *Dark Alliance* as truth," wrote Pipes (1997: 4–5).

An ethnosociological approach suggests that Webb's story had deeper resonance among African Americans, whose experiences lent particular credibility to the operational conspiracy. Their suspicions of conspiracy forced mainstream media and the government to respond seriously to their suspicions that intelligence and policy agencies have little real regard for community, as opposed to "national," security. Vincent Schiraldi, the director of the Center on Juvenile and Criminal Justice, was a lone voice in taking the believers seriously. Schiraldi contended that, in general, African Americans are more likely than whites to believe that the government is "out to get them" *because the facts seem to fit the theory:* "Government surveys show that blacks are slightly less likely to use illicit drugs yet blacks are arrested at five times the rate of whites, and nearly three out of four (74 percent) of those sentenced to prison for possession of drugs are black." Citing other statistics documenting the high rates of imprisonment of black men, Schiraldi argues that the distinction is clear to blacks and makes them "quite ready to believe the government is engaged in a conspiracy." The reasonableness of conspiracy theory is attributable not only to historical oppression, says Schiraldi. "African-Americans tend to view the 'War on Drugs' as a government-sponsored 'War on Blacks.'" That is, the drug war is a race war. "I just mean that, if there was such a conspiracy, it could hardly target blacks any more effectively" (Schiraldi 1996).

The "dark alliance" story might have been quickly buried had not the *Mercury-News* posted the articles on its Internet site, one of the most sophisticated on the World Wide Web at the time. The story took off like wildfire; in one day alone the newspaper site recorded 1 million visitors—quite a phenomenon for a newspaper with a print circulation of only 300,000. The story was also propagated on African American radio call-in programs. For Pipes (1997: 199–201), this is merely evidence that new forms of media have encouraged the proliferation of conspiracy theories, but Internet and "talk radio" formats are perhaps the only mass media that are not entirely passive, that allow ordinary people to achieve voice directly, even if that voice is not entirely unmediated. Their formats lend themselves to control and manipulation by producers and hosts, but the multiplicity of outlets and the immediacy of transmission leave space for the audience to achieve voice to some degree. In other words, they offer potential empowerment—to some extent real, to some extent imaginary—to those who use them.

Historical precedents for the involvement of the national security apparatus in drug deals should have lent more credibility to Webb's story. One of many well-documented studies of CIA participation in the drug trade was written by Gerald Posner, before he emerged as the foremost defender of the Warren Commission and also a critic of the idea that a conspiracy was behind the assassination of Martin Luther King Jr. (Posner 1988, 1994, 1998). Posner described how intelligence operations, not only profited from, but encouraged the expansion of drug production.[4] As with later covert operations, these activities had their consequences for domestic American politics. They found their way into right-wing organizations that fostered McCarthyism and into the presidential campaign of 1968 (Posner 1988: 70–71).

Why did Posner not draw censure for his exposé of CIA complicity in narcotics trafficking, while Webb's career was virtually destroyed for very similar allegations? Posner depicted the drug trade as an aberrant practice of U.S. foreign policy, one mistakenly implemented to foster good intentions. Webb's story challenged the very notion that these activities are aberrant and undertaken to defend the security of all Americans. The insistence of African Americans on accountability threatened to erode support for the national security apparatus among a broader public that has grown increasingly skeptical of government over the last thirty-five years. This is illustrated by the persistent belief of a majority of Americans that President John F. Kennedy's assassination was the work, not of a lone gunman, but of a conspiracy.

The belief in a conspiracy to assassinate Kennedy is so widespread as to defy an ethnosociological approach. Three-quarters of the American public does not constitute a "community"; it is, rather, a mass sharing a myth. The vastness of the alleged conspiracy is exceeded only by the literature treating the subject. Pipes (1997: 16) estimates that over two thousand books have been published in thirty years on the assassination. The persistence and popularity of conspiracy theories about the Kennedy assassination are reinforced by a general decline in trust of public institutions in the wake of the Vietnam War and Watergate. "My paranoia and mistrust of authority came of age during Watergate," says the creator of the popular American science fiction television program *The X-Files* (Marin and Gegax 1996).

There indeed exists a substantial gap between elite and mass opinion regarding the Kennedy assassination. A majority of journalists who covered Kennedy's fateful motorcade in Dallas on 22 November 1963 said thirty years later that they accepted the verdict of the Warren Commission, which concluded that Oswald acted alone (UPI 1993). By contrast, a 1963 Gallup poll showed that 52 percent of Americans already did not believe that one person was responsible for the assassination. The belief seems to have become more widespread with the passage of time. A poll of residents of the state of Iowa in 1992 showed that 74 percent felt that Oswald was not acting alone. Two other polls that same year showed 77 and 73 percent of Americans sharing that view. Of those who watched Oliver Stone's film *JFK*, 82 percent believed that Oswald was part of a conspiracy. It may be a measure of public cynicism that more Americans suspect the CIA than suspect the Mafia of complicity in the assassination (Fogarty 1992; AFP 1992).

A few studies (summarized in Harrison and Thomas 1997) suggest a strong correlation between a sense of powerlessness and mistrust and belief in conspiracies, including doubt about the Warren Commission findings, but we lack sociological or anthropological studies to test this proposition directly. Polling data largely focus on the polarized questions of whether the public believes the Warren Commission or whether Oswald acted alone. We have little data on who believes that there was a conspiracy to kill Kennedy and even less on which versions of the various conspiracies they believe. Nor do we know much about what other kinds of political beliefs the Warren Commission doubters hold. One study (Goertzel 1994), based on a survey of 348 New Jersey residents, finds that belief in one conspiracy raises the credibility of conspiracies in general, but this does not necessarily mean that all conspiracies are given the same degree of credibility or importance.

The release of *JFK* in 1991 boosted the salience of conspiracy theories related to the assassination. The two inspirations for the film were New Orleans district attorney Jim Garrison's closing summation in his unsuccessful prosecution in 1969 of a businessman (Clay Shaw) for allegedly conspiring to kill Kennedy and the views of Fletcher Prouty, a former high-ranking Air Force intelligence officer. Prouty spun out a theory (and coined the term *the Secret Team*) of a conspiracy to control the presidency. "There is a grave conspiracy over the land," wrote Prouty (1975). "This is a game for the biggest stake of all—absolute control of the government of the United States of America; and with control of this government, control of the world. And yet the real crime underlying all of this has not even been identified, stated, and charged. The real criminals still walk the streets, run their corporations, control their banks, and pull strings through their political and financial machines."

In his summation, dramatized in *JFK*, Garrison (1969) called the Warren Commission investigation "probably the greatest fraud perpetrated in the history of humankind." Insisting that he would not "accept power without truth," Garrison claimed that "the strange and deceptive conduct of the government after [Kennedy's] murder began while his body was warm, and has continued for five years." Garrison warned, "There are forces in America today, unfortunately, which are not in favor of the truth coming out about John Kennedy's assassination." The jury, said Garrison, was "the hope of humanity . . . which may yet triumph over excessive government power."

JFK is a feature film using a documentary format that embellishes an actual event, while *The X-Files* embellishes fictional story lines with elements drawn from real events, including many allusions to the Kennedy assassination. Both might be dismissed as popular works of the entertainment industry, but both successfully blur the distinction between documentary and fiction. Less so than with *JFK*, viewers can easily draw a distinction between the plots of *The X-Files* and reality, which probably accounts for why the program was less controversial than *JFK* was on its release. Film and television show share, however, a claim that trusted police and intelligence agencies, more often depicted as "heroic" in terms in popular culture, are agents of a vast conspiracy that operates in the background, behind the facade of ordinary political processes.

Many critics attributed the popularity of *JFK* and television's *The X-Files* to a growing mass pathology in the political culture (e.g., Marin and Gegax 1996). Certainly, the appeal of both reflects a sea change in Americans' trust in government and sense of civic efficacy. Gallup polls show that, between 1958 and 1994, trust in government fell from 73 percent to 19 percent. Data from the National Opinion Research Center show that, in 1966, 42 percent of the public expressed a "great deal of confidence" in Congress; thirty years later that figure had fallen to 8 percent. For the executive branch the decline was from 41 percent to 10 percent in the same period. In 1958, 24 percent said that one could "trust the government to do what is right" only some of the time. By 1996, that figure had risen to 68 percent. In 1958, levels of trust were significantly lower for older people, those with less education, and those with lower incomes. However, by 1996, levels of mistrust had increased among all groups, including those with more education and higher incomes (Bardes and Oldendick 2000: 109–13), suggesting greater receptivity to conspiracism throughout the political culture. After attacks on the World Trade Center in New York and the Pentagon in Washington, D.C., on 11 September 2001 and the subsequent incidents of anthrax infection, approval ratings for the president and Congress and confidence in government soared. However, six weeks later, a *New York Times* poll (30 October) revealed that only half the public believed that "the government is telling the people everything they need to know about the anthrax attacks."

The appeal of *The X-Files* seemed to cut across class and party lines. At the height of its popularity in 1997, 16 percent of all televisions in the nation were tuned to the program, and it is estimated that three of every ten adults between the ages of eighteen and forty-nine watching television were tuned in. A repeat episode was the eighth-most-watched television program in the final week of September 1999. The program tended to attract males slightly more than females, but its attractiveness to advertisers was built on the broad swath of loyal viewers among young adults, regardless of social class. The widespread appeal of the program and the evidence of growing cynicism and mistrust of government among all ages and social classes put in doubt the contention (e.g., Pipes 1997) that conspiracy theory is attractive mostly to minorities and lower-income groups. Its plots fed off widespread doubts about the legitimacy of democratic processes and the possibility of citizen efficacy.

The plots of *The X-Files* are wild and convoluted. World conspiracy theory is at the heart of the show. The images that run behind the opening credits include the flashed messages "Government Conspiracy" and "Government Denies Knowledge." One of the two main protagonists, FBI Agent Fox Mulder, repeats aphorisms expressing a general distrust of American government, including, "All lies lead to the truth," "Trust no one," and "Apology is policy." *The X-Files* built on the popularity of *JFK* and popular skepticism about the Warren Commission by featuring a recurring plot line built around the premise of a secret intelligence team responsible for Watergate and the major assassinations of the 1960s.

Much of the power of post–World War II conspiracism in popular culture can be traced to anxieties about loss of individualism, to what Timothy Melley (2000) calls *agency panic*. *Agency panic* refers to an intense fear among Americans that individuals can be shaped or controlled by powerful external forces. However, the kind of conspiracism that pervades *The X-Files* and many other works of popular culture differs from the kind of fear associated with McCarthyism and with plots such as that found in the film *The Manchurian Candidate*. The international conspiracies of Cold War lore were portrayed as an external threat. If American government officials were involved, they were a fifth column to be rooted out by a partnership of law enforcement agencies and a vigilant citizenry. In *The X-Files*, the fault seems more within us. The main protagonist, Agent Mulder, once ruminated, "What science may never be able to explain is our inflapable [*sic*] fear of the alien among us; a fear which often drives us not to search for understanding, but to deceive, inveigle, and obfuscate. To obfuscate the truth not only from others, but from ourselves" (Alphabet 1999). In an era in which President Bill Clinton seriously questioned the meaning of the very word *is* in a legal deposition, the widespread mendacity of public officials in *The X-Files* resonates with the public.

Deep Politics and Conspiracy

One can hardly imagine a more damaging blow to the legitimacy of the political system than to have Hollywood put Garrison's and Prouty's conspiracy theories into Oscar-winning celluloid. To explain the popular appeal of the Oliver Stone film, journalists and social scientists alluded, following Hofstadter, to a widespread popular misunderstanding of the motives of those holding power and an overdeveloped sense of morality in American political culture. "To a non-American," wrote Henri Astier (1992), "the most striking feature of American conspiracy theories is their populist nature. They rarely reflect the prejudices of a section of society—say one ethnic group—against another, and never the paranoia of a ruler against his people." Astier writes, "People who strongly believe in such powerful ideals as those embodied in the US constitution [*sic*] will not adjust their outrage to the gravity of the offense" (1992: 160).

Peter Dale Scott sees in academic resistance to theories of a conspiracy to assassinate Kennedy "the legacy of the Enlightenment that has left us in this century with the unattractive choices of academic social science and scientific socialism," which he calls *rationalistic structuralism* (1996: 10). He argues that Kennedy's assassination most likely altered the course of American involvement in Vietnam, deepening it, a position adopted in Stone's *JFK*. The assassination, then, would constitute, he argues, a coup d'état. Scott contends that this proposition troubles historians and social scientists, who find it impossible within the positivist tradition to accept that an important historical outcome could have been contingent on an assassination.

Scott contends that a conspiracy to kill Kennedy was hatched in an opaque area of political life "where the processes openly acknowledged are not always securely in control, precisely because of their accommodation to unsanctioned sources of violence, through arrangements not openly acknowledged and reviewed" (1996: xiii). In his analysis of dark events in the post–World War II history of the United States, Scott finds a common thread in traumas like the Kennedy and King assassinations, Watergate, and Iran-Contra. He argues that understanding these episodes will take us, not to a handful of malevolent people, but to "deep politics," defined as "institutional and parapolitical arrangements which constitute the way we are systematically governed. The conspiracies I see as operative, in other words, are part of our political structure, not exceptions to it" (1996: 11). More than just "parapolitics," deep politics includes the shadowy conspiratorial undertakings of national security agencies escaping institutional accountability. "What is really operating here," according to Scott, "is a widely disseminated willingness, not to be blamed on any single individual or agency, private or public, to resort to fraud, violence, or murder to be done." Instead, we have developed a deeply rooted "system of accommodations, one of which is characterized by alliances or symbiosis with lawless forces, such as drug traffickers" (1996: 311–12).

The views of Stone and Scott were specifically addressed in Gerald Posner's *Case Closed* (1994), which defended the Warren Commission's conclusion that Kennedy was assassinated by Lee Harvey Oswald acting as a "lone gunman." *Case Closed* was enthusiastically praised by critics and heavily promoted by its author in numerous appearances on television and radio shows. The book quickly rose to best-seller status. The *New York Times*

Book Review (Ward 1993) proclaimed, "The Most Durable Assassination Theory: Oswald Did It Alone." Its reviewer dismissed Scott's book as the "opaque" meanderings of a literature professor; Posner, by contrast, was validated as a "former Wall Street lawyer." One reviewer contended, "The range and depth of Posner's research is awesome. Nothing essential escaped him." Scott, however, was dismissed as "a longtime leftist critic" who has written just "another conspiracy book" (Reeves 1994: 1378–79).[5]

In its zeal to disparage a particular conspiracy theory, *Case Closed* unintentionally builds an impressive case for the existence of "deep politics."[6] For example, Posner (1994: chap. 3) presents a chilling account of the brutal treatment meted out by Jim Angleton, the CIA official charged with verifying the credentials of defectors, to Yuri Nosenko, a KGB defector who was familiar with Oswald's activities in Russia. Posner (1994: 34–45) claims Nosenko would otherwise have helped corroborate the lone gunman thesis. Posner portrays Angleton and the operations division of the CIA as a dark, violent part of the state, a world of covert activities, obsessed with their own grand conspiracy theory (anti-Communism) and ruthlessness in acting on it.

Posner is a messiah to those refusing to entertain conspiracy theory as an explanation for the assassination, a pariah to those who see no other possible explanation. In reality, *Case Closed* falls somewhere between the logically argued, impeccably researched study seen by his admirers and the distorted apology portrayed by his critics.[7] Posner demonstrates that the evidence and some testimony *can be interpreted* consistently with the Warren Commission, but he does not prove that Kennedy could *only* have been killed by a lone gunman or that the case is closed. Like most conspiracy theorists, whom he disdains, Posner takes what *could* have happened as proof of what *did* happen, and he substitutes a more complex explanation for a more parsimonious one.

The Posner book was part of an elite effort to respond to widespread and persistent public skepticism about the Kennedy assassination. There is little doubt that, from the first, the Warren Commission's charge was to allay public concerns that a conspiracy (foreign or domestic) was behind the assassination, and the persistence of conspiracy theory has been the primary force behind the acceleration of the release of classified materials related to the president's murder. Stone's *JFK*, like Webb's *Dark Alliance,* forced elites to reopen episodes that they would rather remain closed.

Globalization and Conspiracy

In contrast to the Kennedy assassination (an event) or Iran-Contra (a scandal), globalization is a broad, impersonal tendency that seems evolutionary, beyond agency, and impervious to the contingency associated with conspiracism. However, globalization is not merely "happening," any more than American hegemony merely "happened." Its most fervent defenders are liberal internationalists in intellectual and diplomatic circles. William Appleman Williams argues that, beginning with the administration of Woodrow Wilson (1912–20), elites have been aware of the need to plan and seek their goals consciously:

> They very seldom blundered into either success or failure. . . . They were simply powerful and influential men of this world who had concluded, from hard experience and close observation, that all of the truth all of the time was almost always dangerous. Hence they did not use all of the truth all of the time. . . . They thought about economics in a *national* sense; as an absolutely crucial variable in the functioning of the system *per se*, and as the foundation for constitutional government and a moral society. And all of them viewed overseas economic expansion as essential to the continued successful operation of the American free-enterprise system. (Williams 1967: 31)

The liberal internationalist outlook described by Williams has been fodder for right-wing conspiracy theorists with a large following. Television evangelist and power broker Pat Robertson (1991) equates the *New World Order*, a term coined by President George Bush in 1991 after the Persian Gulf War, with the work of Satan. Even more remarkable is the popularity of the outlandish theories of Lyndon LaRouche Jr., who sees the notorious hand of the Illuminati behind globalization (LaRouche 1998). The network of organizations controlled by LaRouche constitutes the most influential movement espousing a world conspiracy theory unapologetically at the center of its worldview.[8] LaRouche organizations have attracted talent from intelligence agencies and other branches of the military-industrial complex, connections that LaRouche has parlayed at times into access to right-wing governments, including the Reagan administration and the (former) apartheid regime in South Africa (King and Radosh 1984). LaRouche's conspiracy theory envisions a sinister cabal of the strangest bedfellows. For example, in a speech made on the eve of the 1976 presidential election to a national television audience, LaRouche contended that the Soviets, the Rockefellers, and the British monarchy are behind the international drug trade (Berlet 1986).

The post–Cold War philosophy of LaRouche is expressed in the *Executive Intelligence Review,* in which hyperbole is in no short supply. In the 9 October 1998 issue of the *Review,* LaRouche proclaimed that political authority must be wrested from the "over-reaching powers assumed by supranational agencies" and restored to "a perfectly sovereign nation-state republic." If not, a world economic meltdown and a "collapse into a global 'new dark age' " are inevitable. The failure of the meltdown to occur within weeks, as predicted, did not deter LaRouche a few months later (in the 15 January 1999 issue of the *Review*) from interpreting impeachment proceedings against President Clinton as a struggle "triggered by what is about to become generally recognized as the worst world depression of the century." The plot, said LaRouche, involved replacing Clinton with Vice President Al Gore, an "act of treason in our nation's political establishment" orchestrated "by President Clinton's foreign (London-centered) and domestic (Wall Street–centered) enemies, such as the circles of Richard Mellon Scaife, Conrad Black's Hollinger corporation, and London's Lord William Rees-Mogg." Various other coconspirators are named, all employing "increasing use of lunatic 'free trade' and 'globalization' ideologies to destroy the economic and other essential functions of the sovereign nation-state."

Despite these outlandish views, LaRouche's following numbers in the hundreds of thousands. His most important cadre organization is the National Caucus of Labor Committees (NCLC). The NCLC participates in elections through a front group, the National Democratic Policy Committee (NDPC). Operating on the fringes of the Democratic Party, the NDPC fielded two thousand candidates in thirty states in 1984. In 1986, the NDPC scored its most significant electoral victory when two of its candidates won statewide nominations: for lieutenant governor and secretary of state in the Illinois Democratic Party primary. In a press conference after their victory, the NDPC candidates accused the Centers for Disease Control in Atlanta of withholding evidence on the ease of transmitting the AIDS virus. They promised to set up "Nuremberg tribunals" to try big business profiteers in the international drug trade. One candidate said that the disappearances and murders of young African Americans in Atlanta a few years before were the work of witches who kidnapped the children and made pornographic movies, a revelation bottled up by connivance between (former) Mayor Andrew Young and Queen Elizabeth II (Oxnevad 1986).

LaRouche's electoral success in Illinois constituted a stealth attack on a slumbering Democratic establishment in an election with an extremely low turnout (22 percent). The victory proved ephemeral, but this should not obscure the fact that his organization garnered over 370,000 votes in the secretary of state race. The appeal of the LaRouche candidates in the 1986 primary must be understood in the context of a decade-long, serious farm-bankruptcy crisis and persistent high unemployment in smaller cities with uncompetitive manufacturing economies. Michael McKeon, a local pollster who had noted growing LaRouche support well before the election, attributed the vote to a rising fear among farmers and workers in small cities that their skills and roles were being marginalized and their economic plight not likely to be remedied by traditional methods. "Hard work just doesn't guarantee success anymore," said McKeon (Oxnevad 1986: A1). An organizer from the rural advocacy organization Prairiefire, often attacked by LaRouche supporters, commented, "I think you can draw a connecting line between the LaRouchers' limited election success and the broad rural atmosphere of despair as well as general right-wing activity in some of these areas" (Malcolm 1986). This line was drawn for rural voters by NDPC volunteers who went house to house, down lonely farm roads, setting up thousands of information tables at fairs and picnics in depressed urban and rural areas.

Who found NDPC most persuasive is suggested by the geographical distribution of support for Robert D. Hart, its candidate for state treasurer in the primary. Hart made no attempt to hide his views, telling the *Granite City Press Record/Journal*, "I have spent the last 11 years mastering the political economy of the American system in association with the world's foremost economist Lyndon H. LaRouche, Jr." (unpublished *Granite City Press Record/Journal* candidate survey). Although losing, he polled a respectable 14 percent (108,452 votes) of votes cast in a four-way race against three well-known Democratic candidates. The Hart vote was concentrated in rural regions in the southern half of the state, where the agricultural crisis of the 1980s hit hardest, and in smaller cities, where traditional manufacturing industries had shed the greatest number of workers from their payrolls. Hart received only 10 percent of the vote in the Chicago metropolitan area but 22 percent of the vote elsewhere. He finished first in 32 and second in 19 of the state's 102 counties, running strongest in the southern and western agricultural regions and in the counties around Rock Island–Moline, where forces associated with the agricultural crisis and manufacturing unemployment converged. He also ran well in the rural counties near East St. Louis, the cradle of right-wing movements such as Phyllis Schlafy's Eagle Forum and the John Birch Society, and in parts of southern Illinois hospitable in the past to nativist movements, such as the Ku Klux Klan.

In a period of hardship and declining confidence in politicians and institutions, it seems that the LaRouche movement found its most secure basis in those areas where voters have felt both politically and economically marginalized in the past, much as Hofstadter depicted them. White voters in depressed urban and rural areas had little trouble fitting the world conspiracy viewpoint of LaRouche into their political cosmology, informed by abandonment and distrust of the Democratic Party establishment. The vote for NDPC candidates may not have much advanced the long-run fortunes of their mentor, but it attracted national alarm and shook the political establishment. It was an early manifestation of the potential of globalization to arouse popular resistance to increasingly concentrated economic power and the loss of national sovereignty.

In the post–Cold War era, conscious and secret economic planning remains a necessity for elites. A series of important international economic treaties on a global and regional scale have been negotiated behind closed doors, then, to the dismay of opponents, passed with relatively little opportunity for public debate. The most recent effort to proceed this way concerns efforts to negotiate the Multilateral Agreement on Investment (MAI). The MAI would limit government regulation of foreign capital by requiring equal treatment for foreign and domestic investors, banning, for example, "performance requirements" in areas of employment, reinvestment, or other conditions (Mayne 1997). So sensitive have been negotiations over the MAI that representatives of the nations negotiating in Paris attempted (unsuccessfully) to prevent the drafts from reaching the public eye. The MAI negotiations might be considered authorized diplomatic meetings requiring confidentiality; however, secrecy in this case is also being used to avoid popular resistance and input through democratic processes.

In 1978, Stanley Hoffmann predicted that such tactics would give rise to populist resistance: "A trilateral policy that would appeal only to the skills of the professional in diplomacy, academia, business, and the media would deepen the gap that, in all the advanced countries, exists between an indifferent or indignant 'next generation,' and the interconnected managers of what Pègey once called the established disorder" (Hoffmann 1978: 249). Although Bilderberg, the Trilateral Commission, and the Council on Foreign Relations carry out many public functions, they also provide forums where economic elites meet behind closed doors to strategize and coordinate efforts to shape global economics and politics (Shoup 1975; Shoup and Minter 1977). Given the secrecy surrounding these meetings, it requires no great leap of the imagination to see fertile ground for operational conspiracies. The opaqueness of these associations suggests at least a hidden agenda. Parenti points out, "A ruling class [that] tries to direct the system for its own interests is, by definition, considered a conspiracy fantasy in mainstream political discourse" (1994: 161). Even if economic globalization is explained less by deep politics than by structural and historical factors, radicals might just as well embrace conspiracism, says Parenti, because "one is likely to be called a conspiracy theorist, not only if one believes that ruling-class leaders sometimes use conspiratorial methods, but if one thinks there is even such a thing as a ruling class that seeks to maintain hegemony" (1994: 160).

Steffen Hantke contends, "Conspiracy theory has demonstrated its enduring usefulness in a climate of shifting ideological alliances. In an ironic reversal of priorities, conspiratorial anxieties based on an ominous threat emanating from a monolithic 'Evil Empire' during the Reagan years have given way to a more broadly defined concern with the U.S.'s own sense of intrinsic coherence." The danger of terrorism "is so firmly rooted in essentialisms and the belief in its own universality that American intervention in the international political arena has never been forced to account for its blatant violation of other countries' sovereignty, the transgressions against international law, or the resistance from those to whose rescue it had supposedly come" (Hantke 1996: 215). With the attacks on Washington and New York of 11 September 2001, for the first time since the Cold War America's principal adversary could be defined again primarily in conspiratorial terms.

Conclusion

Scott (1996: xiii–xiv) contends that social scientists resist conspiracy theories because they cannot be easily reconciled with the underlying assumptions of rationality essential to modern positivism. "The notion that unreason as well as reason rules us from above is psychologically painful" (1996: 12), he says. The studies presented in this collection do not dismiss conspiracy theories as merely delusional; rather, they consider them to be valid for particular communities. Several contributions point out how conspiracy theories may be empowering to those feeling otherwise victimized. By contrast, most historians and political scientists find conspiracy theories wholly pathological and disempowering.

I have argued that the "paranoid style" of American politics is the result of conflating operational conspiracies and world conspiracies, but this does not necessarily render those who share conspiracy theory powerless. World conspiracy thinking in its many variations may be paranoid in many manifestations, but it can also be empowering, even rational, within an interpretative community whom elites would otherwise ignore. Furthermore, recurring scandals born of operational conspiracies lend credence to some theories that social scientists and establishment journalists would rather dismiss. Contemporary conspiracy theories retain credibility because, the further globalization proceeds, the more the promise of democracy seems to recede. The more we are told that power is "transparent" and open, the more people feel the need to say that it is not. Conspiracy theories link structural and historical forces to subjective political action by elites who prefer to confer and operate out of the glare of transparent daylight, in the opaque twilight of deep politics.

Notes

I would like to thank Professor Art Sandler and Professor Britt-Marie Schiller of Webster University, the editors of this volume, and the anonymous reviewers for Duke University Press for their useful suggestions.

1 For all that he derides conspiracism, Pipes describes Leninism as a "powerful conspiracy ideology" (1997: 81) that, like fascism, actually came to power. Indeed, conspiracy is a relevant issue within the thought and practice of Bolshevism, but Pipes has little interest in, and even less respect for, Lenin's views on the limits and potential of conspiracy as a political tool.

2 Pipes dismisses virtually all left-of-center critiques of U.S. hegemony and its political economy as conspiracy theory and paranoia, while he sees international Communism as a genuine real-world conspiracy. Also, since he insists that conspiracy theory began with reactions to the French Revolution and resistance to modernism, he ignores witch-hunts, arguably one of the most significant episodes of world conspiracy theory.

3 For evidence that the Contras qualify as a terrorist paramilitary organization, dependent on the United States for political direction and funding, see Rosset and Vandermeer (1986), especially the former Contra leader Edgar Chamorro's "World Court Affidavit" (235–46) and several other government and independent sources. See also NSA (1997).

4 Posner himself evokes conspiracism with an Orientalist prejudice, e.g., in the preface to *Warlords of Crime*, where he states, "The same ingenuity and dedication of purpose that allowed the Chinese to develop a culture before the pharoes

and to make Hong Kong a commercial paradise are some of the same traits that have been applied by Chinese criminals, through the secret societies, to create massive underworld empires" (1988: xvii).

5   The *Times Literary Supplement* concluded that Posner's contribution "is to awaken us from our reveries with cold facts and sharp logic" so that we can "put the conspiracy-mongers out of business" (26 November 1993, 11). *American Heritage* (February–March 1994, 100) chimed in, "Adult Oswald simply wasn't stable enough to have played a major role in an elaborate far-reaching conspiracy."

6   The reliability of evidence and sources about the Kennedy assassination is difficult to assess. For a carefully compiled compendium of claims, see Assassination Web (1997).

7   There were exceptions. The *Christian Science Monitor* (28 September 1983, 13) praised Posner's forensic research but concluded that he left the case "far from closed." A few reviews specializing in library recommendations (*Choice* 31 [March 1994]: 1210; *Booklist* 90 [15 September 1993]: 107) said kind things about Scott's book.

8   Organizations with a "world conspiratorial" ideology typically have a Manichaean outlook. For example, the right-wing Christian movement of the television evangelist Pat Robertson characterizes opponents as doing the "devil's work." Organizations linked to figures like H. Ross Perot and his Reform Party and the Rainbow Coalition of Jesse Jackson may publicize conspiracies, but they do not espouse a world conspiracy ideology.

References

Adkins, Mark. 1996. "LA Times Deconstructed." http://www.csu.edu/CommunicationStudies/bin/news/cia. Accessed 21 July 2002.

AFP (Agence France Presse). 1992. "Most Americans Believe in Kennedy Conspiracy Theory." 6 January.

Albert, Michael. 1992. "Conspiracy? . . . Not!" *Z Magazine,* May, 86–88. Reposted on http://www.publiceye.org/tooclose/cons_not.html. Accessed 21 December 2001.

Alphabet. 1999. "Deceive, Inveigle, Obfuscate." http://thealph.com/alphabet/d.shtml. Accessed 2 January 2002.

Assassination Web. 1997. "Case Closed or Posner Exposed?" *Electronic Assassinations Newsletter.* http://www.assassinationweb.com/issue1.htm. Accessed 21 December 2001.

Astier, Henri. 1992. "Americans and Conspiracy Theories." *Contemporary Review* 160 (10): 160–70.

Barber, Benjamin R. 1996. *Jihad vs. McWorld: How Globalism and Tribalism Are Reshaping the World.* New York: Random House.

Bardes, Barbara, and Robert W. Oldendick. 2000. *Public Opinion: Measuring the American Mind.* Stamford, Conn.: Wadsworth.

Berlet, Chip. 1986. "Tracking Down LaRouche." *In These Times* 8, no. 8 (2 April): 5, 8.

————. 1997. "Conspiracism." http://www.publiceye.org/rightwoo/rw0026-13.html#P266_102099. Accessed 21 December 2001.

Davis, D. B. 1969. *The Slave Power Conspiracy and the Paranoid Style.* Baton Rouge: Louisiana State University Press.

FAIR (Fairness and Accuracy in Reporting). 1996. "Exposed: The Contra-Crack Connection." *Extra*, October. http://www.fair.org/extra/9610/contra.html. Accessed 21 July 2002.

Fogarty, Thomas. 1992. "JFK Poll Shows Iowans Likely to Believe Conspiracy Theory." Gannett News Service, 29 March.

Garrison, Jim. 1969. "Closing Summation." http://www.astridmm.com/stone/closing.html. Accessed 3 December 2001.

Goertzel Ted. 1994. "Belief in Conspiracy Theories." *Political Psychology* 15 (4): 731–42.

Golden, Timothy. 1996a. "Pivotal Figures of Newspaper Series May Be Only Bit Players." *New York Times*, 21 October, A14.

————. 1996b. "Though Evidence Is Thin, Tale of C.I.A. and Drugs Has a Life of Its Own." *New York Times,* 21 October, A14.

Gramsci, Antonio. 1971. *Selections from the Prison Notebooks.* Translated by Quintin Hoare and Geoffrey Nowell Smith. New York: International.

Groh, Dieter. 1987. "The Temptation of Conspiracy Theory; or, Why Do Bad Things Happen to Good People? Part 1: Preliminary Draft of a Theory of Conspiracy Theories." In *Changing Conceptions of Conspiracy,* ed. Carl F. Graumann and Serge Moscovici, 1–13. New York: Springer.

Hantke, Steffen. 1996. " 'God Save Us from Bourgeois Adventure': The Figure of the Terrorist in Contemporary American Conspiracy Fiction." *Studies in the Novel* 28 (25): 219–44.

Harrison, Albert A., and James Moulton Thomas. 1997. "The Kennedy Assassination, Unidentified Flying Objects, and Other Conspiracies: Psychological and Organizational Factors in the Perception of 'Cover-Up.' " *Systems Research and Behavioral Science* 14 (1): 113–14.

Haygood, Wil. 1996. "True or False, Rumors Spread." *Boston Globe*, 15 December, A1.

Hellinger, Daniel, and Dennis Judd. 1994. *The Democratic Facade.* Belmont, Calif.: Wadsworth.

Hoffmann, Stanley. 1978. *Primacy or World Order: American Foreign Policy since the Cold War.* New York: McGraw-Hill.

Hofstadter, Richard. 1965. *The Paranoid Style in American Politics.* Cambridge, Mass.: Harvard University Press.

Kennedy, Paul. 1987. *The Rise and Fall of the Great Powers.* New York: Random House.

Keohane, Robert O. 1980. "The Theory of Hegemonic Stability and Change in International Economic Regimes, 1967–1977." In *Change in the International System,* ed. Ole R. Holsti, Randolph M. Siverson, and Alexander L. George, 131–62. Boulder, Colo.: Westview.

King, Dennis, and Ronald Radosh. 1984. "The LaRouche Connection." *New Republic,* 19 November, 15–19.

LaRouche, Lyndon, Jr. 1998. "Emergency World Reorganization: What Each among All Nations Must Do Now." *Executive Intelligence Review,* 9 October. http://www.larouchepub.com/eirtoc/1998/eirtoc_.html. Accessed 24 December 2001.

———. 1999. "To Defeat Impeachment, You Must Defeat the New Confederacy." *Executive Intelligence Review,* 15 January. http://www.larouchepub.com/eirtoc/1999/eirtoc_2603.html. Accessed 24 December 2001.

Malcolm, Andrew. 1986. "LaRouche Efforts Had Rural Focus." *New York Times,* 31 March, A14.

Marin, Rick, and Trent Gegax. 1996. "Conspiracy Mania Feeds Our Growing National Paranoia." *Newsweek,* 30 December, 64.

Mayne, Ruth. 1997. "The OECD Multilateral Agreement on Investment." *Oxfam International,* October. http://www.oneworld.org/oxfam/policy/papers/mai.htm. Accessed 24 December 2001.

Melley, Timothy. 2000. *Empire of Conspiracy: The Culture of Paranoia in Postwar America.* Ithaca: Cornell University Press.

Morgenthau, Hans. 1948. *Politics among Nations: The Struggle for Power and Peace.* New York: Knopf.

NSA (National Security Archive). 1997. "The Contras, Cocaine, and Covert Operations." *National Security Archive Electronic Briefing Book No. 2.* Primary documents posted at http://www.seas.gwu.edu/~nsarchive/NSAEBB/NSAEBB2/nsaebb2.htm. Accessed 24 December 2001.

Overbeck, Ashley. 1996. "Media Reacts to Contra/Cocaine Allegations." *Parascope,* November. http://www.parascope.com/articles/1196/media.htm. Accessed 21 July 2002.

Oxnevad, Karl. 1986. "Radical Rights Pull Upset in Illinois." *St. Louis Post-Dispatch,* 20 March, A1.

Parenti, Michael. 1994. *Land of Idols: Political Mythology in America.* New York: St. Martin's.

Parry, Robert. 1998. "*NYT*'s New Contra Lies." *The Consortium for Independent Journalism,* 1 October. http://www.consortiumnews.com/consor26.html. Accessed 24 December 2001.

Peterson, Iver. 1997. "Repercussions from Flawed News Articles." *New York Times,* 3 June, A12.

Pipes, Daniel. 1997. *Conspiracy: How the Paranoid Style Flourishes and Where It Comes From*. New York: Free Press.

Posner, Gerald. 1988. *Warlords of Crime: Chinese Secret Societies—The New Mafia*. New York: McGraw-Hill.

———. 1994. *Case Closed: Lee Harvey Oswald and the Assassination of JFK*. New York: Random House.

———. 1998. *Killing the Dream: James Earl Ray and the Assassination of Martin Luther King*. New York: Random House.

Prouty, Fletcher. 1975. "The Guns of Dallas." *Gallery*, October. http://www.ratical.com/ratville/JFK/GoD.html. Accessed 21 December 2001.

Reeves, Thomas. 1994. "Review of *Case Closed: Lee Harvey Oswald and the Assassination of JFK*." *Journal of American History* 81 (3): 1378–82.

Robertson, Pat. 1991. *The New World Order*. Dallas: Word.

Robins, Robert S., and Jerrold M. Post. 1997. *Political Paranoia: The Psychopolitics of Hatred*. New Haven, Conn.: Yale University Press.

Robinson, William. 1996. *Promoting Polyarchy: Globalization, US Intervention, and Hegemony*. Cambridge: Cambridge University Press.

Rosset, Peter, and John Vandermeer. 1986. *Nicaragua: Unfinished Revolution*. New York: Grove.

Schiraldi, Vincent. 1996. "Black Paranoia—or Common Sense." Pacific News Service, 18 December.

Scott, Peter Dale. 1996. *Deep Politics and the Death of JFK*. Berkeley and Los Angeles: University of California Press.

Sheehan, Michael. 1986. "The World According to Michael Sheehan." Transcript of a speech. http://www.conspire.com/sheehan.html. Accessed 24 December 2001.

Shoup, Laurence. 1975. "Shaping the Postwar World: The Council of [*sic*] Foreign Relations and the United States War Aims during World War II." *The Insurgent Sociologist* 5:9–52.

Shoup, Laurence, and William Minter. 1977. *Imperial Brain Trust: The Council on Foreign Relations and United States Foreign Policy*. New York: *Monthly Review* Press.

Sklar, Holly, ed. 1980. *Trilateralism: The Trilateral Commission and Elite Planning for World Management*. Boston: South End.

Solomon, Norman. 1996. "Media War Erupting over CIA and Cocaine." *Media Beat*, vol. 24 (November–December). http://www.speakeasy.org/wfp/24/Solomon.html. Accessed 24 December 2001.

———. 1997. "Snow Job." *Extra*, January/February 1997. http://www.fair.org/extra/9701/contra-crack.html. Accessed 21 July 2002.

UPI (United Press International). 1993. "Journalists Doubt Kennedy Conspiracy Theories." 22 November.

Ward, Geoffrey. 1993. "The Most Durable Assassination Theory: Oswald Did It Alone." *New York Times Book Review*, 21 November, A1.

Waters, Anita. 1987. "Conspiracy Theories as Ethnosociologies: Explanation and Intention in African-American Political Culture." *Journal of Black Studies* 29 (1): 112–46.

Webb, Gary. 1998. *Dark Alliance: The CIA, the Contras, and the Crack Cocaine Explosion*. San Francisco: Seven Stories.

Williams, William Appleman. 1967. "American Intervention in Russia: 1917–1920." In *Containment and Revolution*, ed. David Horowitz, 26–69. Boston: Beacon.

8

Making *Wanga:* Reality Constructions
and the Magical Manipulation of Power

KAREN MCCARTHY BROWN

In August 1997, Abner Louima, a thirty-two-year-old Haitian immigrant living in Brooklyn and working as a security guard, got in trouble
with the New York City police. The encounter sparked what is now an infamous case of police brutality. Analyzing mainstream media coverage of the
incident and comparing it to the coverage of another case of police violence
in New York reveal an elaborate dance of secrecy and transparency, a contre-
danse if you will, in which secrecy demands transparency and transparency
provokes new forms of secrecy, in spite of itself and at times in the name
of justice. So it goes. When raw power and the most fundamental kinds of
racism are involved, as they are in the Louima case, both victims and perpetrators are at times compelled to hide the factual truth and to keep secrets
while simultaneously making claims on some of the most rudimentary of institutions created to enhance transparency, the news media and the judicial
courts.

The night Louima was arrested, Phantoms, his favorite band, was playing
at the Club Rendez-Vous in Brooklyn. Around four o'clock in the morning,
the almost entirely Haitian crowd spilled out onto the street. As I later heard
the story, two women started exchanging ritual insults about each other's
clothing. Bystanders playfully urged them on; the shouting increased, and
someone called the police. A Haitian friend who was there assured me that,
before the police arrived, no one in the crowd had crossed the line between

play and violence. The police cars nevertheless arrived with lights flashing and sirens screaming. Officers yelling and brandishing nightsticks pushed their way into the crowd. Before Abner Louima knew what was happening, he was face down on the ground with his hands cuffed behind his back. Then, according to witnesses, he was thrown roughly into the back of a police car. By Louima's account, the four policemen involved in the arrest stopped twice to beat him en route to the Seventieth Precinct stationhouse; they used fists, clubs, and even a police radio. Once there, Officer Justin A. Volpe rammed the wooden handle of what appeared to be a toilet plunger into Abner Louima's rectum, yanked it out, and, rudely pushing it at his mouth, told him, "Now you are going to taste your own shit."[1] Louima was then placed in a holding cell, where he sat bleeding for a long time, perhaps hours, before being taken to a hospital. Louima's rectum was perforated and his bladder torn. His injuries required two months in the hospital and three surgeries, including an initial colostomy later reversed. He is now in better health than his doctors had predicted.

Eventually, it was revealed that Officer Volpe had mistaken Louima for someone else in the crowd who had taken a punch at him. At the time of Volpe's trial, David Barstow reported in the *New York Times* (21 May 1999) that, when a nurse at the hospital where Louima was originally taken referred to him as the man who had beaten up a police officer, Louima replied: "Lady, do you think I'm stupid? I'm a black man. Do you think I would beat a police officer in New York City?" From the beginning, the press was suspicious of Abner Louima's accounts of what happened to him. The jury in the initial trial also did not appear to trust him. They dismissed all charges related to the beatings administered on the way to the police station, events for which Louima himself was the only prosecution witness. At times, Abner Louima was treated as if he were the one accused of a crime.

Mama Lola Reconfigures Louima's Reality

In 1997, shortly after he was released from the hospital, Abner Louima was introduced to Mama Lola, a respected Haitian Vodou priestess and healer living in Brooklyn. She is also my teacher in the arts of Vodou and my friend. These days Louima occasionally visits Mama Lola at her home, and that is how I have come to know him. When Mama Lola first mentioned him to me, she said simply, "He' a very quiet, respectable man." Then she mused on what had happened to him: "Maybe they think he some bum in the street. . . .

Like he don't have no family . . . no one to help him." If that is what the police thought, they were mistaken because a significant proportion of the Haitian immigrant community in New York City, along with many non-Haitians, stepped forward to protest what had been done to him.

In April 1999, I interviewed Lola about Louima's situation. It was a strange conversation. At the time, Lola was caught between powerfully conflicting desires. She wanted to discuss Louima with me because we were working on a book on healing and she considered Louima one of her most interesting and important cases, yet the trial of his attackers was just about to begin, and she did not want to say anything that might compromise that process.

Mama Lola chose to deal with her ambivalence by telling me and my tape recorder substantially different stories. With the tape rolling, she spoke with all the caution of a public figure facing the press, yet, at the same time, she signaled further, secret meanings to me. For example, she would occasionally pull down her right eyelid with a finger to signal that I should not take something she said too seriously, or, if I asked a sensitive question, she would silently draw her thumb and forefinger across her lips as if closing a zipper. Once she shut off the tape recorder and whispered to me, even though no one was in the room except the two of us. I have repeated here only the taped version of the interview. For the purposes of this essay, the contorted progress of the conversation and its modes of secrecy production are far more important than any of the particular topics discussed.

When I asked Mama Lola if she were "doing some work" for Louima, a tactful reference to Vodou healing practices, she replied:

MAMA LOLA (ML): Oh, we pray. We do prayer! I always pray for him a lot. . . .

KAREN BROWN (KB): Right.

ML: I . . . uh . . . do something . . . but I don't think he know if I do it or not. . . . I go downstairs to my altar, I pray to the spirits, and do some work with coconut. I use coconut water for clarity. I take the coconut water, and I put some good luck powder. I take lots of *veven* leaves . . . High John the Conqueror root too. . . . I add olive oil, and I make a lamp for him . . . for three days.

KB: So, the lamp has to burn for three days, huh?

ML: Yes. After three days, I put the coconut [shell, with ingredients,] in the sea to sail it away. . . . I go to Coney Island to do that.

KB: Why did you have to take it to the sea?

ML: To wash all the bad thing people . . . [saying] about him. You know, to clear him . . . to clear him . . . in front of everybody.

KB: Don't you also take it to the sea because you can get closer to the spirits there?

ML: Yes, my ancestors, that's right. His ancestors too. . . . The pigeon was after that. I do it in my house . . . in the basement. I talk to the pigeon, and I put Abner' name inside the pigeon mouth, and I let it fly away.

KB: You talked to the pigeon first, like you told it what needs to happen?

ML: Exactly. Exactly. Then I sent it away.

KB: But when you're with Louima, you just pray?

ML: He don't ask me, don't pay me to do nothing. . . .

KB: He's afraid if somebody thought he was doing Vodou, it would hurt his case?

ML: Oh, that's the truth! They will think maybe he come to me to do something. . . .

KB: Something evil?

ML: Exactly, yup!

KB: Is his name on your altar now? [I knew that she did that for her clients.]

ML: No, I don't put his name on the altar. I don't want nobody to come in to my altar to see his name there.

KB: But otherwise you would have put it there?

ML: Yes.

KB: Did you put anything else of his on the altar?

ML: His name. I put it um . . . um . . . behind the statue, but nobody don't see it.

KB: Lola, it's so sad. . . . You're helping him . . . and you have to be so secretive. . . .

ML: You know, people take everything in the wrong way. And they just blah, blah, blah, blah the mouth. . . . So, in this world, you have to be careful.

Mama Lola set out to change Louima's "luck" through the manufacture of two types of *wanga*, "charms," drawn from her repertoire of ritual healing practices, one based on a coconut and the other on a pigeon (see Brown 1995). Her intention was to bring about a situation in which Abner Louima and the things that motivated him would be more transparent to those who were judging him every day in the media and on the streets. In order for her to do this, it was necessary to keep some things secret.

Secrecy and Discretion in the Lives of the Haitian Immigrants

If he did "serve the spirits," the most common expression for what outsiders call *practicing Vodou,* Louima would have denied it when asked about it by journalists pursuing the police brutality case. Thanks to the advice of his community, practically every time Louima was in front of television cameras he was accompanied by a Protestant minister said to be his uncle. This was a politically astute move if not an absolutely honest one. For Haitians, conversion to Protestantism automatically entails a total rejection of the Vodou spirits. So, while the minister's presence communicated many things, chief among them was that Abner Louima is not into Vodou.

Furthermore, even if Louima were not the central character in a major news story, he probably would ask Lola to keep any spiritual work that she did for him secret. Healing work almost always deals with personal problems, so it follows that the most respected healers are those who know how to be discrete. For political, social, and religious reasons, secrecy is an important virtue in the lives of Haitians living in Haiti, a crowded country with scarce resources. In somewhat different ways, secrecy is important in the diaspora communities as well. In general, poor immigrants from Haiti dislike giving out information about themselves. Officially, there are around 250,000 Haitians living in New York City itself, a significant underestimation since many Haitians living in the city are undocumented and resist being counted. Yet even those who have their papers try to avoid bureaucratic accountability. They sometimes have the telephone bill in one name and the mortgage in another, and, when questioned by people they do not know, they frequently give misleading information about age, family, and work history. This practice reflects a deep lack of trust in bureaucracy of any kind, but it is also influenced by everyday social relations. Since so much of what it can mean to be a Haitian (poverty, illiteracy, blackness, Vodou) is liable to provoke prejudicial treatment in New York City, immigrants keep their heads down, and they school their children in secretiveness as a survival strategy in urban America. This old pattern is currently shifting. What happened to Abner Louima and the community response that it evoked have contributed to a new assertiveness among Haitians, a new willingness to take a public stand on issues that affect their lives.

The Haitian Community Acts against Police Brutality

Historically, Haitians in the United States have avoided political activity. This attitude began to change when Jean-Bertrand Aristide, a populist candidate for president of Haiti, won the election in 1990. Much of his campaign was financed by expatriates. Aristide's victory galvanized the diaspora community, increasing their pride and making them bolder participants in U.S. as well as Haitian politics. Even though the United States was complicit in the 1991 coup, afterward Aristide set up his government in exile in Washington, D.C. Then the Haitian political presence in New York City took on a new character as angry crowds demonstrated on more than one occasion. The demonstration for Louima in 1997 was in this assertive mode, but it also marked a new stage in the growing involvement of Haitians in local politics. Many protest signs blamed Mayor Rudolph Giuliani for what happened to Abner Louima. When Louima was first interviewed by the police, he claimed that, while attacking him, Office Volpe bragged: "It's not Dinkins time anymore. This is Giuliani time now." David Dinkins preceded Giuliani in the mayor's office; he is an African American. Louima later retracted this testimony. Apparently, a Haitian community leader told him to use the mayor's name so that the incident would get the attention of the media and not be quickly forgotten, as other cases of police brutality against Haitians have been.

The crowd that marched from Grand Army Plaza in Brooklyn to City Hall in Manhattan to protest the brutalization of Abner Louima at the hands of the New York City Police Department (NYPD) made up one of the largest Haitian demonstrations ever held in New York City. There were many reasons for the size of this August 1997 event. Al Sharpton, a well-known African American minister and activist, stepped in to help organize the march for Louima, while at the same time a half dozen other Caribbean communities in New York chose to stand in solidarity with Haitians on the issue of police violence. Yet I doubt that any circumstance was more responsible for the protest's size and energy than the basic affront to human worth and dignity that the Louima case represented. Haitians were simply fed up. This time the New York City police had gone too far.

Mustering early at the Manhattan end of the Brooklyn Bridge, the police were out in force on the day of the demonstration, and they were nervous. Hours before the protest was scheduled to begin, more than one hundred officers, men and women, gathered in lower Manhattan. A dozen police cars were parked in formation at the end of the bridge, a roadblock ready to be deployed if things got out of hand. Helmets, shields, and batons were in evidence everywhere. Metal gates cordoned off areas for the police along the edges of the demonstration route.

As soon as the crowd appeared over the crest of the Brooklyn Bridge, it was clear that the Haitian demonstrators and the NYPD had quite different scenarios in mind. This was not a crowd bent on violence. Colorfully dressed, carrying a wide variety of protest signs, accompanied by energetic dancers and drummers, singing songs and shouting slogans, the protesters articulated a virtual directory of strategies for handling fear and outrage. In order to contain the awful power of the Louima event and turn it toward something more constructive, the Haitian community was calling on every meaning-making system they had access to, traditional or newly acquired.

Some of the protest rhetoric focused on psychological explanations; "Justin A. Volpe is a sexual sadist," one sign shouted. Other protesters turned to the authority of the Christian religion, terrain that Haitian Americans share with most other Americans.[2] A huge placard, dense with earnest long-hand script, argued for the connection of this terrible event to the Second Coming of the Messiah. Also, rhetorics of justice and human rights were peppered throughout the signs carried by the protesters. Marking it a truly Haitian event were two people in costume, both possessed by Vodou spirits. One had Papa Gede, the spirit of sex, death, and humor, and another had the peasant farmer Azaka, a character valued for his plain speech and blunt truth telling. The first was dressed in black, his face covered in white powder. The second wore the embroidered blue denim outfit that in Vodou temples has become emblematic of Haitians from the countryside.

Many homemade placards castigated the current political climate in the city, a problem for which they laid the blame squarely at Mayor Rudy Giuliani's feet. Because of his "get tough on crime" policies, many people, not only Haitians, hold the mayor responsible for a general increase in racial discrimination in New York City and specifically for an increase in police harassment of blacks and Hispanics. The mayor was depicted on one sign with his head in a toilet bowl. Other signs showed Giuliani, not Louima, as the one whose pants got pulled down. This was not a crowd that was going to gloss over the details of the attack on Louima or turn away from its shaming aspects. At short intervals along the route of the march, a theater group reenacted the brutalization of Abner Louima, albeit in a somewhat abstract way.

Several Haitian marchers had drawn caricatures of the offending police officers on their placards, while other demonstrators, many others, carried toilet plungers that they used in creative ways to comment on the frightening events in the Seventieth Precinct. A couple of men in the crowd fixed the rubber cup of the plunger to the top of their heads. Other Haitian men communicated more directly and attached it to their crotches. Three men carried a coffin with a toilet plunger handle emerging from its lid, positioned like the erection of a corpse, a further signal of the presence of the randy Vodou death spirit, Gede. Dozens of people in the crowd painted their plunger handles red, and sign after sign depicted toilet plungers with blood dripping from the stem.

Late in the afternoon, the crowd gathered near City Hall to listen to speeches about police violence. On the stage were the Reverend Al Sharpton and several leaders of the Haitian community, including the Reverend Philius H. Nicolas, Louima's putative uncle and pastor of the Evangelical Crusade Church in Flatbush, Brooklyn. When one of the speakers made an especially powerful point, a sea of toilet plungers bobbed enthusiastically over the heads of the crowd. A marcher told me it was impossible to buy a toilet plunger in Brooklyn that day. He reported that all the hardware stores were sold out before the march began. The *New York Times,* which otherwise covered the demonstration in detail, made no mention of toilet plungers.

I remember thinking at the time that there was something very wanga-like about the way in which the Haitian protesters used the toilet plungers. One of the most important things that this demonstration accomplished was changing the emotional valence of an instrument of torture. Prior to the march, the toilet plunger was a sign of shame and pain, but, on that hot August day, Haitians took what they feared most, brought it out into the light of public scrutiny, and turned it into an instrument of resistance. What initially appeared to be mere play with the plungers was actually what Vodou practitioners call *working the wanga*. It is true that, as a rule, the making of Vodou charms is a private matter, yet, in some circumstances, it is the public exposure of such a secret thing that gives it real clout. For example, I once heard a story of a Port-au-Prince shop owner who was trying to ruin the business of a competitor by telling false stories about her. A trail of yellow powder across the doorway of the gossip not only served as a serious warning but also moved that person's offense into the realm of the larger community's responsibility.

Issues of secrecy, especially the malevolent kind, are overdetermined in relation to things Haitian, a culture that, in the United States, is often portrayed as virtually synonymous with black magic. Haitians have absorbed the colonial language about magic. These days they refer to both "white magic" and "black magic" in their traditional African-based religion, Vodou.[3] In spite of this superficial rhetoric, Haitian Vodou actually tends to avoid the good/evil dichotomy. Vodou priests and priestesses make wanga in order to help clients with love, health, money, and, not infrequently, legal problems, and giving such help is often morally complex. Helping one person may mean limiting or controlling another. Those who specialize in the Vodou arts of healing are as likely as not to refer to all dimensions of these healing practices as *maji*, "magic." Because such practices are deeply rooted in their culture, it is understandable that the larger Haitian community turned to a kind of maji to deal with the trauma of the Louima incident.

Wanga, such as Mama Lola made for Abner Louima, are simultaneously representations of troubled relationships and the means for solving the problems they represent. The High John the Conqueror root in Lola's coconut wanga, for example, points both to the fact that Louima is under attack and to the resources that he has to fight that battle. The coconut "water," a clear sweet liquid, prefigures the power of the ancestors and spirits to improve the vision of those having trouble seeing Abner Louima clearly and to sweeten their attitudes toward him. Ideally, the person with the problem should "work the *wanga*," that is, maintain a prescribed regimen of ritual practices such as praying and lighting candles before the wanga, but I have seen Lola take over this responsibility for clients other than Louima when they could not conveniently keep a wanga in their own home.

This was the case, for example, with a wanga that Lola made for a woman whose husband was unfaithful. Out of an article of the husband's clothing, Lola made a soft and pliable little doll, complete with male genitalia. Then, using heavy wire and a padlock, she bound the doll into a small wooden chair. For months, it was Mama Lola who kept an oil lamp burning next to the bound figure of the woman's husband. Here also, the wanga describes both the problem and the solution. Lola predicted that, sooner or later, the wandering husband would "bow his head" before his wife just as Santa Clara bowed her head in the image of the saint that, as a finishing touch, Lola placed on the wall directly in front of the male doll.

Bringing an imagined change into reality is what working a wanga is all about. The making of wanga and related diaspora practices are venerable, old traditions. I will never forget the emotional impact of an eighteenth-century wanga that I saw in the Port-au-Prince ethnographic museum on one of my first trips to Haiti. It was composed from an old pitted glass bottle, bound with a short section of old slave chains. Wanga can be traced to ritual practices found throughout West and Central Africa. Among other sources, Haitian Vodou wanga have roots in Dahomean *bocio* (Blier 1995) and Kongo *minkisi* (MacGaffey 1993).

In all cases, the practices associated with wanga are used to manipulate power by changing human relationships. When looked at in this way, the power of the wanga is largely discursive power; it is the power to rewrite the existential narrative at issue. The wanga that Mama Lola made for Abner Louima are not, therefore, all that different from newspaper accounts of Abner Louima's experience with the police or from arguments made by defense and prosecuting attorneys in the courtrooms where the crimes committed against Louima were adjudicated. All, including Mama Lola's wanga, are competing narratives empowered by their various abilities to convince key audiences (including spiritual ones) of their points of view and, therefore, shift problematic situations. This process is complex because each new narrative is unavoidably launched into a sea of old ideologies, automatic associations, and rigid interpretations. Some people have to work against this situation; others profit from it. While some masters of narrative must anticipate and guard against possible points of *meconnaissance* (perhaps by keeping certain things secret), others work at making a narrative say things indirectly, things that otherwise would be unspeakable in this particular place and time. The discussion now turns to what I will call *word wanga* and, thus, to the many ways in which the person and the experience of Abner Louima are reconfigured in the press and in the courtroom. Following the path of the African wanga has led to the magical practices of largely white, bureaucratic institutions in the United States.

The Media Construction: Abner Louima and Amadou Diallo

On 4 February 1999, eighteen months after Louima's encounter with the officers of the Seventieth Precinct, Amadou Diallo, a West African immigrant who worked as a sidewalk merchant in New York City, was fired on forty-one times at close range, late at night, while standing in the entryway to his Bronx apartment. He was unarmed. All shots fired came from four NYPD officers, members of an elite anticrime unit that traveled in plain clothes. According to a *New York Times* (12 February 1999) editorial, the macho slogan of this unit is, "We own the night." Nineteen bullets entered the body of Diallo, and he died shortly thereafter.

Approximately two months after Amadou Diallo's death, in a guest editorial in the *New York Times* (19 April 1999) titled "For Most Brutality Isn't the Issue," New York City police commissioner Howard Safir called the shooting of Diallo "a tragedy" that "only the judicial system can produce answers for. . . ." He added that, even though he does hear complaints about the police, "the complaints . . . are not of officers being brutal, but of officers being brusque." He concluded with the announcement of a police "civility campaign." "We are giving officers tips on how to be more polite," Safir wrote. He made no mention of Abner Louima. Nevertheless, the two cases were immediately linked by the media and by the general public.

The Louima and Diallo cases both involved police violence against recent immigrants to the United States; both victims were black. Given these similarities, it was initially puzzling that the two cases received significantly different treatment from the public and from the media. The Diallo case was in the news continuously starting from the day he was killed. There were dozens of events protesting the shooting: a memorial; demonstrations before and after the memorial; vigils; religious services; and concerts. These events attracted people from across New York's social, racial, and ethnic spectrum. There were several demonstrations for Abner Louima, one of them sizable, yet Haitian immigrants made up the great majority at all events. Also, by contrast with Diallo, Abner Louima disappeared from the newspapers and the evening television news rather quickly. His case actually got more coverage later, during the second trial, for obstruction of justice. By then, the offense against Louima had become so involved with other incidents of police violence, including Diallo's death, that jury verdicts often seemed to be responding more to the larger context of police brutality in New York City than to the specific events that the jury members were asked to judge.

A U.S. film crew followed Diallo's mother at the height of her grief back to Africa, to Guinea, where she took her son's body for a traditional funeral and burial. Long segments of the Africa footage were broadcast on the evening news on several U.S. channels. Since her first visit, occasioned by her son's death, Kadiatou Diallo has become something of a public figure in the United States, speaking out repeatedly against police violence and for gun control. There was an "interfaith prayer and community healing" service for Diallo, a Muslim, at the Brooklyn Academy of Music, and, according to David M. Haiszenhorn, in a *New York Times* article of 15 March 1999 titled "Mayor

Expresses Regret over Police Shooting of Immigrant," at the service Mayor Giuliani referred to Diallo's death as the "loss of an innocent person." He also called the event "a terrible rending tragedy." I do not recall anyone in the media characterizing Louima as an "innocent" person. However, a story on the *New York Times* website on 8 June 1999 reported that one of the attorneys defending the police officers did refer to him as "a 'professional victim' looking for big money damages from the city." Furthermore, neither the names of Louima's parents, nor those of his children, nor that of the place where he was born in Haiti was ever mentioned in the newspapers I read. On the contrary, parts of Louima's identity—his Haitianness in general and especially his religion—had to be muted and handled with discretion. In spite of the fact that the great majority of people in Haiti serve the Vodou spirits in one way or another, any possible Vodou connection to Abner Louima had to be thoroughly hidden so that, in a context of prejudice, he could remain a credible witness against his attackers.

Mayor Giuliani and Police Commissioner Safir honored Diallo by going to his memorial service, held at the impressive Islamic Cultural Center of New York on East Ninety-Sixth Street in Manhattan. That event and the one at the Brooklyn Academy of Music became occasions on which multicultural and religiously pluralistic New York City was put on display, but Abner Louima's case represented nothing about the city that the larger public wanted to honor.

The cases of Abner Louima and Amadou Diallo differed in other ways. Diallo came from Africa, and, in death, he conveniently went back there, sounding an end note for the whole affair, while Louima survived the sadistic sexual attack against him and so must continue to be dealt with, like all the other impoverished people from his country who will not stop knocking at the backdoor of the United States. Furthermore, Louima filed a personal damage suit against the city of New York.

Deeper and more trenchant reasons for the different media treatment given Louima and Diallo have to do with the hypersexualized black body. Viewing blacks in this way is a frequent and historically deep habit of mind among Euro-Americans. Reason might never have been crowned in the aftermath of the French Revolution if Africans (and a few others) had not long been designated to carry the burden of sexuality with all its inherent irrationality and potential for untidiness and loss of control. Partly because Louima was already in place to carry the burden, Diallo escaped evoking this image. His sexuality simply got erased by the media. In fact, it was never an issue. Diallo's body under attack was configured as a clean, fully clothed body. At times, it was represented by an anonymous two-dimensional out-line of a human body crosshatched by nineteen bullet trajectories. The more common visual icon of the violence unleashed against Diallo, however, was a photograph of the empty, bullet-pocked entryway to his Bronx building. Diallo's body, doubly contained (both safely buried and on the other side of the ocean), is gone from this picture, and, thus, Amadou Diallo could be re-configured as deemed necessary by journalists and politicians alike. Via this process, Diallo approached the type of pure victim that motivates politics on both the Left and the Right in America.

Partly because of the comparison with the murdered Diallo, Louima, who is alive, has not been allowed to be an innocent victim. What is more, his body under attack was highly problematic; it had trousers pulled down around the ankles. In newspapers, and on the television news, the most com-mon visual icon of the violence against Louima was, like Diallo's vestibule, empty of a human presence. In this case, however, the iconic photograph showed, not a neutral, public space, but instead an empty precinct bathroom. This scene-of-the-crime photograph functioned as a highly suggestive era-sure, daring the reader to imagine what happened there. The hypersexual, penetrable, and penetrating black (read colonized) body, made excitingly vulnerable and accessible through extremes of social power and physical control, is positioned at the center of Abner Louima's story of torture, as it was at the center of slavery.

In another, related dimension of media word magic, homosexuality can be detected as a partially submerged theme in the narrative of Louima's tor-ture. A *Washington Post* (28 May 1999) article repeatedly refers to Louima as having been *sodomized,* a word whose common usage neatly erases the violence from the incident and accentuates the fact that it occurred between two men. During the two years following Louima's torture by the police, the verb *to sodomize* appeared in several articles, yet, more recently, members of the press (including more than one writing for New York's *Haitian Times*)[4] have almost unanimously fallen into this extended, half-conscious fantasy that Abner Louima is gay. *To sodomize* is now, across the board, the verb of choice in the frequent articles on police brutality that mention Louima's case. In such word wanga, some degree of unconsciousness (a form of keep-ing secrets from oneself) on the part of the writer is essential. Were the lan-guage more transparent to its meaning, its foolishness and lack of integrity would also be more apparent.

A more straightforward charge of homosexuality was at issue in the first trial of Abner Louima's attackers. In his opening statements, Marvyn Kornberg, Justin Volpe's attorney, suggested that Louima might have sustained his injuries prior to arrest, from consensual gay sex in the bathroom of the Club Rendez-Vous. In the weeks of testimony following the opening of the trial, this stunningly irrational argument did not make it back into the courtroom. Never mind. The damage had been done. Kornberg's underlying point, coyly signaled to the jury, was that, if Louima had sex with men, then what happened to him, grotesque as it was, was in some way his own fault. Robert Volpe, Justin Volpe's father, spun his own tale about how Louima shared the blame with his son.[5]

Abner Louima's moral stature was attacked in other ways as well. For example, he was called a liar because of discrepancies between his description of the attack when he was first interviewed in the hospital and his current version of it. According to Joseph P. Fried, writing in an article published on the *New York Times* website on 17 May 1999, one issue was his comment about it being "Giuliani time," while another concerned his body posture at the time of the attack. Was he crouched down and bending over, as he now says, or was he pinned down on the floor, as he said when first questioned? It is not difficult to see how Louima might have initially hedged his story, feeling his manhood to be at stake in these postural differences. Either way, such goings-on do not produce good victims. Sexual tension lies just below the surface in practically everything written about Louima's story, and it is fed by secrecy, silence, and erasure. The biggest erasure was what I kept expecting to see in print but never did: "Justin Volpe raped Abner Louima."

Reconfigurations from the Judge's Bench and the Jury Box

The May–June 1999 trial led to acquittals for all officers involved on charges related to the immediate circumstances of Abner Louima's arrest and to the beatings that he had received on the way to the police station. This is significant because these are the dimensions of the crime against Louima that connect with patterns of police violence widely experienced in the Haitian immigrant community and other such communities. The Louima case, like Diallo's, involved racial profiling (suspecting people of color for no reason other than their color) and street justice (precipitous and unjustified use of force by police on the streets). When these dimensions of the Louima case are taken away, the whole affair shrinks to a weird event that happened in a precinct bathroom, a one-time thing to be dealt with and quickly forgotten. In the first trial, Justin Volpe, who did the deed, got thirty years, and Charles Schwarz, who was convicted of assisting him, received the same sentence.

Even though neither Volpe nor Schwarz pleaded insanity, in the process of the jury sorting out the evidence and deciding whose claims were credible and whose were not, these out-of-control police officers, who routinely operated in an ethos that supported such things as racial profiling and street justice, were transformed into rogue cops at worst and psychologically troubled individuals at best. The systemic corruption of the NYPD was what motivated Louima to resist and what brought out Haitian (and other) protesters in large numbers, yet it was never a real issue in the courtroom.

In February 2000, Amadou Diallo's attackers were on trial for murder. By this time, the Diallo case had become *the* police brutality case, the lightning rod for a city's fear and suspicion of its police force. Around the same time, three of the four former police officers who attacked Louima went on trial again, this time for conspiracy to impede a police investigation. In the trial of the men who shot Diallo, it was word wangas, the way in which the event was reconfigured—what evidence was admissible, what not, and how the defense and prosecution shaped their cases—that determined the outcome. During the trial, the defense repeatedly discredited witnesses not present for the entire event by claiming that they did not have the context to interpret what they saw and heard. There were, however, no witnesses who were present the entire time except the officers themselves. The case against the men who shot Amadou Diallo thus came to rest entirely on the state of mind of the four defendants. It all came down to whether the officers believed that Diallo had a gun and continued to believe that he had a gun for the entire time it took them to fire forty-one bullets. It was no surprise that all four testified in the affirmative on that point. The acquittal of the four undercover officers provoked frustration and anger among Caribbean immigrants, but no real surprise. Many of them have emigrated from countries controlled by their armies. These immigrants have also had firsthand experience with the NYPD. They know that members of the NYPD are rarely held responsible for using excessive force. After the acquittal, groups of young men stood a silent and angry vigil in Diallo's Bronx neighborhood, holding up their black wallets. It was a black wallet that Diallo had in his hand, not a gun.

A leaflet, written in Haitian Creole and circulated in Brooklyn shortly after the Diallo verdicts, announced a protest demonstration. These were the words used to encourage people to come: "Pote Tanbou! Pote Plonje Twalet!" (Bring drums! Bring toilet plungers!). The tie between the Louima and the Diallo cases lives on among the people. I am convinced that it was the offense caused by the acquittals in the Diallo case that ricocheted into the second Louima trial courtroom, producing unexpected guilty verdicts there. Three officers involved in the Louima arrest, Charles Schwarz, Thomas Bruder, and Thomas Wiese, were indicted on charges of conspiracy to obstruct justice. Volpe confessed and plea bargained halfway through the first trial, so he was out of the picture by the time of the second trial, even though he had done more than any of the other officers to impede the internal police investigation. For example, Volpe never came clean about who was in the bathroom with him when he assaulted Louima. In the second round of verdicts, Charles Schwarz got another fifteen years and eight months, and Thomas Bruder and Thomas Wiese each ended up with a sentence of five years in jail. Thus, Louima's attackers received what were probably well-deserved sentences, but, in the trade-off, Diallo's killers, part of a larger structural source of police brutality (an undercover police unit that claimed to "own the night"), sidestepped accountability. As the Haitian proverb says: "Konplo pi fò passe wanga" (Conspiracies are stronger than magic).

Racism in the Shadow of the Fetish

It seems that, whenever Haitians are in the news, a reference to Vodou cannot be far behind. In a 20 June 2000 *Village Voice* article titled "Police Brutality and Voodoo Justice," Peter Noel, a black journalist whose byline appears frequently in the *Voice*, wrote that "the father of Justin Volpe, the white cop who was accused of sodomizing Louima, . . . told friends he was warned by Haitian spiritual healers that Louima is a wicked voodoo high priest bent on deadly revenge." In the same article, Noel also reported that a cop improbably named Ridgway de Szigethy, who spends his time investigating occult organizations, told Noel that, for his son's protection during the first trial, Robert Volpe carried "a little purple crystal . . . and a little vial of holy water." By looking down his nose at crystals and holy water as well as Vodou wanga, Peter Noel exhibited a democratic disdain for all things religious, but, as a result, he missed the depth and significance of the racism in Robert Volpe's attempt to condemn Abner Louima through references to the African-based religion of his homeland. This is an old ploy and one with a long, continuous history. This maneuver is, in fact, a cornerstone in the historic and current structure of European and American racism. A look at the history of the term *fetish*, a word that is in most cases interchangeable with *wanga*, will give a glimpse into the depth and complexity of the racist tropes peppered throughout the coverage of Louima's encounter with the officers of New York's Seventieth Precinct.

More than four hundred years ago, Europeans chose the term *fetish* to stand for powerful material objects used in traditional African religious settings. Chief among these objects were charms related to what would later become Vodou wanga. Not long after, the term *fetishism* or *fetish religion* began to be routinely applied to all aspects of all indigenous African religions. To this day, the Vodun (Fon spirits or deities found in the Republic of Benin, formerly Dahomey) are called *fetiches* and their priests *feticheurs*, another instance of a colonized people swallowing colonial rhetoric. Diviners throughout Benin are routinely called *charlatans*, yet another remnant of the French presence in the former Dahomey.

According to William Pietz, who has written an important series of articles on the history of the concept of fetishism, "the fetish, as an idea and a problem, and as a novel object not proper to any prior discrete society, originated in the cross-cultural spaces of the coast of West Africa during the sixteenth and seventeenth centuries" (Pietz 1985: 5). Fetish theory, Pietz says, "was fully established in European intellectual discourse by 1800" (1987: 23). The term *fetish* subsequently became an unusually influential one in a wide range of intellectual, political, and economic interactions between Europe and Africa. For a remarkably long period of time, fetish theory has provided the most pervasive and broadly influential rationale for racism, colonialism, and general Western cultural chauvinism.

Newton and Locke, figures of the seventeenth and early eighteenth centuries, both had in their libraries copies of the book that introduced "fetish religion" to the European world, Wilem Bosman's 1702 *A New and Accurate Account of the Coast of Guinea* (Pietz 1988). According to the theory of fetishism, "consecrated at the end of the eighteenth century by no less than G. W. F. Hegel in *The Philosophy of History*, Africans were incapable of abstract and generalizing thought; instead their ideas and actions were governed by impulse," and, as a consequence, it was commonly assumed that "anything upon which an African's eye happened to fall might be taken up by him and made into a 'fetish,' absurdly endowed with imaginary powers" (MacGaffey 1993: 32). In the nineteenth century, the concept of fetishism became theoretically indispensable to three of the founders of social science: Comte, Marx, and Freud. It is my purpose here to demonstrate that this intellectual arrangement has, from the beginning, been devastating for black people and that, at the beginning of the twenty-first century, the fetish trope still covertly and overtly shapes the images that Euro-Americans hold of Africans and African Americans in cosmopolitan New York City.

A "theoretically suggestive" term (Pietz 1985), the word *fetish* provided the rubric under which all Africa came to play the Other to Enlightenment rationalism. Most important was the role that the European idea of the fetish played in crystallizing the notion that so-called primitive thinking was characterized by a false theory of causality, a mistaken belief that material objects could be manipulated in such a way as to change the conditions of a person's life (Pietz 1988). When the presumed immorality of the feticheur was added to this mix, the fetish became the perfect foil for making the (illogical) connection so crucial to the Enlightenment, the connection between reason and righteousness. When seen from this perspective, it appears that the humble, antiaesthetic fetish was nothing less than a midwife to the Enlightenment.

Two things are, thus, important to remember from this short history of the fetish/wanga: First is the act of almost unbelievable meconnaissance that led Europeans to characterize all African religions, each one different from the other and each a rich moral universe, as nothing but instrumental magic carried out by bumbling sacerdotes paradoxically characterized as both childlike and evil. Second is the equally inappropriate characterization of African religion as bad science, that is, as primitive thinking or mistaken reasoning.

The European indictment of the African fetish was not merely a matter of slander. The configuration of African religion as fetishism had very tangible political and religious effects. This was the story in Haiti from the beginning of the eighteenth century until long after the end of European domination. In the early eighteenth century, Haitian slaves found making the benign protective charms called *gad-kò*, "body guards," which may consist of nothing more than herbal mixtures put under the skin or small cloth bags pinned inside clothing, were tortured brutally as sorcerers who gained power by deception. Even after the Haitian slave revolution (1791–1804), what Anna Wexler calls *the long shadow of the fetish* did not lift. In 1835, Boyer, then president of Haiti, promulgated a penal code that outlined hideous punishments for all religious practitioners who trafficked in such things as wangas. As late as 1935, Haitian president Vincent launched a campaign against traditional priests for suggesting that they could change people's lives through "occult methods" (Wexler, in press; Hurbon 1987).

It is sobering to realize how important maneuvers such as the misrecognition of African religion and its equation with bad science are to the representation of the African-based religion practiced in Haiti and by Haitians in diaspora today. A microexample: The *New York Times* currently refuses to spell *voodoo* with a capital V (spelling it *Vodou* as Haitians prefer is beyond question) even though it capitalizes the names of other religions, including those of other African-based Caribbean religions.[6] This commitment to a deeply compromised form of the term keeps it handy for use in put-down phrases such as *voodoo economics*.[7]

A more complex and weighty example is to be found in the language of Stephen Worth, a lawyer from the Patrolmen's Benevolent Association. On the same day that jury selection was completed for the Louima case, 3 May 1999, the official coroner's report on Diallo was finally released—three long months after the shooting. An earlier autopsy, requested by lawyers engaged by the Diallo family, concluded that the police continued to shoot after Amadou Diallo was already down and immobilized. The coroner's report confused this issue by initially making no judgments about which shots came first or how fast they were fired.[8] Kevin Flynn, writing in the *New York Times* (4 May 1999), reported that Stephen Worth, attorney for one of the men charged with second-degree murder in the death of Amadou Diallo and at the same time attorney for one of the officers accused of beating Louima, celebrated the second coroner's report, crowing that it "puts the lie to the Dream Team's voodoo autopsy and shows it for the pseudoscience that it is." Thus, Worth called on one of the oldest and most enduring "voodoo" tropes, its equation with bad science, and in so doing managed simultaneously to compromise the authority of scientific evidence in the Diallo case and, in his other case, to cast doubt on the credibility and morality of both the lawyers and the main witness, Abner Louima. Worth sent a potent racist message that demeaned the lawyers working for Louima and the Diallo family (initially Johnnie L. Cochran's infamous Dream Team served as counsel for both) by making an invisible reference to the O. J. Simpson murder case while simultaneously linking the lawyers to a religion whose name is synonymous with *black magic* and, as a result, with Haiti, Abner Louima's country.

Conclusion

Our language and the habits of our bodies and minds carry our history. Such habits as racial prejudice, sexual fundamentalism, and even habitual disdain for all things Haitian are prominent in the U.S. habitus. (Evidence of the latter prejudice is apparent in the similarity, and significant difference, between the treatment of the Diallo case and that of the more recent shooting death of the Haitian Patrick Dorismond.)[9] This prejudice against Haitians began when blacks and mulattoes in Haiti had the temerity to win their freedom from slavery and their dignity by fighting for them and did so during a period when the United States and many European countries were still holding slaves. Habits of the heart and mind, such as the historically rooted prejudice against Haitians, exercise a downward pull on transparent civic values such as those represented by a free press, trial by jury, and police accountability. In the events surrounding Abner Louima, the strategies of transparency set in place actually spawned elaborate strategies of secrecy, and vice versa.

In theory, secrecy and transparency are opposing power dynamics, yet, in the Abner Louima case, they appear to have worked together, evoking one another in a paradoxical dance of increasing complexity. Major players in this drama convinced of the importance of their ultimate goals (or at least equipped with those goals as rationalizing devices) competed for the control of institutions of transparency, such as the press, the judicial system, and police review processes. In the name of keeping peace, Police Commissioner Howard Safir painted a ridiculously mild, even insulting picture of the problems between police and civilians in New York City. In the name of providing their clients with the best defense possible, Kornberg and Worth, Police Benevolent Association lawyers, mounted their defense in the press through innuendo, secrecy, and erasure. In the name of covering the news, the media repeated what Kornberg and Worth said and eventually turned from Louima in order to focus on Amadou Diallo's death. In the name of revealing all the dirty secrets, Peter Noel reported that Robert Volpe, Justin's father, carries a bottle of holy water and used it to make crosses on his own forehead in order to protect against Louima's Vodou powers.

The way in which race interacted with these complex impulses was especially visible in the repeated connection of the Louima and Diallo cases, a linkage that remained in the minds of Haitians and other immigrants. The dense, racially charged images that public personalities and journalists called up so effortlessly in commentary on the cases are representations constructed "in the shadow of the fetish." Like the charms that Mama Lola made to help Louima, they are wanga.

Like wanga, these representations of Louima—spoken out but also present in the silences within the words of police, lawyers, and journalists—characterized complex and troubled relational situations with the intention of influencing them. The police commissioner, the press, and lawyers involved in the Louima case deployed their own word wanga. The Haitian community, in turn, responded to the affront to Louima, and to decades of mistreatment at the hands of New York City officials, by putting their universe of explanations on display, including their much-maligned religion,

Vodou. More to the point, they put their fear-charged, blood-soaked toilet plunger wanga, an externalization of their most intimate and most horrific relational nightmares, on public display. They literally thrust their plungers in the face of the NYPD. This process of exposing wanga power in public worked to some extent like sprinkling yellow powder across the threshold of a troublemaker. It brought Abner Louima's experience to public attention. It threw down the gauntlet in a challenge to the city government to do something about patterns of police brutality while simultaneously tempering the fear of the Haitian community and increasing its political capital. It also contributed to a lengthy legal process that finally got jail sentences for the four men directly involved in the arrest and brutalization of Abner Louima.

In the year 2000, a focus on wanga and wanga-like constructions does a surprisingly good job of revealing the everyday workings of power on all levels of society in New York, an ethnically diverse city with a heritage of racism. One of the most interesting aspects of this comparison is the similarity between the workings of Mama Lola's wanga and the workings of what I have called the *word wanga* of politicians, journalists, and lawyers. All are narrative reconfigurations, and all are constructed in order to control key narratives. It is ironic that the homely African wanga, the very objects used by Europeans at the dawn of the Enlightenment to draw absolute boundaries between themselves and primitive others, should reveal themselves as close cousins of Euro-American "magical" maneuvers.

In the Louima case, the Haitian community won the battle only to lose the war. The police conspiracy of silence and especially Volpe's withholding of crucial testimony, the evidentiary rulings of the courts, the unconscious racism and homophobia of the press, the ancient racist tropes buried deeply in the speech of just about everybody who got near to the case, proved more powerful than what either Mama Lola or the Dream Team could do to bring justice, not only to Abner Louima, but also to the larger Haitian community that experiences continuous police harassment. Institutionalized patterns of abuse, including what could be called *racial profiling* and *street justice,* were identified in a 1994 Mollen Commission report on corruption in the NYPD, but nothing was done to address these problems at that time, and nothing has yet been done to address them. While convictions in the Diallo case could at least have raised these issues of institutionalized racism, the convictions of the four men who brutalized Louima were not seen as relevant to such concerns.

Brian Stevens, writing in the *Haitian Times* (19–25 July 2000), acknowledged that Volpe and his new lawyer had already been to court seeking to cut Volpe's sentence in half. So far, such efforts have not succeeded. Abner Louima turned down more than one offer to settle his civil suit because those offers involved no promises for reforms in New York police practices. In the summer of 2001, Louima finally accepted an offer of $7.125 million from the city and $1.625 million from the Patrolmen's Benevolent Association (PBA). While the PBA payment involved no admission of guilt, it was the first time that a police union anywhere in the country had been forced to pay in a police-violence incident. Yet Louima still got no official promises for police reform. He had to settle for informal promises that had more to do with public relations than with a commitment to changing oppressive police practices.

On 28 February 2002, a federal appeals court threw out the obstruction-of-justice convictions of Schwarz, Bruder, and Wiese because of a technicality. Also, Schwarz's conviction for aiding Volpe in the attack on Louima was set aside because of another technicality, a conflict of interest on the part of his attorney, Stephen Worth. From the moment Schwarz was freed on $1 million bail, the district attorney made it clear that he would be indicted and tried again on these charges.

During the 1999 trials of the cases concerning Louima and Diallo, a large percentage of New Yorkers were deeply concerned about police violence. Then, it was a high-priority issue, but the atmosphere had changed drastically by the time Schwarz's convictions were set aside. Jeffrey Toobin, writing for the *New Yorker,* described the *Times* coverage of Schwarz's return to the Staten Island home of his mother as "a dewy portrait." Toobin also noted that the three leading New York tabloids—the *News, Newsday,* and the *Post*—were also Schwarz boosters. "Free," trumpeted the *News,* while *Newsday* and *Post* cried out, "He's Home," and, "He's Out." It was the events of 11 September 2001 that caused this dramatic change. Because of the attack on the World Trade Center, every police officer, including Charles Schwarz, automatically became a hero, a person larger than life, someone no true patriot would consider criticizing. Thus, in July 2002, Schwarz's third trial ended in a single perjury conviction with a possible five-year sentence, while the jury was unable to reach verdicts on any of the charges that concerned Schwarz's participation in torturing Louima. There may well be another trial; whether justice will be served remains to be seen.

After the attack on the World Trade Center, the United States plunged with astonishing speed into a period of feverish patriotism. The words *At*

War appeared in the *Times* 12 September 2001 headline. What transparency there had been in the U.S. media and in the criminal court system is rapidly being crowded out by yet another word wanga, the War on Terror. On a daily basis, irrational acts of war are being simultaneously revealed and concealed, justified and obscured, in the U.S. media and, at times, in its courts of law.

Notes

1   It was later revealed that the instrument that Volpe used to torture Abner Louima was actually the broken-off handle of a broomstick. The toilet plunger, neverthe-less, continued to be mentioned in newspapers, and its image became the icon of the protest movement that developed out of this case of police brutality.

2   Most of those who serve the Vodou spirits also consider themselves to be good Catholics.

3   The most basic difference between *white magic* and *black magic,* as the terms are used in Haitian Vodou, is that the first is practiced for the good of the family or a larger community and that the second is about the pursuit of selfish and/or individualistic goals.

4   The *Haitian Times,* an English-language newspaper, started by former *New York Times* reporter Gary-Pierre Pierre, routinely refers to the "sodomizing" of Abner Louima.

5   In an article appearing on the *New York Times* website on 2 June 1999, David Bar-stow reported that Robert Volpe claimed that his son's trial was a "modern day lynching." Barstow quoted the senior Volpe as saying: "This was not an unpro-voked situation. . . . There was no innocence on the street that night." Barstow continued: "He said his son took Louima to the bathroom that night because he wanted to hit him, to continue the fight. After assaulting him with the stick, Officer Volpe, his father said, yelled, 'Look what you made me do' at Louima."

6   The oddness of this practice was apparent in a 10 January 2000 *New York Times* article, "Catholics Battle Brazilian Faith in 'Black Rome,'" in which the fol-lowing sentence appeared: "Like Santeria in the Spanish-speaking Caribbean or voodoo in Haiti, Candomble merges the identities of African deities and Roman Catholic saints. . . ." An example of the usefulness of the generic *voodoo* comes from the 15 June 2000 edition of the *New York Review of Books,* which carried a full back-page ad for Robert Park's book *Voodoo Science: The Road from Foolish-ness and Fraud,* published by Oxford University Press. A "blurb" from Richard Dawkins promises that "Park does more than debunk, he crucifies. And the result is huge fun. . . . Not only will you enjoy reading it. You'll never again waste time or your money on astrologers, 'quantum healers,' homeopaths, spoon benders, perpetual motion merchants or alien abduction fantasists."

7   The low-budget film *Voodoo* released in the 1990s is a textbook example of the

first part of the operation by which Europeans positioned Africans in relation to themselves, the one whereby all Africa-related religion becomes fetishism. Oddly enough, there are no black characters in this film, and an atmosphere of fear and dread is created entirely with drumming and quick glimpses of dolls, lighted candles, bits of rafia, and knotted pieces of rope—all the materials of wanga making. That is the only way in which anything connected to Vodou appears in the film that bears its name.

8 A fuller report from the Coroner's Office issued at a later date agreed with the first autopsy report that Diallo was fired on after he had been knocked down by police bullets.

9 According to Roosevelt Joseph, writing for the *Haitian Times* (22–28 March 2000), Dorismond, a twenty-six-year-old security guard, was shot to death by a member of NYPD's Gang Investigation Division. Dorismond, the son of a popular Haitian musician, had just left a midtown cocktail lounge when he was approached by an undercover policeman participating in a marijuana sweep. It was a "buy-and-bust" operation. The plainclothes officer asked Dorismond if he had drugs to sell. Dorismond said no, but the assumptions behind the approach angered him. There was a struggle, and the undercover agent's gun went off. Patrick Dorismond died from a single shot. He had no gun. Neither Police Commissioner Safir nor Mayor Giuliani went to his funeral. Quite the contrary, they went on the attack instead. Giuliani commented that Dorismond was "no altar boy" and instructed Safir to release his criminal record. Dorismond had two juvenile indictments for disorderly conduct. He did not go to jail for either. Both were resolved through plea bargaining.

References

Blier, Suzanne Preston. 1995. *African Vodun: Art, Psychology, and Power.* Chicago: University of Chicago Press.

Brown, Karen McCarthy. 1995. "Serving the Spirits: The Ritual Economy of Haitian Vodou." In *Sacred Arts of Haitian Vodou,* ed. Donald J. Cosentino, 205–23. Los Angeles: UCLA Fowler Museum of Cultural History.

Hurbon, Laennec. 1987. *Le barbare imaginaire.* New ed. Port-au-Prince: Henri Deschamps.

MacGaffey, Wyatt. 1993. *The Eyes of Understanding: Kongo Minkisi.* In *Astonishment and Power: Kongo Minkisi and the Art of Renee Stout,* 21–103. Washington, D.C.: National Museum of African Art, Smithsonian Institution.

Pietz, William. 1985. "The Problem of the Fetish I." *Res: Anthropology and Aesthetics* 9:5–17.

———. 1987. "The Problem of the Fetish II: The Origin of the Fetish." *Res: Anthropology and Aesthetics* 13:23–45.

————. 1988. "The Problem of the Fetish IIIa: Bosman's Guinea and the Enlightenment Theory of Fetishism." *Res: Anthropology and Aesthetics* 16:105–23.
Toobin, Jeffrey. 2002. "The Driver: Did the Prosecutors in the Louima Case Have
  the Right Man All Along?" *New Yorker*, 10 June, 34–39.
Wexler, Anna. 2001. "Fictional Oungan: In the Long Shadow of the Fetish." *Research
  in African Literature* 32 (1): 83–97.

9

Anxieties of Influence: Conspiracy Theory and Therapeutic Culture in Millennial America

SUSAN HARDING AND KATHLEEN STEWART

By the turn of the twentieth century in the United States, neurasthenia, or "nerve weakness," had become a highly fashionable symptomology of characteristically modern anxieties. Its various symptoms—insomnia, lethargy, depression, hypochondria, hysteria, hot and cold flashes, asthma, hay fever, "sick-headache," and "brain-collapse"—graphically marked the effects of urbanization, industrialization, and the rationalization of everyday life. Its fretful preoccupation with bodily vigor and decay articulated the conflicts, contradictions, and haunted sensibilities of pervasive social changes (Lutz 1991: 4–5). As a disorder, neurasthenia embodied a new anxious sensibility of the excitable subject as symptom, mirror, and source of worldly forces; suddenly, both the self and the surrounding world seemed at once diffuse, weightless, floating, and unreal, weighted down with symptoms, haunted, immobilized, and excessively sensory and concrete (Lutz 1991: 15–16). As a discourse, neurasthenia articulated both the mysterious malaise of a subject affected by broad and dimly perceived social processes and the emerging therapeutic dream of revitalization through medicine, self-help, talking cures, and eclectic spiritual cures.

Neurasthenia was an unsteady, fraught structure of feeling, mixing a gothic imaginary of hidden threats and unseen forces and the optimism of a new consumerist-therapeutic ethos of self-realization, personal magnetism, and corporate charisma (Fox and Lears 1983). It became a true cultural lingua franca, not because it provided a unified master narrative for anxious times, but because, on the contrary, it was a site of conjuncture for competing and conflicting discourses, ranging from evolution, civilization, science, technology and medicine, religion and ethics, gender and sexuality, health and disease, class and race, to art and politics (Lutz 1991: 20). It was "a multi-accented story" that allowed many different readings, and, at the same time, as a discourse, it was both heteroglossic and "nervous," articulating diacritical or oppositional forces and sensibilities (Lutz 1991: 15). As the symptomatic space of conjuncture where entrepreneurialism met family-based sentimentality, cultural rationalization met reenchantment, and consumerism, class conflict, feminism, and a newly professionalized therapeutic culture eyed each other with a wary gaze, it was at one moment progressive and at the next apocalyptic, at once optimistic and pessimistic, both productive of new social forms and aggressively conservative.

In its social production, neurasthenia first became a cultural lingua franca among turn-of-the-century cultural producers—artists, writers, and other "brain workers"—men and women with "the most refined sensitivities," and then spread to other classes and sectors through reactions and particular social uses that variously embraced, rejected, subverted, or appropriated it (Lutz 1991: 6, 15). In other words, as a "nervous system," neurasthenia not only expressed or reflected modern anxieties but also participated in their particular and actual production as a set of discursive practices in social and political use (Taussig 1992; Lutz 1991: 20). In practice, neurasthenia both proliferated and contested modernity's angst and its rationalization of the link between the subject and a world of forces and effects.

Now, at the end of a long century's efflorescence of anxious symptomologies within an ongoing nervous system, conspiracy theory has become a new lingua franca to track the tensions and symptoms of the "New World Order." Its idiom is not the body but the body politic; its controlling preoccupation is not with bodily vigor but with human agency and political knowledge in a world of social influences (Melley 2000). Like neurasthenia, conspiracy theory articulates both symptoms and cures in an anxious link between mysterious hidden forces and the redemptive healing force of agency. Unlike neurasthenia, which presumed that its symptoms were the accidental outcome of civilizational progress, conspiracy thinking focuses on the revelation of "the shocking truth": it assumes that our anxieties are *designed*. We are the victims of the hidden persuaders of consumerist culture, a far-reaching technogovernmental complex, a network of demonic forces, an endless swarm of sophisticated social controls and invasive influences. The sensibility of conspiracy, or "fusion paranoia" (Kelly 1995), tracks signs and surges of power, surveils banal surfaces to discover hidden threats and promises, pieces together obscure, disparate details in search of the key to an ultimate puzzle and the moment when the imaginary finally matches the real. It dreams up eccentric paths of return to a pristine past, a redemptive human agency, and a world ordered from on high as if a blueprint of a law, a code, or an urtext could be directly, magically imprinted on matter and society, claiming to heal the wound imprinted by the long-standing sense of disjuncture between the American dream and an always already degraded reality. It is, like neurasthenia, a discourse animated at once by fear and desire.

Postwar conspiracy theory differs from earlier "paranoid styles" of American politics in its tendency toward broad social and cultural criticism rather than disclosing secret cabals and in its nearly unanimous judgment that government power is party to, rather than the innocent object of, conspiracy. Nor is it any longer an episodic or eccentric mode of political attention and articulation. Like turn-of-the-century neurasthenia, turn-of-the-millennium conspiracy theory is an overarching structure of feeling that articulates conflicting political efforts and disparate publics in a multivocalic national space of conjuncture.

Conspiracy theory has become so deeply ingrained in the national political imaginary that it encompasses every point on the political spectrum and is as characteristic of the center as it is of marginal groups and occult knowledges (Dean 1998; Marcus 1999). Conspiracies, secret collusions, clandestine activities, and all manner of treachery are charged and frequently proved or confessed. The federal government builds up elaborate defense systems to protect the nation from free-floating specters of catastrophic terrorisms and weapons of mass destruction (Lewis 1999). We are told of grotesque secret government-run experiments on unwitting citizens such as the Tuskegee syphilis experiments on African American men (Wilson and Mill 1998). Leading figures in government, industry, science, medicine, and the military are directly implicated in cases of social and political corruption, environmental degradation, and consumer fraud and deceit (Schoepflin 1998).

Investigative reports, talk shows, television series, movies, novels, and textbooks present a diffuse, sometimes panicked sense of struggle against unknown forces—a deep worry that normality is not normal any more, that "somebody" has done something to the way things used to be, that we have lost something, that we have—that we have been—changed. We are being influenced, manipulated, regulated, experimented on, watched (Graham 1996). Then, in spite of our suspicions about the police, we become their agents in response to Community Watch programs that solicit us to scan bodies out of place in the neighborhood and television shows like *America's Most Wanted* that ask us to scrutinize the faces in 7–11 for a match. The ubiquitous home video camera is poised to capture moments of conspiratorial forces in motion, such as police brutality, enacting an omnipresent panopticon that mimics the logic of "the system" itself. The dual slogans of *The X-Files*—"Trust no one" and "The truth is out there"—express a heady yet unsettling wedding of a deep skepticism of officially sanctioned truths and the seductions of the sensualization of power/knowledge (Foucault 1980: 44).

Conspiracy theory has spread through so many divergent and conflicting routes that it now articulates a widely shared sensibility of being controlled by an all-pervasive, networked system that is itself out of control. Like neurasthenia, conspiracy thinking is a multiaccented story, an overlapping set of heteroglossic discourses that conjoins contradictory and competing reactions and outcomes in a fraught and fretful structure of feeling that yearns for and despairs of ultimate solutions. It fashions right-wing and left-wing visions with equal vigor. The religious Right mobilized a new "politics of ultimacy" that read politics through a millennialist lens of fateful issues at stake in a once-and-for-all confrontation (Barkun 1998: 459). Pat Robertson joined disparate strands of right-wing conspiracy theories under the rubric of the *New World Order* popularized in his 1991 book of that title. The white male "new war" culture reacted to a feminized New World Order with a paramilitary cultural movement centered on Rambo films, paint-ball games, *Soldier of Fortune* magazine, shooting ranges, militias, and survivalist groups (Gibson 1994). The New World Order quickly accumulated a script of threats including new law enforcement formations directed against gun owners, surveillance through black helicopters and implanted microchips, concentration camps for dissenters run by the Federal Emergency Management Agency, and hundreds of thousands of UN-affiliated foreign troops on U.S. soil to stifle armed resistance (Barkun 1998: 455).

On the Left, political movements fighting the inequalities of race, sex, and class have taken up the practices of conspiracy theory to track the violent effects of unjust subjugation on identities, bodies, and the body politic. In the 1980s, the Cristic Institute brought a lawsuit against a large collection of former U.S. intelligence and military officers who constituted a "Secret Team" operating a vast drug-smuggling and arms-running enterprise that had been directly involved in many of the unhappy events in American history since the 1950s (Kelly 1995: 69). More recently, a broad coalition of environmentalist groups, liberal churches, labor, and social movement activists has launched an international campaign against the World Trade Organization as a secret, conspiratorial world power. Conspiracy theories circulating in the black public sphere posited that HIV was disseminated through black neighborhoods for the purpose of genocide, that the government intentionally spread narcotics into black communities, that food additives in Kentucky Fried Chicken systematically sterilized black men but not white men (Fenster 1999: 72; Kelly 1995: 64). Some feminist discourses tracked a conspiracy of male dominance through institutions, ideologies, and private life (Kelly 1995: 64), while the men's movement embraced men as wounded by the same patriarchal regime and sought therapeutic solutions (Pfeil 1995).

All the voices theorizing conspiracy, Right, Left, and "hard to label," take for granted that the powers-that-be are functionaries of the opposing camp, and none suppose that routine politics ("throw the bastards out") offers much, if any, remedy. For postwar conspiracy has diagnosed structural, not personnel, problems. It is the nervous expression of the idea that social systems affect human action, that large organizations, bureaucracies, social institutions, information networks, ideologies, and discourses shape individuals, and that we therefore are not entirely free, autonomous, self-controlling individuals (Melley 2000: 5). In conspiracy theory, social regulation comes as a terrible revelation, a scandal, because of the challenge that it presents, the threat that it represents, to long-standing notions of the individual as a coherent, rational, autonomous agent. Not only are things not the way they used to be, but "people are no longer what they used to be" (Melley 2000: 42). Postwar paranoid interpretations are, thus, rooted in and articulate "agency panic" (Melley 2000: 12). At the same time, they effect a "postmodern transference" in which the agency depleted from the individual is attributed to the social. Social structures do not simply affect human action; they are mysterious, motivated, intentional, and often malevolent (Melley 2000: 13).

Individuals, groups, and organizations from time to time get so enmeshed in their conspiratorial visions that they act them out, sometimes violently. Charlie Manson, Timothy McVeigh, Theodore Kaczynski, white supremacist militias, J. Edgar Hoover's FBI, and the Branch Davidians and the ATF at Waco are sensational examples, but we have all glimpsed somewhere—in our families, schools, workplaces, and communities—that hypervigilant over-the-edge look in the paranoid eye, that bottomless rage against the system, that obsessive compilation of signs that "they" are up to no good. It may seem that these more and less sensational moments are the only times that anyone seems to do something about conspiracies, that otherwise it's just talk, a lot of wild talk, that never comes of anything, sort of like valves blowing off steam, the effluvia of postmodern life. But postwar conspiracy talk is never idle. It is always also some sort of therapy that has themes of ultimacy and redemption built into it—as dreams, abysmal realities, or intensely polarized unconscious structures. The practices of conspiracy theory form a tensely articulated pact with therapeutic culture through the logics of stress, trauma, injustice, self-made agency, and redemption. Taken separately and together, conspiracy theory and therapeutic culture constitute fields of feeling that channel the contradictions of contemporary social transformations and their effects. They knot together desire and despair, progress and collapse, enchantment and disenchantment, nostalgic and futurist yearnings, and the search for everything from purity to community. This is the nature of a modern nervous system. It is also the nature of metadiscourses of modernity.

Therapeutic culture arose with the shift to consumer capitalism at the turn of the century. It replaced the producer ethic of work, sacrifice, and saving with a yearning for self-realization rooted in the generalized neurasthenic sense that selfhood had become fragmented, diffuse, and somehow "weightless" or "unreal." Advertising, thrill-seeking mass-marketed amusements, and an ethic of immediate gratification helped create a new symbolic universe where the yearning to experience "real life" in all its intensity was both projected as an ideal and frustrated by the contradictions of a deliberate, mass-mediated, market-driven cultivation of spontaneity (Fox and Lears 1983). Therapeutic reactions against the modernist rationalization of culture were themselves symptoms of the rationalization of the helping profession, the talking cure, and an autonomous "self" whose immanent indwelling spirit sought expression and release.

Therapeutic culture and conspiracy theory entwine through their separate and sometimes conflicting or competing uses of a shared set of modernist interpretive practices that oppose the forces of the rational to the irrational, the transparent and true to the arcane and hidden. With a passion bordering on epistemophilia, both claim a sublime pleasure in revealed knowledge and hermeneutic mastery, in the effort to uncover and recover lost or secreted knowledge, cracking codes, sifting through signs, symptoms, and overdetermined webs of feeling in search of the telling detail. Both rationalize the link between the subject and the world by scanning for signs of agency, dysfunction, and fit and by gathering disparate signs into a narrative drama of transformation, encounter, risk, and conversion. Both uncover an underlying plot that combines radical doubt with the sense that the truth is out there. Born of the restlessness and obsessions of modernity's simultaneous overstimulation and numbness, alarm and anesthesia, sapping and celebration of self-control, both breed disciplines and compulsions and take on a life of their own (Berlant 1996; Buck-Morss 1993, 1995; Feldman 1994; Ivy 1993, 1995; Terkel 1988).

Conspiracy theory as a therapeutic practice addresses specifically late-modern anxieties about the perfidies of power/knowledge: uncertainties about the causes of and links between human action and complex social events; about "expertise" and "experts"; about "truth" and "meaning" and "reality"; about the grand metanarratives that gave direction and purpose to history; about how to live as a liberal subject (man) caught in the body of a sociological subject (woman/cockroach). In the same instance that conspiracy thinking addresses these anxieties, it produces them, for every paranoid cure is also a symptom. Whenever conspiracy thinking asserts "the truth" and apprehends "reality," it simultaneously acknowledges their instability and partiality, their social construction and regulation. The postwar culture of paranoia articulates a crisis of agency, of the liberal subject in peril, but every effort to restore it, to disavow subjection, is haunted by traces of influence (Butler 1997). Knowledge of social influence is always built into the postparanoid subject. The ceaseless sign scanning, code cracking, and mastering of logics are a balm, rationalizing, making sense, revealing the meaning of things, and at the same time they agitate, destabilize, and demonstrate empires of conspiracy. The plethora of conspiratorial anti–master narratives that have rushed to fill the vacuum created by postmodern incredulity toward grand narratives also underscores and intensifies a sense of historical fragmentation and disorientation. Paranoid culture, is, thus a therapy of compulsions. Nothing is ever finished. Everything is always starting over, caught in a cycle of endless repetition because each recantation incants the recanted, each autonomous act is the effect of subordination, each step outside is also always a step inside.

We have described contemporary conspiracy theory in the United States, like the neurasthenia at the turn of the century, as an embodied anxiety that articulates the stresses, contradictions, and dreams of redemption of a subject under the influence of diffuse and haunting social, political, and discursive force fields. We also take postwar paranoid culture to be a nervous system or structure of feeling. Internally riven between nightmare and dream, symptom and cure, it becomes a liminal space of conjuncture of myriad discourses, positionings, and reactions. Finally, we note that, like neurasthenia, conspiracy thinking is a metacultural discourse that engages fundamental questions of fear and desire, subjectivity and agency, ideal and reality, through practices of anxious rumination: scanning for signs, symptoms, and sources of dysfunction; fetishizing knowledge; rooting experiences of the uncanny and the unknown in hidden and diffuse structures of power; slouching toward redemption. In other words, we take the culture of paranoia to be a metacultural articulation of the anxiety of influence itself.

Particular cultures, groups, and publics articulate the anxiety of influence in different ways and to varying degrees. They invariably recycle and revise preexisting story lines and tropes, often contribute minor innovations to the larger field of conspiratorial thinking, and sometimes realize stunning breakthroughs, boldly going forth to make connections that no one has made before. Here, we take up two case studies in which a postwar paranoid structure of feeling is embedded in a wider array of practices that fashion "remnant" communities. Both nervous systems are strikingly inventive and generative, metacultural and metaphysical, haunted and dreamy; both sift through signs and influences in complex, critical, uncanny, wondrous ways; and both are especially preoccupied by modern mediated knowledge and "information." They register effects, decipher meanings, predict futures, and fashion stories—small, mid-sized, grand, and cosmic. In the Calvary Chapel case, a nineteenth-century conspiracy theory is given new life in a therapeutic form that meticulously juggles light and dark, fear and desire, indignation and assurance, and that delivers a vision of agency—earthly redemption—through political knowledge. In Heaven's Gate, we have a case of therapy in motion in which agency/earthly redemption is achieved through the miraculous channeling and juxtaposing of assorted metaphysical knowledges, both secular and religious, into charismatic authority and a compelling and really real life-and-death drama.

Calvary Chapel

In 1997, we did fieldwork at the Calvary Chapel church in Orange County, California. Started by Pastor Chuck Smith in 1965, Calvary Chapel grew rapidly as part of the Jesus movement of the 1970s and the growth of suburban evangelical churches in the last two decades (Balmer 1993; Balmer and Todd 1994: 664). It combines conservative fundamentalism, including strict interpretation of the Bible as the word of God and an apocalyptic vision of the End Times, with a soft, or light, pentecostalism and a markedly hip and youthful style. In the early 1970s, Calvary Chapel drew converts from youths and disaffected hippies through Christian rock festivals, go-go clubs, and love-ins, Christian coffeehouses and surfer clubs, baptisms in the ocean, and hotlines for kids on bad trips including a thirty-second cure for heroine addiction. Today, the Costa Mesa campus boasts a congregation of twenty-five thousand members and has spawned a loose federation of four hundred churches, many of which have congregations of over ten thousand people (Balmer and Todd 1994: 693).

Like many of the new evangelical megachurches that rose to prominence in the 1980s and 1990s, the services, style of preaching, and structure of the church have adapted secular therapeutic culture to Christian ends (Miller 1997: 21; Harding 2000) by providing marriage counseling and a wide array of weekly support groups and lifestyle groups, including the Working Women's Joyful Life Bible Study, Proverbs Class for Men, High School Mothers' Prayer Meeting, Korean Fellowship, Becoming Disciples (for new believers), New Spirit/Alcohol and Drug Recovery, Singles' Group, Prison Fellowship, Physically Disabled Fellowship, Elders Pray for the Sick and Other Needs, High School Girls' Bible Study, and the Christian Prophecy Update Meeting. Bookstores on church grounds are filled with a combination of apocalyptic titles warning of the dangers of utilitarian individualism and the decay of moral standards under the regime of liberal humanism, consumerism, and bureaucratization and Christian self-help books with titles such as *Daily Devotions, Everyday with Christ, Self-Confrontation, The Fast-Track: A Manual for In-Depth Discipleship, Marriage the Way It's Made to Be,* and *Men Whom Women Love to Love* (a play on the best-selling secular self-help book *Women Who Love Too Much*).

Services begin with concerts of inspirational Christian pop music complete with electric guitars, drums, and large screens that project the lyrics so that the congregation can sing along. The sermon that follows is given in an informal, vernacular style; the rhetoric moves facilely back and forth between the grand scheme of biblical prophecy and world events and the intimate present day of private life, lifestyle choices, faith, and dreams. A good-news bulletin of mass conversions and fun family events moves into a soft-spoken critique of consumerist values and laissez-faire situational ethics in which "there are absolutely no absolutes"; the world is in a steady moral decline, and the church is becoming more worldly, so Christians have to change the world. Congregants dressed in jeans and T-shirts read along in the vernacular New King James version, marketed as the "Slim Line Version," while the pastor cites Scripture, peppering his comments with hip jokes, friendly smiles, and translations of the signs of the End Times in terms of suburban everyday life.

The pastor encourages people to take notes as he gives them tips on how to be Christians in a world drawing close to the apocalypse. For instance, he might offer a basic three-step plan of Christian action: (1) be Christian, and act as a model for others; (2) get close to non-Christians; and (3) speak out. He gives concrete tips that blend self-help aids with intentional, conspiratorial planning: "It's easier to start a fire with people who are already thirsting," so try talking to non-Christians at holiday parties when the spirit is in the air. We all need to come out of our sequestered suburban and Christian-only lifestyles, so do lunch with a coworker or invite neighbors for dinner, invite non-Christian men to watch the game with you, make contacts when you're working out or at kids' events, contact people you used to know — "though some say it's better not to look 'em up, you know what I'm sayin'?" — and practice "strategic consumerism like going to the same dry cleaner's every day so you learn that person's name." The pastor might also suggest that people write down the titles of Christian self-help books "that will enable you to do these things," such as Paul Little's trio of books *Know What You Believe, Know Why You Believe*, and *How to Give Away Your Faith*. Every Christian should be able to relay the Gospel in a thirty-second to one-minute sound bite.

Calvary Chapel's optimistic apocalypticism — optimistic because it signals the fulfillment of Bible prophecy, the rapture, and the Second Coming of Christ — reads signs of impending doom in a variety of seemingly "good" and "bad" signs, including the growth or development of world population, education, technology, communications, transportation, secularization and ecumenicism, the rise of satanic cults and false prophets, the AIDS crisis, the New Age movement, abortion, pornography, homosexuality, divorce, crime, drugs, UFOs, and alien abductions (Harding 2000: 241). Apocalypticism for Christians such as these is not just a set of beliefs but a specific narrative mode of reading history backward. Future events, which are fixed and known, determine the shape, the content, and the significance of present events and actions (Harding 2000: 230). Economic and political events are read as the fulfillment of biblical prophecy that narrates the return of the Jews to Palestine, the rise of the New Roman Empire, the great tribulation during which the Anti-Christ, or the Beast of Revelation, will rise to worldwide dominance, the rapture of the church in which the saved will be saved from the imminent horrific days, the triumphant return of Christ in the battle of Armageddon, and the final, glorious, millennial reign of Christ from Jerusalem (Fenster 1999: 155; Marsden 1980). Recent world events of specific interest to the church's prophecy updates include, for instance, the Persian Gulf War, anything concerning the fate of Israel and the Jews such as the Mideast Peace Treaty, the election and reelection of Bill Clinton, the fall of the Berlin Wall, the creation of the European Economic Community (the New Roman Empire), and signs of a New World Order in news of the Internet, transnational business and finance, the demise of America as an economic and political power, and the North American Free Trade Agreement (Harding 2000: 233). According to the church's reading of the Bible, we are currently in the Church Age—a suspended time of waiting and watching—and Christians are enjoined to enact their role in God's plan by praying, living right, and saving souls.

Like both therapeutic culture and conspiracy theory, Calvary Chapel's practices of reading back and forth between biblical prophecy and signs in the present find the future in the present, the invisible in the visible, and redemption in a dramatic transformation. In its eschatology, the End is not merely imminent; it is immanent—present in the whole of history—and the individual life holds the promise of the End (Fenster 1999: 177). In the words of Pastor Chuck Smith, "Time is short. I believe God has intended and deliberately designed that every generation should believe that Jesus is coming in their generation. That each generation had that awareness of the immediacy of the return of Jesus Christ. I think God designed it that way" (Smith 1997). The ecstatic promise of predestined events casts concrete Christian interpretive practices as a transcendent experience of the sublime; practicing faith, adhering to moral principles, evangelizing, consuming prophetic interpretations, scanning for signs in current events, and learning to sense the coming of the End Times all bear the mark of a higher order realized in the everyday. Like Weber's Calvinists, Calvary Chapel followers are directed both to hold fast to their faith in salvation, demonstrating it in prayer and otherworldly piety, and to build, prove, and justify their state of grace through action in the world. The belief in predestined biblical prophecy and the premillennial rapture of the saved reproduces the paradox of the Calvinist predestination of the elect; rather than rob Christians of their agency, it infuses them with divinely inspired agency (Weber 1958: 111–14).

Like therapeutic culture and conspiracy theory, then, Calvary Chapel's premillennialism rationalizes the link between the subject and the world by sanctifying the practice of scanning for signs of the End Times and inventing forms of appropriate action. When it connects the banal details of everyday life to an invisible order, it gives voice and reason to a haunting density of floating effects, channeling uncanny resonances and latent forces into routes of engagement and salvation. Fueled by an unstable dialectic of disillusionment and reenchantment, it constitutes a space of conjuncture in which theories of a world order torn between the forces of good and evil and proper agency and passivity or dysfunction meets ecstatic dreams of a peaceful, unhaunted fit between self, society, and spirit. Its very madness from a modern, secular humanist point of view makes it compelling from a Bible-believing point of view; speaking it becomes a political act of dissent, disruption, and critique of dominant theories of history (Harding 2000: 238) at the same time that it lays claim to a new society of Christians.

The nervous link between the practices of conspiracy theory and therapeutic culture was most dramatically demonstrated in Calvary Chapel's weekly Bible Prophecy Update meetings. The study group was attended by a hard core of right-wing conspiracy theorists who gave voice to extremist views that were not otherwise elaborated in the soft, suburban poetics of official church discourse. The study group followed a standard, ritual format that moved from an opening prayer through alarming, vitriolic accounts of secular humanist conspiracies and back to the good-news Gospel of the coming rapture and injunctions for Christians to live calm, holy lives of prayer, soulful preparation, and evangelizing. The leader of the group would open the conspiratorial expressions with a monologue on the evil forces evident in federal gun control, unisex Bibles, environmentalism, sex education in the schools, and the spread of homosexuality through the media. Then the group would watch a video of a professional, official-looking, Christian news broadcast such as *Jack Van Impe Presents* (with Jack and his wife, Rexella, positioned at a "news desk" as anchors) or *This Week in Bible Prophecy* (starring Peter and Paul LaLonde). This was followed by listening to a tape of a prophetic Christian radio broadcast, such as Charles Taylor's *Today in Bible Prophecy*.

The tension in the room would grow thick with the righteous outrage of watching shocking, evil revelations unfold. Then the group leader would invite participants to testify to updates in their own lives. People told violent stories of dark forces at work in their own lives and theorized about conspiratorial cultural, political, and economic trends. They often expressed doubts of their own intelligence and of the little man's ability to track the mysterious moves of the powers that be. But they were sure of one thing: that there were irrational, conspiratorial forces at work in the world and that God had a plan that would turn it all around in the end. When the bitterness of conspiracy theory had reached an unbearable peak, the leader would draw the group away from nascent calls to violent action and back into the fold of the therapeutic Christian community by reminding them that all this bad news was actually blissfully good news because it meant that the Lord was coming soon. Their role as evangelical Christians was simply to go home and pray. Soon they would be released from the torturous knowledge of evil, injustice, and social dysfunction. With this, the tension in the room would visibly deflate, and the feeling of relief, pleasure, and purpose would grow palpable. In the end, the dialectic enacted throughout the session between indulgence in rage and snide comments about the "idiots" in power and an attitude of transcendent Christian self-control would come to a resting point of satisfaction.

Throughout the sessions, both the conspiratorial and the therapeutic sensibilities were fueled by dreams of a triumphant individual agency rising to combat the hegemony of the knowledge industries. Increased knowledge in the world is, in itself, evidence of the imminence of the End Times; time is in fast forward, and this generation is completely different from all others. Knowledge has doubled in each of a string of ever-shortening periods (the years 1–1750; 1750–1900; 1900–50; 1950–60); in the present times, knowledge is doubling every two years. But, in the new secular, consumerist order of things, entertainment, speed, and convenience are the sole values cherished, and change is taken to be a good in itself. Traditional roles and ways of life are materially eroded by dependence on the knowledge industries as a worldly God. Kids who spend all their time on computer games no longer play kick the can and hide and seek. Parents and teachers are no longer the storytellers; huge media conglomerates are. Christians are warned to resist the seductions and distractions of a media-saturated world. On movie night, the church plays Christian horror videos that portray scenarios in which teenagers miss the flight to the rapture because they are distracted by a Walkman and do not hear the final boarding call; businessmen miss the plane because they are on their cell phones and portable computers doing business or playing video games.

Christians have to learn to read between the lines in order to resist the brainwashing of false prophets. Nazis founded the science of semantics; today, they would be able to use Madison Avenue advertising and Hollywood magic. The fact that crime is down but crime reporting is way up is all too convenient for the antigun lobby.

Authorities knew all about the bombs at the World Trade Center and in Atlanta. There were calls to the FBI hotline in Atlanta and photographs of a man rummaging through the duffel bag that held the bomb—was he resetting it? Why haven't they found this guy? Why did they ruin the reputation of the security guard instead—the weak one? They're like the Nazis who burned the Reichstag and blamed it on the Jews. A New Age "expert" on television happily pronounces that we're jumping a stage in evolution, getting rid of millions of weak people; she implies that only the "fit" will survive. Some computers were stolen from U.S. security and offered to Hussein; luckily, a hacker saved the day at the last minute, but there are bad hackers out there too and alarming data leaks every day. The same guy is still running things— the guy in the little red suit.

False knowledge systems, adrift in a world without tradition and Christian values, have produced ludicrous, irrational claims posing as hegemonic values and common sense. Under the new regime of political correctness in the schools, for instance, kids are told that acid rain and global warming are their parents' fault. Kids can be sent home from school for handing out birthday invitations only to boys. There is mandatory teaching of homosexuality as a normal and healthy "alternative lifestyle." (Someone calls out "Why can't the militia be an alternative lifestyle?" and everyone laughs.) These days, a man's computer might actually suggest that he call his wife his "spouse," and the story of Peter and the Wolf is suddenly about an endangered species. Euthanasia is presented in the mainstream media as a *Picket Fences* story about an old man who wanted to be killed to give his son his heart. A person with measles can be quarantined, while a person with AIDS cannot even be legally identified. Gun control nuts want to ban toys that even resemble guns or to ban people from owning a gun if they have ever committed a crime, even if that "crime" is nothing more than a "shouting match with your wife" or a fight at school. Regimes of worldly knowledge come and go, and the old ways of thinking are always delegitimated in the end. In the 1950s, people used X-ray machines as a sales gimmick to see if their shoes fit, and no one had a clue that they were being exposed to harmful radiation. Now, every time scientists find a little bug on Mars, people believe that there is intelligent life in the universe. There are still things that we know nothing about, but biblical prophecy is a constant.

Christian news broadcasts catch critical world events that the mainstream media either miss because they're distracted by soap-opera scandals or actively cover up. There are laws being enacted that will one day overrule national sovereignty. Deadly diseases that are now resistant to antibiotics are spreading unchecked. Police now confiscate all of a person's property if they find a marijuana plant anywhere near their house (and, of course, the police get a cut). They could win the drug war easily, but they don't want to because it's just an excuse to control us. You can be arrested for leaving the country with $1 more than $10,000 if you don't report it. Everyone has to carry identification cards at all times, and they don't want us to use cash because they won't be able to control us and track our every move. The IRS suddenly has the right to access our bank accounts. The Constitution is gradually being eroded to clear the way for a world government. Arabs are attacking the Jews in Israel. They're building up the backbone of the Internet with new fiber, and the government is unable to control its rapid growth and sieve-like structure. A recent study shows that 25 percent of all these women talking about sexual abuse have been implanted with chips that give them vivid false memories of precise events.

Yet, while the media and the powers that be are dangerous forces that spread false consciousness and suppress true knowledge, this is itself part of God's plan. Even the knowledge brokers in the news media, government, high-tech, the United Nations, and big science unwittingly channeled truths. Despite Hollywood's ignorance of God's plan, its apocalyptic blockbusters of disasters are creating images of things to come and preparing non-Christians for the tribulation. New technology might be used in uncovering the secret truths of the Bible. Some say, for instance, that the code of the Word might be decoded by reading every twentieth word of the Bible with the help of computers. Others say that somewhere in the Bible there may be clues to the precise date of the rapture. But, in the end, all the knowledge gathering and righteous interpretations of events will give way to the certainty of the rapture itself as God's force inscribes itself on the world and frees Christians from their vigilant watch. Technologies might begin to track the "earthquake magnitude" of the event with the needles on their instruments going crazy, but, as the world collapses around people, it will be futile to take readings. People can take note of the depletion of the ozone layer, global warming, and epidemics of skin cancer, but, in the end, men's hearts will fail them at the roaring of the rivers and the seas. The rapture will be soon.

The prophecy update sessions end with prayer and light parting comments: "Well, don't bother to pay your taxes because he's coming soon, hopefully it'll be this Pentecost, you never know." Prepare yourself. Make yourself available for whatever the Lord wants you to do. Ask him what he has for you every day when you get up.

Heaven's Gate

In the spring of 1997, as we listened to the people at Calvary Chapel vacillate between righteous outrage at the signs of evil escalating around them and blissful patience in the light of Christ's soon coming, the people of Heaven's Gate acted out another end times scenario, one that fused conspiracy theory and therapy culture in much more demanding terms. While Heaven's Gate drew on a dramatic revision of the premillennialist scenario of churches like Calvary Chapel, its intellectual roots were equally in the UFO/alien discourses that proliferated in the United States after World War II.

Stories of UFO sightings and alien contact were always tinged with suspicions of government cover-up, but charges of conspiracy, cover-up, and repression—social, physical, psychological—became central preoccupations during the 1980s. At the same time, UFO/alien discourses greatly elaborated their therapeutic practices, and they moved from the margins to the mainstream of American popular culture. Among the thousands of stories of UFO sightings, Roswell was the most renowned site of these shifts. Thanks to a series of sensational publications by UFO investigators (Berlitz and Moore 1980; Randle and Schmidt 1991; and see Eberart 1991), the tiny New Mexico town of Roswell emerged from the obscurity of a one-day "flying disc wreckage" story in 1947 to become the centerpiece of an epic/epoch of extensive government cover-up of extraterrestrial contact (Saler, Ziegler, and Moore 1997: 2–29). The process culminated in "UFO Encounter '97" on the fiftieth anniversary of the crash, which, more than anything, was "a celebration of conspiracy thinking" (Dean 1998: 191). In the alien contact lineage of stories, alien abductions were the principle point of entry into more mainstream paranoid and therapeutic culture. In particular, Budd Hopkins and Whitely Streiber published a series of best-selling books in the 1980s that revealed in vivid, visceral detail a terrible history of alien-human contacts that had been doubly repressed—as memory by the aliens and as truth by the powers that be (Hopkins 1981, 1987; Streiber 1987, 1989). The process culminated in 1994 when the Harvard psychologist and therapist John Mack pronounced stories of alien abduction literally true, thereby ending elite academe's regime of stonewalling evidence of alien encounters (Mack 1994).

As if obeying Foucault's critique of the repressive hypothesis, the more it was said that UFO sightings and alien encounters were repressed, the more they proliferated (Foucault 1980). By the turn of the millennium, UFO/alien discourses had become a major clearinghouse for late-modern anxieties regarding threats to human agency, "the fugitivity of truth," the balkanization of "consensus reality," the collapse of grand metanarratives, cultural difference, the origin of meaning, and the all-around dispersion of cultural and political authority (Dean 1998; Dery 1999; Melley 2000; Saler, Ziegler, and Moore 1997: 140–41). They also presented a copious site of conjuncture for all sorts of idioms, enabling connections across a vast field of discourses: space travel; high technology; information; cyborgs; surveillance; mind control; death and life; body and spirit; science; government; reproduction; sexuality; race; immigration; the environment; colonizing and being colonized; fear and desire; trauma and hope; catastrophe and salvation; revealed truth; persecution; and, of course, cover-up (Dean 1998; Bryan 1995; Curran 1985; Darlington 1997; Heseman and Mantle 1997; Lewis 1995; Lieb 1998; Pritchard et al. 1994). And they incorporated a full range of therapies: hypnosis; channeling; meditation; self-help and support groups; psychotherapy; irony; humor; hoax; consumer kitsch; Hollywood films; television series; and investigative reports.

Like Calvary Chapel, Heaven's Gate got its start in the 1970s. Its founders, Bonnie Lu Nettles (also known as Peep, the Admiral, Guinea, Her, and Ti) and Marshall Applewhite (also known as Bo, the Captain, Pig, Him, and Do), were raised in Southern Baptist and Presbyterian churches, respectively, but as adults became adepts in various metaphysical arts—meditation, channeling discarnate spirits, astrology, mysticism, Theosophy, and paranormal contacts with space beings (Balch 1995: 141–42). Sometime in 1974, their peculiar mix of Bible prophecy, metaphysics, contactee/flying saucer culture, TV sci-fi, and high school biology became an unfolding social drama in which they figured, not as mere spectators awaiting the Blesséd Hope, but as major actors. Applewhite had a vision in which he realized that he and Nettles were the two witnesses prophesied in Revelation 11, and they embarked on their mission knowing that they would be assassinated for spreading God's word, that they would rise from the dead after three and a half days, and that they would ascend to heaven in a spacecraft.

The Two, as Bo and Peep also called themselves at the time, began to gather their flock in 1975, invited their followers to "walk out of the door of your life," separate from all human attachments, prepare for the coming "harvest" of souls, and join them in "the Father's kingdom" in spacecraft that would come for them shortly after The Two ascended. For nearly a year, the flock, with and without Bo and Peep, added and subtracted "students," fragmented and reassembled, camped and wandered, waiting for "the Demonstration," the assassination and resurrection, that would prove the truth of The Two's message. Early in 1976, after a particularly bad bout of TV publicity in Las Vegas that made them feel "like they had been shot down by the media and the mission was dead," The Two told their hundred-some students that the Demonstration had in fact occurred already—"at the hands of the media." Not long after that, Peep/Ti announced that "the doors to the Next Level are closed" and the harvest was over. It was time for "students" to enter the "classroom," an indefinite period of growth and preparation for lives of "service" on the Next Level (Balch 1995: 154).

The group disappeared from public view until 1992, when they resurfaced briefly in the form of a website, newspaper ads, television broadcasts, and public meetings in order to make a "final offer" to those who would join them for the "liftoff" that was imminent. Having regathered some "lost sheep," Heaven's Gate, as the group was by now known, disappeared again until the notorious day in late March 1997 when thirty-eight bodies were found rotting in a wealthy San Diego suburban home. From the outside, it was "the largest mass suicide in U.S. history." From the inside, the Captain (Bo, Do, Applewhite) and his crew had left their earthly vehicles behind and joined the Admiral (Peep, Ti, Nettles, who finished her work on the human level and departed in 1985) in a spaceship tucked away in the tail of the Hale-Bopp comet for their journey to the Next Level.

The group's suicide combined with other telltale signs that it was a "cult" to guarantee Heaven's Gate's status as an ultrafringe phenomenon. The group and its spectacular finale figured as a major sign of the times in various paranoid scenarios, such as, "The approaching year 2000 is coaxing all the crazies out of the woodwork" (*Time* 1997), or, "This new hybrid cult [emerged] from a mix of human communications techniques and the latest, newest, and most powerful mass communication technology in human history . . . the Web" (Conway and Siegelman 1997). Prominent UFO/alien contact experts denounced Heaven's Gate not only as a suicide cult but also for its reverence for aliens, that is, for Next Level souls who traveled by spacecraft and whose bodies looked like little gray space aliens. Speaking at the 1997 Roswell celebration, Budd Hopkins rejected any claims about "good, benevolent, transformative eco-aliens," lumping those who make such claims with the Heaven's Gate suicides: "For anyone to accept the idea that we must bypass our fellow humans and look to the UFO occupants as the final source of ecological wisdom and spiritual growth, is, unfortunately, to take a step along the same path" (quoted in Dean 1998: 195).

Hopkins chided Heaven's Gate for its "pronoia," its conviction that aliens were out to help, not hurt, us (Dery 1999: 13), but, as we shall see, its paranoia was equally pronounced. Although itself far from the mainstream, Heaven's Gate fully partook of the mainstreaming of paranoid thinking and therapy culture during the 1980s and presents an exquisite instance of their fusion. Their cosmic metanarrative as it appeared in various webpages during the 1990s (see *Heaven's Gate* entries in reference list) had become much more apocalyptic and conspiratorial than it was in the 1970s as well as much more effectively therapeutic, providing a confident personal voice, a complex historical point of view, and strong plot lines, characters, and motivations.

On the lighter side, Do and his students tell us that "the human kingdom was created as a stepping stone between the animal kingdom and the true Kingdom of God," the Level Above Human, which was a physical place, not a spiritual realm. The human kingdom is made up of "mammalian —seed-bearing—plants or containers," while the Next Level kingdom is made up of "non-mammalian, non-seed-bearing containers for souls." Souls evolve through a series of incarnations in mammalian bodies and progress by shedding human/mammalian characteristics and behavior—sexuality, gender, and all other addictions and ties—through the tutorship of a member, or Representative, of the Kingdom of God who has been through the process. The earth is, thus, a "garden" of plants (containers, vehicles) for souls, which are harvested from time to time by Next Level Representatives. Jesus' body was prepped, or tagged, at birth and incarnated at the time of his baptism by the soul of a Next Level Representative who had come to earth to harvest a few select souls. Do and Ti were, like Jesus, Next Level Representatives, tagged at birth and incarnated by souls in the early 1970s. The bodies of their crew were, like those of Jesus' disciples (his crew), also tagged at birth; in the mid-1970s and early 1990s they were incarnated by Next Level souls who arrived in spacecraft (which humans called *UFOs* and *flying saucers*). For two decades, the crew used their human bodies as cocoons, undergoing the metamorphosis necessary for their assumption of genderless, asexual, nondesiring, telepathic, eternal bodies bound each and only to an Older Member and living lives of service to the Next Level. In the 1990s, Do began to receive ever-clearer signals that their classroom time was nearly over, although he did not know for some time whether they would ascend bodily into a spacecraft that would land on earth or leave their earthly vehicles, their flesh bodies, behind and ascend as discarnate souls (*Heaven's Gate*, "Planet about to Be Recycled").

On the darker side, Next Level "gardening" on earth had long been challenged and corrupted by "malevolent space alien races" who presented themselves to humans as "Gods." They are "Luciferians," descendants of Next Level members who fell away many thousands of years ago, and they are "humans' GREATEST ENEMY. They hold humans in unknown slavery only to fulfill their own needs. They cannot truly create [the Next Level is the only place from which souls, life, and all creating originate], but they develop races and containers through genetic manipulation and hybridization; they make deals with human governments to engage in biological experimentation (through abductions) in exchange for advanced technology." Luciferians keep humans in darkness through their control of religions, above all Christianity, and family, sexuality, and gender. They see to it "through the 'social norm' (the largest Luciferian 'cult' there is) that man continues not to avail himself of the possibility of advancing *beyond* human" (*Heaven's Gate*, " 'UFO Cult' Resurfaces"). When members of the Level Above Human are present, anti-Kingdom forces " 'turn up the heat' in the area of mammalian behavior," binding "human souls to this world through: a preoccupation with sexuality (indulgence in all pleasures/addictions of the human senses); reproductivity (family); service to the human kingdom (within the structure of indebtedness and credit); and non-disputable, 'moral' responsibility to their family, community, race, nation, and their unknowingly distorted *religious* concepts" (*Heaven's Gate*, " 'UFO Cult' Resurfaces," "Organized Religion"). The opposing forces have been so successful that "the weeds have taken over the garden and truly disturbed its usefulness beyond repair—it is time for the civilization to be recycled—'spaded under' " (*Heaven's Gate*, "Overview of Present Mission").

The modal hero in postwar American conspiracy dramas—that is, theories that are fully enacted and inhabited, that become real parallel worlds—is the lone masculine individual who realizes that the system is evil and struggles mightily to get "outside" it, sometimes alone, sometimes with likeminded others. Such figures—Timothy McVeigh, Theodore Kaczynski, the white militiamen—may be seen as vigorously asserting masculinist notions of individual autonomy and self-control against political, social, and technological forces to the contrary. But postwar paranoia accommodated other kinds of responses to the challenge to liberal notions of the individual and human agency, including those like Heaven's Gate that, in effect, actively rejected liberal individualism. Do and his students sympathized with those who publicly scorned "the system" and tried to live "outside" it. They thought that humans such as Randy Weaver at Ruby Ridge and the Branch Davidians at Waco were trying to break away and therefore might not be "spaded under" with the rest of humanity (*Heaven's Gate*, "Last Chance").

But, because they had received no instruction from a Next Level Representative and thus had not shed their mammalian addictions, desires, and ties, such humans were not yet ready to advance to the Kingdom of God and would have to undergo further reincarnations. The quest was not simply to escape "social control"; it was to escape "human" social control and to enter and fully submit to "Next Level" socialization. Heaven's Gate thus doubly reenchanted social control, on the one hand as evil via the Luciferian space alien races and on the other hand as benevolent via the little gray-like souls from the Next Level.

UFO/alien discourses and the postwar culture of paranoia in general are liminal cultural spaces—nervous systems—that accommodate a variety of reactions to the anxieties of the times. Some of them are loose and low cost; others, especially the conspiracy dramas, the inhabitable paranoias, like Heaven's Gate's, are narrow, taxing, intense, and exacting. The entry requirement for Heaven's Gate was total separation from the world—leave behind family, love, sex, work, material possessions, personal names and identities—"everything except enough food and liquids to sustain your vehicle while it is here, and enough rest to give it strength that it needs while it's in a decaying atmosphere such as the Earth's. . . . Anything else, whether it's desire to play the violin or preach a sermon or nurse a child, anything of this world, you must overcome" (Steiger and Hewes 1997: 153–54).

At first, students were, after abandoning all, each expected to figure out on their own via direct contact with the Next Level what else they needed to do to complete the overcoming process. Then, in the summer of 1976, The Two gathered them in a Wyoming campground and launched them on nearly two decades of minutely orchestrated metamorphic therapies, or "disciplines." The disciplines scan as brainwashing techniques, some well-worn, some brand new, but Do presented them as consummate moments of choice in which students decided over and over again to give up their tokens of human agency and autonomy in favor of achieving Next Level consciousness. No one was told to do anything; everyone was free to choose at each moment whether to follow instructions from the Next Level; if they chose to follow them, they would ascend; if not, not.

Students wore hoods "to learn about the 'conning' ways of their visual personalities." Their days were organized into tasks "assigned" every twelve minutes—"each person physically going to a given spot every 12 minutes to concentrate on his or her desire to serve" (*Heaven's Gate,* " '88 Update"). Students were assigned "check partners" with whom they consulted before taking any action. They were given new names. They became meticulous bookkeepers and filled their feeling diaries every 12 minutes. There were frequent fasts, including a three-month fast with a "master cleanser" composed of lemonade, cayenne pepper, and maple syrup. Students entered prolonged regimes of silence called "tomb time." They were asked to abandon all addictions, not only sex, alcohol, cigarettes, and drugs, but likes and dislikes, habits, opinions, judgments, ways of expressing themselves, and personality traits "such as being critical of others or getting down on yourself, having negative responses to situations, needing to talk constantly, having things *your* way or on a particular timetable, or needing human affection or attention" (*Heaven's Gate*, "Total Overcomers"). Finally, detailed "behavioral guidelines" further inscribed a scrupulous regime of self-surveillance. There were "17 steps" for entering the classroom, beginning with "Can you follow instructions without adding your own interpretation" (*Heaven's Gate*, "The 17 Steps"). More advanced "guidelines for learning control and restraint" defined three major offenses (deceit, sensuality, and knowingly breaking an instruction) and over thirty lesser offenses (e.g., "having inappropriate curiosity," "staying in my own head, having private thoughts," and "identifying with influences—using the 'I' or 'me' pronoun in application to an offense instead of recognizing that it was an influence using me") (*Heaven's Gate*, "Major and Lesser Offenses").

At first such therapies were understood as exercises that enabled humans to evolve into members of the next level. Later, Do, or Ti, or The Two, realized that their class members had, as they themselves had, already been incarnated—they "*were not humans* recruited by Ti and Do . . . but *were members of the Next Level before ever meeting them*" (*Heaven's Gate*, " '88 Update"). They were all "walk-ins," all aliens occupying—trapped in—human bodies. If notions of liberal subjectivity cleave to a sense of interiority, self-control, and self-reliance, of a sense that the individual is "a rational, motivated agent with a protected interior core of beliefs, desires, and memories" (Melley 2000: 12), the members of Heaven's Gate sought to vacate that subjectivity as much as they sought to evacuate modern society. Or almost as much. For they conserved the essence of liberal individualism, individual intention (Melley 2000: 30), in their paradoxical mandate to choose perpetually to have no choice.

While Heaven's Gate members became, like Calvary Chapel Christians, adepts at reading the world—and the skies—around them for "signs" that their prophecies were coming true, it was not their signature method of making meaning. Their forte, their peculiar genius, was tacking back and forth among a host of vernaculars—Christian, UFO/contactee, New Age, sci-fi, biology, gardening, teaching—and fashioning a hybrid discourse in which the seams were foregrounded. From the outside, their semiotic moves seemed parodic; from the inside, they seemed like revelation. Their language was overtly double-voiced in a way that highlighted intertextuality and the process of translation in meaning making. With their incessant making explicit of connections and intertwining of terms, Ti and Do taught their students a literary mode of attention. They showed them *how* things were connected, not just that they *were* connected. Indeed, they showed them how to connect things, how to convert similarities across boundaries of difference into similarities always already linked by sameness. They taught them how to convert metaphors into metonymies. How to enchant, or reenchant, the world.

The endless repetition of twinned and twined idioms showed up, not only in the language of Heaven's Gate, but also in their practices and appearances. The group's leaders were of course a pair separated by small differences and were so named, variously, Bo and Peep, Admiral and Captain, Him and Her, Winnie and Pooh, Tiddly and Wink, Nicom and Poop, Chip and Dale, Pig and Sow, Ti and Do, or simply The Two. And the cultural references to the 1970s went way beyond *Star Trek* and *Star Wars* to produce a complex sense of doubling—or cross-referencing, intertextuality, hypertexting—between the then and the now. Heaven's Gate's antifamily, antigender, radical egalitarian celebration of sameness as a form of communion with the other referenced monasticism and mysticism but also the hippie counterculture. Even their radical antisexuality, which seemed if anything a piece of the 1990s, linked to 1970s youth culture in the way that was played out as a quest for a kind of innocent, primordial sexuality and the desire for the intimacy of undifferentiated otherness. "Virginity," Do said, "can be recovered" (*Heaven's Gate*, "'88 Update"). Do himself was a very 1970s father figure, a soft, avuncular father, a Dr. Spock blend of routinization and permission, of Mr. Rogers and Timothy Leary. Do actually looked a little like Mr. Rogers, and he sounded a little like him too. Do also looked a little like Timothy Leary—without hair—a resemblance that was made manifest at the time of the suicide by what we can only hope was a coincidence—namely, the launching of Timothy Leary's ashes, along with the ashes of *Star Trek* inventor Gene Roddenberry, into space the same week that Heaven's Gate ascended to the Next Level.

To this list of allusions to the 1970s—of haunting, channeling, doubling, déjà vus, moments of temporal repetition—we may also add the Grateful Dead. The hippie/drug culture lingo linked Heaven's Gate to the Dead as well as to Timothy Leary. The thoughts, for example, sent down to students from the Next Level were called *flashes* and *hits*, terms once associated with the quintessential 1970s activities, LSD trips and marijuana smoking. Heaven's Gate's greatest mime of the Grateful Dead was its traveling troupe quality. The meandering around the country, the continual process of breaking up and regrouping, the apparent antiorganizational amorphousness and placelessness, all echo the Dead. Heaven's Gate's movements had an edge of flight that the Dead's did not, an edge that recalled yet one more ghost from the 1970s—the television show *The Fugitive*.

The mass suicide of Heaven's Gate was in fact the last moment in a long succession of sudden disappearances, getaways, seclusions, concealments, and disguises. Marshall Applewhite and Bonnie Lu Nettles disappeared, as they became Bo and Peep, from the lives of their already estranged families, friends, and lovers. During 1975, they haphazardly assembled their band of followers as groups of five, ten, and twenty people "suddenly disappeared" from their towns after meeting with Bo and Peep. Some students never contacted their families or friends again; others called them every few years from pay phones or sent them postcards postmarked in cities distant from where they were living. They assumed new names, not one, but two, or three, or more. When they finally materialized in an enduring way for the world to see, it was in cyberspace, the ultimate nonplace, or, rather, the zone of endless virtual places. And, even then, they registered their webpages under false names and addresses.

Fugitives are a kind of outlaw; they occupy spaces outside the law. It is unclear, sometimes more, sometimes less, whether fugitives are in the right or the wrong, and, thus, their flight calls attention to and problematizes the system, whatever system it is, that allots value, meaning, credibility, authority, and rights in such a way that forces flight. Something that is fugitive is also something that is fleeting or that eludes grasp; something evanescent, of short duration, fading, or becoming effaced (*OED*). Perhaps the members of Heaven's Gate would have preferred to leave nothing behind, not even their human bodies, by boarding a Next Level spacecraft on earth, but it did not work out that way. On the other hand, by willing the inevitable—death— perhaps they gained, or recovered, "the suicidal intention depleted from the sociological subject" by Durkheim's "attempt to explain suicide without recourse to individual motive" (Melley 2000: 30, 28). But their "exit statements" do not suggest that individual agency was at stake. Instead, as in the case of their nomadism, the point, aside from getting their souls on board the ship to the Next Level, was to call attention to the meaninglessness of what they were leaving behind, to demonstrate that "the true meaning of 'suicide' is *to turn against the Next Level when it is being offered*" ("Exit Statements").

The student Glnody wrote, "Choosing to exit this borrowed human vehicle or body and go home to the Next Level is an opportunity for me to demonstrate my loyalty, commitment, love, trust, and faith in Ti and Do and the Next Level. . . . There is no life here in this human world. This planet has become the planet of the walking dead. The human plants walk, talk, take careers, procreate, and so forth, but there is no life in them. . . . Suicide would be to turn away from this incredible opportunity I've been given, to turn my back on the Next Level and the life they are offering." Srrody wrote, "As the comet Hale-Bopp brings closure to this visitation, perhaps even this civilization, I am so filled with joy—not only for myself and my classmates, but with the pride that only a son can have for His Father [Do], who has pulled off a Next Level miracle that any of us made it out of this world alive" ("Earth Exit Statements").

Postscript

Conspiracy theory is not an open-ended set of "reading practices" but a particular structure of feeling. It is a nervous system, a split sensitivity, an internally divided cultural space that has force, that generates as well as registers the contradictions of contemporary social transformations. Preoccupied with questions of individual agency, and sometimes yearning for escape, it knows deep down that there is no "outside" to the social/evil influences on earth. Although despairing of a political cure, it seeks one nonetheless in the form of a perfect rationalization of the relation between self and world. As a metacultural discourse—dwelling on fundamental, abstract dilemmas of ideal and real, good and evil, creation and destruction, hope and dejection, purity and pollution, mystery and minutiae—conspiracy theory actively works on, works out, the world, if not the cosmos, in search of its cures. Calvary Chapel rationalizes self and world by sifting endlessly through the signs of the times, while Heaven's Gate channeled and dramatized a medley of stories and tropes—both drawing heavily on "the media," on television, radio, newspapers, magazines, and the Internet, for their raw materials. Their paranoias are/were, not ideologies or beliefs, but practices, remarkably inventive, capacious, and efficacious ones that penetrate deep into the modern subject as modes of agency and float like an ether in a world composed of multiple, contradictory, paradoxical, unstable, but unending influences. This is the Enlightenment with a vengeance. It is also the haunting trace and reminder of the hidden forces and excluded sensibilities that now permeate the force fields of social and cultural life and saturate the sense of the symptomatic self in the world.

References

Balch, Robert. 1995. "Waiting for the Ships: Disillusionment and the Revitalization of Faith in Bo and Peep's UFO Cult." In *The Gods Have Landed: New Religions from Other Worlds*, ed. James R. Lewis, 137–66. Albany: State University of New York Press.

Balmer, Randall. 1993. *Mine Eyes Have Seen the Glory: A Journey into the Evangelical Subculture in America*. Oxford: Oxford University Press.

Balmer, Randall, and Jesse T. Todd Jr. 1994. "Calvary Chapel, Costa Mesa, California." In *American Congregations: Portraits of Twelve Religious Communities*, ed. James Wind and James Lewis, 442–60. Chicago: University of Chicago Press.

Barkun, Michael. 1998. "Politics and Apocalypticism." In *The Encyclopedia of Apocalypticism*, ed. Stephen Stein, 442–60. New York: Continuum.

Berlant, Lauren. 1996. "Face of America and the State of Emergency." In *Disciplinarity and Dissent in Cultural Studies*, ed. Cary Nelson and Dilip P. Gaonkar, 397–439. New York: Routledge.

Berlitz, Charles, and W. L. Moore. 1980. *The Roswell Incident*. New York: Grosset and Dunlap.

Bryan, C. D. B. 1995. *Close Encounters of the Fourth Kind: Alien Abduction, UFOs, and the Conference at MIT*. New York: Knopf.

Buck-Morss, Susan. 1993. "Aesthetics and Anaesthetics: Walter Benjamin's Artwork Essay Reconsidered." *October*, no. 62:3–41.

———. 1995. "The City as Dreamworld and Catastrophe." *October*, no. 73:3–26.

Butler, Judith. 1997. *The Psychic Life of Power: Theories in Subjection*. Stanford: Stanford University Press.

Conway, Flo, and Jim Siegelman. 1997. "Exclusive: Nation's Leading Cult Experts Begin a Web Diary as the Heaven's Gate Story Unfolds." http://www.zdnet.com/yil/higher/cultco11.html. Accessed periodically 1997–98.

Curran, Douglas. 1985. *In Advance of the Landing: Folk Concepts of Outer Space*. New York: Abbeville.

Darlington, David. 1997. *Area 51: The Dreamland Chronicles*. New York: Henry Holt.

Dean, Jodi. 1998. *Aliens in America: Conspiracy Cultures from Outerspace to Cyberspace*. Ithaca: Cornell University Press.

Dery, Mark. 1999. *The Pyrotechnic Insanitarium: American Culture on the Brink*. New York: Grove.

Eberart, George M., ed. 1991. *The Roswell Report*. Chicago: Hynek Center for UFO Studies.

Feldman, Allen. 1994. "On Cultural Anaesthesia: From Desert Storm to Rodney King." *American Ethnologist* 21 (2): 404–18.

Fenster, Mark. 1999. *Conspiracy Theories: Secrecy and Power in American Culture.* Minneapolis: University of Minnesota Press.

Foucault, Michel. 1980. *The History of Sexuality.* Vol. 1. New York: Vintage/Random House.

Fox, Richard, and Jackson Lears. 1983. Introduction to *The Culture of Consumption,* ed. Richard Fox and Jackson Lears, 3–45. New York: Random House.

Gibson, James William. 1994. *Warrior Dreams: Paramilitary Culture in Post-Vietnam America.* New York: Hill and Wang.

Graham, Allison. 1996. "'Are You Now or Have You Ever Been?' Conspiracy Theory and the *X-Files.*" In *Deny All Knowledge: Reading the "X-Files,"* ed. David Lavery, Angela Hague, and Marla Cartwright, 52–62. Syracuse: Syracuse University Press.

Harding, Susan. 2000. *The Book of Jerry Falwell: Fundamentalist Language and Politics.* Princeton: Princeton University Press.

Heaven's Gate. Webpages (accessed 1997–98).

———. "Earth Exit Statements." No longer posted.

———. "'88 Update—the UFO Two and Their Crew: A Brief Synopsis." http://www.zdnet.com/yil/higher/heavensgate/book/3-3.htm.

———. "Exit Statements/Our Position against Suicide." http://www.zdnet.com/yil/higher/heavensgate/letter.htm.

———. "How and When Heaven's Gate May Be Entered: An Anthology of Our Materials" and "Table of Contents." http://www.zdnet.com/yil/higher/heavensgate/book/book.htm.

———. "Index." http://www.zdnet.com/yil/higher/heavensgate/index.html.

———. "Last Chance to Evacuate Earth before It's Recycled (Edited Transcript of Videotape—September 29, 1996)." http://www.zdnet.com/yil/higher/heavensgate/vt092996.html.

———. "Major and Lesser Offenses." http://www.zdnet.com/yil/higher/heavensgate/book/2-5.htm.

———. "'95 Statement by an E.T. Presently Incarnate." http://www.zdnet.com/yil/higher/heavensgate/book/1-4.htm.

———. "Organized Religion (Especially Christian) Has Become the Primary Pulpit for Misinformation and the 'Great Cover-Up.'" http://www.zdnet.com/yil/higher/heavensgate/book/6-6.htm.

———. "Overview of Present Mission." http://www.zdnet.com/yil/higher/heavensgate/book/05.htm.

———. "Planet about to Be Recycled; Your Only Chance to Survive: Leave with Us (Edited Transcript of Videotape—October 5, 1996)." http://www.zdnet.com/yil/higher/heavensgate/vt100596.html.

———. "The 17 Steps." http://www.zdnet.com/yil/higher/heavensgate/book/2-5. htm.

———. "Total Overcomers Classroom Admission Requirements." http://www. zdnet.com/yil/higher/heavensgate/book/5-6.htm.

———. "Transcripts of Two Recent Videos." http://www.zdnet.com/yil/higher/ heavensgate/latest.htm.

———. "'UFO Cult' Resurfaces with Final Offer." http://www.zdnet.com/yil/ higher/heavensgate/book/5-2.htm.

Hesemann, Michael, and Philip Mantle. 1997. *Beyond Roswell: The Alien Autopsy Film, Area 51, and the U.S. Government Cover-Up of UFOs.* London: Michael O'Mara.

Hopkins, Budd. 1981. *Missing Time: A Documented Study of UFO Abductions.* New York: Richard Marek.

———. 1987. *Intruders: The Incredible Visitations at Copley Woods.* New York: Random House.

Ivy, Marilyn. 1993. "Have You Seen Me? Recovering the Inner Child in Late Twentieth-Century America." *Social Text* 37:227–52.

———. 1995. *Discourses of the Vanishing: Modernity, Phantasm, Japan.* Chicago: University of Chicago Press.

Kelly, Michael. 1995. "The Road to Paranoia." *New Yorker,* 19 June, 60–75.

Lewis, Fred. 1999. "The New Antiterrorism." *New York Review of Books* 46 (2): 24.

Lewis, James R., ed. 1995. *The Gods Have Landed: New Religions from Other Worlds.* Albany: State University of New York Press.

Lieb, Michael. 1998. *Children of Ezekiel: Aliens, UFOs, the Crisis of Race, and the Advent of End Time.* Durham: Duke University Press.

Lutz, Tom. 1991. *American Nervousness, 1903: An Anecdotal History.* Ithaca: Cornell University Press.

Mack, John E. 1994. *Abduction: Human Encounters with Aliens.* New York: Scribner's.

Marcus, George, ed. 1999. *Paranoia within Reason: A Casebook on Conspiracy as Explanation.* Chicago: University of Chicago Press.

Marsden, George. 1980. *Fundamentalism and American Culture: The Shaping of Twentieth-Century Evangelicalism, 1870-1925.* New York: Oxford University Press.

Melley, Timothy. 2000. *Empire of Conspiracy: The Culture of Paranoia in Postwar America.* Ithaca: Cornell University Press.

Miller, Donald. 1997. *Reinventing American Protestantism: Christianity in the New Millennium.* Berkeley and Los Angeles: University of California Press.

Pfeil, Fred. 1995. "Sympathy for the Devil: Notes on Some White Guys in the Ridiculous Class War." *New Left Review* 213:115–24.

Pritchard, Andrea, et al., eds. 1994. *Alien Discussions: Proceedings of the Abduction Study Conference.* Cambridge, Mass.: North Cambridge.

Randle, Kevin D., and Donald R. Schmidt. 1991. *The UFO Crash at Roswell.* New York: Avon.

Robertson, Pat. 1991. *The New World Order.* Dallas: Word.

Saler, Benson, Charles A. Ziegler, and Charles B. Moore. 1997. *UFO Crash at Roswell: The Genesis of a Modern Myth.* Washington, D.C.: Smithsonian Institution Press.

Schoepflin, Rennie B. 1998. "Apocalypse in an Age of Science." In *The Encyclopedia of Apocalypticism,* ed. Stephen Stein, 108–39. New York: Continuum.

Smith, Chuck. 1997. "Time Is Short, Cor. 7:29–32." *The Word for Today,* tape 8653. Costa Mesa, Calif.: Calvary Chapel Ministries.

Steiger, Brad, and Hayden Hewes. 1997. *Inside Heaven's Gate: The UFO Cult Leaders Tell Their Story in Their Own Words.* New York: Signet.

Streiber, Whitley. 1987. *Communion: A True Story.* New York: William Morrow.

———. 1989. *Transformation: The Breakthrough.* New York: Avon.

Taussig, Michael. 1992. *The Nervous System.* New York: Routledge.

Terkel, Studs. 1988. *The Great Divide: Second Thoughts on the American Dream.* New York: Pantheon.

Time. 1997. "Special Report: Inside the Web of Death." 7 April, 28–47.

Weber, Max. 1958. *The Protestant Ethic and the Spirit of Capitalism.* New York: Scribner's.

Weber, Timothy. 1983. *Living in the Shadow of the Second Coming.* Grand Rapids, Mich.: Zondervan.

Wilson, Robert Anton, and Miriam Joan Mill. 1998. *Everything Is Under Control: Conspiracies, Cults, and Cover-Ups.* New York: Harper.

Transparent Fictions; or, The Conspiracies of a Liberal Imagination: An Afterword

JEAN COMAROFF AND JOHN COMAROFF

Only connect.
—E. M. Forster, *Howard's End*

Ours, it appears, is an Age of Obsessions.

It is an age in which people almost everywhere seem preoccupied, simultaneously, with transparency and conspiracy. With the lightness and darkness of being. So much is this so that, in 2001, a year that has long signified the cinematic surreal, an outbreak of livestock disease in the United Kingdom was attributed by ordinarily rational people to everything from the secret machinations of the prime minister (Lyall 2001) to the covert operations of animal rights activists, from the illicit importation of cheap meats by the Ministry of Defense to Iraqi biological warfare (Vidal and Brown 2001). No wonder the country was alleged to be "on the verge of a nervous breakdown . . . [that] has no root in real facts and figures, only in a diseased imagination" (Lyall 2001).[1] At the same time, in the United States, after a presidential election that gave the nation much to be *really* suspicious about, the media told their mass publics one thing above all else: "Trust no one" (Bader 2001). Conspiracy, in short, has come to fill the explanatory void, the epistemic black hole, that is increasingly said to have been left behind by the unsettling of moral communities, by the so-called crisis of representation, by the erosion of received modernist connections between means and ends, subjects and objects, ways and means. All this in a global world that is at once larger and smaller, more and less knowable, more and less inscrutable than ever before.

If conspiracy is the autonomic explanatory trope of our age, its conceptual grounding lies in its obverse, in transparency. It is, therefore, with the latter that we begin.

The current preoccupation with *transparency* reveals a distinct shift in our understanding of the term, at least according to Žižek (1997:131). When used in relation to modern technology, he argues, it presumed the possibility of actually uncovering "how the machine works"; but, in its postmodern sense, the word implies the exact opposite. This, Žižek explains, is epitomized in the signifying economy of computer screens, whose cartoon icons may *simulate* everyday reality with beguiling concreteness; yet they conceal the real workings of the machine behind the glass facade, contriving the kind of legibility that renders the technology itself opaque. Is this so? Perhaps, perhaps not. For many of us, the dials on our dashboards and telephones bespeak a mechanical reality only slightly less impenetrable, suggesting that there has been a shift of degree, not kind. But Žižek reminds us of two things. The first is that our obsession with transparency is not unprecedented, the second that changing patterns of illumination cast new shadows and, with them, new domains of darkness beyond their arcs of light. In fact, the more literally we believe in the axiom, "To see is to know," the more haunted we are by what hovers beyond the edges of the visible. The sublime is obscure, according to Burke (Mitchell 1986: 126), eluding ordinary sight. It is precisely the *relation* between the manifest and the inscrutable—or the front and backstage, to invoke Goffman's (1959) more mundane, dramaturgical image—that undergirds the enduring fascination evinced by human beings almost everywhere with the properties of power. As David Graeber (1996: 8) observes, invoking Hobbes on idolatry, the invisible is by nature unspecific and, hence, of infinite possibility. Efficacy and influence, alike in rhetoric and realpolitik, lie largely in controlling the capacity to reveal and conceal, to make "reality" appear or disappear.

The essays in *Transparency and Conspiracy* provide rich, varied evidence of an impulse, palpable across the face of the planet, to reveal the hidden workings of power—and to uncover its tangled complicities. This impulse is part of a more general zeitgeist; Tony Karon (2001) refers to it as *epic paranoia*, describing it as a readiness to connect apparently random, dispersed features of ever more impersonal worlds into tight configurations of collusion and menace, be they local sagas of harassment and corruption or worldwide, even extraterrestrial, cabals of fanatical terror. For most Americans, the cataclysm of 11 September served to confirm—spectacularly, implosively—the global reach of evil empires, of secret networks of crazed killers, of suicide cells that would foment Armageddon by infiltrating the innocent forms of everyday life in the "civilized world." But well before that day, well before that moment of revelation and radical rupture, it had already been noted how educated Europeans have come regularly to be consumed by frightening reports of ever new hazards lurking unseen in the social fabric. Many of them, ironically, are thought to emanate from across the Atlantic (Reid 2001), although Africa, of course, has long been the *ur*-source of epic, epidemic fears, its perennial place beyond the arc of light making it a fertile feeding ground for Eurobsessions with inscrutable dangers of one kind or another. Along with this, as its condition of possibility, goes a passion for "see-through visibility" that stretches from proliferating rites of national and institutional accountability to the aesthetics of public buildings and domestic design.[2]

As we have already intimated, none of this is altogether new, even though the anxieties of the moment may suggest otherwise. While that does not detract from the importance of the studies collected here—quite the converse—it underlines the essential truism that change is always also, in crucial respects, continuity: that cultural creativity involves, not merely incessant improvisation on existing themes, but also the re-presentation of reality in terms that are "almost the same but not quite" (Bhabha 1997, as cited by Humphrey, chapter 6 in this volume). Thus, it might be argued that, while moral panics about the workings of conspiracy have waxed luxuriantly after the Cold War, so did McCarthyism after World War II—and fascism after the war before that. Each was an urgent hyperrationalization of mundane modes of explanation common in the contexts from which it sprung. What is more, these outbreaks bear some resemblance, as populist theories of cause, to the millennialism and witch cleansing that occurred in many non-Western societies after colonial conquest. Paranoia and political theory, Hellinger (chapter 7 in this volume) notes, are often not easy to separate in practice; both exist, in large part, in the eye of the beholder. These diverse manifestations of moral panic *might* be viewed, in other words, as just so many chapters in a long-running narrative, as so many variants on an old modernist theme, as a story that "remains the same, yet is constantly changing" (cf. Comaroff and Comaroff 1999).

At the same time, the proportions of change to continuity, of rupture to repetition, are neither overdetermined nor immutable; they are always labile, always liable to alter. There is, we believe, an immanent historical logic to the current chapter of the story, to the one writing itself just now, that *does* point to an epochal shift, to significant historical *dis*continuities amid the continuities. We *do* seem to be caught up, at the turn of the millennium, in a swelling tide—an *overabundance,* Humphrey (chapter 6) calls it— of claims to discern the destructive hand of evil agents, from devil worshipers, witches, and global jihadistas, through purveyors of death in the name of spiritual truth, to peddlers of human body parts, genetically modified foods, and other nefarious commodities. Their malign machinations are envisaged as cumulatively universal in scale, even though they are made manifest in very particular sites, like the Satanists who target sleepy towns in the South African heartland, or international kidney snatchers with a penchant for New Orleans airport, or faceless felons who pollute the U.S. postal services with biopoisons. It is true that the quests to divine their identities—with their attendant rituals of unmasking, confession, and apology—have precedents in earlier times: times when the pursuit of transparency likewise kindled the popular imagination, prompting a passionate pursuit of hidden truths and moral crusades, times also, as it turns out, of epochal shift. Thus, for example, the great transformation that ushered in the so-called modern world was also a period of feverish effort to find covert connections, to discern the invisible hand that gave design and purpose to a universe made opaque, through great economic and technical change, to contemporary theories of cause and effect—indeed, of history in the making. As we have said elsewhere, we may be, at present, in the formative stages of a social revolution every bit as radical as that of 1789–1848. Several critical features of the current moment reprise, as prefixations, that earlier time; (neo)liberalism and (neo)Protestantism, for instance. Then, as now, ontological categories and explanations were in flux, sparking debate about the definition of personhood and civil order, about the nature of economy and society, about the proper constitution of the state. It was a debate that struggled to frame new vocabularies and to reconcile an enhanced sense of human agency with a concomitant understanding of the "objective" forces of history.

Optical Illusions

It is exactly this kind of reprise—the Enlightenment replayed "with a vengeance"—that Harding and Stewart (chapter 9 in this volume) see in the "paranoid" fixations of millennial America; these fixations show a "haunting trace" of sensibilities excluded by the idioms, the very obsessional explicitness, of our therapeutically minded culture. And it is to the Enlightenment that we must look for the origins of the modernist language of transparency and conspiracy as well as for the signs and concepts that comprise the mis-en-scène of liberal empiricism. For it was the progressive dissolution of the Great Chain of Being, of theodicy and ecclesiastical authority, that cast humankind adrift in a material universe whose mundane truths had to be learned anew by patient, self-willed subjects, equipped only with sense and reason. The blind sage in Eco's *The Name of the Rose* (1983) cedes his place, as the keeper of truth, to a prosaic English empiricist, who, with the aid of vision-enhancing spectacles, produces knowledge by collecting and connecting "clues" lying on the face of the world. In this universe, "seeing *is* believing." Mortal beings, says Foucault (1975), increasingly made themselves both the objects and the measure of knowledge, their lives and deaths to be read less as a sign of cosmic metaphysical forces than as the sum of mundane biophysical processes, knowable primarily through the modest art of observation. Thus it is that the autopsy could become paradigmatic of the forensic gaze; thus it is that the corpse, its vitality, motion, and social connectedness all erased, could provide a "black border" within which the interior logic of life itself might be brought to light. Yet the very exclusions that permitted this illusion of transparency and order—that set the body apart from sociomoral entanglement to proclaim that truth inheres only in concrete evidence contained within the discrete, anatomical individual—ensured that the definition of life captured by biomedicine was endemically limited, bereft of myth and mystery. Less tangible properties of being fell outside its purview. This remains true of radical empiricism, sui generis: it continues to privilege sight over all other forms of perception, to restrict communication about the real to apparently transparent modes of representation, and to dismiss out of hand anything unsusceptible to positivist accounting, from the force of metaphor or moral values to the power of Vodou or paranoid fantasy.

Of course, the dialectical play of visibility and concealment, of darkness and truth, is not just a Dialectic of Enlightenment, so to speak. As we implied earlier, it is probably as old as politics itself. The emergence of the Greek "public," for instance, has been described as a process of "unveiling" in which powers, formerly secreted in the hands of aristocrats, were revealed for all to see (Vernant 1983, cited by Graeber 1996: 11). The quest for transparency, in sum, has a long genealogy. But its technoempiricist connotations were born of optical imagery associated with a specific period in the history of modernity (Comaroff and Comaroff 1991: 185ff.), of its materialities and moral discourses. The likes of Mumford (1934: 124) have gone so far as to argue that the development of large-scale glass production was crucial to the evolution of a modern objectivist worldview. This claim suggests rather too stark a technological determinism for our own tastes. But it *does* seem clear that the phenomenological impact of glass—the everyday experience of its materiality—did much to shape the analytical sensibilities of the age. Spectacles, telescopes, microscopes, became physical extensions of the human eye; as Mumford (1934: 131) notes, they helped render the mysteries of nature "transparent." And they fixed the idiom of all forms of knowing, not least of the workings of society. Mitchell (1986: 166), for one, has remarked on the central place of optical metaphor, of images of "rational transparence," in the writings of post-Enlightenment political theorists of all stripes, from Burke to Marx. This focus on transparency also produced its own obverse: a concern with refraction, distortion, concealment, collusion. And a symbolic lexicon to go with it: note, in this respect, not only the camera obscura—itself a famously telling icon of the dangers attendant on taking visible truths at face value—but also the hidden hand and, most of all, the fetish.

To be sure, it is precisely its revelatory language, its argot of optics, that discloses the dark underside of Enlightenment, its traffic with discourses of unreason, race, and empire. Illumination—a condition of consciousness recognizable only to those freed from be*nighted* savagery—was a key trope of humane imperialism, giving moral force to a host of "civilizing" crusades at once spiritual and secular. Not only did the idea authorize a blanket assault on the "primitive" life ways of sundry others. It also shaped the everyday practices of European colonization at their most substantial. Missionaries to the heathen in Southern Africa, for instance, took great pains to persuade their would-be converts to build large windows into their houses. Why? To illumine the dusky interiors of their lives and beings, leaving superstition and mystery no place to hide; to make the home a place of edification, self-construction, surveillance; to achieve a salvific lightness of being (Comaroff and Comaroff 1997a: 278).

The inverse of transparency in the imperial imagination was, McCarthy Brown (chapter 8 in this volume) shows, the concept of the fetish. This was the standardized nightmare of savage unreason, of depraved idolatry: fetishism evoked a childlike propensity to bestow life on "inanimate things," insisting, with a kind of primitive paranoia, on the sort of essential, fateful connectedness between people, objects, and spiritual forces that had become anathema to a Cartesian consciousness. The primeval status of superstition and witchcraft in evolutionary histories of the modern West is, like the pejorative attitude toward Vodou and other practices likewise deemed "magical" in contemporary America, persuasive evidence of the enduring usefulness of the fetish as a racinated foil to Eurocentric images of clear-eyed reason. This lends ironic power to Marx's reflexive notion of commodity fetishism, that unsettling reminder of our own civilized idolatry, not to mention the alchemy that hides in the light of our own "rational" market economy.

If the genealogy of transparency as trope cuts a revealing swath across the history of the modern empirical imagination—being finely tuned, as we have seen, to the changing registers of ordinary experience—its latest unfolding points squarely to the future. Thus, the mechanical optics of the Industrial Age have been upgraded in, and interdigitated into, the digital era: Windows now come from Microsoft, whose corporate leaders speak as New Age missionaries for the liberating power of knowledge. The e-revolution—or, more properly, e-volution—holds out the promise of a radically democratized McWorld, although some believe that promise to be pure e-lusion, an infantile e-scape from the more concretely pressing political realities of our times. Maybe. More salient for present purposes, the digital age brings with it the dread of ever more extensive, nefarious, tangled webs of cyberintrigue as hackers, militias, fundamentalists, pornographers, syndicated criminals, and schemers of all stripes gain unregulated access to means of mass communication. As the division of labor everywhere becomes increasingly global, local communities across the planet are enmeshed in economies of expanding scale and abstraction, ensuring the ever more mundane experience of realities—like long-distance migration, IDs and credit cards, virtual communities, digital money, electronic frontiers—that eschew any simple division between the legible and the opaque. If ever there was evidence of the dangers of too literal an application of these dichotomies, either as a mode of analysis or as a political call to arms, it is now: now, when the numbing complexity of material, social, and cultural flows across the earth presents us with a plethora of realities that are, at best, trans*lucent*. Realities, that is, that are neither transparent nor opaque, neither in plain sight nor hidden from view. We struggle, as Schrauwers (chapter 4 in this volume) says, to see "through a glass darkly," much like social thinkers did in the ferment of the first Age of Revolution. Now as then, we must be suspicious of the imperious claims of naive empiricism, especially in the name of technical necessity—be it biological, economic, or environmental. We in the human sciences need to fight for multiplicity and polyphony in the ways in which we may come to know the world—and for a broadband sense of what might count as evidence. We must also advocate for the significance of the unseen, for regarding as critical those forces in the world that do not present themselves in technically measurable proportions, from the social effects of abstract capital to the material implications of anomie. Above all, we need to recognize that it is the very complexity of our times, the undermining within them of the architecture of social certainties, that prompts the quest for simplifying truths, for reassuring melodramas of good and evil, for magic that would translate complicated structural influences into the language of personal desire, animosity, forgiveness. All of which is as true of new social and economic theory as it is of new social movements.

Beyond Empiricism

With this in mind, it is instructive to reflect, as several of the contributors to *Transparency and Conspiracy* have done, on contexts in which liberal empiricism has come into contact with rather different local understandings of power and agency, whether among minority communities in Europe and America or in postcolonial Africa, Korea, and elsewhere. Take the African case. Here, as Sanders (chapter 5 in this volume) and West (chapter 3 in this volume) both make plain, the "harbingers of a brave new transparent world" are often unaware of the intricacies of vernacular conceptions of power—and, hence, of the mystifying effects of their own languages and practice, whether they be the introduction of IDs or democratic voting procedures. It is not that local discourses lack their own ideas of visibility and concealment. Much has been written about secrecy and revelation on the continent, past and present; also about ontologies of witchcraft, sorcery, exorcisms, and purges, forms of cultural practice that provide paradigmatic instances of conspiracy theories in action. Yet the ambivalent reception of ballot boxes in rural Mozambique indicates that *transparency* means different things in different places: where communities are used to a public show of hands, for example, the "privacy" of the ballot box evokes suspicions of concealment, especially in places where memories of colonial surveillance still linger. Likewise, party politics often connote a form of cabalistic collusion, a lack of the kind of accountability expected from hereditary rulers or single-party systems (Comaroff and Comaroff 1997b; Karlström 1999). But, even more than this, where understandings of the operation of power are vested in the ongoing interplay of the manifest and the invisible—of humans and spirits, words and deeds, persons and context—discourses about the capacity to act in and on the world assume a distinctive shape.

In fact, as West notes, in much of Africa, politics is taken to be a perpetual "game of hide and seek." Here, leaders are always sorcerers of a kind.

For sorcery, whether turned to good effect or ill, requires a kind of vision more profound than that usually implied by European empiricism, insight like that of Sanders's Ihanzu "seer," who is attuned to the invisible "real realities" thought to animate the tangible, everyday world. Like Freud's paranoic (see Humphrey, chapter 6), the seer sees something that escapes normal people. Only, in his case, the knowledge is made *socially* salient and useful. Such visionaries—and the objects that help them bring things to light, from oracles and "traditional X-rays" to severed heads and identity tokens—are hardly the hostages of an arcane "tradition." They conjure with a wide range of distinctly contemporary forces, forces that manifest themselves in the conflicts and triumphs of lives at once local and translocal, forces that might as well be discerned in the cannibalistic practices of new neoliberal elites as in the mysterious flow of consumer goods or in the capricious capers of the IMF (see Kendall [chapter 1], Bastian [chapter 2], and Sanders [chapter 5]). In so doing, they articulate processes of varying scale and perceptibility, translating the reified abstractions of economy and society into a dramaturgy of such ordinary human motives as desire, ambition, anger, and jealousy—even remorse. Unlike a Cartesian landscape, on which human beings are set apart from matter and nature and act ostensibly as isolates in empty space-time, the experiential terrain of witchcraft and spirit possession is a frenzied field of intersecting influences among persons, environments, spirits, and things. Even cities, as Bastian (1993: 141; 2001) has demonstrated, can assume dangerous, overheated personalities, these being the product of intense commerce and improper accumulation. In these contexts, the modernist injunction to "only connect" is redundant; albeit by grammatical accident, the split infinitive underscores the point. Knowledge requires the constant monitoring of, and action on, already existing connections as they pass in and out of focus and visibility.

Virtual Paranoia: The Return of the Repressed?

What, to return to our opening questions, might any of this tell us about the burgeoning twenty-first-century obsession with transparency and conspiracy? Or about its expression in fantasies, common across the planet nowadays, of righteous, revelatory crusades against invisible evildoers? The obsession itself would seem closely related to another widely noted phenomenon of our times: the rise of a host of new charismatic religious movements that are at once intensely local yet also span vast distances through human migration, the Web, and satellite dishes. These movements, Harding and Stewart (chapter 9) point out, provide richly creative languages for rationalizing the ever more attenuated relationship between self and world. Especially in their more markedly millennial forms, they posit moral certainty and closure in an increasingly limitless, open universe, charting clear causal pathways through a jungle of information, of wildly circulating signifiers, of immaculate deceptions—all this at a moment when the authority of grand narratives of society and history are giving way to the dispassionate, dispersed reign of the market.

In like vein, Hellinger (chapter 7) argues, populist stories of conspiracy and revelation should be seen as serious, sometimes empowering moral allegories that seek certainty amid indeterminacy, surety amid insecurity. As such, they explore the links between invisible structural forces and human action, not least political action; in so doing, they often capture terrors that more cautious analysts fear to name. These moral allegories bear an uncomfortable resemblance to some species of orthodox social thought—especially social thought of a critical bent, which presumes, as a first principle, that, wherever ruling elites exist, they act in various ways to maintain their hegemony (Parenti 1994, cited in Hellinger, chapter 7 in this volume). The Buryat Mongol fable that Stalin was the reincarnation of a Blue Elephant mirrored the "paranoid" discourse generated by Stalin*ism,* says Humphrey (chapter 6), although the former exceeded the latter, she notes, by insisting on the role of individual accountability in history. Humphrey uses *paranoia* less in its commonplace, pathological sense than to describe a genre of enclosed narrative that displaces attributes of the self onto others. Such narratives, she notes, permit people to voice otherwise suppressed, highly ambivalent senses of their own historical agency. This understanding of the term, we would add, contrasts with its more derisive use in the cut and thrust of everyday life, where, like most accusations of unreason, it tends to tell us less about essential truths than about political or confessional contestations. Indeed, to label a person or persons *paranoid* is another, generic form of displacement, one that seeks to locate them beyond the limits of "normal" society; in the case of a group of believers, it is to relegate them to the marginal world of "primitive" superstition. As this suggests, allegations of pathology may, among other things, mark out fault lines of social, cultural, and ideological difference. Like the fault lines of race within many modern nation-states ("Blacks/Jews are paranoid"); or those that distinguish Western rationality from "Muslim fundamentalism"; or those that sustained the reciprocal conspiracies that were spun, by Cubans and exiles alike, around the small body of Elián Gonzalez (cf. Ryer, n.d.).

By connecting disparate dots from across our far-flung universe into often bizarre constellations, however, and by discerning design in a laissez-faire universe, conspiracy theorists may capture strange, startling truths. Thus the myth of the primordial Blue Elephant, whose triumphant return to the post-Socialist scene, recall, proclaimed a crucial flaw in Soviet theories of history: the inability to link structural determinism in any meaningful way to personal agency and morality. It is this will to connect, finally, that distinguishes the various vision quests of the post–Cold War world, be they the therapeutic millennium of an America Calvary, popular Nigerian efforts to expose those who profit from the flesh of compatriots, or the nervous efforts of Korean shamans who struggle in the shadow of the IMF to implicate household gods in financial success and failure. What makes them seem "paranoid," from a liberal-humanist standpoint, is not merely that they tie macrosocial processes to the acts and intentions of particular human beings, impersonal forces to intensely personal effects. Nor is it only that, as familiar oppositions fade and old borders erode, they imagine enemies and evildoers to be ever more pervasive, taking up residence, like X-Files aliens, in otherwise ordinary citizens and neighbors. It is that these vision quests, and the narratives of conspiracy in which they are grounded, presume the eclipse of middle-order social institutions, of conventional sites of production and power, of a collective sense of morality, sociality, and history.

As market forces take on increasing autonomy and local productive relations become ever more subservient to the interests of global capital, the "deep horizontal fraternities" that once shaped ideals of nationhood, class, and community give way to a politics of identity, of technical necessity, and of the consumer rights of a "me generation" turned "we generation" (Comaroff and Comaroff 2000: 305); also, putatively, to the legal regulation of more-or-less everything. History is reduced to "memory," oppression to "victimhood," the latter to be redressed less by empowering *social* reform than by the payment of *financial* reparations. The productive tensions, in modern life and thought, between subject and society, member and congregation, citizen and nation, are reduced to a dialogue of customers and contracts, consumers and rights, clients and therapists. Stakeholders, all, in a vast impersonal order of exchange. Small wonder, then, that the millennium, in neoliberal guise, tends to be radically privatized; hence the planetary popularity of prosperity gospels, national lotteries, pyramid schemes, and technicians of the arcane who "see" into the future. Small wonder, too, that we should be witnessing the widespread pursuit of new forms of moral accountability and of new faiths capable, in Durkheim's (1947: 479) classic terms, of "completing" both the fragmentary knowledge of means and ends afforded by science and the growing abstraction of "man" in "society"—faiths, in other words, that offer in*sight* into, and means of acting on, the mysteries and malign undersides of a rapidly changing world. Neither should we be surprised that God and Satan—ultimate embodiments of invisible, infinite power and, also, of the ultimate Revelation and Conspiracy—should hold so central a sway over popular imaginations in this Age of Transparency, this age in which everyone is suspicious and nobody really knows who the enemy is. Or what the hidden hand is actually doing, how it is doing it, and to whom.

Notes

1 The phrase is a quote from Polly Toynbee, a widely read *Guardian* columnist.
2 Jennifer Connell (2001) notes that even the bedrooms featured in the popular U.S. taste guide *Martha Stewart Living* have become "transparent." Their design conceals nothing, she says, no dust, no clutter, no signs of personal intimacy.

References

Bader, Jenny Lyn. 2001. "Paranoid Lately? You May Have Good Reason." *New York Times*, 25 March, 4.

Bastian, Misty L. 1993. "Bloodhounds Who Have No Friends: Witchcraft and Locality in the Nigerian Popular Press." In *Modernity and Its Malcontents: Ritual and Power in Postcolonial Africa*, ed. Jean Comaroff and John L. Comaroff. Chicago: University of Chicago Press.

———. 2001. "Vulture Men, Campus Cultists, and Teenaged Witches: Modern Magics in Nigerian Popular Press." In *Magical Interpretations, Material Realities: Modernity, Witchcraft, and the Occult in Postcolonial Africa*, ed. Henrietta L. Moore and Todd Sanders. London: Routledge.

Bhabha, Homi. 1997. "Of Mimicry and Man: The Ambivalence of Colonial Discourse." In *Tensions of Empire: Colonial Cultures in a Bourgeois World*, ed. Frederick Cooper and Ann L. Stoler, 152–60. Berkeley and Los Angeles: University of California Press.

Comaroff, Jean, and John L. Comaroff. 1991. *Of Revelation and Revolution*. Vol. 1, *Christianity, Colonialism, and Consciousness in South Africa*. Chicago: University of Chicago Press.

———. 1999. "Alien-Nation: Zombies, Immigrants, and Millennial Capitalism." CODESRIA *Bulletin* 3/4:17–28.

————. 2000. "Millennial Capitalism: First Thoughts on a Second Coming." *Public Culture* 12 (2): 291–343.

Comaroff, John L. and Jean Comaroff. 1997a. *Of Revelation and Revolution.* Vol. 2, *The Dialectics of Modernity on a South African Frontier.* Chicago: University of Chicago Press.

————. 1997b. "Postcolonial Politics and Discourses of Democracy in Southern Africa: An Anthropological Reflection on African Political Modernities." *Journal of Anthropological Research* 53 (2): 123–46.

Connell, Jennifer. 2001. "Martha Stewart and the Millennial Citizen: Regimes of Taste in the Age of the Commodity." B.A. honors thesis, University of Chicago.

Durkheim, Emile. 1947. *The Elementary Forms of the Religious Life: A Study in Religious Sociology.* Translated by J. W. Swain. Glencoe, Ill.: Free Press.

Eco, Umberto. 1983. *The Name of the Rose.* Translated by William Weaver. San Diego: Harcourt Brace Jovanovich.

Forster, E. M. [1910] 1992. *Howard's End.* Edited by O. Stallybrass. London: Penguin.

Foucault, Michel. 1975. *The Birth of the Clinic: An Anthology of Medical Perception.* Translated by A. M. Sheridan Smith. New York: Vintage.

Goffman, Erving. 1959. *The Presentation of Self in Everyday Life.* Garden City, N.Y.: Doubleday.

Graeber, David. 1996. "Beads and Money: Towards a Theory of Wealth and Power." *American Ethnologist* 23 (1): 4–24.

Karlström, Mikael. 1999. "Civil Society and Its Presuppositions: Lessons from Uganda." In *Civil Society and the Political Imagination in Africa,* ed. John L. Comaroff and Jean Comaroff. Chicago: University of Chicago Press.

Karon, T. 2001. "Bush Blows It with Senseless Tenses." *Cape Times,* 13 March, 8.

Lyall, Sarah. 2001. "Soggy Pastures Where All Things Crash and Burn." *New York Times,* 7 April, A4.

Mitchell, W. J. T. 1986. *Iconology: Image, Text, Ideology.* Chicago: University of Chicago Press.

Mumford, Lewis. 1934. *Technics and Civilization.* New York: Harcourt, Brace.

Parenti, Michael. 1994. *Land of Idols: Political Mythology in America.* New York: St. Martin's.

Reid, T. R. 2001. "In Europe, the Ordinary Takes a Frightening Turn." *Mail and Guardian,* 9–15, 17.

Ryer, Paul. n.d. "Tales of Empire: A Tradition of Cuban Conspiracy Theory." University of Chicago, Department of Anthropology. Typescript.

Vernant, Jean-Pierre. 1983. *Myth and Thought among the Greeks.* London: Routledge and Kegan Paul.

Vidal, John, and Paul Brown. 2001. "Rural Myths Catch Military Connections in Their Net." *Guardian* (U.K.), 22 March, 4.

Žižek, Slavoj. 1997. *The Plague of Fantasies.* New York: Verso.

Contributors

MISTY L. BASTIAN is Associate Professor of Anthropology at Franklin and Marshall College, Lancaster, Pennsylvania. She has published extensively on gender, popular culture, media, and colonial history in Nigeria and is the coeditor, with Jane L. Parpart, of *Great Ideas about Teaching Africa* (1999).

KAREN MCCARTHY BROWN is Professor of Anthropology of Religion in the Graduate and Theological Schools of Drew University. She is the director of the Drew University Newark Project, an ethnographic mapping of religious practices in Newark funded by the Ford Foundation. She is also the author of *Mama Lola: A Vodou Priestess in Brooklyn* (1991) and *Tracing the Spirit: Ethnographic Essays on Haitian Art* (1996).

JEAN COMAROFF is the Bernard E. and Ellen C. Sunny Distinguished Service Professor of Anthropology at the University of Chicago. She has published widely on ritual, politics, and society in South Africa, past and present. Recent publications, with John Comaroff, include "Occult Economies and the Violence of Abstraction: Notes from the South African Postcolony" (*American Ethnologist* [1999]) and two edited volumes, *Civil Society and the Political Imagination in Africa* (1999) and *Millennial Capitalism and the Culture of Neoliberalism* (2001).

JOHN COMAROFF is the Harold H. Swift Distinguished Service Professor in the Department of Anthropology at the University of Chicago. He has published widely on African politics, law, and society as well as on colonialism and postcoloniality. Recent books, with Jean Comaroff, include *Of Revelation and Revolution: The Dia-*

lectics of Modernity on a South African Frontier, vol. 2 (1997), and two edited collections, *Civil Society and the Political Imagination in Africa* (1999) and *Millennial Capitalism and the Culture of Neoliberalism* (2001).

SUSAN HARDING is Professor of Anthropology at the University of California, Santa Cruz. She is the author of *The Book of Jerry Falwell: Fundamentalist Language and Politics* (2000) and the coeditor, with Charles Bright, of *Statemaking and Social Movements: Essays in History and Theory* (1984). She has written on narrative politics, rhetorical action, Bible-based speech genres, apocalypticism, and cultural movements.

DANIEL HELLINGER is Professor of Political Science at Webster University, St. Louis, Missouri. He is the author of *Venezuela: Tarnished Democracy* (1991) and *The Democratic Facade* (1992) and has written many articles on Latin American politics and on media and politics in the United States. He is a participating editor for *Latin American Perspectives* and a frequent contributor to the *St. Louis Journalism Review*.

CAROLINE HUMPHREY is Professor of Asian Anthropology at the University of Cambridge and a Fellow of King's College, Cambridge. She has worked since 1966 in Asian parts of Russia, Mongolia, Inner Mongolia (China), India, and Nepal. Among her publications are *Karl Marx Collective: Economy, Society, and Religion in a Siberian Collective Farm* (1983), *Barter, Exchange, and Value*, coedited with Stephen Hugh-Jones (1992), *The Archetypal Actions of Ritual*, with James Laidlaw (1994), *Shamans and Elders* (1996), *Marx Went Away, but Karl Stayed Behind* (1998), and *The End of Nomadism? Society, State, and the Environment in Inner Asia*, with David Sneath (1999).

LAUREL KENDALL is Curator of Asian Ethnographic Collections at the American Museum of Natural History. She also teaches in the Anthropology Department at Columbia University. She has worked in Korea, China, Japan, and Vietnam. She has written widely on shamans, marriage, modernity, gender, and ritual and is the author of *Getting Married in Korea: Of Gender, Morality, and Modernity* (1996), *Shamans, Housewives, and Other Restless Spirits: Women in Korean Ritual Life* (1985), and *The Life and Hard Times of a Korean Shaman: Of Tales and the Telling of Tales* (1988). With Charles F. Keyes and Helen Hardacre, she is a coeditor of, as well as a contributor to, *Asian Visions of Authority: Religion and the Modern Nation State* (1995).

TODD SANDERS is a University Lecturer in the Department of Social Anthropology at the University of Cambridge. From 1998 to 2002 he was a Research Fellow at the London School of Economics and Political Science, and he has also taught at the School of Oriental and African Studies, London, and at the University of California, Santa Barbara. He has published a number of articles on ritual, gender symbolism, witchcraft, and modernity in Tanzania and Kenya and has edited, with Henrietta Moore and Bwire Kaare, *Those Who Play with Fire: Gender, Fertility, and Transformation in East and Southern Africa* (1999) and, with Henrietta Moore, *Magical Interpretations, Material Realities: Modernity, Witchcraft, and the Occult in Postcolonial Africa* (2001).

ALBERT SCHRAUWERS is Assistant Professor of Anthropology at York University in Toronto, Canada. He has published widely on Dutch colonialism and religion in Indonesia and is the author of *Colonial "Reformation" in the Highlands of Central Sulawesi, Indonesia, 1892–1995* (2000).

KATHLEEN STEWART teaches anthropology and cultural studies at the University of Texas at Austin. She is the author of *A Space on the Side of the Road: Cultural Poetics in an "Other" America* (1996) and has written many articles on aspects of the U.S. political imaginary, including the American dream, the materiality of desire, conspiracy theory, banality, apocalypticism, the sensory impact of the new economy, and the aesthetics of the politics of everyday life. She is currently completing a book manuscript entitled "The Private Life of Public Culture," which is based on fieldwork in Las Vegas, Orange County, California, and Austin, Texas.

HARRY G. WEST is Assistant Professor of Anthropology on the Graduate Faculty of Political and Social Science at the New School University in New York. He has been conducting research in Mozambique since 1991 and has published numerous articles and book chapters on the relation between the state and the institutions of rural society as well as on sorcery-related beliefs and practices among the Makonde-speaking peoples of northern Mozambique.

Index

Belief (*continued*)

and Azande witchcraft, 15; and biblical prophecy in the United States,
268; and conspiracy theory, 24–25,
297; modernist language of, 291; and
moral panic, 291; narratives of, 297;
and paranoia in the United States,
208; and "the primitive" in Nigeria,
83; and revelation, 298; systems of, 6,
13; as trope, 288; and truth, 297

Berlet, Chip, 206, 211

Bhaba, Homi K., 182

Blue Elephant, 175–201; and Buddhism in Russia, 175–201; Stalin as
reincarnation of, 181, 296

Bo. *See* Applewhite, Marshall

Borders: and consumer goods in Tanzania, 153; and identity cards in
Mozambique, 106

Buddhism: and the Blue Elephant,
175–201, 200 n.15; in Russia, 23–24

Bureaucracy: obscurity of in Indonesia,
126; and rationality in Indonesia,
124–127, 145–147; and religion in
Indonesia, 144

Buryat, 23–24, 175–201; and politics of
language, 200 nn.14 and 17

Bush, George H. W.: and the New
World Order, 2–3

Cabo Delgado, Mozambique, 92–93,
111

Calvary Chapel church, 27, 265–272,
282–283; and therapeutic culture,
266

Capitalism: "millennial capitalism" in
Tanzania, 154

Captain. *See* Applewhite, Marshall

Central Intelligence Agency (CIA): and
conspiracy theories in the United
States, 24–25; and Iran-Contra scandal, 210; and Kennedy assassination,

216–229; and North, Oliver (lt.
colonel), 212; and secrecy in the
United States, 207, 214

Chama Cha Mapinduzi (CCM revolutionary party in Tanzania): and media
control, 152–153

Charity: and kinship in Indonesia,
135–140

Charms: and conspiracy, 242–256; and
fetishism, 249; and Louima case,
248, 253

China, 175–201; Cultural Revolution in,
187

Christian Church of Central Sulawesi
(GKST): and Dutch colonialism in
Indonesia, 135–137

Christianity, 259–282; and Dutch colonialism in Indonesia, 135–137; and
education in Nigeria, 72; in Indonesia, 20–21, 128; and media in the
United States, 271–272; and morality
in Nigeria, 80, 83; and the Otokoto
affair in Nigeria, 78–83, 87 n.4; and
ritual murder in Nigeria, 73; and
salvation, 180; and social elites in
Nigeria, 72; in the United States,
26–27

Christic Institute, 211–212

CIA. *See* Central Intelligence Agency

Citizenry: in Indonesia, 126

Citizenship, 17, 20; and modernity in
Tanzania, 152

Civil society: in Indonesia, 126

Coercion: and elections in Mozambique, 97, 120 n.30

Cold War, 207; and conspiracy, 219,
223–225; and the United Nations,
2, 8

Colonialism: and modernity in Tanzania, 155–160, 169 n.7

Commercialization: in South Korea,
58 n.5

Communism: and Buddhism, 179; and Buryat hegemony, 181; in Russia, 23–24; and salvation, 180; threat of in Indonesia, 127

Conspiracy: and church power in Indonesia, 141–147; as collective behavior in the United States, 206–210; and elite groups in Nigeria, 67, 79; ideas of in the United States, 5–6; in Indonesia, 127; and the Internet, 3–4; and media, 5; as occult perspective, 7; and paranoia in the United States, 24–27; and popular images in the United States, 208; and power, 5, 15; and religious fear in Indonesia, 132, 145–147; and the "Secret Team," 210–214; stories of in Nigeria, 68, 81–87; and suspicion, 15; and voter cards in Mozambique, 106

Conspiracy theory: and agency panic in the United States, 219; and anxiety in the United States, 264–265; and hegemony in the United States, 24–25, 205; and the Internet, 4; and Kennedy assassination, 204, 226–227; and media in the United States, 5; and modernity in the United States, 27; neurasthenia as, 215, 259; as occult perspective, 17; and paranoia in the United States, 262, 277–278; and pathology in the United States, 204–208, 218; and political imaginary in the United States, 260; and power, 27 n.3; and sorcery in Indonesia, 133–135; as structure of feeling in the United States, 261, 264; as therapeutic practice in the United States, 263–265; and truth, 297; in the United States, 204–228; and witchcraft in Tanzania, 160–169; and *The X-Files* (television show), 217–219

Conspiratorial forces: in the United States, 204

Consumer goods: and modernity in Tanzania, 164–169

Conversion: and conspiracy theory in the United States, 263–264

Corruption: and government in Indonesia, 126, 132; and greed in Indonesia, 21–22, 139–140; and sorcery in Indonesia, 128–129

Cult. *See* Heaven's Gate Movement

Culture: global flows of, 10–12; and tradition in Indonesia, 131

Democracy: and elections in Mozambique, 97; and transparency in Tanzania, 149

Diallo, Amadou: and justice, 242–256; and media, 241; memorial service of, 244; and police brutality, 247

Diaspora: Haitian in New York, 233–255

Discourse, 259; of transparency, 15; of UFO/Aliens in the United States, 273–283

Disorder: and government in Indonesia, 125

Displacement: and paranoia, 296. *See also* Freud, Sigmund

Diviners: in South Korea, 54

Documents. *See* Identity tokens

Doti. See Indonesia

Drug Enforcement Agency (DEA, of the United States): in Nigeria, 80, 87–88 n.11

Eco, Umberto, 3, 291

Elders: and ambiguity in Indonesia, 141, 145–147; and charity in Indonesia, 137–140; and economy in Indonesia, 141–144; and elections in Mozambique, 114 n.45; and identity

Iran-Contra scandal: and the CIA, 210; and conspiracy, 206, 210

Islam: in Indonesia, 127

JFK (film), 217–219

Journalism. See Media

Judicial system: and justice in the United States, 233, 243; and media in the United States, 232, 243; in New York City, 233

Justice: "jungle justice" in Nigeria, 73–79, 82–83; and media in the United States, 5; and police brutality, 25–26, 243. See also Diallo, Amadou; Louima, Abner; New York City Police Department

Kaplonski, Christopher, 191

Karma (üiliin ür): and Buryat reincarnation narratives, 179, 194

Kendall, Laurel, 17–18, 295

Kennedy, John F. (president): assassination of, 216–221; and conspiracy theory, 217

Kin groups: See Kinship

Kinship: and exchange in Indonesia, 136–140; and hidden powers in Indonesia, 134–138; and religious faith in Indonesia, 134; and sorcery in Indonesia, 128–129; vocabularies of in Indonesia, 136–140

Kleinman, Arthur, 53

Kruyt, Albert C.: and anthropological studies 137; and Dutch Protestant missions in Indonesia, 136–137

Labor: and colonialism in Tanzania, 155–160; and zombies in Tanzania, 162, 169 n.10

Language: and conspiracy and transparency, 2–3; of rationalization, 291

LaRouche Jr., Lyndon, 221–226

Louima, Abner, 233–256; and media, 244; moral stature of, 246; and police brutality, 233–56

Magic: and bureaucratic institutions, 242; and Buryat cultural leadership, 182; and Haitian Vodou in New York, 241; "money magic" and conspiracy in Nigeria, 68, 73–79, 83; and ritual murder in Nigeria, 79; substances of in Indonesia, 141–144; word magic in the United States, 245. See also Indonesia

MAI. See Multilateral Agreement on Investment

Makonde African National Union (MANU): and membership cards, 103. See also Mozambique

Makota. See Tanzania

Mama Lola, 26, 234–236

Manchurian Candidate, The (film): and conspiracy theory, 219

MANU: See Makonde African National Union

Marcus, George, 183, 199 n.9

Market economy: in South Korea, 38–39, 48–49

Marketplace: and communication in Nigeria, 76–77

Marx, Karl, 7, 28 n.4

Masculinity: in Nigeria, 81

McCarthy Brown, Karen, 25–26, 292

McCarthyism, 206

McFarlane, Robert C., 212

Media: and Abner Louima, 244–246; and Amadou Diallo, 242, 256 n.8; and Christian news in the United States, 271–272; and conspiracy in Nigeria, 68, 86 n.1; and conspiracy theory in the United States, 215; and editorials in Nigeria, 68–85; and erasure in the United States, 246; and government secrecy in the United States, 209; and justice in the United States, 233–237; and representations of *wanga*, 248; and shamanism in South Korea, 54, 59 n.14; and word magic in the United States, 245

Melley, Timothy, 219, 262

Metahistory, 175–176, 180–189; and allegory and metaphor, 175, 180; and the Blue Elephant, 189; of Communism, 180; and paranoia 183–186; and Stalin, 189; and transparency, 176

Metaphor, 17; and allegory and metahistory, 175; and Buryat reincarnation narratives, 182, 197–198; and identity tokens in Mozambique, 94–98; of optics, 292; and sorcery, 20–21, 24; and sorcery in Mozambique, 109–116, 118 n.15

Metcalf, Andrew, 115

Metonym: identity tokens in Mozambique as, 96, 119 n.25

Misfortune: and shamanism in South Korea, 46

Modernity, 16; and affliction in South Korea, 41; and Buddhism, 23–24; and colonialism in Tanzania, 155–160, 169 n.7; and conspiracy theory, 27; and material goods in Tanzania, 155; multiplicity of, 9–11; and power, 16; and rationality, 7–8; and religion in Indonesia, 131–132; and shamanism in South Korea, 38–41, 56; and state transparency in Tanzania, 148–150; and tradition, 7–9, 22–23; and transparency, 7–8, 16; and wealth in Tanzania, 159, 164–169; and witchcraft in Tanzania, 155–160, 164–169

Modernization: in Indonesia, 126; Soviet, 186

Mozambican National Resistance (Re-

sistência Nacional Moçambicana, RENAMO): 92–93, 111–114, 116 n.3, 117 n.5, 121 nn. 42 and 43

Mozambique: 20–21, 92–121; elections in, 92–121; identity tokens in, 93–116; Nyassa Company in, 99–101, 118 n.18, 118–119 n.20; peace process in, 92, 95; Portuguese administration in, 100–102; power in, 94–98, 101, 112; *shikupi* (medicinal substance) in, 107; sorcery in, 107–121; transparency in, 98

Multilateral Agreement on Investment (MAI), 225

National Caucus of Labor Committees (NCLC), 222

National Democratic Policy Committee (NDPC), 222–223

National Elections Commission (Comissão Nacional de Eleições, CNE): 92, 118 n.14

Nationalism: in Nigeria, 81

NCLC. *See* National Caucus of Labor Committees

NDPC. *See* National Democratic Policy Committee

Nettles, Bonnie Lu, 274–282

Neurasthenia: as discursive practice, 259; in the United States, 258–259

New World Order, 27; as global power regime, 2; and transparency and conspiracy, 3

New York City: Haitian immigrants in, 233–256; police brutality in, 25–26

New York City Police Department (NYPD): and corruption, 247, 256 n.9; and justice, 233–256; and racial profiling, 239, 243; and violence, 238, 243–246, 253, 255 n.5

Nicholas, Philius H. (reverend), 240, 247

Nigeria, 19–20, 65–88; Black Scorpions (elite cult) in, 74–75; cannibalism in, 87 nn.7 and 8; colonialism in, 73; corruption in, 76, 87 n.4; entrepreneurs in, 69–73; FMG, 68, 78, 83; General Abacha, 80–84; IMF structural adjustment program in, 69; "money magic" in, 68, 73–79, 83; National Drug Law Enforcement Agency (NDLEA) in, 80, 84; Otokoto affair in, 65–88, 86 n.3; ritual murder in, 68–87; social elites in, 69–73, 79, 85; transparency in, 68–69, 80–83; "White Paper," 79, 82

NKVD (Soviet Interior Ministry): and secrecy, 185

North, Oliver (lt. colonel), 211–212

Nyassa Company. *See* Mozambique

Nyerere, Julius: socialism in Africa and, 152

Obscurity, 18; of state practices, 21–22

Occult cosmologies, 17; and Christianity in Indonesia, 133–135; as conspiracy theories, 6–7, 12, 15; and ideology, 15; in Indonesia, 22; and power, 6–7, 15; and power in Indonesia, 127–129, 144–147; and transparency, 12

Operational conspiracy, 209–210; and globalization, 226. *See also* Conspiracy theory

Oracles: Azande, 14

Order: discourses of in Indonesia, 121–146; and religion in Indonesia, 144

Oswald, Lee Harvey, 216–219

Otokoto affair. *See* Nigeria

Paranoia, 175–201; as analytical description, 176; and belief in the United States, 208; Buryat narratives of, 175–178, 183–185; and conspiracy theories in the United States, 24–27; and culture in the United States, 264–265; and displacement, 296; and metahistory, 183–185; and pathology in the United States, 208; and political theory, 289; and post-Communism in Buryatia, 196–198; and power, 288–290; and reincarnation narratives in China, 24; and Stalinism in Buryatia, 176; and superstition, 296; and Vodou, 292

Pathology: and paranoia in the United States, 208; and political culture in the United States, 218

PDI. *See* Indonesian Democratic Party

Peace process: in Mozambique, 92, 95

Peep. *See* Nettles, Bonnie Lu

Pemberton, John, 127, 131

Photographs: and identity tokens in Mozambique, 93

Pietz, William, 249

Pig. *See* Applewhite, Marshall

Pipes, Daniel, 5, 206–207, 214, 227 nn.1 and 2

Police brutality: in the United States, 261. *See also* Diallo, Amadou; Louima, Abner

Polimbu (feast): and kinship in Indonesia, 135–144; and sorcery in Indonesia, 135–144

Political process: in Mozambique, 92–121

Politics: culture of in the United States, 205

Popper, Karl, 13

Popular culture: and conspiracy theory in the United States, 217

Posner, Gerald, 215, 220–221, 227–228 nn.4 and 5

Power, 80, 233; anthropological analyses of, 14; as conspiratorial force, 6; and economics in Tanzania, 148–168; and empiricism, 294; ethicalization of in Buryatia, 194–196, 201 n.25; as hidden, 205; as hidden in Indonesia, 127, 135; and identity tokens in Mozambique, 94–95; invisibility of, 27–28 n.3; and legibility in Mozambique, 103–105; in Mozambique, 94–98, 112; and occult power in Indonesia, 127; operations of, 2, 16; and paranoia, 288; regimes of, 2; and the state, 5, 21–22; and transparency, 2; and visibility in Mozambique, 94–95, 101; and witchcraft in Tanzania, 148–168

Premillennialism: and Calvary Chapel church, 268–272; as space of conjuncture, 269

Prouty, Fletcher, 217

Psychoanalysis. *See* Freud, Sigmund

Racism: in the United States, 233–256

Racketeering Influence and Corrupt Organization Act (RICO), 211

Rationality: and government in Nigeria, 68; invisibility of, 12, 21, 26; and modern society, 7; visibility of, 12, 21

Reincarnation: Buryat ethicalization of, 193–196, 201 n.25; and Buryat everyday life, 182; Buryat narratives of, 177, 201; and Buryat political power, 175–201; and karma, 194–196; as metaphor, 180; narratives of in China, 23–24; and paranoia, 187; (*xubilgan*) in China, 175, 194, 198 n.4

RENAMO. *See* Mozambican National Resistance

RICO. *See* Racketeering Influence and Corrupt Organization Act

Risk: and conspiracy theory, 263–264

Ritual murder. *See* Nigeria

Robinson, William, 207

Roswell, New Mexico: conspiracy theories about, 4–5; and conspiracy in the United States, 204; and U.S. government, 4–5

Rumor: and media in Nigeria, 72–78; and ritual murder in Nigeria, 72–78, 85

Russia, 23–24

Sanders, Todd, 22–23, 294–295

Sapir, David, 113

Schiraldi, Vincent, 214

Schrauwers, Albert, 21–22, 293

Schwarz, Charles, 247–248, 254

Scott, James, 101–102, 220

Secrecy: and Buryat ASSR, 185; and conspiracy theory in the United States, 261; and conspiracy in the United States, 209; and Diallo shooting, 252; and elections in Mozambique, 109; and Haitian culture in the United States, 241; and Louima Case, 22, 233; and NKVD (Soviet Interior Ministry), 185; and Vodou, 233–256; and witchcraft in Tanzania, 160–164; and the World Trade Organization, 261

"Secret Team," 210–214

Seeing: and shamanism in South Korea, 46, 54; and sorcery in Mozambique, 107–109

Seers: and witchcraft in Tanzania, 160–169

Sexuality: and African Americans in the United States, 244–246

Shamanism: and business concerns in South Korea, 38–60; and the IMF in South Korea, 52–55; and *kut* (Korean

state institutions in the United States, 205; and tradition, 12; of witchcraft in Tanzania, 165

Tanzania, 22–23, 148–170; Arusha Declaration, 152; colonialism in, 155–160, 169 n.7; conspiracy in, 160–169; IMF in, 148, 153; modernity in, 148–170; secrecy in, 160–164; and state centralization, 152; witchcraft in, 160–169
Tapper, Richard, 5
Taussig, Michael, 46
Technical Secretariat for Electoral Administration (Secretaraido Técnico de Administração Eleitoral, STAE), 92, 93, 119 n.25
Technology: and transparency in the United States, 288
Terror: and Stalinism, 178
Therapeutic culture: and Calvary Chapel church, 266; conspiracy theory in the United States as, 263–265
Ti. See Nettles, Bonnie Lu
Torpey, John, 119 nn.24 and 25
Tradition: and colonialism in Tanzania, 155–156, 167 n.7; and culture in Indonesia, 131; vs. modernity in Tanzania, 23; and occult cosmologies, 6–7; and occult cosmologies in Indonesia, 127; and wealth in Tanzania, 159–160
Transnationalism: and bureaucracy, 3
Transparency: Age of, 298; and Buryat reincarnation narratives, 191; claims of, 16; contemporary obsession with, 288–295; and Diallo shooting, 252; discourses of, 15; discourses of in Tanzania, 148–149; and economics, 19; and elections in Mozambique, 97–99, 109, 117; and global discourses, 11; and globalization, 148–149; and governance, 1; and governance in

Tanzania, 150; and ideoscapes, 11–12, 15–16; in Indonesia, 22; and Loiuma case, 233, 251–256; and market forces, 205; and media in the United States, 252–253; and metaphor, 292; modern pursuit of, 290–291; modernist language of, 291; and modernity, 7; and modernity in Tanzania, 148; multiple meanings of, 294–295; official in Nigeria, 80–83; and politics, 2; and power, 1–2, 12, 16–17; and rationality, 12; and Soviet state, 175; and technology in the United States, 288; trope of, 293; and Vodou, 22, 237
Trust: and IMF in South Korea, 53; and modernity, 11–12; and political culture in the United States, 218
Truth: and conspiracy theory, 297; dialectic of, 291; and modernity, 7; and suspicions of power, 15
Two (Bo and Peep). See Applewhite, Marshall; Nettles, Bonnie Lu

UFO/Alien, 273–283; and anxiety in the United States, 274, 278; and cultural practice in the United States, 277–278; and Heaven's Gate Movement, 273–283; as site of conjuncture, 274
Ujamaa: as Socialism in Tanzania, 152–155, 169 nn.2 and 3
UNDP. See United Nations Development Program
United Nations, 1, 20
United Nations Development Program (UNDP): in Mozambique, 92, 116 n.4
United Nations Operation in Mozambique (UNOMOZ), 92, 114
United States: conspiracy theories in, 1–5, 24–27, 214–215, 260–265, 297; culture in, 205, 217–218, 264–265; judicial system in, 233, 243; justice

Library of Congress Cataloging-in-Publication Data

Transparency and conspiracy : ethnographies of

suspicion in the new world order / Harry G. West

and Todd Sanders, editors.

p. cm.

Includes bibliographical references and index.

ISBN 0-8223-3036-9 (cloth : alk. paper)

ISBN 0-8223-3024-5 (pbk. : alk. paper)

1. Power (Social sciences) 2. Conspiracy.

I. West, Harry G. II. Sanders, Todd.

JC330.T73   2003

303.3—dc21   2002151218